D1614819

SLUMS

SLUMS

THE HISTORY OF A
GLOBAL INJUSTICE

ALAN MAYNE

REAKTION BOOKS

Jude
My companion on the way

Published by Reaktion Books Ltd
Unit 32, Waterside
44–48 Wharf Road
London N1 7UX, UK
www.reaktionbooks.co.uk

First published 2017
Copyright © Alan Mayne 2017

Printed and bound in Great Britain
by TJ International, Padstow, Cornwall

A catalogue record for this book is available from the British Library

ISBN 978 1 78023 809 8

CONTENTS

INTRODUCTION

South Delhi, 2006. We stop beside a dusty though neatly maintained camp of a dozen makeshift tents. They are squeezed between a wall and the verge of a highway that is crammed with honking cars, buses, motorbikes, and auto rickshaws. Washing hangs on lines strung between the tent poles, the wall, and overshadowing trees. Several groups of labourers and their families sit beside the tents and tend cooking fires in the bare earth. They are relaxed. As long as they continue to pay, the police and local politicians are likely to leave them alone.

The men are polite but cool towards us. They have worked hard since early morning in Delhi's booming construction industry, and they are tired. No, they don't want their photographs taken. Other outsiders have taken photographs in the past, and spoken about changes for the better, of model homes to replace the city's 'slums', but things have remained just the same. However one young mother smiles at us. 'Show me to the world,' she says, 'because I am young and beautiful.'

Over half of all humanity now live in urban settings similar to those I saw beside that South Delhi highway and in other nearby places when I lived in India's national capital, where the conspicuous wealth displayed by a few contrasts with widespread and entrenched inequality and outright poverty. The United Nations' Millennium Declaration in 2000 drew attention to the enormity of this situation across the world, estimating that over one billion people were caught in 'the abject and dehumanizing conditions of extreme poverty'. The Declaration adopted the slogan 'Cities Without Slums', and pledged to achieve 'significant improvement in the lives of at least 100 million slum dwellers' by 2020.[1] In 2012 the United Nations Secretary General, Ban Ki-moon, expressed satisfaction that already the living conditions of 'more than 200 million people living in slums have been ameliorated – double the 2020 target'.[2] In 2015 he oversaw the launch of the United Nations' latest initiative to end global poverty, the 2030 Agenda for Sustainable Development, which continues the earlier commitment to 'upgrade slums'.[3]

It is questionable, however, whether 'amelioration' was the best word to describe the interventions, evictions and forced demolitions that have been carried out since 2000 by governments, their business allies and their backers in the United Nations and international development banks in the name of poverty eradication. In any case, 'dehumanizing' and 'slum' are inappropriate words with which to characterize urban social disadvantage. These words, and the constellation of stereotypes within which they sit, misrepresent the lives, livelihoods and prospects of the urban poor. They stand in the way of the fundamental changes in both community knowledge and public policy that are urgently required to overcome social disadvantage in an ever-urbanizing world.

'Slum' is an especially unhelpful word. It misrepresents the complex realities of urban social inequality, whether in New Delhi today, in nineteenth-century London where the word was first coined, or in countless other places across time and space. It marginalizes poor people and low-income areas as supposedly deficient and dysfunctional by-products of urban development. It discounts the knowledge and practices of disadvantaged communities and imposes outsiders' precepts and agendas for change upon their lives. It will forever do so because such thinking has so conditioned the word's meaning over the 200 years of its use that it has become embedded in its very essence.

'Slum' is a fundamentally deceitful construct. A deceit is by definition:

> The action or practice of deceiving; concealment of the truth in order to mislead; deception, fraud, cheating, false dealing.
> An instance of deception; an act or device intended to deceive; a trick, stratagem, wile.
> The quality of deceiving; deceitfulness.[4]

The most obvious deceit associated with the word 'slum' is its use by controlling interest groups to disguise how private capital accumulation benefits a few at the expense of many others, and how the redevelopment of urban 'badlands' into desirable real estate can generate still more profits for the few and yet more misery for others. Advocates of laissez-faire economics and social policy used this approach in the early nineteenth century, as defenders of neo-liberalism continue to do in the early twenty-first century. Proponents of savvy city government in alliance with private sector interests in urban property likewise use the word 'slum' to rationalize rebuilding schemes that might otherwise be called socially coercive and economically manipulative: in England, Birmingham's first massive central city redevelopment project was launched in 1875–6 in the name of clearing away slums; developers and government officials in twenty-first-century Mumbai – the powerhouse of modern India – propose a similar transformation of the city's centrally located Dharavi district, which has often been called Asia's largest slum. Other examples of profitable city redevelopment and infrastructure enhancements undertaken in the name of improving slums are legion across time and throughout the world.

Social theorists and economists, from David Harvey to Joseph Stiglitz, have described the social ill effects of such capitalist economics, and Mike Davis's *Planet of Slums* (2006) highlighted these effects in today's rapidly urbanizing world.[5] My book does not attempt to duplicate their work. Rather, it explores the processes of knowledge formation and policy development which have obscured the causes and effects of urban poverty, and it probes beyond these processes in order to sketch the non-slum lives that really exist in poor neighbourhoods behind the concocted outside stereotypes. That is not its only point of departure from discussions to date. It proposes that the word 'slum' has been historically so overlaid with deceitful meanings that it must be entirely deleted from the construction and implementation of future urban poverty reduction programmes.

There are six key ways in which the word 'slum' misleads and compromises thinking about urban inequality and its possible solution:

First, those who embrace the word apply it to describe what they assume are indisputable realities: warped places and injured or predatory people. But 'slum' is merely a stereotype, a fantasy of its users' imaginations, that generalizes into one abstraction a diversity of settlement types and human conditions. Urban poverty is real and so are disadvantaged neighbourhoods, but slums are not.[6]

Second, slum talk misrepresents poor neighbourhoods and their residents as being deficient, disordered and unchanging, whereas disadvantaged households and communities actually display strategy, energy and resilience in the face of hardship and constrained livelihood choices. The physical arrangement of homes and neighbourhoods reflects a subtle and accumulating vernacular logic that attempts to maximize limited opportunities. Social behaviour likewise demonstrates strands of idiomatic common sense whereby local practice adjusts to and attempts to maximize the restricted chances for individual, household and community well-being.

Third, slums are said to have their own separate existence, and yet to draw parasitically upon their host societies, distorting city growth and economic development, harvesting illicit advantage by trafficking in violence and other crimes, and diverting public resources for law enforcement, public health and job creation. In reality, the labour of poor communities contributes significantly to urban, regional and national economies. These communities are integral, although structurally disadvantaged, parts of cities and the urban networks within which they operate.

Fourth, slum people are always characterized – sometimes with patronizing good intent, sometimes with contempt – as what the dominant culture regards as being the deficient 'Other', or 'the other half' of society. Sometimes the characterizations emphasize life cycle and focus upon intimidation and violence by youth gangs, or aged lives worn down by hardship, or supposedly ingrained pathologies and incapacities; sometimes the emphasis is upon gender, religious difference, or ethnicity and race.

Fifth, although 'slum' is often applied to these 'Other' people and places with a sense of revulsion and is used to justify coercive intervention, it is more generally invoked with some degree of sympathy for those caught in poverty, and with the intention of improving their living conditions. Thus decent people are snared into perpetuating fallacious assumptions and regressive policies. The unhelpful meanings embedded in the concept of slums always compromise the good intentions and short change the urban poor. When Michael Harrington wrote *The Other America* (1962), in the hope that it would expose the widespread extent of poverty in the United States and stimulate social reform, he insisted that

A slum is not merely an area of decrepit buildings. It is a social fact. [It] becomes the environment of the culture of poverty, a spiritual and personal reality for its inhabitants as well as an area of dilapidation. This is when the slum becomes the breeding ground of crime, of vice, the creator of people who are lost to themselves and to society.[7]

This book explores the origins and spread of these misconceptions and misrepresentations. The word 'slum' has been used by governments and property developers to legitimize grandiose schemes of urban redevelopment that have swept away the homes of millions of the poor. It has been used by scholars to describe the apparent blighting of entire city districts (through environmental degradation, inadequate housing and basic services, and limited opportunities for education and employment) and the entrenching in these places of festering subcultures characterized by helplessness, ineptness, violence and crime. It has been used by polemicists who assert that these subcultures exist separately from the vibrant economic, social and cultural life of the mainstream city. It has been used by entertainers in the arts, journalism and tourism to depict an apparent underworld whose forms and behaviours are the antithesis of normal society. It has been used by publicists of the 'big event' – such as, recently, the 2016 Olympic Games in Rio de Janeiro, the 2014 FIFA football World Cup in Brazil, the 2010 FIFA World Cup in South Africa and the 2010 Commonwealth Games in New Delhi – as a reason to remove or conceal embarrassing signs of urban poverty. It has been used by reformers to conjure expectations of a new dawn: 'Cities Without Slums!' Yet poor people themselves rarely use the word 'slum' because it is foreign to their own idioms, and they recognize that it demonizes them in the eyes of others and disempowers them as they attempt to improve homes and livelihoods, achieve good health and education, hold down jobs and help their children to do well in life.

'Slum' misrepresents as chaotic, dysfunctional and debilitating the many neighbourhoods that can be made to work sustainably for the well-being of their inhabitants and for the benefit of the broader culture, economy and environment of cities. Slum stereotypes exclude poor communities from planning how this might happen and trivialize their contributions to the healthy pulse of neighbourhoods and cities. The widespread and enduring currency of slum stereotypes has allowed entire neighbourhoods to be coerced and destroyed in the name of social progress, in the twenty-first century as in past centuries, notwithstanding a mountain of evidence that these interventions further blight the lives of those who are supposed to benefit from them. It is therefore reasonable to conclude that in respect to future reform programmes, 'any proposal in terms of slums becomes unconscious ideological imposition.'[8]

The word 'slum', admittedly, can be used legitimately in an historical sense. It can be used to describe how a misconception came about and has spread across the world. It can be used to demonstrate how a few benefited from its acceptance whereas many poor people were further disadvantaged. It can be used to explain why social reforms have faltered and failed in the past.

But the word cannot be used to describe social disadvantage in modern cities. It cannot underpin effective urban redevelopment and poverty reduction programmes now and into the future. It must be stripped out from the language of academic research, progressive urban public policy and effective neighbourhood collective action. The United Nations itself concedes that 'the catch-all term "slum" is loose and deprecatory. It has many connotations and meanings and is banned from many of the more sensitive, politically correct and academically rigorous lexicons.'[9] Politically correct or rigorously honest? The time has come to ban this deceitful word from today's reform agendas as well as from rigorous research.

There are many other sensible words and phrases that better describe the diverse conditions of urban social disadvantage and that can more effectively underpin reforms designed to empower poor communities. That they may lack the emotive power and short-hand convenience of 'slum' works to their advantage, because they do not mislead. In the English language alone (from which 'slum' is derived) there are other terms that do not carry unhelpful connotations. Disadvantaged areas – which may be located in old city centres, their adjoining inner suburbs and the urban periphery – are often described as tenement districts and shanty towns, as informal, squatter or spontaneous communities, and the United Nations itself uses 'slum' interchangeably with phrases such as 'low-income settlement' and 'informal settlement'. The United Nations Development Programme, a key player in the current 2030 Agenda for Sustainable Development, uses phrases such as 'urban poor communities' and 'poor urban settlements', rather than 'slum', in its English-language publications.[10] Other languages use specific words that match local conditions. We do not need a single master word that overshadows diverse conditions, livelihoods and developmental pathways.

There is a further reason for retreating from the old slum mindsets. I have identified five elements to the deceits about 'slums', but I promised a sixth: all the talk about slums originates with outsiders. The word has to a limited extent been appropriated by grass-roots activists in disadvantaged neighbourhoods, and as a result scholars, journalists and UN bureaucrats have emphasized the activities of community-based organizations such as Shack/Slum Dwellers International, and the longer-running National Slum Dwellers Federation in India. However, by and large 'slum' dwellers do not use the word themselves, or if they do so they parody its meanings or attempt to mobilize support for strategies that reject or reformulate outsiders' assumptions about slums.

In late nineteenth-century London, Mrs Stevens, a mother of six and supporting an infirm husband, explained to a district nurse

> that she always kept an untidy house to ensure the flow of charity. She never put up curtains and she let strips of paper hang off the walls. Before a charity visitor arrived, she dumped coal and rags in the corner and dropped stale cabbage leaves to create a fetid atmosphere.[11]

For some residents of low-income communities the word is so disconnected from their sense of themselves and their neighbourhoods that they do not recognize it as having any relevance in their lives. Thus, in late twentieth-century Mumbai, when a researcher tried to ask residents about their 'slum' experiences,

> The question was intended to be about the slum, whilst the answer was on the personal level. Some of these questions, no matter how carefully phrased, were misinterpreted by the slum-dwellers, especially questions which related to the slum as a whole and to issues of desire and suitability. For example, 'What would you like . . . ?' and 'What do you consider . . . ?' were often answered at an individual level when I intended them to speak of 'the slum' as a whole, of which they had a vague idea.[12]

Others draw lines of differentiation between neighbourhoods that outsiders are unlikely to recognize: in Bangalore, many disadvantaged residents 'thought their own area to be the best in Bangalore, even if they had a low opinion of slums in general. A lot of dwellers obviously did not perceive their area as a slum.'[13]

For most residents of low-income areas, however, the slum construct is an unmitigated embarrassment. In Mumbai, a leading researcher remarked, 'From what I know, slum people disapprove of many notions held about them by non-slum people. They do not want to be considered rotten vegetables of the city.'[14] In the early 1970s, inner-city residents in Liverpool mentioned 'the general stigma felt by everyone because they had an address in the area'.[15] A recent study in Metro Manila found that many residents 'object strongly' to the label 'slum', and another in Rio de Janeiro noted that residents of squatter settlements did not use the word *favela* to describe their neighbourhoods, and felt insulted if called a *favelado* (resident of a favela).[16] For local people, 'slum' is a negative construct that powerful outside forces impose upon them; some of them are oblivious to it, others manipulate it, most of them reject it. The challenge for us is to reject it also, and penetrate the webs of deceit about 'slums' to achieve a better understanding of urban inequality and of strategies to reduce it.

There is a risk, of course, in attempting to redress outsider bias and to reclaim slums as 'normal' communities, of artificially smoothing over the trauma and danger of living in poverty. Happy families and supportive neighbours do not altogether compensate for the sharp-edged realities of inequality, and they are not in any case the experience of everybody living in disadvantaged neighbourhoods. Robert Roberts, who described growing up in Salford in early twentieth-century England, recalled that 'slum life was far from being the jolly hive of communal activity that some romantics have claimed.'[17] Historian Jerry White has powerfully made the same point about poor communities in London.[18] This book identifies contemporary equivalents in sub-Saharan Africa, South Asia and Latin America.

There is also a danger that in reclaiming slum-dwellers from 'Otherness' they are recast according to the expectations of the dominant culture: as law-abiding types and budding entrepreneurs who long to join the escalator ride to bourgeois utopia. Archaeologist James Symonds, tongue in cheek, remarked of recent reinterpretations deriving from 'slum' excavations in places such as London, New York, Melbourne and Sydney:

> it strikes me that when hardship, prejudice, and inter-personal violence are understated or removed, what we are left with are modern-day parables which simply parody the poor, while pushing the moral that hard work and sheer tenacity overcome adversity . . . I would like to encounter more misery, more depravity, and some real failure in their tales. As we enter a global recession it might be worth pointing out that for some people things can never get better.[19]

As it can be in historical writing and archaeology, so too in contemporary social science research and journalism: a leading Indian researcher has warned that good intentions 'sometimes take a sentimental and patronizing turn . . . Much of what is written about the poor in India *miss[es] the points of view of the poor themselves.*'[20]

However, the certainty is that if we do not challenge the misleading mindsets that are fostered by the word 'slum', we doom the world's poor to a continuing and unequal 'dance with the authorities', such as that described recently by one squatter in Jakarta:

> Friday to Sunday, Sana said, the rows of shacks that spread off into the horizon are home. But between Monday and Thursday, the authorities move in, dismantling the homes and sending locals to sleep in the open.
>
> 'If we don't hurry they take our things,' she said.[21]

What a deceitful and miserable word is 'slum', to sanction such a brutal and senseless cycle of destruction that undoes the hard work and sets back the aspirations of the urban poor!

ONE

'SLUM' AND 'SLUMMING'

'Slum' first entered the English language during the early nineteenth century, emerging from the idiom of everyday slang talk in London. It pithily encapsulated ways and conditions of living that seemed to be intolerable. As the American housing expert Charles Abrams explained,

> The word 'slum' is a piece of cant of uncertain origin, little more than a century old. Its derivation may be from 'slump', meaning 'swamp', or it may be a fortuitous blend of 'slop' and 'scum'; it also carries with it the cadence of 'slob', 'slush', 'slovenly', 'slut', and other derivatives of the *sl* combination. Slum reveals its meaning the moment it is uttered.[1]

The word's use spread to cities throughout Britain, and the word was also copied by British colonizers in territories overseas: North America and Australasia, the Indian subcontinent, Southeast Asia and sub-Saharan Africa. Thus a London slang word was adopted in hitherto non-English-speaking societies to describe diverse social conditions in terms that were comprehensible to the new ruling culture. British administrators and their colonial subordinates equated slum with *bustee* in colonial Calcutta and with *kampung* in the Malay Straits Settlements, and imposed it in Nairobi to describe the informal settlements which sprang up when a railway junction was built.

This traffic in words and concepts was not entirely one way. In English-speaking societies during the years of imperial expansion, images from the frontier reinforced characterizations of 'slums' at home: in British Canada, for example, it was suggested in 1897 that the living conditions of the urban poor in Montreal were 'as little known as [those] of natives in Central Africa'.[2] In later times, analogies were drawn with 'slums' in the 'developing' world to highlight how similarly appalling social conditions had once prevailed in 'developed' nations when they went through an earlier 'take-off' stage of economic development and social transformation.[3] Thus historians today can argue that London in the 1880s 'was the heart of empire and it was a damning indictment of the inequality of Victorian Britain that large areas of Europe's most populated city resembled the slums of Calcutta'.[4]

Common-sense opinion holds that today's 'squatter camps and shanty towns are the latter-day slums of the Third World', or, to put it the other way, that the juxtaposition of wealth and poverty that characterized nineteenth-century British and American cities 'persists today in the Third World where the post-war urban explosion replicates the problems and pressures of European industrialization and urbanization'.[5]

This change in the use of the word 'slum', from describing urban poverty in European societies to its almost exclusive application to Asia, sub-Saharan Africa and Latin America today, was significantly influenced by post-Second World War decolonization. The word equivalents and substitutions of the colonial era were maintained by the indigenous elites who inherited governance as the British departed. Jawaharlal Nehru, for example, the first prime minister (from 1947 to 1964) of independent India, deplored 'the degradation of the slums'.[6] Lee Kuan Yew, who was elected Singapore's first prime minister in 1959, used similar language in contrasting conditions under colonialism with the new order promised by independence. In South Africa likewise, the African National Congress's Freedom Charter, adopted in 1955 and still current, vowed that 'Slums shall be demolished,' and in 2010 a senior official in post-apartheid South Africa's Ministry of Human Settlements reaffirmed, 'we dream of South Africa, free of slums.'[7]

With the word's widespread use after the Second World War by new nation states, monetary and aid organizations and the United Nations, 'slum' and its embedded meanings also found expression in nations that English-speakers had never mastered or colonized. 'Slum', cuckoo-like, reshaped the meanings of words such as *banlieue* and *bidonville* in France and French-colonized Africa, *barriada* in Spain and Peru, *quartieri periferici* in Italy, favela in Brazil, *villa miseria* in Argentina and *kampung* in Indonesia. Thus the 2007 annual report of the United Nations agency UN-Habitat referred to the proliferating 'slums (favelas) in the city of Rio de Janeiro'.[8] Elsewhere in the world (in Germany and Russia, for example) the word often appeared as an English import hedged by inverted commas. Influential English-speaking analysts used the word when they discussed events in non-English-speaking nations. David Harvey, for example, describing the redevelopment of Paris under Louis Napoleon in the 1850s and '60s, argued that

> [Baron] Haussmann tore through the old Parisian slums, using powers of expropriation in the name of civic improvement and renovation. He deliberately engineered the removal of much of the working class and other unruly elements from the city centre, where they constituted a threat to public order and political power.[9]

UN researchers have maintained that in Mozambique, which became independent from Portugal in 1975,

> Many residential areas in the urban centers . . . have typical slum characteristics: low-incomes, no basic urbanization, ambiguous or insecure land tenure rights, high population density, poor environmental conditions, poor or very poor building quality, absence of an urban culture, high levels of criminality and delinquency.[10]

It is a sad irony that, by the end of the twentieth century, an emotive English slang term had been so expanded in its application as to define and constrain how the United Nations' Millennium Development Goals should address urban poverty across all nations and cultures. The United Nations' worthy target to halve global poverty was compromised by bracketing to it the neoliberal slogan 'Cities Without Slums'. Slum stereotypes have imposed a spurious generalized 'reality' upon the diversity of form and social action in the poorest districts of the world's cities, and entrenched a reform agenda that fails the needs and wishes of the urban poor.

COMMENTING UPON the wording of the Millennium Development Goals relating to poverty reduction, the geographer Alan Gilbert lamented that

The new millennium has seen the return of the word 'slum' with all of its inglorious associations. After decades when most prudent academics and practitioners had avoided using it, the United Nations thrust the word 'slum' into full focus as the target of their main shelter campaign and as one element of the Millennium Development Goals campaign.[11]

However, Gilbert was perhaps too kind to his colleagues: in framing the Millennium Development Goals the UN General Assembly took wide-ranging professional and academic advice. The Assembly's policy endorsement of slum eradication as a key priority around the world was the sorry achievement of professional planners, architects, public administrators and academic researchers in the social sciences rather than that of politicians and diplomats. Social scientists – anthropologists, economists, geographers, planners, psychologists, sociologists and specialists in community development, public administration and social work – gave international legitimacy to the embedding of slum stereotypes in the postcolonial world. Chinese scholars, for example, have emphasized the 'notorious slums' that existed in China until the Communist victory in 1949.[12] In India, similarly, a pivotal national symposium on slum clearance, convened by the Indian Conference of Social Work and held in Bombay in 1957, concluded by sending a delegation to Prime Minister Nehru to urge the need for a comprehensive national slum clearance and housing policy and for a strong central bureaucracy to oversee it.[13] Half a century later a distinguished group of Indian academics collaborated to produce *India: Urban Poverty Report 2009* for the guidance of the Government of India and the United Nations Development Programme, foregrounding 'slums' to such an extent that the minister for housing and poverty alleviation declared that some 24 per cent of urban India 'lives in slums in inhuman conditions that breed tensions, crime, ill health, and disease'.[14] Likewise in present-day Africa, researchers emphasize 'the proliferation of slums and informal settlements' and contend that sub-Saharan Africa contains the highest proportion of slum-dwellers in the world.[15] In Latin America, academics argue that a key aspect of rapid urban growth since the Second World War has been the proliferating 'slums and shantytowns of Latin American cities'.[16]

Whereas social scientists legitimized 'slum' in the contemporary world, historians popularized the word in our understanding of the past. People tend to look to history for lessons about the past that can shape wise decision-making in the present. Ban Ki-moon used the phrase 'History demonstrates' as he sought to explain current global urban trends.[17] But the history lessons he drew upon were wrong. Historians of nineteenth-century Britain took the lead in translating the slang word 'slum' into a spurious 'environmental reality'.[18] They made the slum stereotypes all the more authoritative by focusing historical attention upon the early social reformers who had seemingly begun to collect the facts about urban poverty and who set themselves the task of 'mapping and organizing the disordered world of slumland'.[19] Historians have until recently disdained the supposedly shallow sensationalism of 'slummer' entertainers and thrill seekers,[20] even though these were the activities in which the word 'slum' first gained currency and through which it achieved its greatest influence upon international public opinion. Yet the facts assembled and the conclusions drawn by the reformers whom historians have studied – including those two pioneers in the mapping of urban poverty, Charles Booth in London from the late nineteenth century and Benjamin Seebohm Rowntree in York from the early twentieth century – were clearly shaped by their class viewpoints. Thus, notwithstanding his sympathy for low earners, 'Booth's social geography was a moralizing geography which linked the poor with dirt and deviant behavior.'[21] So, too, did the compositions of early photographers, such as Thomas Annan in Glasgow from the 1860s and Jacob Riis in New York from the 1880s, which historians have reproduced to illustrate their narratives. The disorder the reformers and publicists saw was a product of their outsiders' gaze rather than mirroring prevailing conditions in disadvantaged communities.

Historians in North America, Australasia and South Africa generally followed the emphases of British urban historians. In American histories, slums were the ugly and savage places where poor immigrants congregated before grasping the opportunity to forge more prosperous lives, and where there collected the residue of those who had missed their opportunity. More than their British counterparts, historians in the United States also considered the cultural production of slums through popular literature, theatre, illustration, song and tourism, although this carried the risk of reifying the fantasies that had circulated about places such as New York's Bowery and Five Points. Thus one popular history, confusing public perceptions of a place with its actual social dynamics, claimed that Five Points was 'the World's Most Notorious Slum'.[22]

These historians, like the social reform pioneers whom they studied, were not intentionally misleading – some, like H. J. Dyos in Britain, were masterful pioneers in exciting new areas of social history research – but an effect of their research was to perpetuate a deceit. They were understandably shocked by the social and environmental consequences of urbanization under early laissez-faire capitalism, and sought words to describe the unequal and unjust society which resulted. Trailblazing books such as Gareth Stedman Jones's *Outcast London* and Richard Dennis's *English Industrial Cities of the Nineteenth Century* did not exaggerate the social disparities that characterized the nineteenth-century growth of cities.[23] Stedman Jones, more so than Dennis, tended to avoid the word 'slum', other than to describe middle-class perceptions. However, for other leading historians 'slum' seemed to fit the bill: a nineteenth-century word that matched nineteenth-century conditions. Anthony Wohl built it into the title of his influential book *The Eternal Slum*,[24] while David Englander used 'slum' unabashedly in describing how the new cityscapes came to

> reflect . . . the play of unbridled market forces, nowhere more so than in the maldistribution of such benefits as could be obtained from grossly inadequate investment in social expend-iture. The needs of the commonalty were sacrificed to the formation of new capital: pressure on working-class con-sumption was ruthless, intense, and unrelenting. The resultant absence of effective demand hastened the deterioration of the environment as workers and their families were packed, layered, and compressed like sardines into the made-down houses of the wealthy, forsaken by their original inhabitants for the safety of the suburbs, or crowded into such accommodation as the speculative builders were willing to provide.[25]

Englander's language is powerfully evocative and his line of argument is convincing, but their effect is undercut by his uncritical use of the very word that has been used to conceal and trivialize the causes and effects that he was studying.

Jim Yelling also sought to describe 'the nature of the slum and its place in the urban structure' of nineteenth- and twentieth-century

England.[26] However, Yelling cautioned that he used slum 'as a political rather than a technical term', and that the word incorporated 'dominant views of the nature of the slum, and of the remedies which should be applied'.[27] Yelling explained that he used the word 'simply to mean conditions conceived of as "unacceptable"'.[28] This was his mistake. The word does indeed simplify, and thereby distorts, complex and varied urban forms and activities; it asserts that 'acceptable' and 'unacceptable' are simple and uncontested universal absolutes. It took another historian, Sam Bass Warner, Jr, to nibble away at this problem and attempt to explain why, because of its inherent contradictions, the word slipped out of general use in the developed world during the 1970s.[29] However, by then social scientists were no longer listening. They were intent on writing about the contemporary slums of the 'developing' world.

WHILE ACADEMIC researchers' use of the word 'slum' has informed the reform agendas of governments, international bankers, aid agencies and the United Nations, the mass-circulation media and the entertainment industry have been still more influential in shaping general understanding of the word. Journalism first entrenched slums in the popular imagination. Henry Mayhew's influential *London Labour and the London Poor* (the first volume of which was published in 1851) initially appeared as a newspaper series in the *Morning Chronicle*, and the Reverend Andrew Mearns's reform pamphlet *The Bitter Cry of Outcast London* (1883) was popularized by William T. Stead's *Pall Mall Gazette*. Walter Besant's *All Sorts and Conditions of Men* (1882) first appeared in the literary magazine *Belgravia*, and George R. Sims's *How the Poor Live* (1883) began as a series in *The Pictorial World*. Journalist Jacob Riis's arresting use of graphic text and photography in *How the Other Half Lives: Studies among the Tenements of New York* (1890) found its first expression as an article in *Scribner's Magazine*. As it was in the metropolitan hubs, so too in regional centres: John Stanley James's *The Vagabond Papers* (1876), for example, first appeared in the Melbourne *Argus* and the *Sydney Morning Herald*. Sir Herbert Brown Ames's *The City below the Hill* (1897) originated as a series in the *Montreal Star*. Two of the best-known 'slums' of the modern world, Kibera in Nairobi and Dharavi in Mumbai, featured in the movies *The Constant Gardener* (2005) and *Slumdog Millionaire* (2008) respectively, and Rio de Janeiro's favelas were likewise introduced to an international audience through *City of God* (2002) and *Elite Squad* (2007). The Parisian *banlieue* had been similarly broadcast to the world through the dark drama film *La Haine* (1995), which quickly became a cult movie. There is also a long tradition of slum entertainment in text, burlesque and song. In 1915, for example, the Australian poet C. J. Dennis used Melbourne's 'scowlin' slums' as the setting for a latter-day Romeo and Juliet humorous romance:

> Wot's in a name? Wot's in a string o' words?
> They scraps in ole Verona wiv the'r swords,
> An' never give a bloke a stray dog's chance,
> An' that's Romance.
> But when they deals it out wiv bricks an' boots
> In Little Lon., they're low, degraded broots.[30]

Dennis's verse sold hundreds of thousands of copies throughout the English-speaking world, cementing the notoriety of Melbourne's 'Little Lon' (Little Lonsdale Street) district as Australia's best-known slum.

The slumland melodramas generated through the mass media and popular entertainment led in turn to an equally long-lived form of 'reality' tourism in the poorest districts of big cities. The 'slummer', the gentleman observer of city 'low life', first presented himself in London during the early nineteenth century (although his antecedents can be traced back well before the 'slum' was invented) and later became a subject of interest for scholars, who borrowed the term *flâneur* that Charles Baudelaire had applied to similar explorers in Paris. The slummer fashion grew and became more organized during the nineteenth and early twentieth centuries, enabling middle-class ladies as well as gentlemen to participate in 'slumming' tours of British, North American and Australian cities. Historians have also drawn attention to slummers from the social elite and the middle classes – many of them women – who worked as volunteers in poor neighbourhoods on behalf of religious groups, charities and social reform networks such as the Charity Organization Society, or who lived for a time in these districts as members of the settlement house movement in Britain and North America, or visited them as government regulators.[31] The efforts of these volunteers were echoed later by sociologists and anthropologists who, by undertaking fieldwork in low-income city districts, 'wanted to know what a slum was like, and how it felt to live in one'.[32] However, it was slummer tourism rather than philanthropy that most shaped public knowledge of urban poverty. New York's Five Points district became the city's 'most alluring tourist attraction' after Charles Dickens highlighted it in *American Notes* (1842),[33] and by the 1920s Harlem had become a popular destination for thrill-seekers. Slumming tours also stimulated a 'flood of writing *about* slums which could be consumed within the safe confines of the home. Writing . . . made the grotesque *visible* whilst keeping it at an *untouchable* distance.'[34]

Slumming shifted gear in the late twentieth century, with the emergence in the cities of the developing world of what has been variously called 'slum tourism', 'reality tourism', 'poverty tourism', 'poorism' and 'dark tourism'.[35] Beginning during the early 1990s in Rio's favelas and South Africa's shanty towns, the phenomenon has widened to cities as diverse as São Paulo, Mexico City, Manila, Jakarta, Singapore, Bangkok, Mumbai and New Delhi. Present-day slumming was encouraged in part by Gregory David Roberts's internationally best-selling novel *Shantaram*, set within Mumbai's poorest districts,[36] but most of all it has been fuelled by the rise of the Internet. Online blogs, articles and tour advertisements share experiences with a still larger audience of sit-at-homes than did the slummer guidebooks of earlier centuries. YouTube clips can take one 'Walking Thru Kibera', or through dozens of others of the world's best known 'slums'.[37]

Sometimes the thrill of slumming, either first-hand or Internet imaginary, is shallow titillation: 'Naughty me stopped at the corner, wanting to snap some photos of the beautifully seductive gals and got scolded by one of the pimps.'[38] However, the chief attraction throughout the long history of slumming tourism and entertainment has been the characterization of slums as an apparently parallel dark universe. Slummers have always highlighted the shock of moving between discontinuous worlds, as the city's familiar vistas suddenly dissolve before the visitors' halting footsteps. They might find themselves in a common lodging-house in nineteenth-century Sydney: 'To enter these rooms and see the heaps of stifling stewing humanity was horrible. The atmosphere choked one with a fearful taste';[39] or they might have to 'stoop and stumble along open sewers and between the press of shacks and houses' in twenty-first-century Dharavi.[40] The allure of such characterizations lies in grotesque difference tinged with menace: during one Rio favela tour 'the guide told everyone to stop taking pictures.

A young man approached the group, smiling and holding a cocked gun.'[41] As the operator of Jakarta Hidden Tours explained, 'there is plenty of interest' to be found by exploring the city's contradiction that 'nearly half the population lives in slums jammed between shopping malls and luxury homes.'[42] Juxtaposition of time as well as place is also offered: slummers in Singapore are invited to explore what Old Chinatown was like before the city 'got nicely sanitised and spruced up'.[43] Slummers insist that such juxtapositions are authentic rather than concocted, and that slum tourism is motivated solely by a 'desire to experience the "real life" of the city'.[44] As one Swiss tourist put it, she wanted to see 'the real Jakarta, behind the façade of fancy buildings and shopping malls'.[45] Some operators give this a further twist, offering views from the protection of comfortable chauffeur-driven vehicles with climate control and door locks, and, in Rio, from upmarket villa accommodation and bars overlooking the favelas so that 'tourists will be able to taste luxury and the gritty life of the slum at the same time.'[46]

Such slumming is designed to entertain. Often the entertainment is also intended to generate interest in providing help for those caught in 'the gritty life of the slum'. Some tour operators, and the aid agencies and community organizations that collaborate with them, return a percentage of tour profits to poor communities, and in Mumbai Roberts assists community development organizations and runs a 'CaringSharing' website that provides advice about charitable giving and volunteering.[47] A lively debate rages as to whether slum tours 'raise awareness rather than provide voyeuristic entertainment for rich westerners'.[48] However, the subtext by the organizers of many such tours is:

> Come with us to gawk at desperately poor people in one of the smelliest and ugliest places on earth. Observe how they scrape by so you can have stories to tell at home and feel better about your own lot.[49]

This is how slum entertainments and slum narratives have always operated, and always will do. As historian Graeme Davison remarked,

> The slum stereotype . . . so pervades contemporary debate, influencing the selection of facts, the classification of statistical information and the construction of explanations, that

it is difficult for the historian to escape its influence. It portrayed lower-class life in essentially negative terms – *dis*ease, *dis*tress, *dis*order, *dis*affection – and always from a lofty middle-class point of view. It acted as a shutter closing the minds of contemporaries to the inner life and outlook of the poor.[50]

Definitions

Mike Davis turned heads in 2006 when he described a 'Planet of Slums'. But how does the dominant discourse today – in popular culture, public affairs and the academy – actually define a 'slum'? Pioneering efforts by the British government during the 1920s and '30s to legislate for the elimination of all slums led the *Times* newspaper to concede that 'slum' was 'a vague term which is used to describe various kinds of unsatisfactory streets'.[51] In the 1960s Charles Abrams likewise remarked that

> The word 'slum' is a catchall for poor housing of every kind as well as a label for the environment. The same word denotes a Chicago mansion turned into furnished rooms and a cardboard carton sheltering a human being in Lima.[52]

Some forty years later the United Nations echoed Abrams's assessment, noting that 'In general parlance, and in the official language, little differentiation is made between types of substandard housing. In practice, all and any such housing is referred to as "slums".'[53] The United Nations, for which Abrams undertook many housing studies in the developing world, now concedes that the 'problem with measuring slums starts with the lack of an agreed definition'.[54] It accepts that today there is still 'no internationally accepted definition of a slum'.[55]

Davis argued that nineteenth-century Britain's 'classical definition of a slum' – which in fact never amounted to a proper definition because usage was emotive, imprecise and volatile rather than objective, specific and fixed – conjured up 'an amalgam of dilapidated housing, overcrowding, disease, poverty, and vice'. He contrasted these meanings with the UN's twenty-first-century usage of 'slum', which was designed to advance the Millennium Development Goals programme to create a fairer world. Davis judged that this reform-driven usage had stripped out the word's 'Victorian calumnies'.[56] But he was over-optimistic here. A recent publication authored by an architect and a city-planning expert asks:

> What response does the word *slum* evoke? For many people there is revulsion, fear, and occasionally outrage. To this we could add an image of filth, crime, disease, slovenliness, helplessness, and poverty.[57]

The Millennium project failed to generate a definition of 'slum' that explicitly rejected these negative stereotypes, but it certainly shifted general thinking about slums in the twenty-first century. One effect of the UN's initiatives has been to erode, although not overturn, conventional associations of slums with feelings of revulsion and fear. In the place of nineteenth-century equations of slums with villainy and vice, the UN substituted sympathy for the apparent victimhood of the urban poor. For the United Nations, the ultimate horror of contemporary slums was that living conditions there were 'threatening the health, safety and well-being of their inhabitants',[58] rather than that the inhabitants behaved like monsters (although recent urban terrorism has influenced the UN to flag the dangers of slum-based 'socio-political unrest').[59] Sympathy for slum-dwellers had, at least in discussions between UN officials and their advisers, triumphed over fear and revulsion. It followed that interventions were needed not so much to coerce slum-dwellers as to save them. The out-of-touch paternalism inherent in such thinking has generated many well-intentioned 'slum-upgrading' projects that have left local residents stranded at arm's length from project design and implementation. Now the United Nations emphasizes the need for community partnerships, but although the rhetoric about participation and empowerment is profuse, their practical expression is rare.

A second effect of UN programmes has been to reinforce the long-standing trend among slummers to impose an artificial assimilationist vision of unified communities upon the social and cultural diversity of cities. Slum-dwellers are to be rehabilitated and drawn into the mainstream. This strategy is influenced in part by recent neoliberal interest in evidence of vigorous small-scale entrepreneurialism within the informal economies of disadvantaged city districts in the developing world. In adopting this line of thought, the United Nations also borrowed from academia an apparent distinction between 'slums of "hope" and slums of "despair"'. This analysis, originating in Latin America but applied by other researchers throughout the developing world, contended that the key difference between these two characteristics of the slum lay in the availability or not of 'escalator and non-escalator [opportunities] to move up through the class structure'.[60] It seemed to follow that interventions could generate hope for aspirational slum-dwellers by providing escalators to improved well-being, because without outside assistance even the entrepreneurial poor were likely to remain caught in dead-end slums. The risk in this assimilationist thinking is clear. As one astute Indian observer remarked,

> Imaginary but well-meant descriptions about the poor and lower caste people have perpetuated myths that are either sentimental or pity-evoking or outright contemptuous. The contemptuous ones depict the poor as downright untrustworthy, lazy, drink-prone and permissive. The sentimental ones run like this: 'Slum people have to be saved from their environment of vice, crime and alcoholism'; or 'slum people are all drunkards – they have to drink, you see, to drown their worries'.[61]

A third effect of the UN's programmes has been to emphasize simply the environmental degradation of slums and the inadequacies of the accommodation available within them, and to neglect the complex social and economic constraints that shape poor communities. Similarly downplayed are the efforts by local inhabitants to make the most of any opportunities that are offered. These effects are a direct consequence of UN policy being driven by the United Nations Human Settlements Programme (UN-Habitat), which has tended to focus on 'the shelter conditions' created by poverty rather than on the underlying causes of urban inequality.[62] The result of this preoccupation has been further to entrench belief in the chaotic material reality of slums and the inability of their residents to improve upon these conditions.

A fourth effect of UN interventions has been decisively to switch the associations of the word 'slum' from European societies in the past to the developing world today. UN-Habitat is based in Kenya's capital, Nairobi, and UN reports and programmes primarily associate slums with the developing world and especially with cities in sub-Saharan

Africa, South Asia and Latin America. Recent academic interest in the 'Global South' and 'Global Cities of the South' has reinforced this trend.[63] The United Nations contends that with this changed usage, 'slum' has lost its earlier sensational connotations: 'In developing countries, the term "slum", if it is used, mostly lacks the pejorative and divisive original connotation, and simply refers to lower-quality or informal housing.'[64] This is a forlorn hope. As a leading Indian economist cautioned, 'Slums are looked down upon.'[65]

UNITED NATIONS activities correspond to general trends in attempts to define 'slum' that had been developing since the middle of the twentieth century. These trends are especially evident among public administrators and social science researchers in India, which, through the Non-Aligned Movement that Nehru launched in the early 1960s, has profoundly influenced thinking throughout the developing world. Fundamental to Indian analysis is the ongoing presumption that slums are, as the director of the Indian Institute of Public Administration once explained, 'a grim reality of our time and perhaps a way of life'.[66] Alan Gilbert's belief that reputable researchers and administrators had abandoned the slum concept does not hold in India. Experts there followed the lead set by A. R. Desai and S. D. Pillai, two pioneering Marxist academics at the University of Bombay, who argued during the 1970s that 'poverty and illiteracy are seen in its [sic] most concrete form in slums, shanty-towns, shack-towns and squatters' colonies.' The slum, they said, 'has come to be accepted as a living reality'.[67] Later researchers echoed Desai and Pillai, taking as a given the slum's 'concrete social reality' or 'living reality'; it was for them 'a fact of the social system'.[68]

After independence, Indian researchers initially drew on academic knowledge from the developed world and sought to translate into Indian public policy a term that had hitherto been discussed largely in terms of urban trends in Britain and the United States. At the pivotal 1957 Slum Clearance Workshop in Bombay, the chairman, P. R. Nayak, the incoming commissioner of the Municipal Corporation of Delhi, drew upon the pre-independence British professional framework within which he had been trained in order to suggest that 'a slum may be defined as a building or an area which is *unfit for human habitation* by reason of serious deficiencies in the nature of the living accommodation or of the environment.' However, he probed beyond this old British legislative phrase, and, drawing upon his own personal observations, added that

> the broad picture is clear enough. A scene of filth and squalor, of dingy streets and unkempt rows of dilapidated houses, of overcrowding in tiny rooms, and of inadequate services rises to our eyes.

Warning of the consequences of slum conditions, Nayak suggested:

> Filth and overcrowding in sub-standard buildings and the paucity or absence of civic amenities and community services have heightened delinquency and arrested or denied opportunities for educational and social development.

Slums had the potential, he warned, to cause 'maladjustment with society' and to upset 'the political stability of the community'.[69]

After the workshop Nayak drew upon its proceedings to formulate a specifically Indian definition of 'slum':

> A slum may be described as a chaotically occupied, unsystematically developed and generally neglected area which is over-populated by persons and over-crowded with ill-repaired and neglected structures. The area has insufficient communications, indifferent sanitary arrangements, and inadequate amenities necessary for the maintenance of physical and social health and the minimum needs and comforts of human beings and the community. There is a general absence of social services and welfare agencies to deal with the major social problems of persons and families, in respect of sub-standard health, inadequate income and low standard of living, who are victims of biological, psychological and social consequences of the physical and social environment.

Nayak added that the flow-on consequences of slum living conditions included impaired health and physical fitness, 'psychological maladjustment to family life and environment', 'social disorganisation' and diminished 'status and dignity of the woman'.[70]

This quirky value-laden definition, which combined echoes from Old World usage in the past with aspirations to describe social disadvantage in contemporary Indian cities more accurately, still held sway at the end of the twentieth century. It was restated in Desai and Pillai's *Slums and Urbanization*, which was first released in 1970 and republished in a second expanded edition in 1990. Desai and Pillai declared that some of 'the worst slums in the world can undoubtedly be found in Indian cities' as a consequence of the national government's encouragement of capitalist development in the post-Nehru era, and they argued that these conditions highlighted the structural imbalances that were being accentuated by free-market economic change and accelerating urbanization in the developing world.[71]

Many other leading Indian planners and academics agreed with Desai and Pillai that slum conditions were the result of structural inequalities in society 'created by [their] rulers' rather than by the supposed 'acts of criminal, vagrant and cunning anti-social elements' in the slums.[72] The urban planners Shveta Mathur and Sakshi Chadha stated, for example, that 'Slums and the urban poor . . . are reflective of the inherent contradictions and inequalities in a city.'[73] Increasingly, too, urban inequality was linked by scholars to the effects of the late twentieth-century free-market surge in what was becoming generally called 'globalization', and especially to its regional impacts upon the 'Global South'. The distinguished economist Amitabh Kundu asserted that Indian slums encapsulated 'the pathetic conditions of the poor in segmented localities in large cities in the era of globalization'.[74]

These trends were influenced by the subaltern studies movement, which had, since the 1980s, given a powerful South Asian twist to academic analysis of marginalized people and places. One trend in this broad movement, 'subaltern urbanism', rejected 'apocalyptic and dystopian narratives' about slums but proposed instead the 'slum as theory'. This approach uses the cities of the 'Global South' to challenge the influence of imperialism, postcolonial nation-building and globalization on the understanding of urban poverty. However, such analysis is still based upon the false proposition that 'the slum stands as a site': a geographical, social and political reality.[75]

The mainstream of conventional Indian scholarship, as elsewhere in the world, has in more shallow ways continued to focus only upon the clichéd assertion of slumland's physical, social and cultural disorder. Such researchers characteristically conclude that reforms are

needed, but their advocacy for these, although superficially sympathetic, is expressed in deeply patronizing ways. The starting point for
such analysis in India is the assertion that

> Slums are cancerous for urban life and no effort should be
> spared to eradicate them . . . Urban slums are a slur on the
> face of the modern civilization. There is a need to help the
> slum dwellers to lead a decent life.[76]

A recurring theme in such research has been the apparent chaos of the
built environment: Indian slums were 'built in a haphazard manner
without any plan'.[77] The general conclusion drawn has been that such
living conditions necessarily debased those who lived there: a sub-
human environment inevitably created 'sub-human and disorganised
life'.[78] In 1994 one neighbourhood study of Hyderabad drew almost
word-for-word on Nayak's 1957 definition of 'slum', and concluded that

> A slum may be described as a chaotically occupied, unsys-
> tematically developed and generally neglected area which
> is over-populated and over-crowded with unattended and
> neglected structures . . . The slum areas breed crime, social
> delinquency and unrest, which are detrimental to the growth
> of a healthy society.[79]

Another study contended likewise that a

> slum is an area where there is overcrowding of houses on land
> and of persons in houses, lacking all sorts of amenities, full
> of unhygienic conditions, disorganised, unplanned and full of
> social evils.[80]

Many researchers built their analysis upon the premise that slums represented 'the other side of our civilization' and comprised a 'sub-standard
culture [that] breeds crime [and] leads to deviation'.[81] Drawing upon
earlier generations of American sociology and anthropology, they
argued that the

> slum is a way of life, a subculture with a set of norms and
> value[s], which is reflected in poor sanitation and health

practices, deviant behaviour and characteristic attributes of apathy and social isolation.[82]

In India and throughout the developed world, the emphases contained in academic depictions of slums have been accepted by aid agencies, which, although they did not directly seek to define 'slum', perpetuated and reinforced unhelpful characterizations of them through their wide networks of supporters. When, for example, in 2005 the charitable organization WaterAid undertook a social survey of social disadvantage in Delhi, its report was introduced by Kundu, who referred to 'the city population living in slums [as living] mostly in sub human conditions'.[83] Similarly, Oxfam's web news, magazines and shopping catalogues regularly feature 'slums', ranging from Christmas catalogue items made by Delhi 'slum' women (2008) to vignettes about children in Nairobi's Mukuru 'slum' (2015). The intentions of Oxfam, WaterAid and Kundu are all deeply humanitarian, but they are compromised by using an artificial construct in pursuit of social justice. The same is true throughout the developing world. In a feature story about Jakarta, for example, the IRIN Humanitarian News and Analysis service, which is based in Nairobi and backed by the United Nations, reported that the huge Indonesian capital 'is dotted with slums . . . Many people live without running water in shanty towns built in the shadow of gleaming skyscrapers, and gutters are clogged with rubbish, causing foul smells.'[84] Likewise in Africa, a church organization working in Kibera stressed that its inhabitants 'live every day in an environment whose conditions are degrading and dehumanising, where corruption and violence are commonplace. They are ignored and forgotten by society.'[85] This is the old sensational 'slummer' language of the nineteenth century, still skewing philanthropic action in the twenty-first.

IT IS REASONABLE to conclude that although public opinion and expert knowledge have generated many characterizations of 'slum' in the modern world, they have produced no clear and credible definition to replace what Davis aptly described as the 'Victorian calumnies' of the past. This is precisely because – as Abrams remarked and the United Nations acknowledged – 'the term "slum" [functions as] an easily understandable catch-all'.[86] The word's power lies in its use as a shorthand term that subordinates rigorous thinking to the simple assertion of one's preconceptions. The word's currency has had the effect of perpetuating broad and unhelpful stereotypes rather than generating precise definitions of shelter conditions among the urban poor that are capable of underpinning the rigorous research and effective community development projects needed to achieve a fairer world.

Some experts, like Gilbert, therefore abhor the word and regret its continuing currency. The sociologist AbdouMaliq Simone, a key figure in scholarly thinking about cities in the Global South, worries that

> The designation 'slums', while important to the work of political advocacy and political development, tends to group particular kinds of urban spaces across the world into generalizations that end up obscuring important features about how the poor actually live and use cities.[87]

Such reservations are not entirely new. In the early twentieth century, for example, the authoritative *Chambers's Encyclopaedia* decided against including an entry for 'Slum', and directed readers instead to its essay on 'Housing and Town-planning'.[88] Likewise, in mid-century India, C. Govindan Nair, the director of town planning at Madras, referred to *Chambers's*, and mused:

> The term [slum] connotes something extremely ugly, repugnant, repulsive – in fact amounting to something slimy – filthy. It carries with it a great deal of loss of dignity. While this is absolutely true of slum areas as we know them, to my mind, I feel that we should not use the term otherwise than in a non-technical and non-legislative sense. I . . . submit that in its application in the technical and legislative sense, any mention of the term as such should be avoided. I feel that the free use of the term cannot remove from it the stigma that will attach to it and, in the sociological sense, any labelling of an area or the resident dwellers of the area with such a stigma would be consonant with loss of prestige. They are there as a matter of circumstance; but as equal citizens their dignity needs safeguarding. The psychological reaction which the continued use of the term may induce, may not, I am afraid, be a desirable feature.[89]

In Latin America in the twenty-first century, veteran anthropologist Janice Perlman, who has studied poor communities in Rio de Janeiro since the late 1960s, declared, 'I find it objectionable to refer to favelas – or any other squatter settlements – as "slums",' and criticized the United Nations' Millennium Development Goals programme for rehabilitating a word that 'had rightly fallen into ignominious disrepute'.[90]

In the resulting vacuum of credible academic definitions the *Oxford English Dictionary* has become a standard reference point in discussions about slums, although its entry has not been substantially revised since 1912:

> A street, alley, court, etc., situated in a crowded district of a town or city and inhabited by people of a low class or by the very poor; a number of these streets or courts forming a thickly populated neighbourhood or district where the houses and the conditions of life are of a squalid and wretched character.[91]

A parallel UNESCO definition, used by Desai and Pillai in the 1970s, revolved around similar concepts:

> a slum is a building, a group of buildings, or area character-ized by overcrowding, deterioration, unsanitary conditions or absence of facilities or amenities which, because of these con-ditions or any of them, endanger the health, safety or morals of its inhabitants or the community.[92]

A recent Government of India report, having struggled to find an all-encompassing definition, turned to the *Encyclopædia Britannica*: 'residential areas that are physically and socially deteriorated and in which satisfactory family life is impossible'.[93] It is unfortunate that all these definitions echo value judgements from the past that Davis thought had been consigned to the dustbin of history. In an effort to weed out such slighting references to behavioural abnormality, India's Registrar General and Census Commissioner recently explained:

> A Slum, for the purpose of the Census, has been defined as resi-dential areas where dwellings are unfit for human habitation by reasons of dilapidation, overcrowding, faulty arrangements

and design of such buildings, narrowness or faulty arrangement of street, lack of ventilation, light, or sanitation facilities or any combination of these factors which are detrimental to . . . safety and health.[94]

However the Registrar General's continuing reliance on the nineteenth-century phrase 'unfit for human habitation' leaves his updated definition still anchored in Davis's past.

This is not simply a matter of semantics; it goes to the heart of knowledge formation and progressive reform. A good example of how 'slum' concepts compromise such work is the Cities Alliance, an international network established in 1999 in partnership with UN-Habitat and the World Bank, which initiated 'a Cities Without Slums Action Plan' – subsequently included in the Millennium Development Goals – to remove the world's 'squalid, unhealthy, unserved and vulnerable urban slums'. The Cities Alliance has struggled to find a practical definition for target neighbourhoods that

range from high density, squalid central city tenements to spontaneous squatter settlements without legal recognition or rights, sprawling at the edge of cities. Some are more than fifty years old, some are land invasions just underway.

Its best effort at synthesis has been to declare that all such settlements 'share the same miserable living conditions'.[95] This is no advance upon reformers' comments of a century earlier.

The paradox of using an inherently deceitful word to promote an equity-based reform agenda led the United Nations in 2002 to draw up its own 'operational definition of a slum'.[96] This comprised five 'slum definition indicators' or 'shelter deprivations used to measure slums – lack of access to improved water, lack of access to sanitation, non-durable housing, insufficient living area, and insecurity of tenure'.[97] In applying this new definition, UN-Habitat explained that it would identify 'any specific place, whether a whole city or a neighbourhood, as a slum area if half or more of all households' were deficient in these five key variables.[98] However, the United Nations soon acknowledged the insufficiencies of a definition that focused only upon the physical and legal but 'does not fully capture the degree of deprivation experienced by a given household or slum community,

or the specific needs of that community [nor] the severity of combined deprivations'.[99] More reluctantly, it conceded that its 'slum'
definition was 'restricted to the physical and legal characteristics of
the settlement, and excluding the more difficult social dimensions'.[100]
The United Nations is left with the rallying cry of 'Cities Without
Slums' for programmes that aspire to achieve fundamental social
reform but which, because of the contradictions inherent in defining
the word upon which they rest, cannot adequately express and address
the needs and aspirations of the urban poor and cannot build upon
their substantial achievements.

Implications and consequences

It is easier to identify the inadequacies of the word 'slum' than it is to
explain why the term nevertheless continues to be so widely, although
unevenly, used. It persists in part because it is used by powerful elites in
politics, public administration, academia, the mass media and business,
and it is endorsed by the comfortably well-off in mainstream society.
To them it is immaterial that the word is not accepted by the vast
majority of those who live in places that are called slums.

It also persists because places to which it is applied, from
nineteenth-century Five Points to twenty-first-century Dharavi, were
and are indeed environmentally compromised and the life chances
of many of their residents unambiguously constrained. However, we
would much better understand such local environments, and assist
their inhabitants to modify them for the better, if we removed the
distorting 'slum' prism from the way we perceive and prioritize issues
of social and environmental development.

The term 'slum' also persists because it masks the improprieties of
economic, political and legal regimes that enable profits to be made
out of cities' inequalities. It is abhorrent, for example, that even as
Slumdog Millionaire won eight Oscars and became a box office hit
around the world, the homes of two of its principal child actors were
pulled down in 2009 and their families left to live in the streets as the
result of slum clearance drives by city and railway authorities.[101] The
innumerable projects of urban redevelopment undertaken throughout
the world since the nineteenth century under the guise of eliminating
slums have delivered profits and new city infrastructure for governments, entrepreneurs and private investors, but have usually worsened

the lives of those who lived and worked in the targeted communities. Demolitions are the most visible and traumatic of the daily injustices perpetrated on 'slum' communities, injustices that include impediments to health care, education, jobs and legal aid, and petty tyrannies and harassment by local officials and the police.

Such injustices are symptomatic of basic inequities in the functioning of market economies that no regulators have had the will to resolve. Englander's comment that the nature of nineteenth-century urban economics in Britain left the poor 'packed, layered, and compressed like sardines' into districts of entrenched disadvantage is not only true of the past he described but is echoed (as Desai and Pillai pointed out) in the cities of the developing world today, and it especially resonates with the social geography of the cities of the Global South. Simone points out that

> global economic trends and policies do have an effect on where people live and what they are able to do. The problems of accumulation – of generating sufficient profit – have been displaced onto the poor. This happens by cheapening labor and disinvesting in public services.[102]

Kundu suggests that in Indian cities these trends have set in train 'a process of segmentation' that has created high-tech industrial zones, chic shopping complexes and high-income residential enclaves on the one hand, and poor communities and polluting industries on the other.[103] The intensification of these contrasts – even as the national GDP of developing nations such as India and Brazil rises – has prompted some experts to warn that 'globalization might be creating rich countries with poor people.'[104]

But, most of all, 'slum' persists because we, mainstream society, use and embrace it. Sometimes we embrace it in order to do nothing: in our contempt for 'losers' and 'users' we feel righteously justified in neglecting the 'underclass'. Sometimes we embrace it in the name of humanitarian action: donating to an aid agency, heeding the latest journalistic exposé or perhaps participating in a slummer tour. For the most part, however, we perpetuate slum stereotypes because they help us to define (and congratulate) ourselves in juxtaposition to our imagined opposite. Thus, in our imaginations, the slum is necessarily an abhorrent and dysfunctional realm, because it was fashioned as the antithesis of commonsense understandings of decency and utility in the modern city. It was fashioned thus because the slum genre sought to contain social contradictions by mobilizing public opinion around core principles about individual and collective behavior that purported to identify and explain the causes and effects of urban poverty, and that offered solutions for these social ills.[105]

Peter Stallybrass and Allon White well described how 'what is *socially* peripheral is so frequently *symbolically* central' in the high–low, us–them, good–bad juxtapositions and constructions of 'Otherness' that underpin the processes of 'ordering and sense-making in European cultures'.[106] Pillai argued that the same dynamic operates in other cultures as well. In India, he suggested,

> Looking at slums from the middle or upper class or upper caste milieu, a writer may see the opposite of many things he holds 'dear' and 'correct'. By showering pity on the poor, his own values and culture-class levels are brought into an elevated level of empathetic dignity [because] 'they' are not 'normal' people with a 'decent' culture 'like us'.[107]

Today the more comfortable sections of the 'developed' world no longer apply the word 'slum' to their own nations but use it in reference to community development or reality tourism in the 'developing' world. This use is underpinned in part by sympathetic concern. However, there is also a strong element of self-congratulation: 'advanced' nations have supposedly moved beyond slums to a higher stage of development. There is, moreover, an element of denial: of continuing and intensifying social polarization and unrest at home. Meanwhile, in the developing world today, slum stereotypes are used by the elite and the rapidly expanding middle classes to rationalize inequality and to draw a line between it and 'normal' modernizing society. 'Slum' and 'slumming' thus continue to operate today as they did when they emerged during the beginnings of modern urbanization in the nineteenth century.

TWO

THE ATTRACTION
OF REPULSION

The first known inscription of the word 'slum' is in *A Vocabulary of the Flash Language* (1812, 1819). Its compiler, James Hardy Vaux, was an outcast: a convict banished to Britain's penal settlements in Australia. Vaux's *Vocabulary* was intended to help his guards understand the London slang talk used by his fellow prisoners.

Widening use of the word 'slum' during the nineteenth and twentieth centuries, from local Cockney idiom in the East End of London to the language of English-speakers throughout the world, was a result of the transformation of Britain and its settler offshoots in North America and Australasia from predominantly rural to urban societies. That transformation led the world. It was an outcome of the massive growth of commerce and industry during the take-off phase of modern capitalism and the subsequent consolidation of capitalist economies during the twentieth century. Urbanization – the increase of urban populations at a faster rate than population growth for society as a whole – was equated with progress and modernity by many contemporaries. In 1899 the pioneering American statistician Adna Weber described the aggregation of population into cities as 'the most remarkable social phenomenon of the present century'.[1] However, for many people it was an uncertain and unsettling phenomenon to live through. The rapid growth of towns and cities, generated by expanding markets for goods and services but insufficiently overseen by government regulators, created habitats that were ugly, inconvenient and sometimes dangerous. They resulted in appalling living conditions for many of the working classes. The word 'slum' was adopted to encapsulate those conditions and to rationalize the resulting gulf between comfort and affluence on the one hand and hardship and destitution on the other.

Lewis Mumford argued that 'The two main elements in the new urban complex were the factory and the slum.'[2]

The word 'slum' was thus value-laden from the outset. It was not a straightforward and uncomplicated descriptive label for the aggregations of social disadvantage that accompanied rapid urban growth. Slums were not a tangible material outcome of the inequitable operation of the markets for labour and housing, although those outcomes were plain to see. Rather, the word 'slum' was an envelope for an accumulating set of concepts that was employed in order to try to comprehend and explain those outcomes. It was thus a product of popular imagination, or, as Charles Dickens put it, of the 'attraction of repulsion'. The word 'slum' encapsulated fear: anxieties that rapid urban growth was degrading natural environments and dissolving long-standing social norms and relationships, generating ill health, crime and disorder. It also expressed bewilderment and embarrassment that such conditions could exist in the very vortex of modernity. In 1934, digging the first sod for a new public housing estate in Birmingham, Britain's minister of health spoke of the 'great effort to rid this country of the disgrace of the slums'.[3] However, as the minister's words suggest, 'slum' simultaneously expressed hope: slum conditions could be eliminated. The word was used by researchers and reformers as they sought to describe the inequities and contradictions in modern society and to mobilize support for their efforts to overcome them. In like manner, it was used by well-intentioned citizens who agreed with the reformers that urban social conditions, albeit deplorable, were improvable. However, to a still greater extent, and as Dickens recognized, the slum entertained.

Sensational depictions of slums enthralled the mass audiences that urbanization had created, and in doing so they also engaged those audiences in reaching a loose consensus regarding the ideal forms – spatial, functional and behavioural – that were appropriate to modern times. The slum's 'attraction of repulsion' was thus played out as a kind of shared performance that was shaped in large part by the social elite, but participated in and actively perpetuated by the mainstream of urban society. Slums were depicted as residual places to which the positive influence of freely operating markets and complementary state regulation had yet to be comprehensively applied; slum-dwellers were the misfits who accumulated in these unreformed places through misfortune, incapacity or deviant obstinacy. The slum thus took root in the imaginations of English-speaking societies as an unambiguous marker of what was and was not appropriate to the modern urban world: nowhere else have slum stereotypes 'been so tightly packaged in an opposition to city ideals as in the Anglophone world'.[4] Appropriateness of form and behaviour was made clear by juxtaposition with its imaginary polar opposite. Slum behaviour was characterized as the antithesis of responsible and effective citizenship in the modern city; slum environments were a travesty of the decent homes, productive workplaces, handsome public spaces and efficient municipal services that framed the lives of normal citizens. Characterizations of slums simultaneously acknowledged that inequality existed in modern cities and fashioned a moral consensus that responsible citizenship could largely eliminate it. This powerful consensus transcended divisions of gender, class and status, because by directing slum stereotypes against one's supposed inferiors, even financially stretched working-class families could affirm their self-esteem by measuring themselves against the dwellers of the slums. Thus, for example, Winifred Foley's memories of growing up in a poor English coal mining community during the 1920s contrasted the 'middling families' of struggling mine workers such as her parents' with 'the "slums" at the feckless end' of town.[5]

This chapter traces the development of the slum concepts that conditioned general understanding of urban social disadvantage where the urbanization of the modern world began – in Britain and British-settled societies – from the early nineteenth century, when the word 'slum' was first coined, until the 1970s, by which time its shock value had faded in favour of other norm-reinforcing constructs in what by then called itself the 'developed world'. The chapter also begins to explore the public policies that resulted from these deceits.

The urban kaleidoscope

When the French architect Le Corbusier first visited New York in 1936 he described the city as 'certainly the most prominent manifestation of the power of modern times'.[6] It was considered to be 'an index and instrument of moral progress in American society'.[7] The modern city has been described as 'our greatest creation'.[8] The pace of urban change during the nineteenth and early twentieth centuries was most evident in the English-speaking world (Britain, North America and Australasia). In 1890 eleven, and in 1920 thirteen, of the world's thirty most populous cities were located in these nations.[9] The census of 1851 recorded that, for the first time, a majority of the British population lived in urban places. London became the world's metropolitan hub during the nineteenth century, and New York took over that position in the early twentieth century as the United States, like Britain, increasingly became an urban nation (in 1920 a majority of Americans were recorded as living in towns and cities). Chicago, Philadelphia, Boston, Detroit, Manchester, Birmingham, Glasgow and Liverpool developed into huge centres of industry and commerce. San Francisco, Vancouver, Melbourne and Sydney became regional hubs in an emerging global shipping network. So rapid was their rate of growth that New World cities like these have been called 'instant cities'.[10] Unlike the urban places of the Old World, they were born modern. Melbourne, for example, which was founded only in 1835, so harnessed the new technologies and opportunities of the modern world that by 1890 it had become one of the largest cities in the world, bigger than Birmingham or Boston, bigger than Madrid, bigger than Madras. Some of these modern city powerhouses contained huge populations, some of them sprawled over vast tracts of land. All of them were characterized by rapid growth. All of them inspired pride for the vitality of their economies, the rich diversity of their cultural life, the grandeur of their public architecture and the modernity of their technological infrastructure. There was a sense of comfort and achievement, also, in the private domestic sphere that underpinned the public life of cities and which found expression in the neat suburban homes and gardens of the new urban middle and skilled working classes.

However, these modern cities also generated apprehension and ambivalence. Cities were bewildering in the unprecedented and relentless rapidity of their growth and in their scale. As historians Maury Klein and Harvey Kantor said of the urban transformation of the United States, contemporaries 'saw their world dissolving and re-forming about them'.[11] City dwellers struggled to comprehend new habitats whose extent, diversity and density of population eroded the patterns of movement, the cycles of work and leisure, the environmental relationships of people to place and the social relationships of small communities that had prevailed for centuries. People's sense of pattern, purpose, position and limitation dissolved in the face of the kaleidoscopic open-endedness of the modern city, and new formulas for action more appropriate to the new conditions were not at all clear.

Direct sensory experience – of the air, land and waterways – drew attention to this new imbalance: urban environments degraded as city dwellers slowly learned, from the consequences of their neglect, the need to manage on vastly larger scales the supply of water, food and fuel and the removal of waste. Edwin Chadwick's pioneering *Sanitary Condition of the Labouring Classes of Great Britain* (1842) comprehensively documented those consequences and their possible regulatory remedy. In 1848 the Health of Towns Act provided local authorities with the first tools for doing so, but any attempt at regulation was long characterized by neglect and evasion. Cities remained noisy, congested, smelly and filthy. They were profoundly unhealthy. Urban congestion made explicit to all that it 'was beyond the practical imagination of the governing classes . . . to provide sufficient housing for the population at rates which the bulk of the people could afford'.[12] The insufficiencies and inadequacies of urban housing highlighted the uneven social outcomes of city growth. In modern cities, prosperity jarred spectacularly with abject poverty.

The fundamental cause of these environmental and social problems is now clear. It was the result, as historian H. J. Dyos said of nineteenth-century London, then the world's largest city, of accumulated private capital 'being ploughed heavily back into the commercial machine instead of being distributed in higher wages' for all.[13] It was the result of profit margins being heeded by employers and investors rather than the social costs of generating them. It demonstrated the incapacity of unregulated private enterprise 'to create or maintain the social investment and services that were the essential cornerstone of the city'.[14] This ethical malaise was not only a feature of early capitalism in the Victorian era. Visiting the manufacturing cities of Edwardian Britain early in the twentieth century, the Australian novelist Vance Palmer sensed 'the pressure of an industrial machine, grinding on incessantly and giving no adequate return, in leisure, warmth, decent food, to the people who kept it going'.[15] In the 1960s, as Dyos was writing about the nineteenth century, Michael Harrington turned his attention to the contemporary world and pointed out that, still, every 'big city in the United States has an economic underworld' of workers caught in insecure and low-paying jobs and deficient housing.[16] Management and shareholder preoccupation with profits – increasingly generated across global operations – had led to the restructuring and relocation of entire sectors of urban and regional economies, and in some cases to their virtual eclipse. Commentators in the United States and Britain spoke of urban decay, rust belt decline and deindustrialization. Once-dominant industrial cities such as Liverpool and Detroit seemingly imploded during the 1960s and 1970s as their economies unravelled. New York City teetered on the edge of bankruptcy in the mid-1970s. In Britain, the population of Liverpool – the core city within the broader Merseyside industrial region – peaked at 726,000 people in 1921 but had declined to 330,000 half a century later. Although Liverpool's city centre, rebuilt after the Second World War, continued to thrive, the city's docks, railways and manufacturing industries were decimated, creating some of the highest concentrations of poverty in the nation.

Although the cause of these social upheavals is now clear, their diagnosis in the past was not. The Canadian businessman and philanthropist Sir Herbert Brown Ames, who undertook a household survey of poverty in Montreal during 1896, cautioned that reform efforts 'cannot interfere with the inscrutable law of supply and demand to raise the workingman's wages'.[17] Although a minority of perceptive medical practitioners, philanthropists and housing reformers had since the early nineteenth century drawn attention to the environmental and social problems resulting from unrestricted market-driven urbanization, they did not command sustained public attention. Instead of addressing urban social problems, the beneficiaries of the emerging urban social order sought 'to put a distance' between themselves and the problems that urbanization had created.[18] From as early as the 1830s, the urban middle classes had begun to build suburban homes on the urban periphery, far away from the social and environmental problems that urbanization was creating. Skilled working people joined the migration, initially living in inner suburbs within walking distance of their city workplaces, but following the middle classes to more distant commuter suburbs as public transport systems expanded during the later nineteenth and early twentieth centuries, and as automobile ownership became a mass phenomenon from the middle of the twentieth century. In 1901, for example, it was said of leafy suburban Edgbaston, initially home to many of Birmingham's business elite, that the district was becoming

> crowded with terraces, many of them very pretty and attractive in their way. The tenants are a good class. They cultivate their little gardens; they plant trees; they twine creepers round

their doors; they take care of their dwellings, and are proud of their aspect.[19]

In the United States, the National Advisory Commission on Civil Disorders noted with concern in 1968 that a massive and accelerating 'outflow' of better-off families from the central cities to the suburbs had been evident since the Second World War.[20] It seemed that suburbanization everywhere was creating a social vacuum in the city centres and undermining any common ground between mainstream society and the poor. As one academic study in Melbourne warned in 1967, 'However much we idealize life in the suburbs, there is still the fact that in the centre of this constellation of garden suburbs are acres of slums.'[21]

Social commentators throughout the nineteenth and twentieth centuries noted with concern an apparent weakening in social ties and responsibilities as a consequence of urban growth and the suburban diaspora, and urged 'public-spirited men' to show greater leadership in civic affairs.[22] Occasionally their voices were heard. The take-up of George Dawson's 'municipal gospel' by Birmingham's business and professional leaders during the 1870s is a good example,[23] and in North America polemics such as W. T. Stead's *If Christ Came to Chicago* (1894) and J. K. Galbraith's *The Affluent Society* (1958) sparked widespread debate about the appropriate balance between private profit-making and public service. However, in the long term the private profit motive and social complacency prevailed, even in regions where the ill consequences of urban and economic change were most apparent. In the Massachusetts cotton manufacturing city of Lawrence – one of many in the New England region that struggled for viability as textile production shifted to cheaper production sites in the American South – the authors of a wide-ranging social survey lamented in 1912, 'what an extremely weak, and exceptionally broken assembly of peoples the city is.'[24] In the struggling English manufacturing city of Liverpool, likewise, social analysts concluded in 1972 that 'the social disintegration of the community has been both dramatic and alarming.'[25] The 1977 Liverpool Inner Area Study referred to

rundown slums, almost ghettos, sandwiched between redeveloped city centres and the suburbs, seen by people only on their journey to work as they look down from the railway across the backs of terraces, or across the vacant land from main roads.[26]

In *The Other America* (1962), Harrington not only pointed out that 'tens of millions of Americans are . . . existing at levels beneath those necessary for human decency,' but drew attention to the paradox that such poverty had become 'increasingly invisible' to affluent suburban America.[27] John Stubbs made a similar point in relation to the widespread extent of poverty in Australia. *The Hidden People* (1966) begins thus: 'At least half a million Australians are living in poverty. We have little contact with them, yet they are everywhere.'[28]

Within the largest cities there had existed since at least the middle of the nineteenth century whole regions of disadvantage that were barely known to outsiders and only glimpsed by others as a blurred zone traversed quickly in the commuter train and (from the middle of the twentieth century) the expressway. Even in smaller cities, direct knowledge of poor neighbourhoods was only skin-deep. The English city of York, for example, comprised just 76,000 inhabitants in 1899 when B. Seebohm Rowntree embarked upon his pioneering social survey that was intended 'to throw some light upon the conditions which govern the life of the wage-earning classes in provincial towns, and especially upon the problem of poverty'.[29]

It took the shock word 'slum' to transcend the ignorance, indifference and complacency of the majority of city dwellers concerning the poverty in their midst. Rowntree had used the word to encapsulate what he found in York's overlooked and disadvantaged Hungate neighbourhood:

> Hungate [is] one of the main slum districts in York . . . Though not large in extent, it is still large enough to exhibit the chief characteristics of slum life – reckless expenditure of money as soon as obtained, with the aggravated want at other times; the rowdy Saturday night, the Monday morning pilgrimage to the pawn-shop, and especially that love for the district, and disinclination to move to better surroundings, which, combined with an indifference to the higher aims of life, are the despair of so many social workers.[30]

By the 1930s, 'slums' in American cities were being called 'the most glaring symptom of urban disintegration'.[31] Depictions of slums cut across the social and geographical distance that separated city dwellers. Slum sensationalism commanded attention. Their 'attraction of repulsion' harnessed the anxieties and curiosities that city dwellers felt about the unfamiliar places that were inhabited by the urban poor.

When in 1883 the Reverend Andrew Mearns first spectacularly drew mass attention to London's slums in his Congregational Union pamphlet *The Bitter Cry of Outcast London*, which depicted a 'great dark region of poverty, misery, squalor and immorality', he caused a sensation not only in London but throughout the English-speaking world. For although Mearns's evidence was drawn from London, his conclusion was universal:

> the discovery that seething in the very centre of our great cities, concealed by the thinnest crust of civilization and decency, is a vast mass of moral corruption, of heart-breaking misery and absolute godlessness.[32]

Robert A. Woods, a leading figure in the settlement house movement in the United States, said of *The Bitter Cry*, 'All classes were moved by it. The state of the London poor was felt to be to English civilization something like an imputation of failure. It touched British pride.'[33] In faraway Australia, the *Sydney Morning Herald* remarked that the effect of *The Bitter Cry* was to highlight the 'vast wealth being accumulated on the one hand, and an immense amount of poverty staring us in the face on the other', and fretted lest people conclude 'that our civilisation is a failure, and that we are going from bad to worse'.[34]

The Bitter Cry, and subsequent shock publications about other cities in the English-speaking world, did indeed lead some to question unfettered capitalist development. Commenting on Mearns's pamphlet, *The Congregationalist* argued 'that slums stood as testimony to the results of the "iron bondage of this dry science" of *laissez-faire* economics'.[35] It led others to ponder the structures of a society in which the comfortable mainstream could be unaware or unconcerned that such inequalities existed. In Britain it mobilized philanthropic housing reformers, sparked the setting-up of a royal commission to investigate working-class housing conditions and paved the way for the passage of important housing legislation. Most of all, however, polemics such as *The Bitter Cry* entertained. It stimulated, and was in turn showcased by, sensationalist newspaper and magazine commentary, and further slumland exposés, throughout the English-speaking world. Dyos had no respect for such entertainments, contending that the reason for this shallow interest, 'tacitly accepted at the time, is that the slums helped to under-pin Victorian prosperity'.[36] It is more accurate to say that the concept of slums commanded attention as no other could during much of the nineteenth and twentieth centuries because it rationalized the inequalities and environmental degradation underpinning modern capitalist cities. This was the fundamental deceit of the slum.

Inventing the slum

The early meaning of the word 'slum' is obscure because it originated in spoken rather than written English and had a limited currency. It first appeared in written form in dictionaries of 'flash language', slang and the 'vulgar tongue' in early nineteenth-century London, which sought to explain 'the cant of thieves, prostitutes, and vagabonds' by translating the obscure colloquialisms from marginalized groups that were 'often used to exclude or mislead others'.[37] The power of slang lies in the freedom it gives speakers 'to play with and enjoy the language, make words up, adopt new expressions indiscriminately, and use language for humour, irony, sarcasm, and irreverence'.[38] Dictionary definitions lag behind and struggle to encapsulate such word play.

The earliest attributed meanings for the noun 'slum' range across obscure places and 'gammon' talk, to illicit or deceitful behaviour.[39] Vaux's *Vocabulary*, which was compiled in 1812 and published in 1819, describes a slum ambiguously as 'a room', but brackets it with a (criminal) 'racket' and with 'lodging-slum', or 'the practice of hiring ready-furnished lodgings, and stripping them'.[40] Vaux, unambiguously a rogue himself, was well positioned to furnish these meanings. The word possibly derives from 'slumber' (Middle English 'slumer'), which was reapplied by slang to out-of-the-way city places whose apparent sleepiness masks a darker underside.[41] Depictions of such places mentioned the 'drowsy air about even the worst neighbourhoods' and routinely drew attention to thieves and prostitutes 'Lounging at the doors and lolling out of windows and prowling about street corners'.[42] It was in this sense that 'slum' was first used colloquially to refer to hidden-away rooms of 'low repute'.[43]

As its use increased, this meaning widened to include whole houses, alleys and neighbourhoods in seemingly out-of-the-way and unsavoury parts of the city. Thus, as the word's circulation expanded beyond the idiom of its first users, it was applied pejoratively to what outsiders regarded as unfamiliar, insanitary and undesirable places. W. G. Hoskins argues that it was in this context that

> The slums were born. The word *slum*, first used in the 1820s, has its origin in the old provincial word *slump*, meaning 'wet mire'. The word *slam* in Low German, Danish and Swedish, means 'mire': and that roughly described the dreadful state of the streets and courtyards on these undrained sites.[44]

An association was thus born in slum usage between somnolent backwaters, deviant behaviour, poverty, misery and squalor. Pierce Egan's monthly journal *Life in London* (1821–8) set some of its tales among the 'back slums' of London's St Giles district and described such places as being 'low, unfrequented parts of the town'.[45] In 1825 Charles Westmacott ('Bernard Blackmantle') likewise referred to 'the number of desperate characters who inhabited the back-slums lying in the rear of Broad-street'.[46] But as such mass-circulation publications gave 'slum' a wider currency and evolving meanings, it is likely that its original use in the street slang of London's poorer classes became compromised and was abandoned.

By mid-century the phrase 'back slum' – often bracketed with inverted commas in acknowledgement of its fading slang origins – was appearing in publications not only in London but in other cities in Britain, North America and Australia. In 1857, for example, parts of Melbourne, then scarcely twenty years old, were being called 'back slums' and likened to 'the most crowded parts of Spitalfields and St Giles' in London.[47] By then, in general usage the phrase was beginning to be shortened to the single word 'slum', a trend that owed much to the widely publicized denunciation in 1850 by Cardinal Nicholas Wiseman, the newly appointed Roman Catholic archbishop of Westminster, of the 'labyrinths of lanes and courts, and alleys and slums, nests of ignorance, vice, depravity and crime' that surrounded his diocese.[48] However, 'back slum' retained a general, though declining, currency throughout the English-speaking world for the remainder of the century, and dictionary definitions of 'slum' in the twentieth century continued to lay emphasis upon the 'foul back street' at its root.[49] The use of inverted commas by publishers to denote the word's slang origins also declined from the 1840s, although they continued to be used into the early twentieth century.

The word's early use by Londoners to characterize discrete and out-of-the-way localities persisted and was applied in this way in other cities across the world and over time. In 1933, for example, Melbourne's 'slums' were described as being scattered about the inner suburbs in 'pockets':

> A visitor . . . may pass by, in numbers of places, what appear to be innocent-looking right-of-ways, whereas, if he entered they would often be found to lead into other rights-of-ways, or maybe narrow streets, in which there are the most dilapidated houses, inhabited by people who are on the poverty line, many of them slovenly and vicious.[50]

However, this sense of slums as forming discrete backwaters was increasingly used in parallel with, and subsumed within, a broader sense of slums sprawling across entire districts that encroached upon ever-wider areas. As the BBC broadcaster Howard Marshall said of Britain in 1933, 'the slums are not small localised areas – a few streets here and there in the great industrial towns – but . . . they sprawl in black patches over the whole country.'[51]

'Slum' swept aside, but did not entirely replace, other words that had been used since the eighteenth century to characterize the poorest city neighbourhoods. 'Rookery', for example, connoted congestion and hubbub, and 'den' added the implication of predation and criminality. Both words, translated from their original meanings in the natural world, gave a non-human hue to depictions of urban poverty. This pejorative meaning was absorbed by 'slum'. Thus W. T. Stead, railing against 'the horrors of the slums', declared in 1883 that London's poor were being 'brutalized into worse than beasts by the conditions of their environment'.[52] 'Slum' and 'rookery' were still being used interchangeably in Britain during the 1880s and '90s, and 'rookery' remained in use throughout the English-speaking world during the early twentieth century.

The words 'slummer' and 'slumming' entered the formal English vocabulary during the 1880s and '90s. They referred in part to those who lived in poor areas (the New York *Voice*, for example, referred in 1889 to 'some shirtless slummer').[53] Increasingly, the words were also applied to those who visited disadvantaged neighbourhoods out of curiosity or philanthropic intent. Thus 'slum' became a verb as well as a noun. Some of those who undertook 'to slum' were seeking to help. Charles Masterman lived in a London tenement building and a university 'slum' settlement before writing *From the Abyss* (1902). Cyril Forster Garbett (subsequently the archbishop of York) undertook four hours per day of house-to-house visits among the poor both when he was a young curate and then as vicar of a dockyard parish in Portsea between 1900 and the First World War. The bishop of London, Arthur Winnington-Ingram, reminiscing about his appointment in 1888 to head the university settlement of Oxford House in London's East End, told a *Times* reporter in 1933 that 'it was exactly 45 years this month since he went into slumland himself, and he would never forget that first journey, setting off in a hansom cab from Euston to find Bethnal Green'.[54] Queen Mary, wife of George V, also toured Bethnal Green as the campaign to eliminate slums gathered momentum in 1919. However, most slummers were drawn by idle curiosity. The *Boston Journal* noted in 1884 that a 'party of young fashionable people of New York thought they would go a slumming', and in London Joseph Hatton referred in 1889 to '"Slumming" [as becoming] a modern fashion'.[55] It was remarked in the 1930s that 'sightseeing trips to the East End are a feature of tourist London.'[56]

IT WAS SIGHTSEEING in London's East End that had first whetted Dickens's sense of the 'attraction of repulsion'. His biographer John Forster noted that Dickens had from an early age been drawn to congested places such as London's St Giles district:

> he had a profound attraction of repulsion to St. Giles's. If he could only induce whomsoever took him out to take him through Seven Dials, he was supremely happy. 'Good Heaven!' he would exclaim, 'what wild visions of prodigies of wickedness, want, and beggary, arose in my mind out of that place!'[57]

Dickens had used the same phrase in his own writing, before Forster's biography was completed, to explain the pulling power of the churchyard of St Ghastly Grim.[58] His interest in the phrase thus encompassed both human and environmental corruption. It dovetailed neatly with the widening usage of the word 'slum' during the second half of the nineteenth century, and resonated with the ambivalent public mood about the urban transformation of human society.

The theatricality of Dickens's concept perfectly matched the qualities of performance that underpinned the cultural construction of slums in popular imagination. As even Charles Booth remarked of one study area in his pioneering social survey of London, 'There is in this part a great concentration of evil living and low conditions of life that strikes the imagination and leads almost irresistibly to sensational statement.'[59] Slum performances – whether expressed in novels, theatre, speeches, polemics, social surveys, journalism, visual media or slummer tourism – described and sought to make sense of the indeterminacies and contradictions of modern cities by 'fixing and framing . . . social reality'.[60] They attempted to establish clear lines of 'continuity and predictability in a world of endless change'.[61] These were performances without a master director and a single authorized script. The 'attraction of repulsion' genre was only loosely controlled by the emerging collective common sense of urban popular culture. 'Making sense' of cities and slums meant building up blocks of knowledge that corresponded with one's own experiences, assumptions and priorities, and anchoring these within broader expectations that could be loosely shared by elite, middle- and working-class society. The many strands of the slum genre that shaped public knowledge in the English-speaking world therefore contained contradictions, inconsistencies and differences of emphasis. However, characterizations of slums, whether contained in the analytical approach of a Rowntree or the flamboyant journalism of a Riis or Stead, had key traits in common. They used shock to galvanize attention: Henry Mayhew's seminal *London Labour and the London Poor*, first published as a series of articles by the *Morning Chronicle* in 1849, was applauded for providing 'revelations so marvellous, so horrible, and so heartrending'.[62] They all sought, as Riis did most famously in *How the Other Half Lives*, to explain 'other' people and places. They all did so by fashioning 'Otherness' as an imaginary opposite to their own familiar worlds, activities and value systems. Thus the 'attraction of repulsion' functioned not to challenge and reformulate the social dynamics of modern cities, but to clarify, justify and reaffirm them through juxtaposition with 'the evil of the slums'.[63] Its blurred but loosely shared vision was sustained by ongoing cross-referencing between cities. Ames, for example, when he sought to arouse public concern about the conditions of the poor in Montreal, remarked in 1897 that the citizens of Montreal should, for a time, cease discussing the slums of London, the beggars of Paris and the tenement house evils of New York and endeavour to learn something about themselves and to understand more perfectly the conditions present in their very midst.[64]

Slum depictions, which emerged as a clear genre in the English-speaking world during the late nineteenth century and persisted into the 1970s, characteristically included theatrical signals to alert the audience that a doorway into an alien world was opening before them. Beyond this threshold – 'secret', 'hidden', 'unsuspected' – lies slumland. To proceed is to risk confronting multiple horrors, and the faint-hearted are cautioned, melodramatically, to go no further: 'At this point we respectfully but earnestly ask our lady-readers to read no further unless they are quite prepared for pain and shock.'[65] The American writer Stephen Crane warned readers of his novel *Maggie: A Girl of the Streets* (1893) that they might be 'greatly shocked' if they followed his narrative into New York's infamous Bowery district.[66] Illustrators and photographers sought to dramatize these threshold moments and juxtapositions: a forbidding tenement building, an empty alleyway, or perhaps a pen-and-ink sketch for a newspaper or periodical showing a group of Salvation Army evangelists, illuminated by the glow of a street lamp, while grouped about them in the dark are the hunched figures and gloomy encircling buildings of the slum. In narrative form, an imaginary rite of passage unfolds as the public world of the city is replaced by the hidden world of the slum: a sudden turn off the main street; a disorientating, gasping stumble along stinking narrow alleyways; uncertain footsteps up rotting stairs or through dark entranceways into the most intimate places of the urban poor. Mearns encapsulated this new slumland style:

> You have to grope your way along dark and filthy passages swarming with vermin. Then, if you are not driven back by the intolerable stench, you may gain admittance to the dens in which these thousands of beings . . . herd together.[67]

Time magazine was still echoing this slummer style in the 1970s, describing how, hidden amidst the wilderness of America's inner cities, there is a different world, a place of pock-marked streets, gutted tenements and broken hopes. Affluent people know little about this world, except when despair makes it erupt explosively onto Page One or the 7 o'clock news. Behind its crumbling walls lives a large group of people who are more intractable, more socially alien and more hostile than almost anyone had imagined.[68]

THE SLUMLANDS THUS REVEALED are typically presented as forming a foreign and topsy-turvy territory, the antithesis of the cityscapes and lifestyles with which audiences are familiar. They are 'queer places'.[69] They delineate the borders of 'slumdom'.[70] Descriptions of slums often categorize themselves as 'explorations' and are narrated by a guide (often accompanied in turn by policemen, sanitary inspectors or social workers with detailed local knowledge and survival skills) who leads the 'journey through the slums'.[71] Journalists frequently accompanied government officials on actual inspection tours of poor neighbourhoods, and their reports, sometimes reprinted in the newspapers of other cities, spread the genre of slum sensationalism throughout the urban network. Stories about slumland discovery often echoed popular narratives of European exploration and imperial expansion. The opening passage of George Sims's *How the Poor Live* (1883) is typical:

I commence with the first of this series of papers, a book of travel. An author and an artist have gone hand in hand into many a far-off region of the earth, and the result has been a volume eagerly studied by the stay-at-home public, anxious to know something of the world in which they live. In these pages I propose to record the results of a journey with pen and pencil into a region which lies at our own doors – into a dark continent that is within easy walking distance of the General Post Office. This continent will, I hope, be found as interesting as any of those newly-explored lands which engage the attention of the Royal Geographical Society – the wild races who inhabit will, I trust, gain public sympathy as easily as those savage tribes for whose benefit the Missionary Societies never cease to appeal for funds.[72]

The 'dark continents' thus described are unambiguously repugnant. James Cuming Walters, who wrote a series of articles called 'Scenes in Slum-Land' for the *Birmingham Daily Gazette* in 1901, called the city's slums 'a blighted region' within which the poor eked out a miserable existence

> amid the rank and rotting garbage, in the filthy alleys, and within the time-blackened old-fashioned dwellings, near the ill-smelling canal, or in the vicinage of factories which pour out their fumes in billowing masses from the throats of giant-stacks.[73]

Environments such as these are squalid and unordered. They are 'labyrinthine' and 'maze'-like. Buildings are surrounded by rubbish, slush and slime. Some are derelict and boarded up. They box out the light, and the stagnant air is difficult to breathe. Washing and toilet facilities are primitive and worn out by heavy common use; waste removal is defective. Homes – the word often qualified by inverted commas, as was 'dwelling', to emphasize what a travesty of real homes such places are – are poky and crowded, lacking furniture, the walls discoloured and mouldy, the floors dirty and swarming with vermin. The inhabitants of such vile places are likened to 'savage' and 'primitive' tribes, because the 'law of the jungle operates in the slum'.[74] Its streets are dangerous places where fights erupt and passers-by are assaulted; by the 1950s British audiences were being warned about violent youth gangs, and by the 1970s – with the spread of crack cocaine – commentators in the United States were drawing attention to 'the near anarchic violence on many ghetto streets'.[75] Slum narratives stressed that degraded environments debased those who inhabited them, with the result that 'slum-dwellers, with certain exceptions, are . . . filthy in their habits, and behave with less decency than animals.'[76] Subhuman analogies pepper the descriptions of both people and place: neighbourhoods are 'rat-holes', 'warrens' and 'dens'; their occupants are 'bestial' and herd together 'like swine'.

The 'attraction of repulsion' genre also emphasized the vast extent of slums. Walters's description of Birmingham's 'slum-region' is typical:

> They stretch out, with infinite ramifications, from the most crowded centre of Birmingham to the uttermost boundaries.

You may walk for a day, and not come to the end of the main thoroughfare which, like a polluted river, is fed by a thousand infected tributaries; and you may walk for a week and not have traced the in-and-out convolutions of streets, by-ways, alleys, and courts, which in the mass form the black and festering cancer, ever slowly widening, and sapping the life and strength of the city.[77]

Thirty years later in 1933, when Howard Marshall toured British cities, he concluded that two million families lived in slums 'in the utmost squalor and wretchedness'.[78] Another forty years later, little had seemingly changed when in 1972 a Shelter report cautioned that in Britain 'there are more than a million people living in communities dominated by their slums and blighted by other social problems.'[79] The enormous scale of the problems thus revealed invited generalization. As Sims had said, 'The story of one slum is the story of another.'[80]

This common storyline emphasized not only the scale of the encroaching slums but their terrible intensity. The universal slum acted like a destructive vortex. Those caught in it, wrote Sims, 'are sunk in the misery and degradation of slum life'.[81] In turn, as like attracts like, Mearns wrote that the 'low parts of London are the sink into which the filthy and abominable from all parts of the country seem to flow'.[82] Bernard S. Townroe warned in 1936 that 'the slum-minded class' were 'not normal members of the community. Often they are mental defectives who have sunk down and down until they occupy the cheapest and most verminous lodging obtainable.'[83] In 1956 a British government report cautioned that slum housing 'creates conditions in which the weaker families lose heart and sink'.[84] The word 'sink' (which is analogous in part with seepage, cesspools and sewage pits, and thus readily links to the 'slime of slums') was repeatedly used in slum narratives, and in Britain by the second half of the twentieth century it was also being applied to the public housing estates with which local government authorities had sought to replace run-down neighbourhoods. Thus new slums arose in place of the old. *New Society* commented in 1976 that

in every town that has council houses at all, there's a 'sink' estate – the roughest and shabbiest on the books, disproportionately tenanted by families with problems, and despised both by those who live there and the town at large.[85]

Sink estates were synonymous with violence, lawlessness and misery. Walter Besant, whose *All Sorts and Conditions of Men* (1882) had portrayed similar conditions in the nineteenth century, warned in 1896 that the poor were 'falling lower and lower still into the hell of savagery'.[86] Such conditions of life, contended Walters, constituted 'a seething mass of horrors' within which 'the innocent are soon contaminated, and . . . crime and violence are rampant.'[87] The Australian social reformer Frederick Oswald Barnett in 1933 likewise described a descending spiral through low-skill and intermittent jobs to 'the lowest depths of drunkenness, criminality or prostitution'.[88] In 1977, in the aftermath of an 'orgy of looting and burning' that swept through New York's poorest neighbourhoods during an electricity blackout, *Time* provided a 'portrait' of one of the participants:

> In Brooklyn's grimy Bedford-Stuyvesant ghetto, a welfare mother surveys her $195-a-month tenement apartment, an unheated, vermin-ridden urban swamp. The bathroom ceiling and sink drip water on the cracked linoleum floor. There are no lights, no locks on the doors. Disheveled and 35, the woman has been on welfare ever since her five-year-old son was born. She joined in the looting during July's traumatic blackout, and calls the episode 'convenient. We saw our chance and we took it.'[89]

Slums were variously likened to 'infernos', 'hells', 'the abyss', 'the underworld' and 'the depths'. The slum was 'the volcano crater . . . of an underlying wrong method and ideal in our city development'.[90] In these slumland netherworlds were to be found 'abominations' of all kinds. Here dwelt the 'submerged', the 'substratum', the 'residuum', all of them characterized by 'the filth of body and mind, the depth of depravity, the collapse of manhood and womanhood, the loss of moral fibre, in the region of despair, desolation, and corruption'.[91] During the 1970s the Reverend Jesse Jackson, referring to Chicago, declared: 'It is bad to be in the slum, but it is worse when the slum is in you. The spiritual slum is the ultimate tragedy.'[92]

The slum-dweller performs

Slum performances typically identified a recurring cast of unambiguous slum 'types' whose role in acting out this 'spiritual slum' was to make explicit the pernicious 'slum habits' that were adopted by 'slum-minded' people.[93] Their behaviour – wary of, and sometimes threatening towards, outsiders – represented a fundamental subversion of the behaviour deemed appropriate to both the public life of the city and the private life of the home. Their way of life demonstrates that it is 'the bad man and the bad woman [who] make the slums'.[94] Thus slum types are habitually presented as drunkards: 'Strong drink is a builder of slums.'[95] Slum women are untidy, wan, drawn and dejected; their children are squalid, thin and haggard; the men are 'low-browed and evil-visaged'.[96] These communities belligerently eyeball even the best intentioned of slummer visitors: 'Forbidding-looking men and women with folded arms, too often nursing their wrath to keep it warm, or giving full vent to it, stand at open doors.'[97]

Mothers gossip, drink and fight rather than budgeting for their families, cleaning their homes, preparing meals and caring for their children; in the slum narratives of the 1970s they might also sell heroin. Often they are single mothers or have husbands or partners who regularly beat them, and who turn to crime rather than productive work. Teenagers drop out of school, join street gangs and indulge in 'rowdy behaviour'.[98] A married woman from Manchester's Moss Side declares in 1972, 'It's pretty bad this area; the big lads come and blackguard around.'[99] Invariably, slum performances depict children as 'the most pitiable element of slum-life' because of their initial innocence and their vulnerability to the 'polluting' effects of the slum.[100] In a typical journalistic vignette, in which a 'child tumbles into the dirty little lane, which forms his sole playground', the moral is drawn: 'What chance has he to make a man of himself?'[101] Often the owners of slum dwellings are vilified for charging exorbitant rents while neglecting to maintain their properties, because their disregard for the ethical rules of decent society, rather than the fundamentals of free-market capitalism, can readily be blamed for contributing to entrenched urban poverty. Thus the plight of the American 'underclass' during the 1960s and '70s could be attributed in part to 'the extortionate sums charged by many slumlords'.[102] Slum performances also commonly drew attention to a minority of slum-dwellers, poor but respectable, who are patterns of cleanliness and models of good citizenship. Though they lack this world's goods, some of the old women not only take a great pride in their homes, but in character are nothing less than 'saints'.

However, characteristically, the gradual contamination of such folk by their neighbours, or the stark juxtaposition of their honest and hard-working standards and those of the slum as a whole, proved the rule that the 'typical slum-dweller is either slovenly or vicious'.[103]

THE RECURRING USE of easily recognizable 'types' to personify slumland encouraged the circulation of crude ethnic stereotypes to describe and explain the 'Others' who personified urban poverty. Caricatures of different and supposedly inferior national types fitted well into slumland performances. In nineteenth-century Britain, ethnic stereotyping was the result in part of large-scale Irish immigration. Hence Sims's word-picture of Mrs O'Flannigan, 'the most notorious "drunkardess" . . . in the neighbourhood', who exclaims "I ain't been sober for five years – ha! ha! ha!"'[104] In *The Bitter Cry*, likewise, a symbolic doorkeeper to Outcast London comes in the form of 'a repulsive, half-drunken Irish-woman'.[105] Anti-Irish stereotypes also circulated widely in Britain's settler societies overseas. Ethnic slum caricatures in Britain during the late nineteenth century drew as well upon the large-scale settlement of European Jews in London's East End. The chairman of the London County Council's housing committee complained in 1932 'that in the past thousands of aliens whose standards of life were not British had been allowed to dump themselves into the Metropolis'.[106] In Canada, the English-speaking majority used French-Canadian ethnic caricatures to visualize urban poverty. However, it was the mass emigration of the European poor to North America during the late nineteenth and early twentieth centuries that entrenched ethnic stereotyping as a central component of slum representation. Americans prided themselves that urban inequality could not be home-grown; it was surely caused by foreign poverty being transported to the New World. Some of this poverty was attributed to Irish immigrants, but increasingly attention focused upon a 'vast and motley horde' of non-English-speaking European immigrants.[107] Robert Hunter remarked in 1904, 'we have Russia's poverty, Poland's poverty, Italy's poverty, Hungary's poverty, Bohemia's poverty – and what other nation's have we not?'[108]

This unsettling combination, on a huge scale, of both cultural difference and social disadvantage was greeted with dismay by Americans. Here was rich new material for the 'attraction of repulsion' style to draw upon. The Reverend William T. Elsing, a city missionary in New York's East Side, worried in 1892 that 'the English language is rarely heard in some of the lower parts of New York.'[109] Others pointed out that this trend was not limited to the nation's largest city. In 1906 Howard Grose cautioned that

> New York is a city in America but is hardly an American city. Nor is any other of our great cities, except perhaps Philadelphia. Boston is an Irish city, Chicago is a German-Scandinavian-Polish city, Saint Louis is a German city, and New York is a Hebrew-German-Irish-Italian-Bohemian-Hungarian city – a cosmopolitan race conglomeration. Eighteen languages are spoken in a single block.[110]

For Grose, the proliferation of foreign languages was symptomatic of a deeper social malaise. He argued that immigrants, by settling in city slums, were 'forming foreign colonies which maintain foreign customs and are impervious to American influences'.[111] Hunter also contended that because of the immigrants' poverty,

> their colonies are usually established in the poorest, the most criminal, the most politically debauched, and the most vicious portions of our cities. These colonies often make up the main portion of our so-called 'slums'.[112]

Chicago sociologists Robert Park and Herbert Miller reported in 1921 that the immigrants' home cultures broke down upon exposure to 'the American melting-pot', leaving them receptive to 'demoralization, maladjustment, pauperization, juvenile delinquency, and crime'.[113] In American popular culture, pejorative caricatures of immigrant ethnic types put an ugly face on the inhabitants of slumland and explained the persistence of poverty in progressive American cities.

Slums in the United States were associated especially with the southern and eastern European poor. Encouraged by the multi-volume findings of the Dillingham Commission on Immigration in 1911, Americans identified a hierarchy of immigrant types, the most superior and assimilable being British and northern European migrants (such as Germans, who were 'thrifty, intelligent and honest') who had the skills to work their way out of the slums, but ranging downwards to eastern and southern Europeans ('darker in pigmentation, smaller in stature, more mercurial, more attached to music and art, more given to crimes of larceny, kidnapping, assault, murder, rape and sex-immorality').[114] Slum performances focused on Jewish immigrants from central and eastern Europe and southern Italians. The latter were despised as being 'more ignorant than the negro and a great deal more vicious'.[115] The former were regarded with heightened suspicion because they came from regions that were regularly ravaged by cholera. As the head of the u.s. Public Health Service commented in 1921,

> For many years a very large number of emigrants from central Europe have arrived . . . in an inexcusably unhygienic condition and with a very considerable percentage of them infested with vermin.[116]

Americans responded with immigration restriction laws, culminating in the introduction of a nationality-based quota system in 1921 and still tighter restrictions in 1924. Henry Cabot Lodge, a leading advocate of immigration restriction, urged that 'we must sift the chaff from the wheat':

> Any one who is desirous of knowing in practical detail the degrading effect of this constant importation of the lowest forms of labor can find a vivid picture of its results in the very interesting book just published by Mr. Riis, entitled 'How the Other Half Lives.' The story which he tells of the condition of a large mass of the laboring population of the city of New York is enough to alarm every thinking man. [The immigrants] tend to lower the quality of American citizenship, and . . . in many cases gather in dangerous masses in the slums of our great cities.[117]

Similar concerns were expressed in Australian cities as European immigration increased after the First World War. Inner suburbs such as

Carlton in Melbourne were resettled first by European Jews and, from the 1950s, by Italians. Newspapers railed against these 'slum colonies' within which immigrants were 'thrown back on themselves, [and] virtually denied any opportunity of assimilation'.[118]

ETHNIC PREJUDICE against European immigrants overlapped with even cruder currents of racism. Explaining the complacency of public opinion in the United States regarding urban inequality, Woods remarked that Americans 'are kept from a full sympathy with their poorer brethren not only by the barrier of different social position, but by the more impassable barrier of alien race'.[119] Woods was writing in the 1890s, but it could equally have been the 1960s or the 2010s. In part, the slum's racialization occurred in the abstract and at a distance from the direct experience of city dwellers. Thus characterizations of the urban poor had since the early nineteenth century implied that poor people constituted a different and inferior race. Slum narratives often equated slum-dwellers with savage tribes in primitive societies, a genre that historian Bill Luckin calls 'racially tinged urban tribalism'.[120] Henry Mayhew's descriptions of London's mid-nineteenth-century poor are a classic example. This trend to racialize the slum was reinforced by nativist concern in the United States from the late nineteenth century that mass immigration was not only producing an undesirable ethnic hodgepodge but was creating the conditions for a 'struggle of the races'. Hunter predicted Americans' 'race-suicide' as the 'direct descendants of the people who fought for and founded the Republic . . . are . . . displaced by the Slavic, Balkan, and Mediterranean peoples'.[121]

More alarming still than the prospect of a struggle between the races was that of 'race . . . degeneration [through the] intermarrying and intermingling of peoples, which will indefinitely lower the standard of American . . . manhood'.[122] Such thinking gained credibility throughout the English-speaking world from the late nineteenth century. It overlapped with the older parallel idea of the urban poor as a race apart, and combined with newer degenerationalist concerns about race enfeeblement as a result of urbanization. Thus in 1912 it could be seriously contended in Australia that this

> race-suicide evil . . . is the direct result of over-urbanisation, and is more pronounced in Australia then elsewhere in the

British Empire, because excessive urbanisation is a more
marked feature of the social conditions in Australia than anywhere else. The people who live on the land continue to have
families of healthy size, simply because they live a healthy
natural life, which the people of the great cities do not.[123]

In 1942, thinking ahead to a better post-war world, Australia's federal
minister for social services maintained that

> the greatness of a nation is determined by the character of
> its people, and . . . the environment of dirty streets and ugly
> homes and bad drainage, not only undermines the health of
> the occupants but robs them of pride, honour and hope, and
> is thus the surest road towards national degeneracy.[124]

Proto-degenerationalist thinking had originated in Britain during
the early nineteenth century, but strengthened in the English-speaking
world from late in the century as Social Darwinism grew in popularity
and as investigations into the health effects of urban living proliferated. It was increasingly asserted that slum-dwellers were not only a
different race, but a degenerate race. Riis cautioned in 1902, 'They
drag one another always further down. The bad environment becomes
the heredity of the next generation.'[125] This degeneracy seemingly
threatened to contaminate national racial vigour and strength. These
spurious assumptions were legitimized by the new science of eugenics, which was founded in Britain by Sir Francis Galton, and which
developed from the turn of the century in the United States under the
leadership of Charles Davenport into what would eventually become
the science of genetics. Concerns about urban racial degeneration first
achieved national prominence in Britain when, as a result of the embarrassing setbacks of the Boer War (1899–1902), a British Committee on
Physical Deterioration was set up which reported damningly upon the
racial decline of urban-bred recruits. British anxieties were noted elsewhere in the English-speaking world. U.S. immigration officials drew
attention in 1904 to 'a decided increase in . . . physically and mentally
defective [immigrants] from Great Britain and Ireland'.[126] In Australia,
the Salvation Army's *War Cry* noted in 1907 that among 'the most pronounced traits of the average slum dweller's character is instability and
enfeebled will-power'.[127] Degenerationist concerns were reinforced

during the First World War when it was widely reported that battalions recruited from the countryside fought better than their city counterparts. The British minister of health maintained that wartime military service highlighted 'certain weaknesses [in the] organisation and physical capacity' of recruits from the slums, whose 'undersized and unfit' constitutions represented 'a real danger to the State'.[128] Worries about racial degeneration continued to strengthen throughout the interwar period. As one Australian social reformer remarked in 1936,

> The dwellers in our thickly congested districts have little or no chance of developing their good instincts, these being crushed, and often completely destroyed by the dirt, squalor and crime that surround them, the finer and better instincts becoming less and less potent in each succeeding generation.[129]

The credibility of pseudo-scientific assertions of racial degeneration persisted after the Second World War, notwithstanding the horrors of Nazism. Planning a better post-war order, another Australian reformer cautioned that 'the great majority of the slum population is comprised of those who for mental and physical reasons cannot satisfactorily compete in the economic battle for existence.'[130] Talk of racial decline in this battle for existence continued to be echoed into the 1960s and '70s.

TALK OF CITY-BRED racial degeneration was nonetheless an abstract concept. In popular culture the racialization of the slum owed much more to the incorporation of non-European racial elements into the crude performances by recognizable slumland types. This trend was the result in part of the influence upon public opinion of racially prejudiced comments made by British colonial administrators (an argument that is developed further in Chapter Four). Thus, in Australia, it was taken for granted that a 'considerable number of Australian aboriginals and half-castes' lived in slum areas such as Fitzroy in Melbourne after the Second World War, and this was played out in slumland exposés.[131] The trend was influenced also by recurring alarms about epidemic diseases spreading globally from Asia (a concern that is considered further below). However, it was mainly the result of the movement of non-European people into the European settler societies of the New World. Consequently, characterizations of the urban poor were

'increasingly filtered through racist and nativist lenses'.[132] Melbourne's
Herald newspaper remarked in 1908 that the nation's slums comprised
'a most undesirable class of Asiatics and degraded Europeans', and the
Argus elaborated in 1910 that the slums were 'largely Chinese, with a
considerable sprinkling of Syrians and Southern Europeans, and only
a very small proportion of the British race'. *Punch* added a sprinkling
of 'Hindoo' people to this alien racial mix.[133] The prospect of such
a racial mishmash gave definition to abstract talk about urban racial
degeneration, for as the u.s. commissioner of immigration remarked
in 1899,

> The Anglo-Saxon, Latin, and Semitic races mix, and in time
> make respectable men and women, even from the lowest con-
> ditions, but the Oriental races do not mix well with the people
> of Europe, and the mixture, unless made among people in
> affluent circumstances, is always degrading to the European.[134]

Racial prejudice during the nineteenth and early twentieth centuries was directed especially against the most numerous and widely
travelled non-European racial group, the Chinese. Australia and the
Pacific coast of North America were obsessed with Chinese immigration and sought legislation to restrict or eliminate it. Port cities around
the Pacific Rim also lobbied for ever stronger quarantine restrictions
to protect themselves from infectious diseases spreading along the
shipping routes from China. Anxious discussions probed the likely
consequences of race competition and the predicted degenerative
effects of racial interbreeding. Slum sensationalism directed popular
attention to caricatures of debauched and disfigured European women
'decoyed' into Chinese opium dens.[135] The outbreak of bubonic plague
in San Francisco and Sydney in 1900, which in both cities was blamed
upon the Chinese, drew comment around the world, and prompted
the local authorities to undertake rigorous cleansing operations in the
poorest waterside districts and especially in the Chinatowns of both
cities. In San Francisco, its commerce disrupted by strict quarantine
restrictions imposed during the prolonged plague emergency, public
health officials and journalists agreed that 'Chinatown forms a slum
from whose emanations there is hardly any escape.' Distraught San
Franciscans equated local conditions with the nation's apparent worst,
contending that New York's most infamous 'sore spot, Five Points,

a haunt and breeding place of filth, disease and vice, [is] similar to Chinatown'.[136] California's State Board of Health, urging the removal of San Francisco's Chinatown, declared that

> the presence in the heart of a great city of a large alien and unassimilable population is a constant and serious menace to the health, commerce, and industries, not only to the city itself but also of the State and even the nation at large.[137]

Chinatown, whether in San Francisco, Vancouver, Sydney or Melbourne, seemed to be an explicitly foreign community in 'the very heart of the city',[138] with different foods, smells, dress and language. There was rich slumland material here for illustrators and photographers to use in books, newspapers and magazines: sinister street scenes, trap doors into opium dens and police squads chasing pigtailed criminals, breaking open gang hideouts with axes and sledgehammers and displaying captured arms caches. There was rich scope as well for narrative embellishments to the 'attraction of repulsion' genre. Hostile Chinatown stereotypes circulated widely until well after the effects of immigration restriction laws against China became evident from late in the nineteenth century in Australia and North America.

San Francisco's newspapers exemplified the style. The city's Chinatown contained 'every imaginable foul odor and stench', and 'labyrinths of maze-like passages'.[139] Such shocks and surprises for the newspapers' readers embellished the theatricality of the rites of passage into slumland: the reinforced gate 'closed upon us' as the visitors enter 'another world' to discover a 'transplanted bit of the Orient' in the midst of a seemingly European city.[140] As the slummers penetrate into dark and stifling places they are surrounded by 'jabbering', 'chattering' and 'howling' Chinamen. They discover 'the mysterious nooks and corners of underground Chinatown, where few white men ever penetrate. It is a strange labyrinth of burrows – more like the Roman catacombs'.[141] These performances powerfully reinforced the topsy-turvy character of slum descriptions:

> The highbinder tongs [criminal gangs] have turned almost the whole of Chinatown into a gigantic Chinese puzzle of trap doors, mysterious electric wires, trick stairs that fall to pieces when certain steps are pressed upon, and floors that are made

of paper, painted to look like boards, with nothing underneath but a twenty-foot drop.[142]

Thus in Chinatown the vortex of the slum is intensified as 'its labyrinths twist and become more complex.'[143] Habitations in such a place are explicitly subhuman: the Chinese reside in 'nests', 'lairs', 'rat holes', 'dens' and 'burrows'. The deceptive sleepiness of slums by day is given a further racial twist: in Chinatown the sanitary inspectors and police are confronted by the 'wily ways' and 'bland obstinacy of the race',[144] and find the hatchet-men of criminal gangs supposedly 'deep in slumber' and 'feigning sleep'.[145] By night, however, Chinatown's opium and gambling dens come alive, 'white slaves' are on offer in the brothels, and criminal gangs fight turf wars in the streets.

The identification of Chinese with slums had faded in North America and Australia by the middle of the twentieth century. In Britain, however, the racialization of slum stereotypes was given impetus from the 1950s and into the 1970s as immigrants from the Caribbean and South Asia began to arrive in large numbers, swelling the expatriate community from around 100,000 people to over one million. This migration trend had gathered momentum after the 1948 Nationality Act, which made British citizenship available to migrants from British colonies, and the London Declaration of 1949, which paved the way for former colonial possessions to become member states in the new Commonwealth of Nations. The resulting racial backlash in Britain, first expressed in the Notting Hill riots of 1958, was famously articulated by Enoch Powell in 1968 in the so-called 'Rivers of Blood' speech, whose strident nature led to his dismissal from the Conservative shadow cabinet. Powell's language was crude, but both Conservative and Labour governments had since 1962 imposed increasing restrictions upon new Commonwealth immigrants, and the Immigration Act of 1971 virtually ended the immigrant flow. Racial discrimination nonetheless continued to harden against new Commonwealth immigrants already settled in British cities. In 1977 the Liverpool Inner Area Study warned that young Liverpool-born blacks were responding by 'developing an aggressive culture and life-style of their own that is in effect creating a new community where none existed before'.[146] Meanwhile in the United States the 1965 repeal of the interwar immigration restrictions based on national origin resulted in another wave of immigration into North America, much of it non-European, and this reignited racial characterizations of urban poverty there.

THE UNITED STATES added a further element to the racialization of slumland: the black ghetto. In *How the Other Half Lives* Riis described the 'color line' that had developed in New York City since the civil war as a trickle of southern blacks migrated into the cities of the northern states.[147] However, black American migration to northern cities was negligible until the First World War, when increasing migration triggered a racial backlash, culminating in race riots in Chicago and discrimination against them throughout the 1920s and '30s that created highly segregated Black communities. When sociologist Louis Wirth wrote about Chicago's ghettos in 1927 he used the word 'ghetto' interchangeably with 'slum', arguing that the historical Jewish ghetto, translated to American cities by European immigrants, now functioned more broadly as a reception area for each new wave of poor immigrants as they adjusted to American society. Jewish immigrants had

> been displaced by the Poles and Lithuanians, the Italians, the Greeks, and Turks, and finally the Negroes . . . The latest invasion of the ghetto by the Negro is of more than passing interest. The Negro, like the immigrant, is segregated in the city into a racial colony; economic factors, race prejudice, and cultural differences combine to set him apart.[148]

The mass migration of African Americans into the cities during and after the Second World War intensified this segregating trend. However, black American experience did not fit Wirth's slum-based '"elevator" model of the immigrant experience [which] implies that each group takes its turn in the process of social mobility and suburbanization'.[149] Black Americans remained stuck on the ground floor, in the poorest city neighbourhoods, and in turn the increasingly race-specific word 'ghetto' gradually replaced 'slum' in the American vocabulary. The resentments and bitterness generated within black communities by across-the-board racial discrimination exploded in the inner-city riots of the 1960s that galvanized the world's attention every summer. However, the subsequent investigations that sought explanations for such widespread and intense rioting did not blame the slum. In the United States, racialism had so conditioned thinking about urban disadvantage that 'slum' had become subsumed within the black ghetto.

That 'mass of ugly and venomous slums'

The slum's 'attraction of repulsion' was coloured everywhere by apprehensions about the pace, scale and unpredictability of urban change.[150] These in turn fed further anxieties: that diseases generated in the slum's disordered environment might at any moment spread across entire cities, nations and the globe; that race degeneration originating in slums might spawn nihilistic youth cultures and in the longer term sap national character and strength; that deviant slum-minded behaviour might readily transmute into broader workplace disaffection and political extremism. Such were the common-sense understandings of 'slum' that one passionate social reformer remarked in 1966: 'We experience an almost instinctive revulsion when confronted by the few poor people we do come into contact with.'[151] Revulsion and fear influenced investigative and reform initiatives that sought to document, contain and alleviate the slumland menace.

FEAR OF EPIDEMIC DISEASE underpinned nineteenth-century thinking about slums, and the legacy of this fear persisted well into the twentieth century. *The Bitter Cry* called slums 'hotbeds of vice and disease'.[152] That phrase had widespread and enduring currency. Notwithstanding ongoing uncertainty and disagreement until the early twentieth century about the origins and transmission of disease, a broad consensus quickly emerged amongst the middle-class sanitary reform movement during the nineteenth century that a correlation existed between slums and the generation of 'filth diseases' such as cholera, typhus and typhoid that periodically ravaged cities, and the diarrhoeal illnesses and infectious fevers that especially threatened infants. Slum environments were routinely depicted as maggot-ridden, cancers and sores. The journalist and philanthropist Ada Chesterton remarked in 1936 'how deep the sore of the slum has eaten into the very bones of the city. Like terrible scabs those courts fester, destroying the bodies, blighting the souls of those imprisoned within.'[153]

From the middle of the nineteenth century, and especially during its last quarter and into the twentieth century, elaborate state health bureaucracies evolved with the task of cleansing and ordering city environments, removing 'nuisances' and waste, overseeing drainage, sewerage and water systems, combating overcrowding and rooting out dwellings 'unfit for human habitation'. In so doing they became increasingly 'an awesome force for the surveillance of the poor'.[154] Their meshing of scientific investigation, technological innovation and regulatory intervention was increasingly driven by confidence that community health and urban environments could be manipulated and controlled, that 'the identification and investigation of social problems would automatically reveal their solutions'.[155]

Despite confidence that the domestic spread of epidemic diseases from slums was being arrested, there still existed in the early twentieth century the nagging worry that slums might transmit diseases originating in unclean places elsewhere. This anxiety reinforced ethnic and racial stereotyping where slums were specifically associated with impoverished immigrants. The emergence of an efficient high-speed global shipping network during the second half of the nineteenth century brought the risk of highly contagious diseases such as cholera and plague originating from as far away as China, Japan and India. As one U.S. Senator remarked in 1882,

> with our rapid modes of communication . . . and the cheapness
> of transit from every quarter of the earth to this country, we
> are liable to be infected every year by these dread pestilences
> that strike terror to the heart of all nations of the earth.[156]

In 1896, as it celebrated the opening of what was reputed to be the most modern and effective maritime quarantine station in the world, San Francisco's *Call* newspaper explained:

> The diseases with which the Angel Island quarantine [station]
> has to deal are those of the Orient, principally China and
> Japan, and they are the deadliest known. Cholera, black plague,
> smallpox, leprosy and half a dozen others almost as bad are
> constantly making efforts to get into San Francisco.[157]

Cholera had first impacted upon the English-speaking world during 1831–2, when it spread in an epidemic wave from India across Asia and Europe to Britain. In the United States, 'a day of general humiliation and prayer to Almighty God' was held, that Americans might be spared this pestilence.[158] Their prayers were in vain. In Sydney, quarantine restrictions were hurriedly enacted to regulate incoming shipping, and this British-derived statute became the basis for all subsequent Australian quarantine barriers. More global cholera pandemics would follow in the late 1840s, the mid-1850s and 1866, all of them originating in India, and introduced to Britain and North America by impoverished European immigrants. In New York additional emergency quarantine measures in 1865 barred cholera's widespread importation into the United States. The year 1866 was the last time a cholera epidemic occurred in London. However, further waves of epidemic cholera spread throughout Europe during the early 1870s, mid-1880s and early 1890s.

These European epidemics were barred from Britain by strict quarantine restrictions. The United States responded to these epidemics by appointing medical officers to its European consulates during the mid-1880s to check all steerage passengers embarking for the United States. When cholera next ravaged Europe during the early 1890s and was imported to New York by Russian immigrants in 1892, compulsory inspection and disinfection of all American-bound passengers was enforced at European and Asian ports, and was followed up by a virtual suspension of all immigration. In 1900 the appearance of bubonic plague throughout Asia and then Europe led to the dispatch of u.s. health officers to Chinese, Japanese, European and British ports to inspect all passengers and disinfect their luggage. In 1904 medical inspectors were also appointed to Calcutta and Bombay. During 1905, for the first time, over one million 'alien' immigrants were examined by u.s. medical inspectors. The reappearance of cholera in Russia and Italy during 1910 led to an intensification of immigrant inspection, disinfection and detention in European ports and upon their arrival in the United States. These precautions remained in place until the First World War, and were resumed once the war ended. Still more stringent measures were enforced upon Asian immigrants to West Coast American cities and were perpetuated when public health and immigration restriction laws were consolidated in the restriction laws of the 1920s.

CONCERN OVER SLUM-BRED pestilence overlapped with anxieties that slum-dwellers might initiate riots and revolt. Sims predicted in 1883 that the slum's fevers and its filth may spread to the homes of the wealthy; its lawless armies may sally forth and give us a taste of the lesson the mob has tried to teach now and again in Paris, when long years of neglect have done their work.[159]

Similar predictions were still being made half a century later. In 1930 the British housing reformer B. S. Townroe warned that

We cannot expect those who live under bad conditions to be proud of our Constitution and of our Empire[;] our slums are breeding-grounds not only of physical disease, but of mental rebellion.[160]

Such rebellion might conceivably take the form of individual delinquency and crime. Drawing upon his second social survey of York, in 1941 Rowntree cautioned that there were 'danger signals' that orderly working-class culture was disintegrating, and he gave as examples of this trend a decline in church influence and the increasing independence of juveniles from parental control.[161] In the 1970s, local government officials in Liverpool, Manchester and Birmingham, alarmed by rising crime rates, 'maintained that the real problem of the inner urban areas was the "feckless" character of the people'.[162]

However, slum-minded behaviour might also find collective expression in outright riot and revolt. Well-to-do New Yorkers were long traumatized by the 1863 draft riot, which they blamed upon mobs originating among slumland 'hives of sickness and vice'.[163] Concerns that slum-dwellers constituted a 'dangerous class' were highlighted by the u.s. social reformer Charles Loring Brace in *The Dangerous Classes of New York* (1872), although the concept had been current since at least the middle of the nineteenth century.[164] English-speakers regularly pointed apprehensively to Paris, where the storming of the Bastille in 1789 and the establishment of the Commune in 1871 provided alarming examples of what the poor might do to their masters. As John Freeman warned the citizens of Melbourne in 1888,

We, too, have a dangerous class in our midst, lurking in holes and corners away from the public gaze, where they mature undisturbed their plans against society; and where vice in every form flourishes unchecked by aught that might have a restraining influence over it.[165]

U.S. moral reformer Helen Campbell, author of *The Problem of the Poor* (1882) and *Darkness and Daylight, or, Lights and Shadows of New York Life* (1891), likewise drew attention to the 'smouldering elements of riot and revolt down among the slums'.[166]

Thus slums might spread not only infectious disease but social disaffection, contaminating the respectable working classes and radicalizing their trade unions and the political labour movement. Historian Gareth Stedman Jones has described how real this possibility seemed in Britain during the economic recession of the 1880s, when class tension and disorder gripped London in 1886 and came to a head with the 'bloody Sunday' riot of 1887.[167] In 1928, after participating in a London slummer tour, the Liberal former prime minister Lloyd George described the places he had visited as 'a Bolshevist munition factory'.[168] As one London housing reformer announced later in the year, 'There was no better breeding-ground of social unrest than bad housing. The problem was not merely one of the city, but was one of the nation.'[169] Social disorder was still more a feature of U.S. cities, which 'have been in a state of more or less continuous turmoil since the colonial period'.[170] Nowhere was this more the case than in Chicago. In 1886 the nation was stunned when a rally of striking workers was interrupted by an anarchist's bomb thrown at police and was then shattered by retaliatory police gunfire. Chicago stunned the nation again during the bitter Pullman Strike of 1894, when federal troops and national guardsmen were mobilized to maintain order and rumours flew that 'tens of thousands [had] reportedly organized for a march from the slums of Chicago.'[171] The city shocked the nation yet again with the bitter race riot of 1919. That riot's 'explosive mixture' of white racism and black resentment was repeated one hundredfold across the nation's cities during the ghetto riots of 1964–8, when television news showed to the entire world images of fire, mayhem and of soldiers in armoured vehicles patrolling the centres of America's main cities.[172]

THESE MANIFOLD APPARENT dangers stimulated a snowballing investigative response throughout the English-speaking world that had in common a desire better to understand and to control the slumland threat. Many social surveys were undertaken by concerned citizens and philanthropic organizations, but increasingly the perceived slum menace prompted investigation and action by all tiers of government. As a corollary, emerging professional groups in public health, social work, architecture, urban planning, education and the social sciences played influential roles in defining slum problems and devising remedies. Public knowledge was increasingly shaped by 'faith in the authority of the expert and in the transformative power of the social sciences'.[173] The combined weight of public anxiety, expert opinion and state authority was a powerful stimulus for slum reform. The u.s. ghetto riots of 1964–8, for example, prompted President Lyndon B. Johnson to appoint a National Advisory Commission on Civil Disorders, whose voluminous 1968 report gave added weight to Johnson's War on Poverty. The British government responded to the turmoil in America's inner cities by launching its own Poverty Programme in 1968. This pattern of perceived slum threat leading to investigative response and attempted solutions had its origins during the nineteenth century. Mearns's *The Bitter Cry* prompted the setting-up of the 1884–5 Royal Commission on the Housing of the Working Classes, whose exhaustive investigations paved the way in turn for the Housing of the Working Classes Act of 1885, and its elaboration in 1890, which formed the basis for subsequent housing regulation in Britain and its overseas territories. During the nineteenth and twentieth centuries an accumulating body of city-specific, national and comparative international data, analysis and proposed remedies became available about the living conditions of the urban poor. Each new study, statute and government programme drew upon, and in turn fed into and reinforced, the knowledge base and conventional wisdom by which slum problems were identified and reforms were devised to address them.

These investigative and reform responses to slums were generated in part – as is highlighted in the case of *The Bitter Cry* – by deep anxieties about the polarizing effects of urbanization and by dismay at the tarnished ethics and uneven benefits of modern capitalism. In Australia Barnett and his colleague A. G. Pearson argued in 1944 that

> The present economic system demands a vast pool of idle labour. Into the pool men are thrust when times are slack, out of the pool they are drawn when times are good. Those in the centre of the pool are the unemployed, and they may be there

for some continuous period – a week, a month, or a year, or even more. Towards the side of the pool are the casual or part-time workers. They are not in the pool for a long continuous period, but are constantly scrambling in and out. Maybe they work for a few days every week, and then are unemployed for the rest of the week.[174]

Historians have stressed fear and pessimism as the drivers of slum reform. However, slum investigations and the suggested reforms were sustained less by disillusionment and fear than by confidence that slums were controllable and reformable, that the existing social order was fundamentally just, and that the reformers had the knowledge, skills and resolve to overcome the slumland menace. The reform movement confirmed the popularizers' contention that slums were a real and terrible presence in urban society, and that comprehensive reforms were required in order to contain and normalize them, as well as ensure that slum-dwellers were given 'the opportunity to really live'.[175] Yet, at the same time, most reformers believed that radical restructuring of society was unnecessary and that long-term social progress was inevitable. Rowntree, for example, whose 1900 survey shocked Britain by concluding that '26 per cent of working-class families lived in slums, or in houses little better than slums,' expressed satisfaction when he repeated the survey in 1936 that York's slum population had fallen to under 12 per cent.[176] His third social survey in 1950 identified a further 'remarkable decrease in poverty'.[177] The influential 'Chicago School' of urban sociology had argued since the 1920s that American slums were functional elements within the overall ecology of cities and served as stepping stones for immigrants into the mainstream. Investigating the social conditions and opportunities that enabled people to escape poverty, Charles Stokes identified 'escalator and non-escalator' determinants that created either 'slums of "hope"' or 'slums of "despair"'.[178] Gerald Suttles, one of a later generation of Chicago sociologists, said of the slum in 1968 that 'public stereotypes convey a sense of certainty.'[179]

Not only have historians identified anxiety rather than confidence as the trigger for slumland investigations; they have contrasted the reformers' professionalism and serious purpose with the shallow theatricality of slum entertainers and have distinguished between slummer tourism and slummer philanthropy (the latter increasingly undertaken by professionals working for state agencies). Booth's pioneering social survey of London, for example, has been hailed for 'rejecting the sensationalism of Mayhew, of Stead, of the *Pall Mall Gazette*' and for paving the way instead for factual analysis of urban social disadvantage.[180] However, the reformers, by so confidently contrasting what seemed to them to be the social and environmental chaos of slums with the intrinsic good order of modern society, reinforced rather than challenged the 'attraction of repulsion' milieu through which the apparently repulsive reality of slums was fashioned. Many reformers used theatricality to get their message across. In Britain, Raymond Unwin railed in 1909 against 'the old unhealthy slums', and across the Atlantic the New York housing reformer Lawrence Veiller thundered in 1931 that 'the United States has probably the worst slums in the world.'[181] Barnett said of the report prepared for the Victorian state parliament by the Slum Abolition Board in 1936–7 – a board that he had lobbied to have created in the first place – 'I'd written a number of pamphlets, and they were all collected and shoved in wherever it was necessary.'[182] Barnett also used slum tourism to generate support for reform, taking people 'down to actually see the slums, and they were all aghast. They'd never known.'[183] The distinction between slum reformers and slum entertainers was thus more apparent than real. Both were responsible for peddling slum stereotypes.

Among the most widespread and influential of philanthropic reform interventions were those of the Charity Organization Society (established in 1869) and the university settlement house movement (originating in 1884), both of which began in London and spread across the English-speaking world. Both reasoned that by providing role models within the slums the urban poor could be led to better lives. Thus, at the famous Hull House settlement in Chicago, which began in 1889, the poor could 'learn . . . to live good, clean, temperate lives . . . through the demonstration of the enduring beauty and gayety of such a life as contrasted with the lurid and fleeting joys of the other'.[184] Historians have queried such motives. The university settlement movement, for example, 'captured all too well the paradoxical blend of arrogant self-confidence and anxious self-doubting of the late Victorian ruling classes'.[185] It is easy to jibe at outdated mindsets. The charity workers and settlement house residents were in the main well-intentioned and knowledgeable people, snared in the slum deceits of their times. Such were Octavia Hill, the influential co-founder of the Charity Organization Society, and Jane Addams and Ellen Starr, who established Hull House; so too were the Oxford and Cambridge students who lived in the world's first university settlement of Toynbee Hall, founded in East London in 1884, and their equivalents in other settlements throughout Britain and North America. The settlement in Bristol is a representative example. It was established in 1911, its first warden being Hilda Cashmore, the daughter of a wealthy industrialist. In 1937 a new warden was appointed, Hilda Jennings, who led the organization for the next twenty years. Like Cashmore, she was educated at Oxford, and while undertaking further study at the London School of Economics she had lived at a settlement in Bethnal Green. Arrogant self-confidence and anxious self-doubt? Probably in part. But these philanthropists undertook useful work for low-income communities as intermediaries, advisers and advocates.

Equally well intentioned, and still more ensnared in slum deceits, were church initiatives to establish city missions and outreach activities to help the urban poor. Australia's best-known non-government social welfare, research and advocacy group for disadvantaged Australians, the Brotherhood of St Laurence, was established by the Anglican clergyman Gerard Kennedy Tucker during 1930 in Melbourne's inner suburb of Fitzroy because the district contained 'the poorest and most poverty-stricken slums in Australia'.[186] Tucker's declared purpose was 'to rescue the slum-dwellers from their squalor'.[187] Another good man caught in slum deceits. Likewise the Nonconformists: it was said proudly that Presbyterian deaconesses 'burn brightly as beacon lights guiding folks to the Harbour of Better Things in those dim, drab and dismal localities of our great metropolis known as slums'.[188] The Salvation Army, which was established in London's East End in 1865 and spread throughout the world, undertook similar slum rescue work, visiting homes and leading Bible reading and prayers. The Army's 'slum sisters have been freely going in and out like sweet angels among the haunts of the lost', so much so that slum families were said to 'almost worship' the slum sisters who guided them.[189]

The clearest examples of the self-confident energy of the slum reformers were the overlapping housing and urban planning movements, and the statutes and state agencies that were generated by them. Housing advocates argued that the slum problem would be largely overcome by moving slum-dwellers into better housing. In Britain, Howard Marshall argued during the 1930s that 'ninety-five per cent of slum-dwellers will form fresh habits and take the greatest pride in their new homes.'[190] This objective was pursued in part by philanthropic model-housing companies working within the private housing market. In London the Improved Tenements Association, which bought, reconditioned and managed hundreds of dilapidated houses, reported that through their work 'Slum conditions are abolished . . . and many bad tenants through the growth of self-respect and a pride in their homes become good tenants.'[191] Yet, for all the well-intentioned effort, such philanthropic associations made an 'infinitesimal contribution to the total urban housing stock'.[192]

Beginning in the middle of the nineteenth century and becoming stronger since late in the century, housing reformers also pursued legislative options to regulate the private housing market and to stimulate it to provide better and more affordable housing. In Britain especially, tentatively at first, legislation enabled local government to provide public (state-owned) housing. The early twentieth-century achievements of the London County Council, cautiously undertaken, were nonetheless 'quite remarkable'.[193] In 1919 Christopher Addison, Britain's first minister of health, steered through the Housing and Town Planning Act, which launched a massive public housing programme by local authorities. Nearly half a million council houses were built during the 1920s and over a million by the late 1930s. By far the largest public housing provider was the London County Council – whose programme was called 'the most spectacular example of municipal housing in Europe'[194] – followed by Liverpool, whose public housing programme dated back to 1869. In the United States, the New York Housing Authority, established in 1934, became the nation's first municipal housing agency, and others soon followed. The Chicago Housing Authority, for example, was created in 1937, the same year that the federal Housing Act of 1937 provided funding for public housing.

By the late nineteenth century slum reformers were becoming sufficiently confident about their ability to design an entirely new modern spatial order that they prepared plans for entire communities and cities and lobbied for legislation to create stronger city and metropolitan authorities to put such planning into full effect. The phrase 'town planning' was first used by the Australian architect John Sulman in 1890 and first enshrined in legislation by the British Housing and Town Planning Act of 1909. Introducing this legislation to parliament, the radical Liberal politician John Elliot Burns explained that 'The object of the Bill is to provide a domestic condition for the people in which their physical health, their morals, their character and their whole social condition can be improved.'[195]

The reform movement powerfully influenced the understanding of slums and the direction of policies to deal with them. In some respects, reformers merely extended, and lent authority to, concepts that were already in place. However, they were responsible for important changes of emphasis as well. The most important of these was the 'keen sympathy with the poor' which reformers introduced to the discussions of slums, their 'sympathetic understanding' of those who were compelled to live in such appalling environments.[196] It was the reformers who began to change the public perception of slum-dwellers from villains to victims. For example, left-leaning doctor and politician Christopher Addison (Viscount Addison), the architect of the 1919 Housing and Town Planning Act, and who served the Liberals as president of the Local Government Board and minister of health before switching to the Labour Party, spoke passionately during the 1920s of slums being a 'betrayal' in that they sapped the lives of the city poor.[197] Increasingly, reformers derided stereotypes of slumland villainy and argued that most of the urban poor had not brought upon themselves

> a 'descent' into the slums. That was their starting place, and their condition was not the result of their evil living but due to the 'accident of birth'. [They are] ordinary decent citizens, whose only crime is their abject poverty.[198]

Such was the repulsion generated by the prevailing slum stereotypes, however, that the reformers' sympathy was abstract and condescending. Their confidence in the facts they accumulated and their strategies for change distanced them from the communities they aimed to help. It seemed to them that slumland had so seared its victims that they were reduced to powerlessness and dysfunctionality. Barnett described slums as 'prisons surrounded by the walls of an environment that is entrenched in heredity, that encompass the life of its inhabitants from the cradle to the grave'.[199] He said of the slummer tours he organized, 'Everywhere we went in the slums was a sense of utter hopelessness, of absolute futility.'[200] In reformist discourse, it seemed axiomatic that 'the slum-minded class' needed interventions on their behalf, because they were inert, apathetic and deficient.[201] As Walters remarked, 'most of these people in the slums have lost their anchorage. They have neither hope nor ambition.' No wonder, he said, that slum homes 'are never dusted, never tidied, never made cosy, but smell like pigeon-pens and dog-kennels'. No wonder that such dirty overcrowding 'favours bestiality in general, and the relations between fathers and daughters, uncles and nieces, mothers and their own sons, is such as we dare not describe'.[202] Charles Stokes's sympathetic and influential 'Theory of Slums' (1962) cautioned that in advanced societies such as the United States the previous escalator function of slums was fading because those left at the bottom comprised 'a class more and more composed of the "incapable"'.[203] As late as 1979, a British geographer could still assert that in Britain 'the slum dweller is inadequate and unable to cope,' and lacked 'the personal resources to cope with the everyday pressures of life'.[204]

Notwithstanding reformist sympathy, slum deceits remained entrenched in the English-speaking world; notwithstanding reform interventions, inequality was on the rise at the end of the twentieth century.

REFORMERS AND ENTERTAINERS had together created the slum deceits. Whereas reformers did so while attempting unsuccessfully to eliminate slumland, many entertainers simply magnified its presence. They embellished its attraction of repulsion. As one book publisher, in rejecting the manuscript for *Maggie: A Girl of the Streets*, told Crane, 'the effect, I presume, that you wished to produce [is] a kind of horror.'[205] The general public, however, revelled in such horrors. By the early twentieth century 'the slum was on a par with the department stores and theaters as the newfangled attractions of the city.'[206]

The entertainers pursued a wide range of styles and objectives. They had much greater influence on public opinion than the reform movement and the state-sanctioned reform programmes that emerged from it. Some entertainers were serious reformers. Walter Besant's novels *All Sorts and Conditions of Men* (1882) and *Children of Gibeon* (1886) sought to draw attention to poverty in London's East End, as did Jack London's *People of the Abyss* (1902). George Gissing's social realist novels *The Unclassed* (1884), *Thyrza* (1887), *The Nether World* (1889) and *New Grub Street* (1891) also emphasized urban poverty. James Cuming Walters, likewise, was no shallow voyeur. In common with Mearns and Riis, the journalist sensationalized slumland, but in so doing all three sought to improve it. Walters was 'an ardent Dickensian', with an instinct for harnessing repulsion to galvanize the attention of an audience, and 'for twelve months [he] lived in various disguises in the worst of the slum dwellings' in order to write authoritatively about *Scenes in Slumland*.[207] Walters's call for reforms went largely unheeded, but his stories certainly entertained.

Walters's articles in the *Birmingham Daily Gazette* were similar in style to the mass-circulation newspapers' frequent 'explorations' of city slums, which provided their readers with spurious first-hand encounters with slumland in the comfort of their suburban homes. In San Francisco, for example, newspaper readers could imaginatively join with government law enforcers as they penetrated 'the horrible side of the town' to launch 'raids' on Chinatown's 'slave den' brothels and opium palaces.[208] During the 1930s *Time* magazine photographer Margaret Bourke-White became one of the highest-paid women in America, making 'her living as a voyeur, as a middle-class tourist among the neediest people, sending dispatches back to the comfortable living rooms of *Life* magazine's readers'.[209]

The 'exoticism' of vaudeville theatre and musical comedy provided other avenues for contemplating the slum's horrors from a safe distance.[210] Melodramatic social sketches, often taking the form of pseudo-guidebooks through the slums, also proliferated during the nineteenth century. The *Mysteries and Miseries of New York* (1848) and *Darkness and Daylight, or, Lights and Shadows of New York Life* (1891) are examples of this style. Novels provided another means of imaginatively living through first-hand encounters with the slum. Novels such as George G. Foster's *Celio: or, New York Above-Ground and Under-Ground* (1850) assured readers that their slumland dramas were 'drawn from real life'.[211] Ruth Park's well-known novels *The Harp in the South* (1948) and *Poor Man's Orange* (1949) were set in the slums of Sydney.

Slum tourism offered the most extreme form of slum entertainments. London and New York attracted the greatest interest, and their poorest districts figured on international tourist itineraries. For much of the nineteenth century New York's Five Points was regarded as 'the nation's foremost slum', and European tourists flocked there to draw comparisons with slum tours undertaken at home.[212] During 1933 one Melbourne slum reformer shook his head disapprovingly about those 'Australian tourists who partake of . . . "tours by night of London's slums and underworld"'.[213] These tourists, however, were in good company: 'On a visit to the London slums . . . the Prince of Wales exclaimed, "My God . . .! What can we do to end this?"'[214] Most cities had their local slum tour attractions. In 1900 a tour group of fashionable gentlemen and ladies in San Francisco was arrested when their guide led them into a Chinatown brothel. The *Examiner* newspaper remarked disapprovingly that slum tours had given the city 'a bad name over the country. The tens of thousands of visitors who have been conducted through the dens have gone away to tell of San Francisco as one of the worst cities on earth.'[215]

Slum entertainments of all varieties were sustained in part by the 'curiosities' they uncovered about different ways of life.[216] The sights, the sounds, the smells and the body language were all excitingly alien. Hence the new fad during the 1920s for well-to-do New Yorkers to visit Harlem's nightclubs in order to listen to jazz and absorb the local atmosphere. Melbourne's Little Lon, with its brothels and large Chinese community, likewise drew visitors because it seemed to represent

> the centre of romance. Sometimes we summoned up courage and strolled down the hill around Stephen-street, just as infamous, or threaded our way through the lanes which connected Big Lon. and Little Lon., most infamous of all.[217]

San Francisco's Chinatown was 'the delight of the tourist and the unclean abode of a thousand smells, with all its bizarre effects and all its contempt of Caucasian law and civilization'.[218] Celebrations of the Chinese New Year regularly attracted crowds of curious bystanders, and

> the sightseer was forced to . . . jostle [through] narrow sidewalks among the crowds of Chinese [amid] native hucksters hawking their wares in the Chinese tongue and the firing of crackers filled the air with strange sounds.[219]

Crucially, however, few of these one-off slummers would have wished to cross these borders of otherness permanently. By showcasing slumland's mysteries and miseries, slum entertainments crystallized belief in its opposite, the slummers' orderly city and their way of life within it. Herein lay the entertainments' power. Riis's illustrated lectures on slumland have been described as 'simultaneous entertainment and ideology'.[220] The slum's 'attraction of repulsion' acted like a hall of mirrors, its grotesque distortions of one's own sense of normalcy serving to reinforce conventions about what should be celebrated and enacted in modern cities.

The urban poor were so stereotyped in these entertainments that they were largely excluded from effective community engagement and reform. Mainstream society drew comfort instead from the thought that while deviant 'slum-minded' character traits could be modified through philanthropic guidance and contained by firm state action, they were beyond the scope of either community action or state intervention to resolve. As the Scriptures confirmed, the poor would always have a presence in even the most advanced societies. This explains the apparent paradox of community enthusiasm for slum entertainments on the one hand and indifference regarding efforts to scale back urban social injustices on the other. This indifference frequently translated into electoral resistance to costly reform initiatives by government. Another key consequence, repressive intervention, is explored in the next chapter.

USE OF THE WORD 'slum' to describe disadvantaged areas in English-speaking cities diminished during the 1960s and virtually ceased in subsequent decades. However, the word was not entirely forgotten. Suttles's authoritative 1968 sociological study of Chicago's West Side was titled *The Social Order of the Slum*, and described the study area as 'generally labeled an impoverished Negro slum'.[221] In 1971 it was still being said of Leeds – which throughout the twentieth century contained the highest proportion of Victorian era back-to-back housing in England – that its 'main problem . . . centred on its legacy of Victorian slums'.[222] Increasingly, the word seemed to reference only the past. By contrast, Ronald Henderson's trailblazing *People in Poverty: A Melbourne Survey* (1970) – which probed present-day social indicators – made no reference to 'slum' in either its social analysis (based on survey work in 1966) or its guiding principles.[223]

Slum stereotypes eroded in part because of the emergence of more professional and sophisticated social science research. Henderson, for example, a professor and director of the Institute of Applied Economic and Social Research at the University of Melbourne, was appointed by the Australian government in 1972 to chair its wide-ranging Commission of Inquiry into Poverty. 'Slum' concepts appear nowhere in any of its main reports and research papers. Slum stereotypes also eroded because of the long drawn out opposition of working-class communities to slum clearance, and because the old Jewish ghettos, Little Italys, Chinatowns and more recent immigrant 'slums' were being redefined in popular imagination as places of tourist charm and gourmet delight. The focus on slums also faded because the reformers' earlier confidence evaporated, as city problems proved more entrenched than expected and indeed proliferated. Simultaneously a new generation of social workers, educationists, sociologists, planners and architects during the 1960s, '70s and '80s challenged the orthodoxies upon which their professions had hitherto been based. By the late 1970s there had taken root a sense of 'widespread professional guilt at what had been done to cities in the name of slum clearance and redevelopment'.[224] To a still greater extent, the stereotypes faded as places once regarded as slums were 'gentrified' by affluent professionals who wanted to live amid the cosmopolitan excitement of the inner city. These trends are discussed further in Chapter Three. Henderson, one of the new breed of social reformers, recognized all these trends in his Melbourne study of people below the poverty line:

> The hard work and skill of many migrants, especially the Italians, have helped to transform some of the inner city areas of Melbourne. Twenty years ago, Carlton looked dingy and depressed. Now, very largely due to the work of Italians, many of the old houses have been restored to something of their former charm, and it is an attractive suburb with a style of its own. Ironically enough, this has made it popular with Australians as well, and many business and professional people now compete for the old terrace houses. This raises the price and often puts them beyond the reach of migrants.[225]

However, it is less the case that slum concepts were explicitly rejected and discredited than that they lost popular relevance in local affairs. 'Slum' ceased to resonate as its shock value in relation to domestic social anxieties faded amidst the post-1945 trend towards mass affluence. Moreover, the word 'slum' became less and less firmly anchored to the places it had once described. By the 1960s and '70s, grinding chronic poverty had substantially reduced and much of the decayed nineteenth-century housing stock that had accommodated this poverty had been replaced, or reconditioned as levels of homeownership rose. In Britain much inner-city housing had been obliterated by wartime bombing, and city centres in Britain, North America and Australasia were comprehensively redeveloped into business, administrative, retailing and entertainment hubs as well as places for high-income and high-density living.

New shock words overshadowed 'slum' in domestic affairs as public attention turned to prevailing social issues and to other city districts where these issues were seemingly concentrated. In the United States after the inner city riots of the 1960s, attention focused on the ghetto. Tellingly, in the *Report of the National Advisory Commission on Civil Disorders*, the index entry for 'slums' says '*see* ghetto'.[226] In Britain, social problems were no longer associated with the infamous slum names of the old central city areas – now rebuilt, transformed and even forgotten – but with the new municipal housing estates, the 'sink' estates of the urban periphery. In Australia, likewise, Stubbs predicted that the new suburban public housing estates were becoming the 'slums of tomorrow', because their inhabitants had 'imported the culture of poverty' from the old slums where they had previously lived.[227] Peter Hollingworth, director of social research at the Brotherhood of St Laurence (he later became its executive director, a bishop and Governor General of Australia), pointed out in 1972 that although 'the old slums of the inner suburbs of a generation ago' had disappeared, new areas of disadvantage were emerging in the outer suburbs, far away from employment opportunities and deficient in public services.[228] The pressure points of contemporary urban living were becoming more geographically distributed, socially differentiated and culturally complicated than the old slum genre could accommodate and explain.

Public debate about urban friction points was moving beyond the old preoccupation with central city areas to focus on entire city regions. In the United States the post-1960s preoccupation with 'the racial ghetto' encompassed not only long-standing concerns about 'the continuing economic and social decay of the central city' but, more alarming still, the apparent unravelling of American society into 'a divided nation'.[229] On both sides of the Atlantic, commentators began to speak of a broad-ranging urban crisis. Michael Harrington, in the introduction to an updated edition (1971) of his *The Other America*, suggested that the slum problem had been overtaken by the larger problem of 'the plight of the cities'.[230] Other American observers drew attention to the multiplying effects of economic restructuring and deindustrialization upon entire cities and the urban networks within which they had functioned. In 1972, the British Department of the Environment commissioned inner-city studies of Liverpool, Birmingham and London to pinpoint the transformations unfolding in these urban heartlands as their docks and industries closed down. In Scotland, deindustrialization wiped out Glasgow's manufacturing base. The 1973 global oil crisis and accompanying recession brought New York City to the verge of bankruptcy in 1975. However,

> it was saved from bankruptcy by national governmental and financial institutions that dictated unprecedented cutbacks in spending for collective services such as health, education, public transportation and housing. This was in direct contrast to the reduction of poverty and the enhanced spending on public health and education in the 1960s. In fact, it reversed more than a century of progressive social policies in New York.[231]

Most commentators, however, rather than criticizing this emerging neoliberal orthodoxy, spoke of a spiralling cycle of housing deterioration, abandonment and arson in American cities and a widening urban underclass.

In Britain, the oil crisis intensified domestic social tensions and industrial unrest, culminating in the 1978–9 'Winter of Discontent'. When Conservative leader Margaret Thatcher became British prime minister in 1979, the nation's industrial base was in freefall. As the docks closed and the factories shut their doors the viability of the urban heartlands where modern capitalism had begun was under question. Thatcher's government and its successors, and neoliberal governments across the English-speaking world during the 1980s and '90s, responded by winding back public expenditure and stimulating the private sector. Social polarization intensified. Yet paradoxically, in a twist to the old slum deceits, 'slum' was no longer used to describe the social disadvantage and alienation in the East London neighbourhoods where the term had first been applied in the early nineteenth century during a similarly unsettling age.

But there was a further twist: characterizations of slums in the late twentieth century were still alive and well. From the middle of the century the focus of the entertainers and many of the reformers had changed from the old slums of the developed world to the new slums of a postcolonial developing world.

THREE

THE WAR ON SLUMS

During the late nineteenth and early twentieth centuries slum stereo-types became a dominating influence shaping public awareness of urban poverty throughout the English-speaking world. In Britain, where the word 'slum' originated, the bishop of Winchester remarked during 1933 that 'the country to-day was conscious in a way in which it never had been before of the appalling nature of the slum problem.'[1] So intense was the dramatic contrast drawn between slumland evils and the image of the modern metropolis that only one progressive response seemed possible: the slum must be obliterated. This conviction remained firmly and widely held until the 1960s.

Opinion-makers used language akin to that of a nation state at war to mobilize public opinion in support of so large a task. The New York journalist and social reformer Jacob A. Riis wrote in the style of a war correspondent reporting battle news back to the homeland when he published *A Ten Years' War* (1900) and *The Battle with the Slum* (1902).[2] Some reformers advocated flanking operations, such as planning legislation to control city growth, and the construction of affordable modern accommodation in multi-storey flats or on suburban housing estates. Other reformers emphasized education, training and welfare support. However, all sides of politics and the labour movement agreed that, in the overall battle with the slum, its sordid environments must first be cleared away and its inhabitants dispersed throughout mainstream society. By the 1970s, after a century of slum clearance activity, inequalities nonetheless remained obstinately entrenched, although broadening prosperity made poverty less visible. Yet notwithstanding the slum war's faltering offensives, its social impact upon inner-city communities was immense. In Britain, where the war on slums had been pursued with the greatest vigour, some two million homes, accommodating five million people, were demolished between the 1930s, when the war on slums began in earnest, and the 1970s when it ended in stalemate.[3] In the United States, 'renewal' projects sanctioned under the pivotal Housing Act of 1949 had by the mid-1960s targeted over 400,000 'blighted' housing units and caused the relocation of over 300,000 families.[4] Urban sociologist Herbert Gans estimated that between 1950 and 1980 about 735,000 American households were directly displaced by slum clearance projects.[5]

This chapter traces the development of slum clearance schemes in the English-speaking world from their beginnings in the nineteenth century until their gradual abandonment during the 1960s and 1970s. It outlines legislative efforts to harness state powers for the comprehensive removal and rehousing of poor communities, and the parallel efforts, increasingly urgent as the huge cost to the public purse of such undertakings became clear, to harness private enterprise more effectively to the task of redeveloping cities. It looks at the origins of slum 'reconditioning' as a supplement or alternative to slum clearance and at the escalating resistance to the slum war by local communities.

Local resistance complicated but did not unravel the scripts for the war on slums. It still seemed plausible that decent citizens should applaud the slum clearance teams, not stand in their path and file legal challenges. When the war on slums eventually faltered during the 1960s and '70s it was more because of the failure of the language of war to sustain the broader community's interest than because of the influence of community resistance upon public opinion. Mobilization for the slum war, like slumland, its supposed adversary, was an artifice. Both were entertainments that reinforced prevailing societal values and diverted attention from the social costs of maintaining those values. The war on slums helped to win elections, sold newspapers, crammed public meetings, filled slummer tours, provided profits for land developers and builders and forged careers in politics, the civil service, the professions and reform organizations. However, it was a proxy war because it did not require active engagement on the part of its supposed main recruits, the general public. That deceit could not prevail indefinitely.

The pretence of a general mobilization for a war against the slums helped to mask society's culpability in tolerating the underlying causes of social inequalities in free market economies, and indifference regarding the evictions and relocations that slum clearance projects were causing. Even this phoney war struggled to maintain interest when it veered too close to real social issues, as Cyril Forster Garbett, the Anglican bishop of Southwark in London (and later archbishop of York), acknowledged in 1925. Chairing a meeting about housing reform, Garbett bemoaned

> the large amount of apathy and ignorance in regard to it. A large number of people had no idea what the housing conditions were like in the worst parts of London. The slums were a blot on our civilisation and a scandal to our Christianity.[6]

The slum war was eventually overshadowed during the 1950s and '60s by a graver confrontation, the Cold War, and public attention also switched to new and more compelling domestic issues.

Unfit for human habitation

No legislation in English-speaking nations has ever used the word 'slum' as a formal measure of marginality or as a trigger for intervention (although the u.s. Housing Act of 1937, for example, did include a definition of the word).[7] Instead, public health, housing and urban planning regulations focused on the concept of unfitness. The widespread acceptance of 'slum' concepts during much of the nineteenth and twentieth centuries made it seem self-evident that the places to which the word was applied were intolerable for normal human life and must be removed. Slums were understood to be repulsive sub-human places that reduced their inhabitants to beasts. These brutal environments would need to be swept clean and their sites redesigned before decent people could reoccupy them and worthwhile activities begin there. Slum reform was thus predicated upon the unfitness of slums to sustain normal human life and the scandal that such grotesque environments should persist in modern society. This thinking was reinforced from the mid-nineteenth century by the broader preoccupations of the public health movement, which focused on the 'intolerability' of unregulated urban environments.[8] The starting point for slum reform thus became the phrase 'unfit for human habitation', which was introduced into the general British legislative framework by the Public Health Act of 1848 and incorporated into housing legislation during the 1860s and '70s and which still provided the basis for housing and urban planning policy throughout the English-speaking world a century later.

By adopting the term 'unfit for human habitation' to measure housing quality (and, by implication, quality of life), slum reformers reasoned that 'some places are fit for demolition only.'[9] The regulatory term 'unfit for human habitation' therefore empowered local authorities in Britain to take action against insanitary and structurally unsound housing. In most cases, however, they initially sat on their hands. Some city corporations quickly used the term in their by-laws and local improvement acts to clear away 'slum' housing. Liverpool led the way in 1864, and city improvement acts in Scotland applied slum clearance on a broader scale. Implementation of Glasgow's 1866 Improvement Act displaced some 25,000 people over the following decade. Improvement schemes in Edinburgh demolished some 3,500 houses between 1867 and the 1890s. Most local authorities, however, hesitated to act against unhealthy areas or to condemn insanitary buildings within them. General enabling housing legislation provided a more uniform basis for local initiatives, but in the absence of clear guidelines and realistic financial incentives, and with no likelihood of central state intervention to enforce compliance, little slum clearance work was attempted by British local authorities before the 1930s.

William McCullagh Torrens's Artisans' and Labourers' Dwellings Act of 1868 was the first general housing law that explicitly empowered local authorities to condemn, demolish or repair houses 'unfit for human habitation'. Torrens was an independent Liberal. His bill was watered down by the dominant factions in parliament and thereafter ignored by most local authorities, with the result that the statute initially achieved little. However, after the furore provoked by *The Bitter Cry of Outcast London*, its provisions were tightened and incorporated into the Housing of the Working Classes Act in 1885 and the consolidating Housing of the Working Classes Act in 1890. The Torrens strategy was perpetuated in the key Housing Acts of 1924 and 1930, and continued to influence post-war housing legislation.

A broader strategy than that of the Torrens Act, applied to entire 'unfit' areas rather than individual buildings or adjoining structures, was introduced by Richard Cross (later Viscount Cross), home secretary in the Conservative government of Benjamin Disraeli. Cross's Artisans' and Labourers' Dwellings Improvement Act of 1875 enabled local authorities to repossess and clear 'unfit' places and to assist private housing associations to provide improved replacement dwellings. The statute thus sought to build upon the attempts of local improvement acts in Glasgow and Edinburgh (and less explicitly of municipal street-widening schemes and of private enterprise redevelopment such as railway construction in London) to compulsorily purchase and remake undesirable areas, even if not all the houses within them could be condemned as 'unfit'. The Birmingham City Council, led by the reformist Liberal mayor Joseph Chamberlain, moved immediately to implement the Cross Act, redeveloping much of the old city centre. In 1913, with the major works completed, Joseph's second son, Neville, hailed 'the great improvement scheme which drove Corporation Street through a mass of slums'.[10] In London, improvement schemes undertaken by the Metropolitan Board of Works under the auspices of the Cross Act demolished some 7,400 dwellings and displaced 29,000 people up to the board's replacement by the London County Council (LCC) in 1889. The LCC embarked upon a further round of slum clearances, amounting to over 23 ha (58 acres) before the First World War. On a national scale, however, very little was achieved under the permissive provisions of the Cross Act.

The Cross Act and its later amendments were consolidated by the Housing of the Working Classes Act in 1890. This law, which has been called 'the first real attempt to deal with the slum question',[11] provided a clearer pathway for local authorities to compulsorily purchase areas, undertake reconstruction schemes and build and operate model working-class housing. In parallel with the LCC, Liverpool embarked upon 'a bold attempt' to apply the Act in order to clear away slums and rehouse their residents.[12] However, most local authorities still ignored their new powers, as they did the later slum clearance provisions of Labour politician John Wheatley's 1924 Housing Act. Local government shied away from the complexities of slum clearance undertakings, and owing to the post-war national housing shortage 'local authorities were subject to practically no pressure to clear slums, either from the public or from the Ministry of Health.'[13]

This inaction only began to change during the Great Depression, when Arthur Greenwood, minister of health in Ramsay MacDonald's second minority Labour government of 1929–31, steered a new Housing Act through parliament in 1930. Greenwood's legislation is generally regarded as providing the 'foundations of modern slum clearance'.[14] It translated the slum war from rhetoric into practice. Greenwood's Act strengthened both the Torrens and Cross provisions for local authorities to clear 'unfit' houses and housing areas and for the first time provided state subsidies to local authorities for slum clearance activities. It also introduced some measure of accountability to the Ministry of Health for municipal activities. This approach was strengthened by the Housing (Financial Provisions) Act of 1933, and in 1935 a new Housing Act explicitly made it the 'duty' of local authorities to survey overcrowded districts and to prepare plans for the redevelopment of 'unfit' areas.[15] Historian Jim Yelling called this 'a re-assertion . . . at a much larger scale' of Cross's original principles, noting that it

> allowed the compulsory purchase, clearance and redevelopment by local authorities of large areas in the working class parts of cities in which only one-third of the houses need be unfit or overcrowded.[16]

These strategies for demolishing individual unfit buildings and clearing entire unfit areas continued in Britain after the Second World War, with the large-scale revival of slum clearance from 1955 once the massive post-war housing shortage had been overcome (some four million houses were destroyed or damaged during the war). An updated definition of the key concept 'unfit for human occupation' was built into the Housing Act of 1957 and reaffirmed in the Housing Act of 1969, ensuring the phrase's ongoing currency throughout the period of Britain's slum wars. The term was still being used by British parliamentarians in 2015.[17]

BRITISH REGULATORY INTERVENTIONS against 'unfit' homes and neighbourhoods were echoed in its overseas settler societies. In Sydney the Improvement Act of 1879 enabled the city council to launch a systematic drive against houses 'unfit for human habitation', the first significant slum clearance programme in Australia, and a similar provision was included in the Public Health Act of 1896. Melbourne's town clerk noted in 1912 that local regulations against houses 'unfit for human habitation' in the Victorian capital had also

> effected a considerable improvement in the old condition of things in this regard, and ha[ve] resulted indirectly in the

abolition of a large number of dwelling houses in certain parts
of the City and the erection of factories and stores on the sites
thereof.[18]

Municipal by-laws were underpinned by state public health laws. A
parliamentary select committee on 'unfit' housing in Melbourne was
appointed in 1913 and was followed in 1914 by a Royal Commission,
whose work was interrupted by the First World War. A Housing
Investigation and Slum Abolition Board was appointed by the Victorian
state government in 1936 to reassess the problem, and its 1937 report,
emphasizing the proliferation of 'unfit' housing, led immediately to the
creation of the Housing Commission of Victoria (HCV). The 1938 Slum
Reclamation and Housing Act, which spelled out the new commission's powers, drew in large part upon the Torrens and Cross provisions
of English legislation.[19] The subsequent Housing Act of 1958, which
underpinned the HCV's post-war slum crusade, likewise echoed British
precedents, enabling the commission to declare 'reclamation' areas
if they contained 'houses which are unfit for human habitation or
insanitary or unhealthy in the opinion of the Commission'.[20]

The United States was also influenced by the concept of unfitness,
and a strong slum abolition movement developed during the nineteenth and twentieth centuries amongst legislators, lobbyists and the
urban planning profession, intent on rooting out slum areas 'in which
the housing is so unfit as to constitute a menace to the health and
morals of the community'.[21] As in Britain, the term 'unfit for human
habitation' was enshrined in legislation and retains its currency to
the present day. Even Jane Jacobs, who fiercely critiqued U.S. urban
planning in the early 1960s, accepted the reality of 'slums' and 'unfit
neighbourhoods'.[22] Most Americans, however, considered British-style
interventions against slums to be 'wildly radical and confiscatory'.[23]
City authorities, denied the compulsory purchase powers of their
counterparts in Britain and its former colonies, had to pay market
value for properties in projected improvement zones. Very few city
governments therefore embarked upon slum clearance (New York
City and Chicago undertook limited clearance schemes), and instead
private enterprise was relied on to drive the cityscape's ongoing renewal.

During the 1930s and '40s, however, Americans coined a new
phrase to describe the apparently escalating consequences of private
enterprise disinvestment and slum encroachment in inner cities: 'urban

blight'. Concerns about blight generated a more receptive climate for interventions against unfit neighbourhoods. In the aftermath of the Great Depression, 'a more soul-searching attitude became apparent' among Americans, and it was suggested that, 'for the first time, we are becoming blight-conscious as a people.'[24] In 1934 the New York City Housing Authority was created to undertake 'the clearance, replanning, and reconstruction' of the city's slums.[25] The 1937 federal Housing Act provided the first nationwide tools for clearing away slum-bred blight. City planning commissions drew up ambitious plans for the clearance and redevelopment of blighted areas, in order to counteract what Lewis Mumford in 1938 called 'the accumulated physical and social results of . . . ravaged landscapes, disorderly urban districts, pockets of disease, patches of blight, mile upon mile of standardized slums'.[26] Policy analysts, business interests and public officials all agreed with this gloomy diagnosis. As *Business Week* declared in 1940, each big city 'shows symptoms of identical dry rot at its core'.[27] In 1944, Chicago School sociologist Louis Wirth described a 'catastrophic downward spiral' within city centres and advocated their large-scale redevelopment.[28]

Business interests began to recognize that slum clearance projects could generate handsome profits for redevelopers who worked in partnership with city governments. And so another new phrase was born: 'urban renewal'. American ideas about 'blight' and 'renewal' reshaped thinking about slum clearance in Britain and throughout the English-speaking world. In Australia, for example, Melbourne's Housing Investigation and Slum Abolition Board in 1937 referred to the '"blighting" [of] whole areas' and commentators quickly began to speak about 'Melbourne's blighted and slum areas'.[29] Dr Ramsay Mailler, founder of the Victorian Slum Abolition League, warned during 1943 of 'the "blight" which covers so many parts of our bigger cities'.[30] Referring to disadvantaged neighbourhoods in Australian cities, another Australian expert commented in 1945, 'The authorities call this a "blighted area." We call it "the slums."'[31] Blight magnified the effects of unfitness within slumland and spilled them over into surrounding areas. In Britain, planners and architects formed the Society for the Promotion of Urban Renewal in 1958 to push slum clearance and modernization through urban regeneration of the 'twilight areas' in Britain's inner cities.[32]

In the United States, New York City embarked on over a dozen redevelopment projects to counteract blight between 1935 and 1942, more than any other American city, and by the late 1940s most big cities had established redevelopment agencies. The federal Housing Act of 1949, reinforced by the Housing Act of 1954, provided the necessary authority for them to undertake wide-ranging urban renewal programmes, harnessing the resources of the public and private sectors 'to eliminate slums and blighted areas, and to realize as soon as feasible the goal of a decent home and a suitable living environment for every American family'.[33] The statute provided federal subsidies for city redevelopment projects, which, coupled with powers of compulsory purchase, enabled local agencies to clear and then sell 'blighted' areas for redevelopment and renewal. The Act

> extended the power of eminent domain, traditionally used in America only for government-built projects, so drastically that governments could now condemn land and turn it over to individuals – for them to build on it projects agreeable to government. Under Title I, whole sections of cities could be condemned, their residents evicted, the buildings in which the residents had lived demolished – and the land turned over to private individuals.[34]

During 1948, anticipating the new law, New York mayor William O'Dwyer appointed Robert Moses to chair a new coordinating body, the Committee on Slum Clearance. Moses 'did to New York what Haussmann had done to Paris'.[35] By the time Moses relinquished his 'dictatorial command' over the city's urban renewal programmes in 1960, New York had racked up more renewal projects against 'blighted' areas than the combined total of all other American cities.[36]

UNFITNESS WAS UPHELD for over a century as a solid, reliable and measurable term, but its utility as a legislative basis for urban redevelopment was fundamentally compromised.

First, it rested on the assumption that slums comprised a finite 'backlog of unfit houses . . . which would naturally come to an end' as these ageing dwellings were identified and dealt with.[37] By the twentieth century dealing with this backlog was generally understood to mean eradicating the 'Victorian slum legacy'.[38] Gradually, however, policy-makers realized that the task was not so straightforward, because 'Every year new slums were created.'[39] In Britain, for example, with the updating of the definition 'unfit for human habitation' after the Second World War, and the takeover of accounting by Whitehall from local government in 1967, estimates of unfit housing spiralled upwards and ever more out of reach of even the most ambitious and costly slum clearance programmes. The government conceded in 1968 that there were 'more unfit houses and sub-standard houses than had been known before, and they were not so much concentrated as had been believed before, but more spread out'.[40] It was estimated during the mid-1970s that with around 100,000 houses becoming 'unfit' per year, existing programmes to eliminate slum housing could make 'very little impression'.[41]

Second, the experiences of local authorities in Britain and over-seas in attempting to deal with 'unfit' places gradually demonstrated that the measuring stick 'unfit for human habitation' was actually a 'highly subjective' characterization of homes and neighbourhoods.[42] In 1937 Victoria's Housing Investigation and Slum Abolition Board, for example, defined a 'slum "dwelling" [as] one which, judged by present standards of living and amenity, is not fit for human habitation'.[43] The board did not, however, attempt to explain how it could objectively identify those 'present standards', and in 1969, during the fight to pro-tect the Carlton district of Melbourne from the HCV, it was telling that residents argued that the regulatory basis for the HCV's interventions was nothing more than 'cultural prejudice'.[44] Many slum crusaders, though, asserted, in denial of such claims, that the term 'unfit for human habitation' did not go far enough. In 1934, for example, one alderman in northwest London was reported as saying that what he and his colleagues 'called slums were not slums in the terms of the Act. They were fretting to get on with slum clearance, but were bound hand and foot both by the Act of Parliament and by the Ministry.'[45] Increasingly, however, officials and commentators became concerned that the term was indeed too sweeping in its application. In the United States, Gans cautioned in 1959 that 'federal and local housing standards which are applied to slum areas reflect the value pattern of middle-class professionals.'[46] His warning was initially treated with scepticism, and in Britain similarly it was not until a government report on 'housing fit-ness' appeared in 1966 that policy began to 'get away from the concept of the "unfit" house [and] the "slum"'.[47] Even so a key 1968 government policy paper continued to maintain that the concepts of 'slum' and 'unfit' homes and housing areas were 'in the main still the right ones'.[48] It was a last hurrah. When in Melbourne the HCV launched another slum clearance drive in Carlton during 1969, residents objected that

> The Housing Act does not define what renders a house unfit for human habitation . . . The Housing Commission has not inspected any of the houses and therefore it cannot have determined if any of the houses are unfit for human habitation. The Carlton Association . . . has carried out a survey of the houses, and DID NOT FIND ONE HOUSE UNFIT FOR HUMAN HABITATION.[49]

Community researchers in Liverpool likewise ridiculed the likelihood, by the early 1970s, that 'a building can be declared unfit for human habitation in Liverpool . . . while the self-same building, if transported to Chelsea, would command an astronomical sum on the market.'[50]

There were other paradoxes about the enforcement of 'unfit' housing regulations. Notwithstanding the rhetoric about an all-out war against slumland, most state-sanctioned slum clearance was undertaken by condemning individual structures as 'unfit for human habitation' and relying on their owners to demolish or repair, rather than by government authorities intervening directly to clear and redevelop whole 'unfit' areas. Many more of these condemned houses were repaired by the private sector than were demolished. In Britain the minister of health estimated in 1933 that during the previous three years 1.5 million 'unfit' houses had been reconditioned at the order of local authorities in England and Wales.[51] The figure, like the definition, was rubbery and was probably inflated to serve the government's interests: it was independently calculated in 1945 that only 751,000 condemned houses had been made 'fit' for habitation between 1930 and 1939.[52] The general pattern, however, is clear. First, regardless of the exact figures, a massive intervention in working-class communities had taken place; second, many more 'unfit' dwellings were repaired than were demolished; and third, most of this rehabilitation was undertaken by private enterprise rather than by the state.

Although such outcomes are now commonly equated with urban renewal policies that were forged in the United States after the discovery of 'blight', efforts to rehabilitate 'unfit' neighbourhoods had been pioneered in Britain during the late nineteenth and early twentieth centuries. Notwithstanding American reservations about the scale of state intervention in British cities, slum regeneration in Britain originated as a partnership between the public and private sectors, within which the extent of public intervention was strictly limited.

British practice was influenced in part by the activities of philanthropic housing associations in London, and by municipal initiatives in provincial cities such as Manchester and Birmingham. The Liberal Unionist housing reformer and town planner John Sutton Nettlefold, who chaired Birmingham's municipal housing committee during the early twentieth century, was especially influential. His *Practical Housing* (1908) recommended that Birmingham's approach be incorporated into a national system for rehabilitating 'unfit' areas. The Chamberlain political dynasty reaffirmed this argument. Neville Chamberlain (who, like his father Joseph, served as lord mayor of Birmingham, and was subsequently prime minister in 1937–40) stated in 1920 that the Birmingham city council was applying the Torrens provisions of the 1890 Housing of the Working Classes Act to issue closing orders against 'unfit' dwellings more extensively than in any other city, compelling owners to repair their properties and producing 'a very marked improvement in the general conditions of the town at a comparatively small expense to the public'.[53] His older stepbrother Sir Austen Chamberlain likewise argued in the 1930s that, by applying Birmingham's landlord-driven slum-repair approach nationally, 'they would have a vast area of many hundreds of thousands of houses which could be made decent at small expense.'[54] Manchester, too, adopted a policy of 'reconditioning' unfit dwellings, resulting in a 'very considerable campaign of piecemeal destruction and reconstruction' of slums by the city corporation and property owners.[55]

By the 1920s and '30s, 'reconditioning' (or 'mending') was being advocated by many in Britain (and copied by others throughout the English-speaking world) as a pragmatic and across-the-board strategy for winning the war against slums:

> Reconditioning, as a housing term, is a new word in the English vocabulary. It implies something more than normal repairs and something less than new reconstruction, though where one ends and the other begins may be difficult to determine.[56]

It was argued that with some three million people living in British slums, the problem was too big and expensive for universal clearances and the rehousing of the occupants in new public housing. The Marquis of Salisbury, whose father had steered through the pioneering housing enactments of 1885 and 1890, was also by the early 1930s advocating reconditioning over slum clearance:

> There was an enormous number of houses at present unfit for decent habitation which could be made fit. Reconditioning presented tremendous advantages over rehousing. To recondition a house cost less than one-third of the cost of rebuilding.[57]

Reconditioning not only spared the public purse; it demonstrated that in a private enterprise society the state could work constructively with private property owners rather than intervening punitively against them and that private enterprise could behave ethically and deliver public-spirited outcomes as well as generating private profits. Both Liberal and Conservative politicians supported reconditioning as a modern-day equivalent of the widely respected philanthropic work by Octavia Hill in the late nineteenth century, which had sought to demonstrate that philanthropy and private enterprise could work together in attacking slumland. The Improved Tenements Association in London, for example, which had been established in 1899 with Hill's backing, regularly paid its shareholders a 4 per cent return by buying in 'slumdom [and] turning hovels into decent dwellings'.[58] Hill's system drew admiration because

> She aimed at reconditioning not only their dwellings but also their lives. With that object she determined that all her rent collectors should be women, and women of an educated class, capable, on the one hand, of seeing that the property providing the rents was properly managed and kept in repair, and, on the other, of becoming friends and domestic advisers in case of need of the wives by whom as a general rule the rents are paid.[59]

In 1921 the Unhealthy Areas Committee, appointed by the minister of health and chaired by Neville Chamberlain, argued that such were the financial and logistical obstacles to clearing slums wholesale and rehousing all their inhabitants that 'no clearance and reconstruction of a complete or drastic character can be expected for a good many years to come.' Chamberlain and his colleagues proposed that

> since they cannot be cleared, the areas can at least be temporarily improved [and] kept under proper supervision [so as to] provide as good homes for working class families as new houses, the rent of which is necessarily so much higher.[60]

In making its recommendation the committee acknowledged the positive effects of the Octavia Hill system but doubted that it could sustain a national system of slum reconditioning. It proposed instead that local authorities purchase, repair and manage slum housing on Hill's principles. In 1933 the Departmental Committee on Housing, chaired by the Conservative politician Baron Moyne, also adopted Hill's system and proposed a public–private partnership for putting it into general effect. The committee recommended the granting of state subsidies for housing societies to recondition slum housing on a large scale and manage them as rental properties under the Hill system, thus transforming 'many bad tenants through the growth of self-respect and a pride in their homes'.[61]

Modifications of Hill's approach continued to be advocated throughout the English-speaking world after the Second World War, but Hill's system lost traction as the British concept of reconditioning was gradually redefined from a policy that required a response from landlords to one that assisted the home improvement efforts of owner-occupiers. Britain's 1949 Housing Act offered grants to owner-occupiers for home repairs, and by the early 1970s these grants had contributed to the repair of over one million 'unfit' houses.[62] In postwar Australia the Brotherhood of St Laurence argued that a similar 'attention to housing would . . . tend to make slum areas into reasonable working class suburbs'.[63] In the United States Gans similarly advocated from the late 1950s that 'greater emphasis should be placed on the rehabilitation of low-rent housing, and less on its clearance.'[64]

Increasing levels of homeownership after the Second World War provided endorsement for a parallel housing strategy that had helped to underpin the war on slums throughout the nineteenth and twentieth centuries. It was calculated that by encouraging private enterprise to build attractive new houses, mostly in the suburbs, 'there will be a filtering up of poorer people into the houses vacated by the purchasers' and thus an inexorable eroding of slumland.[65] As the HCV explained during the 1960s, 'The Commission concentrated on Slum Reclamation and largely left the building of villas in the metropolitan area to private enterprise.'[66] Filtering was attractive both to middle-class progressives and the labour movement. Addison's Liberal-leaning 1919 Housing and Town Planning Act in Britain, for example, has been described as a 'conscious decision to neglect the slums themselves and to focus instead on new suburban housing estates based on garden city ideals'.[67] That strategy was also popular with Conservatives. The 1923 Act (sponsored by Neville Chamberlain, the then minister of health) used state subsidies to encourage private enterprise to make good the interwar housing shortage. By 1933 some two million new houses had been built by private enterprise since the First World War, over half of which were subsidized. However, even the Ministry of Health conceded that most of this new housing was not affordable by the lowest paid.[68] As Sir Ernest Simon, a progressive politician and former lord mayor of Manchester, pointed out in 1933, 'private enterprise . . . never has built, and never will build, decent houses to let for the lower-paid workers.'[69]

'The Great Crusade'

The years of most intense slum clearance activity in the English-speaking world, from the 1930s to the '60s, were widely characterized as a 'Great Crusade' or the 'Good War'.[70] This was, for Westerners, the most just of wars, and calls for an 'anti-slum crusade' had a long currency.[71] At the beginning of the intensified crusades of the 1930s, British Conservative politician Sir Edward Hilton Young, minister of health in MacDonald's cross-party national government during the Great Depression, urged a national front to support 'a great attack upon the crying evil of the slums'.[72] Young announced 'a declaration of war upon the slums'.[73] Thirty years of campaigning later, as the slum war began to flag in the United States during the early 1960s, left-wing social critic Michael Harrington likewise called for a 'crusade' to launch 'an all-out attack upon the slums',[74] and President Lyndon B. Johnson announced a 'War on Poverty' in 1964. Calls for a slum war conjured up the most fundamental of struggles: civilization versus savagery. Such analogies drew in part upon a long legacy of colonial-inspired juxtapositions between civilizers and savages that had helped to shape the meaning of the word 'slum' since the nineteenth century.

Characterizations of the slum crusade were influenced still more by two twentieth-century world wars and the subsequent tensions of the Cold War period. Moses's Committee on Slum Clearance, for example, 'saw modern rebuilding projects as a way to make Manhattan a symbol of American power during an age of metropolitan transformation and the Cold War'.[75] Most of all, the talk of battle encapsulated the instinctive response that the slum-world's 'attraction of repulsion' demanded: normal folk must mobilize against slumland's evils. Even by the late 1960s, after a decade of grass-roots challenges to the viewpoints of social elites and governments, it still seemed to many that slum eradication was 'one of the few progressive causes which remained uncomplicated and, without question, desirable'. Once officialdom declared an area a slum, opposition appeared 'wrong-headed and almost incomprehensible to the outsider'.[76] In Britain, Herbert Manzoni, who directed Birmingham's massive slum clearance programme during the 1960s and '70s, maintained that 'slums weren't only slum buildings, they were also slum conditions of all sorts including a slum mentality . . . [We must] get rid of the lot [and] make a new environment'.[77] As Hubert Humphrey, mayor of Minneapolis, had remarked pithily during 1948, 'Either we lick the slums or the slums will destroy the city.'[78]

Advocates of a decisive 'attack upon the slums' spoke both of 'flanking movements' to wipe out unfit houses and of more intensive 'campaigns' and 'direct assaults' to retake entire districts.[79] In Britain, all sides of politics sought to position themselves as leaders of this great crusade. Greenwood urged 'a nation-wide attack on slums', and Young, providing a radio commentary on the progress of this 'battle' with the slum, declared that 'the news from the front was good.'[80] In 1936 Bernard Townroe, a member of the LCC's housing committee, explicitly compared the fight against slums to the conflicts of the First World War:

> The Whitehall officials, who have had over fifteen years' general experience of housing difficulties, are like the General Staff. The actual hand-to-hand fighting against the slums falls upon the front line troops, the officials and members of local authorities, while the voluntary Housing Societies are like the Territorials. The actual strength of these fighting forces is about 50,000 men and women, who have to attack the Hindenburg Line of slums and overcrowding.[81]

The Second World War and the Cold War gave continuing currency to these analogies. Australia was a case in point. It had been shaken by the prospect of Japanese invasion during the 1940s and rocked by Soviet espionage exposés during the Petrov defection and the subsequent Royal Commission into espionage during the 1950s. Thus when in 1966 Victoria's Minister of Housing launched the HCV's emotive report *The Enemy within Our Gates*, it was with the assurance that the Commission was fighting back against Australia's enemies and 'is attacking slum clearance'.[82]

In calling for Britain to mobilize for 'a successful war upon the slums', Townroe had argued that in wartime Britons had 'learned by experience that the whole nation had to be mobilized in order to avoid defeat'.[83] Such analogies with wartime mobilization resonated in part because of widespread acknowledgement of the magnitude of urban poverty. One member of the House of Lords marvelled in 1928 that 'there were no fewer than three million people in this country living in slum areas,' and as late as 1965 a Labour government could still base its entire urban programme on the premise that there existed a 'huge social problem of slumdom and obsolescence'.[84] Talk of mobilization for war also reflected an emerging consensus that previous approaches had proved insufficient. As *The Times* pointed out in 1931, the 'cost and the difficulties of the work are so great that, except on a small scale, generation after generation has tacitly shelved it till a more convenient season'.[85] The situation seemed little different in 1979: 'Despite forty years of slum clearance, the slum problem in England and Wales appears to be considerably larger than it was when its extent was first comprehensively measured in 1933.'[86]

Most of all, however, mobilization for war resonated because of the theatricality of slum performances. The analogy served the agendas of entertainers, politicians, bureaucrats, reformers and city developers. Newspaper campaigns, radio, illustrated public lectures and propaganda films underpinned their messages. New York reformers staged two massive exhibitions in 1900 and 1908, the first having as its centrepiece a large cardboard model of a crowded tenement block, and the second displaying 'not only photographs of New York's slums, but models and interiors . . . bringing home the fact that the housing law had barely touched the living conditions of a large proportion of the population'.[87] In London, a major exhibition in 1931 on 'New Homes for Old' had as its showpiece 'A mechanically worked diorama [showing] old slums being demolished and new houses built on their site'.[88] In Melbourne, when the Housing Investigation and Slum Abolition Board was appointed in 1936, the *Herald*'s front-page banner headline read 'Attack on Slum Evil Launched'.[89] Such sensationalism, however, was deeply misleading. In 1933 Melbourne's town clerk, quoting from the British journal *The Medical Officer*, cautioned:

> On paper there is a nation-wide campaign against slumdom ... though the amount of slum clearance actually done is infinitesimal and not likely to be excessive this side of the millennium.[90]

The key result of such entertainments was not mobilization at all but acquiescence, and, as Harrington realized in the United States in 1962, 'a well-meaning ignorance':

> A good many concerned and sympathetic Americans are aware that there is much discussion on urban renewal. Suddenly, driving through the city, they notice that a familiar slum has been torn down and that there are towering, modern buildings where once there had been tenements or hovels. There is a warm feeling of satisfaction, of pride in the way things are working out: the poor, it is obvious, are being taken care of.[91]

Yet the consequences of this phoney slum war for inner-city communities are staggering: during 1939 alone, at the height of Britain's first slum campaign, some 90,000 houses were demolished or closed in England and Wales. The British slum war resumed in 1955 and continued uninterrupted until the mid-1970s, during which time some 1.3 million people were evicted from their homes. Across the Atlantic, it has been suggested that in New York alone during the Moses regime almost half a million people were evicted. Although Moses released no detailed official figures, one independent study estimated that in the ten years 1946–56, 320,000 people were evicted:

> He tore out the hearts of a score of neighborhoods, communities the size of small cities themselves, communities that had been lively, friendly places to live, the vital parts of the city that made New York a home to its people.[92]

Summing up Moses's achievement, David Harvey remarked that he took 'a "meat-axe" to living communities'.[93]

TALK ABOUT A WAR on slums first translated into wide-ranging action following the 1929 British general election. MacDonald's incoming minority Labour government pushed the 1930 Housing Act through parliament, and Greenwood instructed local authorities to implement the Act immediately in order to clear the nation's slums within five years. In 1933 MacDonald's new cross-party government of national emergency, heeding calls by the Prince of Wales and the archbishops of Canterbury and York to intensify the slum war, announced a fresh assault, redirecting state funds from public housing to slum clearance. Young, who replaced Greenwood as minister of health in the coalition government, set about 'encouraging the more active administration of the Act of 1930 by the responsible local authorities', requiring them to detail 'their programmes for dealing with the slums in five years by clearance and reconditioning'.[94] When Young's deadline was reached it was estimated that 'More people living in slums had been rehoused in the five years ending in the spring of 1939 than under all the earlier official slum clearance scheme[s] since 1890.'[95]

Some 273,000 houses were demolished during the 1930s, and it has been suggested that by 1939 'the slums were being demolished at a rate never exceeded since.'[96] These results were spread unevenly across the nation. Scotland quickly developed a reputation for energetic action, and in England Leeds embarked upon a major slum clearance campaign to remove its ageing stock of back-to-back housing. By contrast, Birmingham's slum clearance activity during the 1930s was the smallest of any in the nation's largest cities. Notwithstanding the overall scale of the slum war, the targets that local authorities had set when Young demanded a five-year campaign to end the slums had still not been met when in 1939 a real war brought the slum war to a halt. Many more homes were subsequently destroyed by German air raids than had been removed by all the 1930s campaigns to end the slums.

There were echoes of the British slum war in its territories overseas. In Australia, talk continued as a substitute for action. A Minimum Allotment, Anti-Slum and Housing Crusade Committee was active in Melbourne before the First World War, and during the early 1930s regular news reports of the homeland's war on slums prompted the formation of a Committee for Slum Clearance in Sydney. A similar committee was established in Adelaide. In Melbourne, the news from 'Home' coincided with F. O. Barnett's local slum abolition campaign beginning in the late 1920s, and in 1935 G. K. Tucker, head of the Brotherhood of St Laurence, designed a dramatic new letterhead with the words 'The Brotherhood of St. Laurence has Declared War on the Slums'.[97] A Slum Abolition League was formed in Melbourne during 1936 to coordinate the local campaigns, which culminated in the establishment of the HCV. However, as the HCV later conceded, 'With the intervention of World War II little could be done to attack the problem massively.'[98]

When the slum war resumed after the Second World War, its chief battlefront was initially in the United States, where massive 'urban renewal' schemes sought to roll back the spread of 'blight'. One million Americans had been evicted as a result of these schemes by the mid-1960s.[99] Backed by the federal Housing Acts of 1949 and 1954, big city governments forged partnerships with private enterprise to commence massive schemes of slum clearance and urban redevelopment. Baltimore and Philadelphia embarked upon huge renewal projects during the 1950s, and in 1957 Boston's new redevelopment authority began the destruction of the West End district. In the same year, the *New York Times* could nonetheless boast: 'City Leads Nation in Slum Clearing'.[100] New York mayor Robert Wagner launched 'Operation Bowery' in 1961 to sweep away the blighted Bowery district in Lower Manhattan, which had been characterized as an infamous slum since the nineteenth century.[101] In Chicago, similar schemes of massive 'renewal' took place during the late 1950s and '60s.

Across the border in Canada, Toronto led the way on another front of the slum war, with schemes such as the Regent Park clearance project in 1947 and the opening in 1965 of a new city hall on the site of the old slum district 'the Ward'.[102] In Canada's British Dominion partner, Australia, a short-lived Commonwealth Housing Commission urged the federal government in 1944 to 'recognize the clearance of slums as partly a national responsibility', but the recommendation was ignored and clearance was left in the hands of state governments and local authorities.[103] In Sydney, the New South Wales Housing Commission undertook slum clearance projects in the inner suburbs during the 1950s and '60s, but these were dwarfed by those undertaken in Victoria. Before the Second World War had even ended, Tucker reignited the campaign in Melbourne for the HCV to reclaim the slums. The Brotherhood funded research reports, three films (*Beautiful Melbourne*, *Gaol Does Not Cure* and *These Are Our Children*) and sponsored public meetings, sermons and weekly radio broadcasts – as well as persuading the mass-circulation *Herald* newspaper to reproduce its research findings in a series of articles – to hammer home its key theme: 'we set up a Government authority [the HCV] to get rid of the slums in 1937 and now 17 years later, the slums are not only still with us, but they are more extensive than ever before.'[104] Whereas the state Labor government procrastinated, the Liberal (conservative) opposition endorsed the campaign and in 1956 the incoming Liberal government under Henry Bolte, encouraged by the Conservative example in Britain, sought to restart the slum campaign. The HCV had cleared less than five acres by the end of 1955, but in 1960 two HCV officials, J. H. Davey and G. Shaw, drove through Melbourne's entire inner-suburban ring and produced a 'Report on Slum Reclamation and Urban Redevelopment of Melbourne Inner Suburban Areas' (popularly dismissed as the 'windshield survey') which comprehensively condemned the entire region as a slum and scheduled its proposed wholesale redevelopment.[105]

In post-war Britain, influenced by American trends, a renewed slum war was talked up by the Conservatives when they returned to government under Winston Churchill in 1951. With the post-war housing shortage overcome, housing policy could refocus on 'attacking once more the wretched conditions which still restrict and darken too many lives'.[106] The minister for housing and local government, Harold Macmillan, stated in 1953,

> we can no longer afford to put off, to put aside, the question
> of the slums. We can no longer leave people living in cramped,
> dark, rotten houses with no water, sometimes no lavatories,
> no proper ventilation and no hope of rescue.[107]

Macmillan's pledge was emphasized by the Conservatives during the 1955 general election, which they won with an increased majority under the leadership of Sir Anthony Eden. Closures and demolitions of 'unfit' houses in England and Wales thereafter rose rapidly, from 18,000 in 1954 until levelling out at 60,000–62,000 per annum during the early 1960s under Macmillan's prime ministership. In total, over one million dwellings were demolished during this renewed slum war.[108] Leeds resumed its demolition campaign against back-to-back tenement rows during the 1950s and '60s, but nowhere was the new slum war more intense than in Birmingham, whose new chief engineer and surveyor, Herbert Manzoni, was reported in 1958 to be 'concerned about the sea of slumdom which encompassed the city centre, [and who] had the vision of sweeping it all away in one operation'.[109] In 1964 the incoming Labour government led by Harold Wilson embarked upon an even more intense national campaign, lifting the rate of closures and demolitions to 90,000 per annum (where it had stalled at the outbreak of war in 1939). Glasgow's Gorbals district, once known as 'Britain's most notorious slum', was cleared away.[110] Labour's minister for housing and local government vowed in 1968: 'There will be slum clearance at well over 100,000 a year. We cleared 90,000 slums in Great Britain last year . . . I want to step up clearance by 50%.'[111]

The long-running British slum campaign, however, was running out of steam. The change in mood was influenced in part by the winding down of the slum war in the United States, where community resistance in Philadelphia, Boston and other cities to expressway and renewal projects during the 1950s was starting to attract attention. In New York Moses was discreetly removed in 1960 and his Slum Clearance Committee disbanded. The changing mood was also shaped by belief within the political elite that the main slum war had been won, and that full employment and state welfare supports had 'largely eliminated' chronic poverty.[112] It seemed that only mopping-up operations were now needed. In Britain a Labour government white paper in 1968 highlighted a renewed interest in repairing rather than demolishing the remaining old housing, and this approach was reflected in the Housing Act of 1969. Although the Conservatives under Edward Heath won the 1970 election and announced a new ten-year deadline to clear the nation's remaining slums, the annual demolition rate tapered off to approximately 70,000 houses in England and Wales, and slumped to 49,000 in 1975 under Wilson once more. On both sides of the Atlantic, the slum war had ended in stalemate.

We are not slum-dwellers!

War requires an adversary, but the slum's defenders were largely invisible in the reports and commentaries on the slum crusades. Although

the foreign abominations of slumland territories are repeatedly emphasized, and its cowed inhabitants are mentioned with sympathy (albeit
mingled with derision), their overlords are absent. There is no massed
enemy force to be confronted and overcome. Slum entertainers and
reformers often referred to (and sometimes named) the absentee
landlords who rented out hovels unfit for human habitation, and
they hinted at an overlap between property interests and politicians.
However, over time, slum crusaders sought to build alliances with
property interests rather than fight with them, in order to 'improve'
slums and redevelop cities.

Although the archetypal slum was characterized as a place owned by
absentee landlords and occupied by poor renters, by the second half of
the twentieth century, a time of rising real incomes, a small but significant proportion of inhabitants of the clearance areas were working-class
owner-occupiers who protested against the condemning of their homes.
Even tenants, who formed the majority in the clearance areas, could
seem ambivalent about their 'liberation'. A former British minister
of health said of his experiences during the 1920s, 'People who lived
in the slums were not so anxious to remove as might be supposed.'[113]
The slum's inhabitants were generally characterized as a subservient
and cowed class rather than as actively belligerent. It was they, after
all, whom the crusaders were liberating, although the liberators were
often exasperated that the clearance of 'unfit' areas left untouched
the 'problem of individual reformation' of the inhabitant: 'Various
are the epithets used to describe him – "anti-social", "unregenerate",
"unemployable", "incorrigible", and "problem citizen".'[114]

By the 1960s the slum crusaders found themselves ambushed by
an unexpected adversary among slumland's inhabitants. Affluent and
articulate middle-class professionals, many of whom had settled in
the inner cities for the lifestyle there, took the lead in resisting the
clearances. In 1969 the Carlton Association in Melbourne, speaking
on behalf of one local neighbourhood in the district, objected that
it 'should not have been proclaimed a Slum Reclamation Area. The
houses are not slum dwellings, the people are not slum dwellers, and
the block in no way conforms to any definition of a slum.'[115]

Throughout the slum crusades, the working-class communities
most targeted by the clearance projects expressed apprehension about
the disruption to their lives. Owner-occupiers were indignant that their
homes should be seized without adequate review and compensation.

At a public meeting in Bristol during the mid-1950s, one resident from the Barton Hill neighbourhood,

> amid general applause, complained of the failure of the Corporation to give advance information or to furnish Barton Hill people with precise facts, with the result that many people had bought property recently at high prices. 'I was proud', said one woman, 'that we were able to buy our own house; we thought we could settle here and get our money back by saving rent. It was a shock to us to hear that it was going to be taken from us.'[116]

A Bristol University Settlement researcher recorded that

> Much bitterness was aroused by one official who endeavoured to console families to be removed by such remarks as 'Surely you don't want to stay in this "slum".' The immediate reaction was to say 'We're not a slum; we're respectable, and so is Barton Hill.'[117]

In Boston's West End during the 1950s, immigrant households 'could not understand how the buildings they had worked so hard to own could suddenly be taken away from them'.[118] By 1968, a key British policy paper reported that

> A growing proportion (now about 20 per cent nationally and much higher in some areas) of owners of houses in clearance areas are owner-occupiers; and they have a special grievance. Often they bought their house when it was not possible to get anything better, and they have put their savings into it. In any case, it is their home which is being demolished.[119]

In the following year, when much of Carlton was declared a reclamation area, over half of the affected housing was owner-occupied. According to the Carlton Association,

> Our survey shows very considerable expenditure [by home-owners] since 1960. The same rehabilitation of terrace housing has occurred throughout the inner suburbs, following an influx

of migrants with strong aspirations to home ownership and often possessing the skills to improve their newly-bought houses. More recently young professional people have started to buy and renovate terrace houses, especially in Carlton.[120]

Cruel paradox that redevelopment authorities should disregard grass-roots house improvements when state-sanctioned reconditioning of old housing stock had been recommended time and time again by politicians through much of the nineteenth and twentieth centuries.

Many tenants also reacted with alarm. Boston's West End renters had, 'during the [years of] postwar prosperity, [been] able to modernize the interiors of their apartments'.[121] In Britain likewise, those

> who had invested time and money in maintenance and repair of their houses and convinced themselves that 'it's good enough for us' found it difficult to accept that their houses had become 'unfit for human habitation' overnight.[122]

Tenants well knew the insufficiencies of the rental accommodation that was available to low earners through the private market, and many cautiously welcomed relocation to modern public housing estates. At Barton Hill, for example,

> a minority of the inhabitants, amounting to just over a quarter of the occupants, already wished to move and were on the Corporation's waiting list for rehousing. Their reasons were mainly connected with the structural condition of their houses, nearly half of which were designated as 'unfit' or with the fact that they were sub-tenants and desired a separate house.[123]

As one Liverpool woman remarked during the early 1970s, complaining about her family's long wait for public housing, 'These houses are finished. If they don't knock 'em down they'll fall down. We're just waiting and waiting. Can't do any decorating. Just hanging on all the time waiting.'[124]

Norman Dennis, who interviewed residents of clearance areas in the northern English city of Sunderland during the mid-1960s, found that 65 per cent of families reported structural defects in their houses; 80 per cent of households had no piped water, and only 2 per cent had an

SLUMS

indoor toilet. When he undertook a follow-up survey in the late 1960s, he found that 86 per cent of households were dissatisfied with the structural condition of their homes.[125] A woman from Leeds who had lived in a back-to-back for over thirty years remarked in the early 1970s that the 'landlord could have put baths in years ago, but they don't break their necks even to do repairs'.[126] However many of these people regretted the forcible break-up of their communities. John Waite, who was born in York's Hungate district in 1923, recalled later in life what Hungate had been like before the demolition crews moved in during 1938:

> I'm not saying that the way of life was good, the conditions that they were living under, they were certainly a lot better when they moved them out. But they lost a way of life once they split Hungate up.[127]

Such reactions perplexed the slum crusaders. As one leading reformer in Chicago mused, 'It was strange to find people so attached to homes that were so lacking in all the attributes of comfort and decency.'[128] In Britain, Townroe acknowledged that as soon as 'a slum area is threatened, the inhabitants protest violently', but he sought to explain away these protests, saying that the slum-dwellers 'are naturally conservative, clinging to the corner of the world they know best, and where they have friends near'.[129] Other commentators contended that home improvers formed only a small fraction of slum populations, and that the houses they treasured as homes were by any objective measure miserable hovels. It seemed only common sense that normal folk would rejoice at being rehoused in modern flats in the city centre or on suburban cottage estates.

It was generally agreed that only the 'slum minded' residuum could possibly mourn their former homes. James Cuming Walters said of Birmingham's slums early in the twentieth century, 'An animal-like attachment seems to tie them to the places, however bad.'[130] Sheffield's Social Survey Committee, reviewing the effects of slum clearance in 1931, likewise sneered that

> The old intimate and interflowing life of the slum . . . and the pleasantries of the corner beer shops [have] gone and their going was regretted, sometimes bitterly, sometimes wistfully by a number of the inhabitants.[131]

Such people seemingly could not free themselves from their 'old and deep-seated habits'.[132] Newcastle's city planning officer argued in 1963 that

> we are dealing with people who have no initiative or civic pride. The task, surely, is to break up such groupings even though the people seem to be satisfied with their miserable environment and seem to enjoy an extrovert social life in their own locality.[133]

Ethnic and racial prejudice coloured these opinions. In the United States, immigrant neighbourhoods such as Boston's West End were targeted for renewal, along with those where African Americans and Puerto Ricans had congregated. Gans remarked that in the United States, 'By 1960, slum clearance was predominantly "Negro removal".'[134] In London's Tower Hamlets district, a local government area which included the notorious Bethnal Green and which by the early 1970s was heavily settled by Indian and Pakistani immigrants, researchers concluded: 'It was clear that the local authority regarded the area as a "problem" area and that the position of the Asian residents was their major cause of concern.'[135]

NOTWITHSTANDING THE ENTRENCHED prejudice that sustained it, the slum war was gradually undermined by the realization that merely obliterating 'slum' environments would not overcome either the social inequalities or the alleged social pathologies that had accumulated there. Attention therefore focused upon devising affordable rehousing schemes for evicted residents, given that few people were prepared to address the deeper issues of housing reform or to advocate higher wages, income redistribution and a comprehensive social security safety net.

Even slum crusaders said that clearance projects needed to be accompanied by the rehousing of evicted residents in affordable housing convenient to their work. The rub, however, was that the replacement housing delivered by clearance projects rarely housed the actual people who had been displaced. This was an awkward acknowledgement for the crusaders to make. It had begun to be recognized during the nineteenth century that slum clearance without affordable rehousing simply increased pressure on low-cost housing in neighbouring inner-city areas. A British government report noted in 1921 that the effect of slum clearances had been 'merely to push the old tenants into the surrounding areas and so create new overcrowding and new slums'.[136] However, notwithstanding the emerging consensus that to 'clear an area without adequate provision being made for re-accommodating the inhabitants is to shirk the real problem', it was not until Greenwood's Housing Act in 1930 that local authorities faced any meaningful requirement to ensure the rehousing of people displaced by slum clearances.[137] As late as the 1970s, it was contended that so 'long as a local authority acknowledges a general responsibility to rehouse displaced residents there is no central government interference in the way this obligation is to be met'.[138] In the United States, similarly, Gans objected during the late 1950s that

> American redevelopment planning so far has proceeded on the assumption that relocation is secondary to redevelopment. Thus, great pains are taken with planning for clearance and the reuse of the site, but plans for the present occupants of the site are treated as by-products of the redevelopment proposal.

In consequence, he said, too many former residents were 'encouraged to buy houses in the suburbs at prices beyond their ability to pay'.[139] Harrington complained in 1962 that post-war renewal projects had 'not provide[d] enough [housing] units for those who had been driven out to make way for improvement. The projects thus created new slums and intensified the pressures within the old slums.'[140]

Working-class dissatisfaction with proffered rehousing alternatives also alerted some slum crusaders to the constrained housing choices available to the poor and the affection felt by them for their neighbourhoods. Some reformers sought to provide alternative low-cost rental accommodation on part of the slum clearance areas, despite the property market redefining such areas as expensive inner-city land. Thus they built flats of multiple storeys and – as construction technologies improved – high-rise towers. The financial bottom line dictated these outcomes in order to recoup the costs of redevelopment and maximize the number of tenants who could be fitted into the reduced spaces reallocated for low-cost housing. The HCV, a world leader in post-1945 public housing construction, calculated not only that rehousing 'must be in the form of flats', but opted over time for increasingly higher densities of public housing: from 'walk-up flats, to a combination of 4-storey walk-up flats and high-rise elevator blocks. Walk-up flats are now being replaced by high-rise blocks.'[141] However this direction in public housing options was opposed by many working people, the labour movement and some middle-class progressives. When a review of slum clearance programmes was undertaken in London's Stepney district in 1925, the residents'

> behaviour at the inquiry was very rude; but they certainly made it evident that they are passionately attached to their poor little homes, and are strongly prejudiced against block dwellings, where they would not be able to keep pigeons, fowls, and rabbits in 'a bit of back garden'.[142]

A report to Sir Anthony Eden's Conservative government in 1956 found that too many flats were being built without regard to the needs of families with young children or those of tenants who had previously kept pets or engaged in backyard hobbies such as gardening, carpentry or pigeon-keeping. The report suggested, 'Alternative hobbies which might be encouraged are the keeping of budgerigars, or tropical fish, and window gardening.'[143]

Progressive politicians and the labour movement had since the nineteenth century championed an alternative strategy: building cottage-style rental housing on suburban cottage estates. The LCC won praise for its 'splendid work [in] building houses on the outskirts of London', where it was said that more people lived in municipal housing than the entire population of Nottingham.[144] However, as the bishop of Southwark commented in 1928,

> the building of the new houses had so far affected the slum problem very little. That was due to the fact that the rents of the new houses were too high, and the cost of moving back-wards and forwards from the suburbs to the place of work was too high.[145]

Relocated residents also had to adjust their meagre budgets to allow for rents, but rents payable quarterly rather than weekly as they were accustomed to, and to purchasing furniture and appliances for their new homes. Tenants at the LCC's model dwellings estate in Peckham staged a rent strike in 1931 and formed a 'passive resistance army'.[146] There were broader readjustments to be made, for example, in the areas of friendships, leisure-time activities, shops and schools. As one woman in Bristol remarked during the 1950s, after being relocated from Barton Hill to a new suburban housing estate out 'in the wilds', her husband 'misses . . . his evenings in the "local". He and Bill Smith were keen on darts and it wasn't many evenings when they didn't have a game. He pines for it all.'[147]

Slum crusaders tended to dismiss such talk as mere sentimentality: idle nostalgia for frivolous ways of life amid 'the gay hubbub of the city' that were best avoided.[148] However, a fuller appreciation of working-class neighbourhood preferences gradually coloured the paternalistic sympathy of some outside observers. According to *The Times*, Sir Austen Chamberlain acknowledged in parliament in 1932 that

> The homes of the poor were often as dear to them as the homes of the wealthy, and within the neighbourhood in which they lived were all their friendships. If their houses were pulled down and they were rehoused in some other district they would have to start a life as strange to them as it would be to him if he were transferred . . . to Australia or Canada.[149]

One woman who had lived in London's Bethnal Green all her life told investigators during the mid-1950s that she 'had been shocked to hear that the authorities might be labelling her beloved court a "slum", and was now terrified lest they pull it down'.[150] As an official in Leeds said of the residents whose lives were disrupted by slum clearances during the 1970s, 'You've got to remember that these are people. They've lived there twenty years. All their friends and memories are there.'[151]

Such concerns deepened with the gradual development of a new style of social science analysis which was better equipped to uncover sensible reasons for working-class neighbourhood preferences: housing affordability, transport, jobs, shopping, family associations. Professor J. H. Fleure, chair of Manchester University Settlement's Survey Committee, concluded after his colleagues had studied Manchester's ill-reputed Ancoats district in the late 1930s, 'Compulsory clearance would inevitably break up the intricate economic and social pattern of their lives':

The dismayed had much to say. They knew the rents of the new Corporation houses. Higher rents meant less money for food, and the careful housewife knew that she needed every penny she was spending on food if her family was to be fit for school and work. In Ancoats, work was often near at hand, they could 'pop home', and see to the children's dinner and the shopping. They dreaded the thought of weary and costly daily journeys. In Ancoats they had learned to manage, they knew the cheapest shops, they could make their purchases every day . . . The corner shop was kind and purchases might be entered 'in the back of the book' for a few days if money was short. And there were friends in Ancoats who could mind the children, come in for a game of cards, look after invalids, share the news.[152]

When Britain's slum war resumed during the 1950s, Hilda Jennings at Bristol's University Settlement was one of the first observers to document its mixed effects sympathetically. She had been the settlement's warden since 1937 and directed social research on the city's Barton Hill district when the city council announced its redevelopment in 1953. Michael Young and Peter Willmott's *Family and Kinship in East London* (1957), which studied the unravelling of Bethnal Green as the slum war proceeded, achieved a much greater impact. Subsequent researchers heeded its insider's perspective, such as the explanation given by one resident: 'I suppose people who come here from outside think it's an awful place, but us established ones like it. Here you can just open the door and say hello to everybody.'[153] Across the Atlantic, Gans's fieldwork in Boston's West End during 1957–8, on the eve of its destruction by the city authorities, was equally influential. Gans set out to describe how slum clearance needlessly 'destroys . . . a functioning social system'.[154]

Academic arguments like these began to shift public opinion. When Dennis studied the north of England during the 1960s, he quoted a local newspaper, the *Sunderland Echo*, which asked provocatively in 1965,

families are turned out of their cherished cottages in mis-named 'slum-clearance' schemes. Why is it that having been brought from under the shadow of the dole, we now have to live under the shadow of the bulldozer?[155]

A spate of similar grass-roots studies was released during the 1960s and 1970s throughout the English-speaking world. Sidney Jacobs, a social worker who studied the effects of tenement-block clearances in Glasgow's Maryhill district during the early 1970s, recorded the residents' bewilderment:

> We were very happy there and people couldn't believe that they were taking the place apart . . . To me it was like a wee village and everybody knew what was happening to people and everybody was interested in each other. It was like a death sentence that kind of thing coming to us.[156]

Social science researchers identified an especially embarrassing and unexpected consequence of the slum crusaders' activities: the unravelling of otherwise viable communities by the blight caused by redevelopment. The phenomenon had first become apparent in Britain during the late nineteenth century. George Sims, for example, had damned

> the working of the Artisans' Dwelling Act. Space after space has been cleared under the provision of this Act, thousands upon thousands of families have been rendered homeless by the demolition of whole acres of the slums where they hid their heads, and in scores of instances the work of improvement has stopped with the pulling down. To this day the cleared spaces stand empty – a cemetery for cats, a last resting-place for worn-out boots and tea-kettles.[157]

America's preoccupation with the concept of 'urban blight' from the 1930s and '40s vastly increased the potency of such criticisms during the second half of the twentieth century. New York's East Tremont district is a case in point. East Tremont was identified by planners as the route for a new expressway during the early 1950s, and thereafter its houses stood empty for years as demolition and construction work slowly proceeded and its deserted streets were 'roamed by narcotics addicts in gangs like packs of wolves'. The Women's City Club, appalled by the results of these renewal schemes, declared that 'Manhattan looked like a cross section of bombed-out Berlin right after World War II.'[158] Gans noted that when plans for the redevelopment of Boston's West End were first released in 1950, landlords were advised not to make extensive repairs on their properties. Many residents claimed – with some justification – that parts of the area deteriorated rapidly as a result, especially where apartments or entire buildings became and remained vacant in the years that followed.[159]

Concerns about urban blight also increasingly conditioned assessments of post-war slum clearance in Britain. Jennings recorded the 'gloom' in Barton Hill during the 1950s among the residents of houses that had not been scheduled for immediate demolition, and who were living amidst

> rubble-covered sites and boarded-up houses . . . 'It's like a graveyard' said one woman, as she stood solitary on her doorstep looking at the empty houses opposite. 'A bomb site isn't it' said another.[160]

As the Barton Hill redevelopment scheme continued into the 1960s, Jennings described

> the efforts of solitary inhabitants, living in streets in which only a few isolated homes remained in occupation, to maintain standards by keeping the curtains clean and putting the vase of flowers in the front window.[161]

In Glasgow, slum clearance during the 1960s left 'much of the Gorbals . . . a vast, empty sea of rubble awaiting the next attempt at building Utopia'.[162] Dennis identified similar outcomes in Sunderland in the 1960s. One resident told him: 'They keep saying "another five years". But then it goes on for twenty.' Another confided his suspicions about the delay: 'The Corporation is very crafty. They let it go down. They let it deteriorate. A little bit worse! A little bit worse! Then they can get them cheap.'[163] A woman lamented:

> Every night of the week . . . boys and girls invade the [vacant] houses. They throw stones at the shattered panes of glass. When the stone throwing is over they adjourn to the houses, drinking beer and singing and shouting.[164]

Birmingham also adopted this staged approach, buying up dilapidated housing well in advance of planned demolitions, when it embarked upon slum clearances of a vastly larger scale in 1954. By the early 1970s some Birmingham residents had 'endured fifteen years of planned blight and appalling living conditions'.[165] In Newcastle, likewise, the city council's policy of buying and boarding up condemned properties ahead of redevelopment was blamed for creating a 'cycle of blight' in adjoining neighbourhoods.[166]

Neighbourhoods in Liverpool were described in similar terms during the late 1960s and early '70s:

> Life in the new urban deserts is rapidly becoming unbearable for those who remain. Half-demolished houses and broken drains harbour rats, which make their way into still-occupied dwellings. The small number of residents leaves many areas unsupervised and hence subject to vandalism and crime.[167]

These nightmarish consequences were showcased by the Liverpool Inner Area Study in 1977:

> For those who have to live with the day to day reality of large, rubble-strewn sites the impact is immediate, unsavoury and depressing. Packs of half wild dogs scavenge among bags of abandoned household refuse. Pools of water collect where badly filled cellars have subsided. Children build fires with cardboard cartons and the abandoned timber from demolished houses and play among the piles of brick rubble and broken glass. Half bricks provide a ready and almost endless supply of ammunition for the frequent destruction of the windows of surrounding houses. Mattresses, furniture, gas cookers, prams and even cars that have outlived their usefulness are dumped. There is a pervading smell of old town gas from the partly buried gas pipes of demolished houses and the stopped off gas mains. It cannot be surprising that nearby residents, faced with five to ten years of dereliction, feel abandoned by an impersonal and uncaring bureaucracy.[168]

'I was fighting for my home'

So declared Lillian Edelstein, leader of New York's East Tremont Neighborhood Assocation, when she unsuccessfully lobbied city hall during the early 1950s not to build an expressway through their homes. 'It was like the floor opened up underneath your feet,' said Edelstein.[169] Resistance to slum clearance programmes came in large part from the working-class and lower-middle-class residents of condemned houses and neighbourhoods. New York's Sunset Park was called a slum by Moses and obliterated by an expressway in 1941, but a former resident had seen it differently: 'A slum! That wasn't a slum! . . . That was a very nice neighborhood. It was poor, but clean poor.'[170] It is probable that such reactions had also been common during the late nineteenth and early twentieth centuries, but they were idiomatic to the neighbourhoods directly affected and received little or no wider recognition unless they served to entertain. In Sydney, for example, during a municipal inspection tour in 1884 aimed at condemning houses 'unfit for human habitation', an accompanying journalist reported tongue-in-cheek that one woman

> took up a commanding position on her own doorstep, and as the municipal procession passed along, delivered an address to her congregated neighbours, which was received with many marks of sympathy and satisfaction. She took for her subject the City Council in general, and Mr Seymour [the Inspector of Nuisances] in particular, and drew short but trenchant historical parallels between the former and 'a den of thieves', and the latter and 'the evil one himself'.[171]

Such local reactions proliferated as the slum campaigns intensified during the twentieth century, and increasingly took organized form during the 1960s and 1970s. As Dennis summed up the reactions of working-class communities to the British slum war in the early 1970s, 'It would be difficult to exaggerate the anger and depth of insult felt by many home-centred and house-proud residents when they discovered that their own cottages were described as poor.'[172]

Local anger and resistance were routinely overlooked or trivialized by officials, journalists and politicians during the slum crusades. As *The Times* had remarked in 1933, supporting the 'speeding-up and

... intensification' of slum clearance under the Greenwood Act, 'The authorities will have to reckon with and to overcome some obstruction on the part of slum dwellers themselves.' The leader writer added smugly, 'omelettes cannot be made without breaking eggs.'[173] Edelstein's East Tremont Neighborhood Association bussed in over 200 local women to protest outside New York's city hall in 1953 and 1,000 people attended another rally. No one listened to them. By 1955 the community had given up and was largely dispersed.[174] Few listened either to New York's Lincoln Square Residents' Committee during the 1950s when it objected to the Rockefeller-sponsored Lincoln Center redevelopment project. Over 5,000 families were displaced. In Harlem, organized resistance to evictions was likewise evident during the early 1950s, and a coalition of residents' groups was formed in 1956, but few outsiders listened and the slum crusades continued.[175] In Chicago, urban renewal amid the 'slums' of the Near West Side began in 1959, despite court appeals, with the creation of a new campus for the University of Illinois.[176] Across the border in Canada, residents of Toronto's Cabbagetown mobilized unsuccessfully during the 1940s and '50s.[177] So did working-class residents of Vancouver's Strathcona neighbourhood – initially composed mainly of eastern European and Italian immigrants, but gradually transformed into the city's Chinatown – when city authorities announced a massive slum clearance programme in the late 1950s and pursued it through the 1960s. The residents protested that Strathcona 'was a low-income working-class area, it was not a slum'.[178] In Australia, residents of inner-Melbourne working-class communities such as Collingwood, Fitzroy, Richmond, Prahran, and North, South and Port Melbourne reacted similarly during the 1950s.[179] All their protests went unheeded.

Another source of opposition, entirely unexpected and much harder to ignore, emerged during the 1950s. It comprised well-connected sympathizers from the social elite. In Britain, community groups such as the Barton Hill Planning Protection Society, established during the mid-1950s in Bristol to oppose slum redevelopment plans, also held public meetings and lobbied city officials, without success. Yet the Barton Hill protests were not rejected out of hand, because they were backed by the University Settlement and the Protection Society was chaired by the local vicar. In New York, too, middle-class liberals started to heed grass-roots protests. In 1959 the progressive Citizens Union demanded details about the private sponsors who partnered the city's redevelopment schemes. When the *New York Post* took up the issue and revealed that one project was backed in part by underworld leaders, the Slum Committee's days were numbered. The mayor appointed an outside consultant, J. Anthony Panuch, to review the city's urban renewal programme. Panuch's report acknowledged that 'slums, after all, are neighborhoods and communities.'[180] Gans, recalling his West End fieldwork during the late 1950s in Boston, wrote, 'I became so angry that at one point during my field work, I considered dropping my study and joining the small band of West Enders who were trying to halt the bulldozer.'[181]

By the early 1960s, in New York, Boston, Philadelphia, Chicago and San Francisco, protests by residents' groups were becoming more widely supported, reported and, as a consequence, heeded by officials and policy-makers. This trend further encouraged opponents of the slum crusade in Britain. Community protests in Liverpool during the 1960s began to be reported and they became better organized, leading in 1971 to a council reassessment of its renewal programme and a subsequent winding-back of slum clearance in favour of rehabilitating old housing.[182] Manchester's grandiose slum clearance plans in the late 1960s likewise ignited a spate of widely reported neighbourhood protests. These protests produced a receptive context for the formation of a federation of residents' groups, and this contributed to the abandonment during the mid-1970s of Manchester's post-war clearance drive.[183] In Birmingham during the early to mid-1970s the number of residents' groups increased from under a dozen to over forty, united in a federation of community groups.[184] Meanwhile in Sydney, Australia, a coalition of resident action groups was formed in 1971 to fight the destruction of inner-city neighbourhoods.[185]

These protest movements enjoyed greater publicity and credibility during the 1960s and '70s because the leadership and membership of residents' groups was increasingly middle class. Journalists, academics, professionals, artists and writers were able to look at the supposed slums not as slummers did from the outside, but from the inside. They were residents; Gans called them 'cosmopolites'.[186] They were attracted by the cosmopolitan ambience of inner cities. Among the first wave were university students. One such was the Australian poet and academic Chris Wallace-Crabbe, who studied at the University of Melbourne during the 1950s and lived among the adjoining 'slum' districts of Carlton and Parkville in 'student digs (four or five to an

1880s terrace house)'. He loved the Jewish kosher butcher shops and Italian delicatessens and cafés, and he frequented the local pubs and wine bars where, 'After a few bottles we could almost dream that we had been written by Proust.'[187] This emerging fashion for inner-city living, as it became driven by affluent middle-class professionals, was by the mid-1960s being called 'gentrification' (a term coined by Ruth Glass in 1964 to describe social changes occurring in London) and linked with 'trendy' and 'yuppy' lifestyles.[188] The trend found an early champion in Jane Jacobs, a resident of New York's Greenwich Village, whose *Death and Life of Great American Cities* (1961) quickly became an international best-seller. Jacobs became a leader of local residents' protests when city hall identified the West Village neighbourhood as blighted and in need of redevelopment. The protracted opposition eventually prevailed and West Village was given blanket protection in 1969.[189]

The West Village fightback became an inspiration for gentrifiers around the world. In Toronto, Cabbagetowners remobilized during the 1960s, supported this time by Jacobs, and in 1969 their candidates were elected to the city council. In 1972 the reformers won the mayoralty.[190] In Vancouver, the Strathcona Property Owners and Tenants Association, launched in 1968, began a sophisticated publicity campaign that forced the city to cancel its renewal programme.[191] In Australia, residents in Melbourne took courage from the international protest movement that arose when during the mid-1960s the HCV identified a huge ring of inner-Melbourne suburbs as ripe for redevelopment in its bid to consolidate itself as Australia's leading urban redevelopment authority, armed with sweeping powers to repossess and redevelop 'whole districts at a time'.[192] In 1969 formal notices of the HCV's intention were sent to residents in Carlton, which was becoming increasingly a home for staff and students at the nearby University of Melbourne rather than, as it had been for much of the century, a place of first settlement for Jewish, Italian and Greek immigrants. Angry residents formed the Carlton Association to fight the commission. Ian Robertson, a member of the new association and a lecturer in history at the university (he became a distinguished historian of Renaissance Florence), wrote to the *Age* newspaper protesting against 'the arbitrary invasion of a bureaucrat-driven bulldozer'.[193]

The Carlton Association contended that the HCV's slum clearance proposal was based on 'an out-moded idea, abandoned in other States and overseas'. The association used meticulous research and analysis to demonstrate that the commission's benchmark of 'unfitness' was unmeasurable and therefore indefensible, and to argue that the HCV's 'destruction of the historic heart of Melbourne' was insensitive to the heritage value of the late nineteenth-century cityscape which was 'cherished by the people of Melbourne and admired by visitors to the city'.[194] The HCV's announcement of another scheme later in 1969 to redevelop the Brooks Crescent area in neighbouring Fitzroy led to the establishment of the Fitzroy Residents' Association, which similarly pitched its campaigns on the theme that Fitzroy was 'not a slum'.[195] By 1973 the Victorian government, embarrassed in particular by the Carlton Association's publicity campaigns, formally abandoned its redevelopment plans for the district. Announcing the government's change of heart, the *Age* drew attention to the fact that the state premier, Rupert Hamer, 'went out personally to tell the residents that the Housing Commission had dropped its slum clearance plans in favour of preserving the existing Victorian terrace houses'.[196] The decision was hailed as signalling 'the virtual death of both Slum Reclamation and Urban Renewal on a large scale' in Australia.[197] The urban planning establishment throughout the English-speaking world, less effusive about such policy backtracks, conceded that a new 'image of a cosy secure community ravaged by the "planners" [had] replaced that of the miserable slum fit only for the bulldozer'.[198]

The gentrifiers' opposition campaigns marked the end of the slum war in the English-speaking world. Their resistance turned the heads of policy-makers as the opposition of working-class residents never could. Other events and trends gave indirect support to the gentrifiers' arguments. The Cold War focused the attention of politicians and the general public upon international strategic issues over domestic entertainments. Fiscal pressures during the 1960s, and the economic crisis of 1973–4 caused by a global hike in the price of oil, made governments receptive to putting expensive redevelopment and rehousing schemes on hold. Increasing real wages and their wider distribution made 'Dickensian' slum talk appear anachronistic, and newsmakers concentrated on stories about the affluence of modern societies rather than the persistence of entrenched social disadvantage. In the eyes of progressive reformers, slum problems had become subsumed within the bigger problem of the decline of whole cities and urban regions. With the most notorious 'slum' neighbourhoods either obliterated by redevelopment or transformed by gentrification, the entertainments of slumland sensationalism refocused upon their imagined equivalents in the postcolonial cities of the developing world.

Although the gentrifiers' campaigns signalled the end of the slum war in the English-speaking world, they did not mark the end of the misrepresentations that had underpinned it. Indeed, the gentrifiers never fundamentally challenged them. Instead of contradicting the very notion of 'slum', they drew distinctions between their own neighbourhoods and slums elsewhere, and argued that localities could be 'unslummed' if their residents' energies were respected and harnessed by officialdom. Jacobs popularized this argument in her *Death and Life of Great American Cities*, pointing to the revitalizing potential of neighbourhoods such as Boston's North End, San Francisco's North Beach and her own Greenwich Village, 'the unslummed former slum in which I live'.[199] By implication, the generations who had previously lived in these districts had created the festering slum conditions which needed to be 'unslummed'. Residents' groups in Melbourne such as the Carlton and Fitzroy Associations used similar arguments later in the 1960s when they argued that their revitalizing neighbourhoods were very different from slums. Homes there were redefined by them no longer as hovels 'unfit for human habitation' but as places rich in history and architectural heritage. In response to their arguments, the *Age* reflected:

> It may be that many of the . . . houses are 'sub-standard' according to some convenient bureaucratic yardstick. But do they constitute an incurable slum? Given a reprieve, many of them, perhaps the majority, could be renovated.[200]

Victorian-era housing in hitherto 'slum' neighbourhoods such as Paddington in Sydney and Carlton, Fitzroy and North Melbourne in Melbourne were repaired and modernized, and began a dramatic price rise. Gentrification had unleashed a crusade of an entirely different sort: a 'Heritage Crusade'.[201]

WHEREAS GENTRIFIERS engaged heritage architects to convert the run-down villas used as rooming houses back into fashionable single-family homes, others advocated the repair of old homes to shelter the disadvantaged. Thus renovation and rehabilitation, trialled in the nineteenth century, championed by British Conservatives as 'reconditioning' during the 1920s and '30s and opposed in the post-war period by the British Labour left as 'an excuse for putting off clearance',[202] reinserted itself throughout the English-speaking world during the late twentieth century as a progressive alternative to the slum wars of the 1930s to the '60s. As J. B. Cullingworth put it in 1963, in an influential study funded by the Joseph Rowntree Memorial Trust:

> The nineteenth-century concept of 'slum clearance' is becoming increasingly outmoded. The majority of the remaining old houses in Lancaster are basically sound, and with adequate maintenance and improvement could usefully provide for local needs for at least another generation.[203]

The progressive rethink about the emphases of urban social policy was initially most pronounced in the United States, where the slum war had first been halted, and replaced by a better-intentioned 'War on Poverty', declared by President Lyndon B. Johnson in 1964. This saw the creation in 1965 of a federal Department of Housing and Urban Development, and in 1966 the rolling out of a federally funded Model Cities Program designed to address the issues of social disadvantage that it was now conceded previous urban renewal programmes had ignored. In Britain, influenced by American thinking, the Housing Act of 1964 signalled 'the beginnings of a move away from slum clearance towards the rehabilitation or improvement of both dwellings and areas',[204] and the 1968 policy paper *Old Houses into New Homes* confirmed this trend. The subsequent Housing Act of 1969 was called 'a watershed' that marked 'a new era in British housing policy' by crystallizing the reaction against wholesale redevelopment and stressing housing improvement instead.[205] This new direction was further consolidated by the Housing Acts of 1971 and 1974. As one commentator remarked in 1976, a correction had been needed for 'the mistakes we made in the 1950s and 1960s of believing we could bulldoze our housing problems out of the way by demolition and new building alone'.[206]

The achievements were more apparent than real, because the slum deceits persisted. Community groups complained that the new-found attention shown by urban planners to 'community participation' was tokenistic at best. In the United States the election of a Republican president, Richard Nixon, in 1968 set in train a 'nationwide melt-down of a liberal political order' that had shaped federal thinking on urban social policy since the 1930s.[207] Nixon proceeded to dismantle the model cities programmes and to reassert the primacy of private enterprise in redeveloping the inner cities. Nixon's disgrace in 1974 did not halt the neoliberal winding-back of the urban public policy that he had championed. In Britain, the Conservatives' victory under Margaret Thatcher in 1979 led to the dismantling of state interven-tion in urban affairs, whose beginnings earlier in the century had so dismayed Americans, and in its place the encouragement of private enterprise in revitalizing cities. In both nations the rhetoric of com-munity consultation and participation sought to mask the continuing marginalization of local communities from the development process.

FOUR

ORIENTALIZING
THE SLUM

The 'slum', an English linguistic deceit, was exported to English-speaking settler societies and consolidated there during the nineteenth and early twentieth centuries. However, by the 1960s and '70s it was struggling to maintain relevance in English-speaking nations as a symbol of pressing domestic social problems. The word had also been exported during the nineteenth century to British colonial possessions in which English-speakers comprised only a tiny controlling elite rather than a settler majority and where most of the indigenous populations lived in rural areas. Here also slum stereotypes took root, among the local elites as well as the colonizers. Thus as the original meanings of the word 'slum' eroded in English-speaking nations they grew in currency as urbanization accelerated in their former colonies. Slum deceits thus became a feature of what Europeans began to refer to in the postcolonial era of the 1950s and '60s as the Third World, and – in the Eurocentric paternalism of the 1970s – as the developing world.[1]

A two-way process of slumland imposition and transformation took place during the nineteenth and twentieth centuries. On the one hand, the word 'slum' was used to describe the living conditions of the races that Europeans encountered in the cities of the British Empire. The word was imposed by the British in their colonial possessions, overlaying a diversity of idiomatic words and meanings in other languages, and was adopted by the English-speaking professional, academic, business and political elites who led these societies as they moved towards independence. Thus, by the Second World War, the word 'slum' had attained its widest circulation, and the fullest elaboration of its meanings about desired and undesirable arrangements of urban space, expressions of collective behaviour and individual life choices, through its grafting upon Britain's Oriental possessions.

On the other hand, this new use of the word gradually translated its meanings from European to non-European societies. The slum was 'Orientalized'.[2] As colonies became independent nations and incorporated slum stereotypes into their postcolonial development programmes, forged partnerships with international aid agencies and explained their social policies and modernization strategies in international networks and forums, 'slum' became a familiar and credible term throughout the world in non-English-speaking as well as English-speaking nations, and well beyond the sphere of influence of the former British Empire. In both its original and new meanings, however, 'slum' was a label that was imposed upon socially disadvantaged neighbourhoods. Nowhere was the concept organic to the places it described, and nowhere was it unreservedly accepted by the inhabitants of these neighbourhoods.

This chapter traces these transformations from their beginnings during the nineteenth century until the Second World War. The next chapter discusses the consolidation of slum stereotypes as former colonies became independent nations, and traces these developments up to the 1970s, by which time slum stereotypes were firmly entrenched throughout the world. Both chapters focus principally on India, which in the nineteenth century became the centrepiece of the British Empire and in the twentieth century the world's largest democracy. During both colonialism and the post-independence drive for modernization, the state played a crucial role in translating the foreign word 'slum' into indigenous thinking and policy formulation. Whereas in English-speaking societies the slum's attraction of repulsion was generated by class difference and misunderstanding (Chapter Two), which then informed state policy (Chapter Three), in 'the Orient' the process was reversed: slum deceits were introduced by a foreign state and were gradually adopted as an instrument of control by indigenous elites.

Strange places

The overwhelming strangeness of foreign settings induced British colonial administrators, residents and visitors to reapply the stereotypes of slumland difference and repulsion that were familiar to them in their homeland. Thus they attempted to make sense of the jarringly unfamiliar cityscapes of their colonial possessions. As was pointed out in a

1902 report on sanitary conditions in Hong Kong (which the British had occupied since 1841), 'In a tropic country and with an Eastern population whose tendency is to herd together, the conditions are so different from those obtaining in England.'[3]

Colonial thinking about 'the Orient', which seemed simultaneously alluring and abhorrent, transformed the word 'slum'. It was used to describe a vastly expanded range of human habitats in a multiplicity of non-European societies, it shaped usage in non-English languages and it became more explicitly grounded in notions of racial difference and European superiority. Colonial notions of Oriental difference were grounded in time as well as in place and race. It seemed that colonial cities were characterized by extremes of wealth and poverty that English-speaking nations had supposedly progressed far beyond and now equated with a distant 'Dickensian' era of hard times. The progressive English architect and town planner Henry Vaughan Lanchester, lecturing in Madras during 1916, suggested that

> Bad as you may consider some of the congested quarters of the larger Indian cities to be, when looked at from all points of view they can hardly be regarded as worse than some of the industrial quarters built in England in the earlier half of the nineteenth century. In India epidemics claim a heavier mortality, but in every other respect the life of the factory hand [in Britain] of three generations back was almost inconceivably devoid of all that makes life worth living.[4]

In Hong Kong, a government report in 1950 stated that 'In some ways conditions in this modern and wealthy tropical city of Hong Kong are worse than they were in England in 1840.'[5]

Oriental slums seemed to be mired in living conditions that had prevailed in British cities a century earlier. According to Hong Kong's governor, Sir Geoffry Northcote, in 1938, 'The two principal causes of human ill-being, malnutrition and slum housing conditions, dominate, I regret to say, the lives of a very large majority of Hong Kong's population.'[6] In Singapore (which the British East India Company had occupied since 1819, and which became Britain's Straits Settlements colony in 1867 after its administration was separated from that of India), a report on social conditions concluded in 1960 that 'one quarter of a million people lived in badly degenerated slums in the city centre and another one-third of a million lived in squatter areas on the city fringe.'[7]

The colonial cityscapes which so mesmerized British observers were the product not simply of European intervention and township formation but also of long-term indigenous urban development and urban practice (largely ignored by the colonizers) within mainly rural hinterlands. In Hong Kong and Singapore, for example, the precolonial history of human settlement stretched back hundreds and even thousands of years. In western Africa, the port city of Lagos had originated within the local Benin empire during the sixteenth century, becoming a major embarkation port for the slave trade until it was captured by the British in 1851 and formally annexed a decade later as the capital of Lagos Colony. Similarly in South Asia, Delhi, which was made the capital of British India in 1911, had first been established by Shah Jahan in 1638 as the capital of Mughal India (which the British formally ended in 1858), replacing the earlier Islamic cities of the Delhi Sultanate that dated back to the twelfth century. To the east, the city of Lucknow had, according to ancient lore, been founded by Rama's brother Lakshmana, and it became the glittering capital of the Nawabs of Awadh in 1775, even as the Nawab exchanged nominal fealty to the Mughals for subordination to the British East India Company. In the south, Hyderabad had been founded by the Qutub Shahi sultanate in 1591 and during the early eighteenth century became the capital of the Mughals' southern viceroy, the Nizam, to whose court a British Resident was appointed in the late eighteenth century to represent the East India Company as the Nizams acted more and more independently of the Mughals.

Pre-colonial cities existed alongside others founded by Europeans. Some of these newer cities were the creations of early European mercantilism. The site of Bombay (Mumbai), for example, was acquired by the Portuguese during the sixteenth century, transferred to the British crown in 1661 and leased to the East India Company. Cape Town, on Africa's southern tip, was established by the Dutch East India Company as a port and refuelling station in 1652 and was captured by the British in 1795 (and permanently occupied from 1806). Accra, which is today the capital of Ghana, also began as a Dutch trading post during the seventeenth century within the territories of the Ashanti empire, and was captured by the British and made capital of their Gold Coast colony in 1877 during their expansionist clashes with the Ashanti. The British East India Company established Madras (Chennai) as Fort St George in 1640, and set up Calcutta (Kolkata) as another trading post in 1690. Other colonial cities had more recent foundations. Malaysia's capital, Kuala Lumpur, began in 1857 as a Chinese tin-mining settlement within the territory of the Selangor sultanate, and as British oversight of the peninsula tightened, became headquarters for the British Resident from 1875 and capital of the Federated Malay States in 1896. Johannesburg, similarly, originated as a gold-rush camp in the Dutch Transvaal during 1886, and was captured by the British in 1900. Kampala, the capital of present-day Uganda, grew up around a port which the British East Africa Company established in 1890, and Kenya's capital, Nairobi, took form around a railway depot built by the Kenya Uganda Railway in 1899.

British reactions to the congested living conditions of colonial cities were nowhere more intense, and more broadly influential upon the expanding usage and evolving meaning of the word 'slum', than in South Asia, which the British East India Company had begun to dominate during the eighteenth century, and which Britain directly governed between 1858 and 1947. Benjamin Disraeli (Britain's Conservative prime minister in 1868 and 1874–80) famously called the region the 'brightest jewel in the crown' of the British Empire, and at a pageant in Delhi during Disraeli's prime ministership in 1877 Queen Victoria was proclaimed Empress of India. However public knowledge about South Asia was conditioned as much by accounts of squalor as by those of pomp and ceremony. Squalor was largely a rural phenomenon: in 1901 only 11 per cent of the population was classified as urban, a figure which inched upwards to 14 per cent in 1941 and 17 per cent in 1951. However, it was urban squalor that caught British attention, because the concentration of people living in towns and cities was huge and without precedent: 26 million in 1901, rising to 44 million in 1941 and 63 million in 1951 (a level that the entire population of Britain would not reach for another sixty years). Dr James Cleghorn, a Surgeon-General of the Indian Medical Service, commented after his retirement in 1898 that throughout his career 'I had never seen anything so bad as existed in the chawls [tenement buildings] of Bombay.'[8] The overcrowding there, he said, was over double that to be found in the most densely settled parts of London.[9]

Striving for words to describe the crowded, noisy and smelly living conditions of Indian cities, some expatriates used the term 'rookeries'. Increasingly popular, however, was the word that was supplanting 'rookery' in general English usage: 'slum'. E. P. Richards, the first chief engineer of the Calcutta Improvement Trust, noted in 1914 that whereas in European cities 'the English expression "slum" means generally a group or a few acres of city dwelling-houses,' in India 'slums' were of an entirely different magnitude, and were 'absolutely appalling and unprecedented' by European standards.[10] The standard tropes of slumland representation in English-language usage matched perfectly the extremes of Oriental otherness that the British sought to encapsulate in descriptions of their Indian possessions: the 'filthy dens' whose inhabitants 'lie like sardines in a tin', accessed by passageways 'that were . . . nearly dark and . . . filthy with moist mud and human excrement'; and the accompanying degenerate patterns of 'slum life' in which 'poverty, ignorance, insanitary habits, improper and insufficient feeding . . . worry and alcoholism follow on one another in a vicious circle.'[11]

The Orientalizing of the noun 'slum' was duplicated with the verb 'to slum', as Dickens's 'attraction of repulsion' drew shocked European visitors to inspect first-hand the poorest and most congested districts of South Asian cities. Some slummers were drawn by idle curiosity, others by the urge to reform and improve. Thus the second Marquess of Linlithgow, viceroy of India from 1936 to 1943, showed

> the keenest interest in improvement schemes of Old Delhi[, and] made extensive visits to the works in progress undertaken by the Delhi Improvement Trust and to slum areas where further schemes of improvement are to be worked out.[12]

The Viceroy's inspections had many precedents in the subcontinent. The second Baron Sandhurst, a progressive Liberal politician, went slumming in Bombay soon after his appointment as governor in 1895 'to acquaint himself at first hand with the slums in Bombay and the sanitary condition of the city'.[13] However, it was in Calcutta, the centre of British administration in India until 1911 and commonly called 'the second city of the Empire', that slummers sought out the most extreme juxtapositions of urban squalor and modernity upon which slum stereotypes had always rested:

> Calcutta has a prosperous and dignified business centre of which it is justly proud; yet the same city . . . in its combination of chawls, tenements and narrow lanes has some of the worst slums in the world.[14]

When the Calcutta Improvement Trust was established in 1912, Richards set about compiling a 'Slum Map' of the city, and

> during six or seven months, walked some 600 miles in and about these streetless areas, and was profoundly impressed by their sad, dirty, intensely ugly, ramshackle, and degraded aspect; by the disorder, irregularity, and grave defects of the buildings; by the inhabited dens; by the innumerable weakly men and women, ricketty children and sick babies, the interminable coughing and expectoration, the depressed unsmiling faces; the stagnant heat and polluted over-used state of the air in those countless dark, unventilated, narrow passages; daily so thronged in parts with every kind of people, that clean and unclean are obliged to jostle closely and breathe and re-breathe each other's direct emanations. It is certain that the Calcutta congested areas must constitute a great disease-breeding radial centre, perhaps the greatest in India.[15]

THUS ENGLISH, the new language of power, was imposed upon the linguistic landscapes of Britain's subjugated territories. In some places it filled a vacuum where no idiomatic expression had existed before. In other places, 'slum' overlaid and redefined a wide range of idiomatic expressions in other languages that described the diversity of local building styles and living conditions in societies around the world. In Singapore, for example, 'slum' became the conditioning term to describe vernacular housing, and *kampong* (meaning a rural village) became its ancillary. In India 'slum' subordinated idiomatic words such as *bustee* in Calcutta and Dhaka, *basti* in Delhi, *cheri* in Madras and *ahata* in Kanpur (all meaning village-style mud and thatch huts), *chawl* in Bombay (a large tenement building divided into small rooms which were let out separately to tenants), and *katras* (single-room tenement rows) and *jhuggis* (squatter camps) in Delhi. Moreover, as 'slum' and 'slumming' gained currency in the Oriental heartlands of the British Empire, they became reference points in the thinking of British colonizers in Africa during the late nineteenth and twentieth centuries.

This process of linguistic transfer was not merely one way. British officials often adopted local terms such as *kampong*, *bustee* and *chawl* in describing what they considered to be 'slum' conditions in colonial cities. Furthermore, slum and slumming were readily adopted and independently perpetuated by English-educated indigenous elites. In Bombay, for example, the local intelligentsia were by the early twentieth century earnestly imitating their British counterparts and undertaking outreach activities intended to 'improve' the lives of the urban poor.[16] The 'slum' was actively propagated by indigenous recruits to the colonial civil service, rather than simply imposed on local populations by British expatriates. The Cambridge-trained doctor K. Raghavendra Rao, who was appointed acting health officer of Madras in 1915 when the British medical officer resigned and who was finally confirmed in the position in the early 1920s, repeatedly drew attention to the problems of the 'over-crowded slum'.[17] He fretted that 'more and more of such slum areas are growing up wherever a small open space is available,' a result, he said, of 'poverty, environment and training, improvidence and drink'.[18] The Edinburgh-trained doctor C. S. Govinda Pillai, who replaced Rao as health officer in 1926, likewise drew attention to the city's 'slum areas' and repeated Rao's warning that 'More and more slums are created every day.'[19]

Rao and Pillai did not merely echo their British teachers; they wished to use their training to further reforms that might improve living conditions in their own country. Thus Britain's slum deceits were magnified by well-intentioned advocates of liberalization and community development abroad. In an address to the Bombay Sanitary Association in 1904, Sir Bhalchandra Krishna (dean of the Faculty of Medicine at the University of Bombay and at various times a member of the Governor's Council and the City Improvement Trust) drew extensively upon British sources and precedents to highlight the 'most pernicious effect' of the 'indiscriminate herding of men, women and children' into the poorest districts of Bombay. He drew also upon direct experience, reporting that 'I have visited many of these slums,' and attesting to their 'demoralising influence'.[20] Krishna advocated the adoption in Indian cities of British philanthropic interventions such as those of Octavia Hill, together with British-based housing legislation and urban redevelopment projects like those undertaken in London by the Metropolitan Board of Works and in Birmingham by the city corporation. In Birmingham, he noted approvingly, the city authorities 'drove the great Corporation Street right through the former "slum area", thus rendering a splendid service to the moral and physical health of a great number of people'.[21]

Some Western-educated members of the local business and professional elite went a stage further, drawing upon slumland concepts
even as they queried some of the effects of British colonialism. Chunilal
Bose, who served a term as sheriff of Calcutta, suggested in 1928 that

> The awful insanitary condition of some of the *bustees* and dark
> congested plague-spots of Calcutta does not reflect much credit
> on the efficient administration of the Health Department of
> this great city and would be considered a standing reproach
> to any enlightened self-governed municipality in the world.[22]

Jawaharlal Nehru shared this opinion. An Indian National Congress
activist who went on to become the first prime minister of independent
India, Nehru had been educated at Harrow and Cambridge and studied law in London before returning to India in 1912, as, he said himself,
'a bit of a prig'.[23] While chairman of the municipality of Allahabad
in the early 1920s, however, he became aware of the huge imbalance
between the well-serviced residential areas of the city inhabited by the
European and Indian elites and 'the poorer parts of the city [that] are
almost ignored'.[24] Simultaneously fascinated and repulsed by slumland,
Nehru became determined to improve the lives of its inhabitants even
as he threw himself into the politics of the independence movement.
He was haunted by the memories of 'visiting some of these slums and
hovels of industrial workers, gasping for breath there, and coming out
dazed and full of horror and anger'.[25] In Singapore likewise, Tommy
Koh, who graduated as a lawyer in 1962 and undertook postgraduate
training in Britain and the United States, recalled visiting relatives
in the Bukit Ho Swee squatter district (before the devastating fire of
1961), and dreamed that once independence was realized, 'Singapore
would be without slums and all Singaporeans would have access to
good housing, clean water and modern sanitation.'[26]

It was only Mahatma Gandhi who was clear-sighted enough to
reject slum stereotypes and the skewed concept of modernity upon
which they rested. Gandhi had graduated as a lawyer in London in
1891, and lived in South Africa from 1893 to 1914, when he returned to
India and joined the freedom struggle. He never used the word 'slum'
to describe the disadvantaged city neighbourhoods he knew so well,
and when he attended the second Round Table Conference in London
during 1931, attempting to thrash out with the British government a

pathway towards Indian self-rule, he pointedly stayed at Kingsley Hall amid the supposed 'slums' of London's East End. However, in the main the indigenous elites, acculturated to British concepts of slums, 'viewed the public norms and practices of the poor with a mixture of distaste, contempt and anxiety'.[27] Thus were the racially coloured attitudes of expatriate Britons absorbed into local social structures and expressed in the layout and governance of cities.

The mental line that most Europeans instinctively drew between their own and Oriental lifestyles found tangible expression in the spatial arrangement of colonial cities. In India, for example, the East India Company had by the early nineteenth century established a clear division within its city jurisdictions between 'native' city populations on the one hand and the formal city centre on the other. The latter included its associated European garrison or cantonment and nearby 'Civil Lines' or European residential areas (in which, however, 'many upper middle class Indians, professional men, officials, etc., live[d]'[28]). British officials thus resided in the 'distant civil lines, aloof from "native" life in all its horror'.[29] The layout of New Delhi highlighted this 'rigid social segmentation'.[30] In Singapore, which Stamford Raffles established as an outpost of the East India Company in 1819, the settlement was carefully planned to ensure a similar separation of European zones from the native kampongs. In Hong Kong, when Chinese settlement began to encroach upon European residential areas, a law was passed in 1888 to preserve a European-only zone.

Cantonment regulations in India were later incorporated into the township rules of British Africa. The concept of separate European living areas was especially championed by the first Governor General (1914–19) of the new consolidated colony of Nigeria, Sir Frederick Lugard, resulting in cityscapes in which

> European quarters or reservations have low-density housing, large gardens, golf courses, wide, straight and curvilinear avenues, while African sections, in contrast, are characterized by unpaved grid iron streets and crowded housing.[31]

In Kenya, similarly, Africans were barred from Nairobi's formal residential areas, forcing them to squat in informal settlements which were largely unserviced by local authorities. Kiberia, which is today probably Africa's most notorious 'slum', thus began with British encouragement as an informal settlement established by Nubian returned soldiers on the periphery of Nairobi, after the First World War. In Uganda, too, the 'racialization of space' was expressed in municipal regulations designed to exclude Africans from the formal city boundaries.[32] Racial segregation was still more clearly expressed in South Africa (which was created by the union of four colonial territories in 1910), where it was entrenched by the Natives (Urban Areas) Act of 1923. Throughout the British Empire, the effect of such practices was to establish formalized and well-ordered parts of colonial cities, largely inhabited by Europeans and the local elite, and informally arranged 'native' areas which were either crammed into the central 'slum' areas of historic old cities or into the proliferating squatter settlements around their periphery.

This racial geography was paralleled and perpetuated by systems of governance. Colonial cities were characterized by distinctions of governance between European areas (with comprehensive and accountable regulation) and indigenous zones (with indirect rule through the local elites, and occasional arbitrary intervention). In India there evolved a complicated and overlapping system of direct rule in the original presidencies of Madras, Bengal and Bombay, and indirect governance through princely states, the latter emblematic of a generally hands-off approach to local administration in 'native' areas. As Nehru remarked, 'The British conception of ruling India was the police conception of the State. Government's job was to protect the State and leave the rest to others.'[33] Notwithstanding the development of elaborate systems of city administration during the late nineteenth century, the British 'remained relatively unresponsive to the social and political consequences of industrial urbanization'.[34] So, too, were the local elites, whose representatives to the

> municipal corporations were elected on a limited franchise from a narrow group of Western-educated professionals and businessmen. The various boards and trusts which reshaped the docks and cleared the slums were controlled by appointed members and British officials . . . who only took account of local political opinion when forced to.[35]

BRITISH RACIAL ATTITUDES, and the disdain felt by most of the indigenous elites for the urban poor, were influenced in part by concern that disobedience, disorder and even outright resistance to colonial rule might be nurtured by Oriental slumlands. These associations, especially evident in India after the upheaval sparked by the 'Indian Mutiny' in 1857, strengthened from late in the century as industrialization created a strike-prone mass urban working class. They were further reinforced from the early twentieth century as a mass civil disobedience movement developed in defiance of British rule. Elsewhere in the empire, Trinidad's Slum Clearance and Housing Ordinance of 1938 was enacted in the wake of mass rioting; housing shortages and resulting high rents sparked nationalist rioting in Accra (the Gold Coast) during 1945; and urban planning in Uganda during the 1940s and '50s was likewise influenced by recurring strikes. In South Africa nervous white administrators devised urban policy in the knowledge that the 1946 census showed for the first time that all its cities contained majority black populations. Colonial rulers in Singapore during the 1950s worried about secret societies and left-wing associations, and in Hong Kong during the 1950s and '60s slums and squatter settlements were blamed for nurturing organized crime, rioting and tacit support for mainland China. During the Mau Mau uprising in Kenya between 1952 and 1960, the most serious indigenous rebellion in the British Empire since 1857, it was argued 'that "slum conditions" had provided a "breeding ground" for "subversive activities"' by Kikuyu nationalists.[36]

Racially prejudiced commentary on colonial slums was more generally influenced by the enormous flow of rural migrants into cities. British town planner James Linton Bogle expressed alarm in 1929 that in India the 'rapid growth of the towns has been uncontrolled'.[37] Singapore's migration chain stretched into both India and China, and although immigration restrictions were introduced during the 1950s, approximately one-quarter of Singapore's population was living in immigrant kampong settlements by the early 1960s.

Refugees compounded the apparent chaos of rapid and under-regulated population growth. The Japanese invasion of China in 1937 flooded Hong Kong with a million refugees, and from 1949 the Chinese civil war swelled the colony's squatter camps with another half a million refugees. Hong Kong's refugee-driven squatter problem persisted through the 1950s and '60s. Singapore's kampongs were likewise enlarged during the 1950s by Chinese refugees from the Malayan Emergency guerrilla war. Natural disasters such as flood and fire generated still more headaches for colonial administrators. Hong

Kong's Shek Kip Mei fire in 1953 (the worst of many fires in squatter settlements) left over 50,000 people homeless and led to the Hong Kong Housing Authority public housing programme. Fires were also endemic in Singapore's kampongs, the worst of which – in Kampong Bukit Ho Swee in 1961 – left 15–16,000 people homeless and initiated the city state's massive public housing programme.

By far the greatest influence upon hostile stereotypes in regard to Oriental 'slums' was fear of epidemic disease. As the health officer for Madras remarked at the end of the First World War, referring to outbreaks of influenza, cholera and smallpox, and anxieties about bubonic plague, 'Public health in the city during 1918 is a tale of distress, disease and death.'[38] Outbreaks of infectious disease in colonial cities exacerbated the ongoing problems of refugee resettlement. When bubonic plague spread from China to Hong Kong in 1894, 50,000 people fled to the mainland. Plague reached Bombay in 1896, and as it took hold

> Business was paralyzed, offices were closed, and thoroughfares, ordinarily teeming with life, were characterised by a desolate emptiness. By the end of January 1897 some 400,000 people – about one-half of the entire population of the City – had fled.[39]

Epidemic disease traumatized colonial cities. 'Asiatic' cholera was especially dreaded for much of the nineteenth century, as was bubonic plague from late in the century. Over 2,000 people died during the first year after the plague's emergence in Hong Kong in 1894, and the epidemic persisted until 1901. More than 250,000 people died in Bombay during the three years following the outbreak of plague in 1896. The epidemic subsequently spread across India, and some experts calculated that by 1918 the pandemic had caused some 12–13 million deaths.[40] It spread to Africa early in the twentieth century, surfacing in Johannesburg during 1904 and causing hundreds of deaths in Accra in 1907. This prompted a major report on sanitary conditions in Britain's West African possessions.

This trauma was blamed on slums. The Scottish urban planning pioneer Patrick Geddes, who undertook a series of reports on Indian cities during the early twentieth century and was subsequently appointed professor at the University of Bombay in 1919, called plague 'that most fearful of all the slum-diseases'.[41] The epicentre of Bombay's plague epidemic was believed to be 'a notoriously evil district' inhabited by 'the poorer classes', its houses 'old, ill-drained, badly ventilated [and] occupied by a narrow-minded, prejudiced class, ignorant of the most primitive laws of health[,] crowding together and careless in habits'.[42]

Colonial administrators looked to British medical experts for advice on disease prevention and suppression. The Indian Plague Commission, which was appointed by the Government of India (GOI) in 1898, was led by the professor of medicine at the University of Edinburgh, Calcutta-born Thomas Richard Fraser. British medical officers directed local cleansing operations and the hunt for fresh cases of disease. Recurring emergencies of infectious disease led to ever more systematic oversight by health officers, interventions by cleansing squads and stricter public health regulations. As one British expert in Hong Kong noted during 1938,

> The only supervision for the slum dweller in Hong Kong is that provided by the law, mainly through the Sanitary Department, who, periodically, see that houses are cleaned out and white-washed, and inspect to prevent overcrowding and nuisances.[43]

Epidemic disease prompted otherwise hands-off colonial administrators to attempt to regulate the Oriental slum and to ensure that a safe distance was maintained between Oriental living places and the neighbourhoods where European expatriates resided. For example, Sir William J. R. Simpson, professor of hygiene at King's College London and previously Calcutta's health officer between 1886 and 1897, advocated racial segregation in cities to protect the colonizers from tropical diseases. He promoted this policy throughout the empire, serving on key commissions in Hong Kong, Singapore, western and eastern Africa, South Africa and Northern Rhodesia between 1900 and 1929. The logical corollary was for colonial officials, drawing upon British public health precedents, to attempt to destroy the Oriental slum. As Geddes remarked, the response of 'European sanitationists, and their western-educated Indian colleagues' to the catastrophic Indian plague pandemic that began in 1896 was to embark upon 'a long period of sanitary reform, but this unfortunately [was] characterized by mere slum-demolition instead of home-building'.[44]

A new slum war

The rapid and ill-regulated growth of Oriental cities, and the perceived correlation between unprecedented human congestion and pandemics of social disaffection and infectious disease, led colonial administrators to borrow from urban policy in Britain and attempt to begin another 'attack on slum areas'.[45] As the governor of Madras, Baron Pentland of Lyth, pointed out in 1918, 'It is but natural that we should turn for guidance in these matters to the West.'[46] J. P. Orr, chairman of the Bombay Improvement Trust, likewise emphasized that

> Eight years' study of the slum question in Bombay has convinced me that new legislation on the lines found necessary for dealing with slum evils in western countries will be required, if there is to be a substantial advance towards the ending or mending of Bombay's slums.[47]

Following British precedent, no laws were passed in any British possession to name and define 'slum' in order to legitimize this new slum war. Rather, efforts initially concentrated upon enforcing British-based regulations against buildings 'unfit for human habitation'. In Hong Kong a cholera epidemic in 1883 led to the establishment of a sanitary board to oversee the identification and removal of 'unfit' buildings. This was the beginning of 'a process of policy transfer from the UK to the colony' which saw the local authorities using street improvement projects and applying regulatory pressure upon the owners of insanitary buildings in order to undermine 'slum' districts.[48] From 1894, the bubonic plague emergency in Hong Kong prompted revised building regulations and the Public Health and Buildings Ordinance of 1903. This borrowed from the Imperial Housing of the Working Classes Act of 1890 and strengthened regulations for the compulsory purchase of buildings 'unfit for human habitation'. The ordinance provided the basis for building regulation until the mid-1950s, when the Hong Kong Housing Authority was established. In South Africa, the appearance of bubonic plague in Johannesburg's poorest black neighbourhood in 1904 led the city's incoming British authorities to destroy the area, evict its inhabitants and appoint a Sanitary Commission to recommend further action.

However, it was the Indian plague pandemic which established the main rules of engagement for the new war on slums. The pandemic, beginning in Bombay in 1896, induced British health officers to undertake systematic house-to-house inspections. They identified thousands of buildings as unfit for human habitation, marking them with the initials 'UHH' and ordering their owners to close, repair or demolish them.[49] In the early 1920s, after the pandemic had ended, examinations for the Diploma in Public Health at the University of Calcutta still included questions on how to administer closing orders for houses 'unfit for human habitation' under the Housing of the Working Classes Act of 1890.[50] In issuing closing notices against 'unfit' dwellings, officials pushed the law to its limits and beyond. Bombay's long-serving municipal health officer, Lieutenant-Colonel T. S. Weir of the Indian Medical Service, admitted that during the plague emergency 'Not only had they been as active as the law permitted, but we had done and were doing a great deal that was illegal to improve dwellings.'[51] Residents and property owners in Bombay regarded the plague suppression measures as 'cruel' and resisted them, and when similar measures were adopted after plague spread to Calcutta, health officials acknowledged that the community response 'was always . . . passive opposition'.[52] Hundreds of 'huts' in Calcutta's 'worst quarters' were nonetheless demolished using the city's plague regulations and thousands of residents were evicted.[53] Despite opposition and protest, authorities in Bangalore also undertook 'improvements on a large scale', demolishing several thousand houses 'in order that over-populated districts might be opened out'.[54] City authorities in Bombay, Calcutta, Lucknow and Ahmedabad imitated their British counterparts by using street-widening projects to tear down 'unfit' properties. Geddes complained that

> like too many other endeavours of municipal regulation in India, [street realignment schemes] are too simply imported from English manufacturing towns [and are] here in every way unpractical.[55]

The plague emergency also triggered more comprehensive and premeditated measures of area 'improvement'. Hong Kong's plague epidemic, which began in the Tai Ping Shan tenement district, led to the Tai Ping Shan Resumption Ordinance of 1894, under which the neighbourhood was demolished in the colony's first area-wide slum clearance project. In India, still wider powers were demanded. Bombay, where the plague pandemic had begun, took the lead. The City of Bombay Improvement Act of 1898 established a City Improvement Trust under whose authority it was intended that 'a large number of tenements will be cleared away.'[56] Redevelopment trusts had been active in Britain's slum wars since the mid-nineteenth century, and the groundwork for the Bombay statute was provided by the Torrens provisions of the Housing of the Working Classes Act of 1890, thereby enabling 'improvement schemes' to clear and redevelop areas in which houses had been identified as unfit for human habitation.[57] Improvement schemes in India were explicitly designed 'for the elimination of bad types of housing – "slums", as we term these'.[58]

Bombay in turn provided a model for Calcutta, which,

> In spite of demolitions under plague regulations, *bustee* improvements and all the thousand and one activities of the various departments of the Corporation . . . is still a rat-infested, overcrowded city, with slums and alleys in which veritable 'plague spots', potential if not actual, still lurk. Let us hope that the Improvement Trust, which is shortly going to be constituted, will so transform the city that, once free from the plague, it will always remain so.[59]

The Calcutta Improvement Act of 1911 established a Bombay-style Trust which began operations early in the following year. As in Bombay, the enabling legislation was 'based almost word for word' on the Torrens provisions of the Housing of the Working Classes Act of 1890, giving authority to the trust to undertake improvement schemes if 'any buildings in any area which are used as dwelling places are unfit for human habitation'.[60] Other Improvement Trusts were established in Hyderabad in 1914, Lucknow in 1919 and Allahabad in 1920, and these trusts undertook slum clearance schemes throughout the 1920s and '30s. By contrast, the government of the Madras Presidency continued to rely on the city authorities in Madras to police closing orders against buildings 'unfit for human habitation' as their principal weapon for combating the plague, but in 1920 a British-modelled Town Planning Act was passed to expedite the city corporation's escalating 'slum campaign'.[61]

In Delhi, which formally became the new headquarters of the GOI in 1931, the local municipal authorities had initially collaborated with the GOI's public health commissioner during the early 1920s to launch an anti-plague campaign in insanitary neighbourhoods and they undertook a series of small improvement schemes during the 1930s designed to remove 'slums'. However, the city authorities acknowledged that, at a time when the war on slums was in full swing in Britain, and the construction of India's imperial capital was well advanced,

> The limitations of British India town improvement acts to deal with the problems of slum clearance and abatement of poor class over-crowding are manifest and it would seem that a satisfactory remedy can only be found in fresh legislation along the lines of the British Housing Acts.[62]

In 1936, lobbying for enlarged powers, they presented the GOI with a report on overcrowding in Delhi, arguing that

> the city contains numerous well-defined slum areas of the meanest type and abounds in insanitary lanes and dwellings constituting a menace to the public health of the whole urban area of Delhi.[63]

The GOI responded by establishing a Delhi Improvement Trust in the following year to tackle what the city's Indian municipal health officer called the 'grossly insanitary slum conditions [which] have frequently been reported upon and have long evoked public criticism and stirred the public conscience'.[64]

Geddes had always been critical of the slum campaigns in India that relied upon municipal regulations against 'unfit' housing or street 'improvement' schemes, stating that

> all this well-meant line of municipal action, so common throughout Europe and America during the past generation – and also among Indian municipalities within more recent years . . . – has been on the whole disastrous, as increasing the very overcrowding, and its consequent diseases, which it sought to remedy. I might point to various Indian towns, in which positive house-famine has been created, essentially by a benevolent Municipality, aided by subsidies from a no less well-intentioned Government.[65]

However, Geddes was still more scathing of the new Improvement Trusts, calling their establishment a 'dubious advantage' because in applying their enlarged powers they repeated the municipalities' mistakes on a larger scale.[66] Many others also criticized the trusts, among them jealous municipal officials, landlords and ratepayers. However, with the exception of the tenants evicted by Improvement Trust redevelopment schemes, whose opposition neither expatriates nor the indigenous elites heeded, nobody questioned the trusts for their preoccupation with 'slums' and their draconian plans for eliminating them.

The Bombay Improvement Trust, established in 1898, immediately embarked upon a slum clearance scheme in the First Nagpada district, a working-class neighbourhood of over 11,000 inhabitants that had been ravaged by plague. The trust reported in 1906 that the First Nagpada scheme 'may now be considered complete'.[67] As this and other slum clearance schemes gathered momentum, Bombay's health officer observed that 'practically every day houses are being acquired by the Improvement Trust and occupants are being turned out.'[68] By early 1909 it was estimated that over 14,500 families had been 'dishoused'.[69] The Calcutta Improvement Trust began its first clearance scheme in similar style during 1913–14, targeting the Surtibagan area, a neighbourhood of some 5,000 people, the most densely settled in the city and among the areas worst hit by plague. However, the trust's activities stalled during the First World War and thereafter encountered fresh difficulties. Chief among these was the vast magnitude of the city's housing crisis, alongside which the trust's efforts appeared puny. Frustrated trust officials attributed the housing crisis to the habits of the poor, which they claimed had created 'the most appalling housing conditions imaginable'.[70] Thus the slum deceits multiplied. Other difficulties further undermined the trust's efforts. Inadequacies in the trust's enabling legislation were blamed for financial shortfalls and procedural delays that were exploited by landlords and tenants who opposed the trust's projects. As schemes in the English-speaking world had already discovered, the cost of buying and redeveloping land in the city centre was quickly found to be prohibitive.

The profit-and-loss ledgers of the Calcutta Improvement Trust were further complicated because the trust had initially decided – 'as an experiment' – to build a three-storey 'chawl', modelled on those already built by the Improvement Trust in Bombay, to rehouse some of those evicted by its first clearance scheme.[71] The trust was careful to emphasize that it had 'not so far decided to embark on a policy of re-housing, which would involve a financial loss', and acknowledged that, in order for its projects to break even, the rents of trust housing would have to be set too high for the poorest tenants and would thus only 'indirectly' assist those whom the trust displaced.[72] Thus another British slum deceit – that those evicted would be rehoused, and that in any case the beneficial effects of providing housing to better-off market segments would trickle down to the poor – was exported to its colonies. The Calcutta Improvement Trust contended 'that it would be impossible to re-house these people in masonry dwellings at rents which they could afford . . . if a fair commercial profit were expected'.[73]

Such pessimistic predictions were influenced by prior experience not only in Britain but in Bombay. In launching the First Nagpada Improvement Scheme, India's first Improvement Trust had also undertaken to rehouse 'the poorer and working classes' in model tenement blocks that would be located 'as far as possible in the same vicinity'.[74] In November 1899 the foundation stone for the first housing block was laid by the governor, Lord Sandhurst, who was accompanied by the viceroy and backed by a message of support from another English slummer, the Prince of Wales. These 'experimental Chawls for the housing of the poor' were opened in 1901 and the building of additional blocks was foreshadowed. However, drawing upon the collective wisdom of philanthropic housing experts in Britain, the trust cautioned that

> The smallness of the wages of the poorer and working classes and the high price of land, make the problem of housing these people a difficult one to solve, and the difficulty is accentuated by the peculiar habits of these classes.[75]

Thus did the slum preoccupations of one nation take root in another and gain legitimacy from the transfer. Some within the Bombay Trust suggested overcoming the difficulty, as local authorities had sought to do in Britain, by building public housing on cheaper outlying land in order 'to encourage and largely develop the migration of the population to the suburbs'.[76] Others recommended that, as the trust was not required by law to rehouse the evicted tenants, it should eschew rehousing schemes entirely and rely instead on the trickle-down effects of the general housing market. Cowasji Jehangir, a Cambridge-educated leader of Bombay's Parsi community and a city corporation representative on the trust,

> stated that in view of the impossibility of providing for the dishoused the Board should go ahead without attempting to make provision for the dishoused, leaving them to find their way to any new quarters available.[77]

Key officials in Bombay had begun, even before the First World War, to advocate an entirely different strategy, proposing an 'indirect attack on the slums' by translating to India the 'reconditioning' approach to neighbourhood improvement schemes that was becoming influential in Britain.[78] Explaining its experimental switch from clearing entire areas to selectively demolishing 'unfit' houses so as to improve the amenity of those remaining, the trust reported in 1912 that Orr had undertaken a study tour in Britain to assess

> the applicability to Bombay of the methods that have superseded in England and elsewhere the now generally condemned method of wholesale demolition and reconstruction which seems to have been the only method originally contemplated by the Trust Act for dealing with insanitary areas. It is now generally recognised that the wholesale demolition method is too costly to be applied to more than a few small areas here and there.[79]

Orr argued that 'In the earlier years of the Trust, too much stress was perhaps laid on the Trust's functions as a slum destroying agency' and that the trust's experimental chawls 'sufficed for only a fraction of the total dishoused'.[80] Orr's arguments were eventually accepted by the trust, but in reality it had little choice. Unable to fund wholesale slum clearances on the scale required to undertake a 'direct attack', and becoming unpopular because of the clearance projects already undertaken (in the first five years of resuming clearances after the First World War, almost 5,000 tenements were demolished), the trust 'was compelled to resort to "slum-patching"'.[81] The overall effect of the trust's slum war in Bombay was to worsen the city's low-cost housing crisis.

The Calcutta Improvement Trust followed Bombay's lead, warning that the task of demolishing all the city's slums and 're-housing by means of "tenement" or barrack dwellings (chawls) erected on the site of cleared slums' would be 'excessively costly'.[82] Advocating a 'slum-repair system' instead, the Calcutta Improvement Trust looked to the example of Birmingham, so 'admirably described' by John Nettlefold's *Practical Housing* (1908), and which 'now possesses perhaps the most extensive area of "reformed" slum, in any English city'.[83] Richards, the trust's chief engineer, visited Birmingham and, impressed by the combined effects there of selective municipal interventions and incentives for property owners to repair or replace 'unfit' buildings, became 'convinced that this method is the sole means of salvation for two-thirds of present built-up Bombay and Calcutta'.[84] Richards maintained that the Calcutta Improvement Trust could not afford to provide more than 'a small sample of exemplary chawl-building on cleared slum-sites';[85] private enterprise would have to do the rest. During the 1920s and 1930s, this Birmingham-based 'slum repair system' of selective repairs became the new orthodoxy of the emerging cohort of urban planning experts in British India.[86] The Indian example was watched in turn with keen interest by colonial officials throughout the British Empire.

Larger-scale area redevelopment schemes in British India's slum wars nonetheless continued to be undertaken periodically during the 1930s. Delhi's Improvement Trust launched a three-year programme in 1938, the most ambitious element of which was the appropriation of some 28 ha (69 acres) behind the old city walls between the Ajmeri Gate and Delhi Gate, displacing over 3,400 families 'in the interests of public health and slum clearance'.[87] Although improvement trusts and city corporations always declared themselves to be 'fully conscious of the urgent necessity of providing more houses for the people displaced', the practical difficulties standing in their way seemed always to disappoint these pious hopes.[88] Moreover, the parallel objective of 'city improvement' invariably overshadowed interest in ameliorative social improvements. Delhi's Ajmeri Gate Slum Clearance Scheme 'met with a great deal of opposition from the citizens of the area concerned' because the project contained 'not the slightest hint . . . of . . . rehousing . . . those persons who are likely to be ejected'. A municipal committee reported that

> the Improvement Trust has committed a blunder in including
> a very large area from Delhi Gate to Ajmeri Gate which is not
> exclusively confined to slum[,] extending its operation to other

than purely slum areas . . . just for the purpose of aesthetic development.[89]

On the eve of the Second World War, as the independence movement gathered strength, city authorities in British India continued to lobby for 'greater powers for . . . dealing with insanitary houses, slum areas and improvement schemes, and with the regulation of hutments'.[90]

The slum war in British India was copied elsewhere in the empire, but on a much smaller scale and with indifferent results. Sometimes, former British India officials played a direct role in the transfer of ideas. In Singapore in 1907, in response to W. J. Simpson's *Report on the Sanitary Condition of Singapore*, new legislation empowered the municipal authorities to undertake improvement schemes for the 'reconstruction of unhealthy areas'.[91] No schemes were forthcoming, and in 1918 another report proposed the establishment of an independent Improvement Trust. E. P. Richards, who had left India in 1914, was appointed in 1920 as chief engineer and deputy chairman of the resulting trust (which initially functioned as a department within the Singapore municipality). He drafted enabling legislation for a permanent trust, proposing sweeping new powers for 'dealing with slums'.[92] The Singapore Improvement Trust was formally established in 1927, and sought to launch a programme of improvement schemes as 'the most satisfactory method of dealing with slums'.[93] Little was achieved before the Japanese occupation during the Second World War. Wartime devastation and depopulation further complicated the trust's operations after 1945 as priorities shifted from clearance to rebuilding. Nevertheless, in 1948, the trust reaffirmed its intention to 'abolish the fearful slums of the town with their terrible overcrowding and their attendant evils of crime and disease'.[94] The resumption of large-scale post-war immigration prompted the trust and municipal authorities to undertake clearance drives against squatter settlements during the 1950s, triggering resistance and, in 1955, the formation of the Singapore Wooden House Dwellers' Association to oppose the authorities' heavy-handed interventions. The protesters readily aligned themselves with the developing independence movement.

In Hong Kong, the slum war was still more muted. A Housing Commission was established in 1935 to investigate slum conditions and recommend a strategy for dealing with them. It became one of the many casualties of the Second World War. In 1949 Sir Patrick Abercrombie, the architect of London's post-war strategic plan, was commissioned to prepare a comprehensive strategic plan to guide Hong Kong's orderly post-war development, but his blueprint became redundant as half a million refugees poured into the colony, fleeing from China's civil war. Hong Kong's population increased from some 600,000 people in 1945 to over three million by 1961. The authorities responded by harassing the proliferating illegal squatter settlements. Efforts began in 1947 to clear the largest squatter settlement, at Kowloon Walled City, leading its residents to form an association and ask China for help. In the following year, when the Hong Kong police moved in to evict the squatters, an eyewitness reported that 'the police met an enraged mob and a shower of bricks and stones and had to use tear gas bombs and open fire.'[95] For the time being, the government abandoned its drive in Kowloon Walled City, but continued its broader programme against squatters. Some 3,000 squatter structures were torn down during the year in 1955/6, and 10,500 in 1961/2. Kenneth A. Watson, an independent member of the Legislative Council, complained during 1964, 'If they try to squat on the pavements, they are driven away by the Police, and if they take to the hills, their huts are torn down by the squatter control squads.'[96] Watson also worried about the effects of government supervision upon the colony's older housing stock, arguing that

Through exclusion orders, made under the Landlord and Tenant Ordinance, about 100,000 people a year are faced with having to find new homes as a result of the demolition of old tenements. Most of them are unable to afford the highly-inflated rents prevalent today.[97]

In the main, however, the Hong Kong authorities disregarded the housing of Chinese residents, and relied upon private enterprise both for housing supply and for redevelopment. Private sector redevelopment schemes and tenement construction, which boomed from the mid-1950s as the colony's economic growth accelerated, were later said to have been 'so poorly executed that an additional generation of slum building has been bequeathed'.[98] By contrast, the government's redevelopment schemes were small-scale and half-hearted: the 1959 Tai Hang Village slum clearance project quickly halted because of opposition from property owners, and the Sheung Wan scheme, begun in 1969 to implement the recommendations of a government

Working Party on Slum Clearance in 1966, dragged on for two decades. A mental divide opened up between the modern environment and lifestyles of Hong Kong's new towns and 'the poor conditions in the old and run-down districts', and this strengthened during the 1960s and 1970s.[99] The fundamentals had not changed by the time of Hong Kong's transfer to China in 1997.

In Britain's African territories, unlike Hong Kong and Singapore, only a tiny minority of the local populations lived in urban areas. In the colony of Nigeria, which was established on the eve of the First World War, less than 5 per cent of the population lived in urban areas at the war's end, a proportion that had increased to some 20 per cent during the early years of independence after 1960. Colonial regulations in Africa therefore sought primarily to prevent rather than eliminate slums, by excluding Africans from living within the formal zones of cities. The regulations were unenforceable, and so the local authorities periodically sought to break up illegal hut settlements and relocate their inhabitants to the urban periphery. In 1936, as the slum war gathered momentum in Britain, a slum clearance scheme was launched in Jinja, Uganda, provoking local anger until it ground to a halt during the Second World War. In 1954 a Ugandan African Housing Department was established to ensure the continuing orderly development of separate European and African city zones.[100] Similarly in the Gold Coast, colonial development planning during the 1950s allocated large sums to municipalities for slum clearance and the rehousing of their inhabitants to suitable zones, in an attempt, as one British official put it in 1953, 'to control and eventually to replace the disorderly shack communities springing up in and around towns'.[101] A United Nations Housing Mission (among whose members was the u.s. housing expert Charles Abrams) criticized this policy in 1956 and recommended that funding for slum clearance be redirected to support 'self-built housing' by low-income families.[102] However, the UN report was largely ignored by the colonial authorities.

The slum war in colonial Africa was pursued most vigorously in South Africa, where British redevelopment blueprints were followed, for example, in the Slums Act of 1934 and schemes by Cape Town's colonial authorities to redevelop the city's shoreline districts by destroying old mixed-race areas such as District Six. These were grafted on to the polarized racial landscape that had been produced by long and sustained European immigration. The racial separation of urban wealth and poverty became still more evident after the National Party won government in 1948 on an explicitly apartheid platform, and proceeded to enact and then consolidate Group Areas legislation from the 1950s into the 1980s so as to enforce compulsory urban segregation. In Cape Town some 150,000 people – including the entire population of District Six – were evicted from the city centre and moved to the out-lying Cape Flats. Popular opposition to these laws and other apartheid discriminatory practices culminated in the Sharpeville police shootings of 1960 and the subsequent banning of opposition movements. White electors voted in that year for their country to become a republic, and in 1961 South Africa left the British Commonwealth. Ongoing area relocations and the repression that accompanied them (including the 1976 police shootings at Soweto, which received worldwide condemnation) continued throughout the 1970s and into the 1980s.

FIVE

NEW SLUMS
IN A
POSTCOLONIAL WORLD

Whereas English-speaking nations first popularized the concept of slums and tore down entire city neighbourhoods in the name of a 'war against slums', it was postcolonial India that first explicitly gave the word 'slum' legal authority, and made slum clearance a central plank of national development planning. India's first prime minister, Jawaharlal Nehru, vowed that 'Looking at these slums and the sub-human conditions in which men and women live there, we feel that immediate action must be taken to change all this.' Nehru added that in planning for future urban development in independent India the 'problem is not merely . . . old slums but . . . the creation of new slums. It is obvious that we shall never solve it unless we stop completely the formation of new slums.'[1] India's approach was widely shared throughout the developing world during the second half of the twentieth century.

The granting of independence to Britain's colonial territories, which began in India and Pakistan in 1947 and was largely completed by the late 1960s, had the paradoxical effect of reinforcing colonial slum stereotypes and inserting them explicitly into the legislative framework and city-building activities of the new nation states. This chapter traces these developments from the late 1940s to the 1970s. Postcolonial leaders, rather than rejecting slum labels as an alien construct that had been artificially imposed by colonialism, adopted slum metaphors to encapsulate the old colonial order that they claimed to be breaking down through democratization and modernization. They embarked upon large-scale schemes of 'slum' redevelopment, and when these projects faltered they experimented with the 'slum upgrading' strategies that had also been widely trialled in the English-speaking world. In initiating these new slum wars, postcolonial nations were encouraged and supported by a post-war network of international agencies – the United Nations and monetary and aid organizations – that had been established with the intention of creating a better-ordered and fairer world. The resulting partnerships not only entrenched slum deceits in the former colonial territories of English-speaking nations, but legitimized these deceits in developing-world nations that had hitherto been free from them.

Nation-building and the colonial legacy

In many former colonies after the Second World War, independence brought little change in urban policy because energies were concentrated on overall national development. These new nation states continued the colonial governments' hands-off approach to the social issues that affected only city-dwellers, who made up a small fraction of their total populations. When Nigeria won independence from Britain in 1960, the new government fenced off 'slum' areas in Lagos before the arrival of the queen's representative, Princess Alexandra of Kent, lest the sight of them compromise the independence celebrations. Many newly independent nations 'adopted a policy of benign neglect' towards the urban squatter settlements that proliferated as rural migrants sought jobs in the cities. This policy was based on the assumption that 'slums are [an] illegal, . . . unavoidable but temporary phenomenon . . . that can be overcome by economic development.'[2]

However, the situation was different in other newly independent nations. The apparent new dawn of democratic modernization led governments to equate slums with the old order that had to be swept away before new democratic nations could be created in its place. The postcolonial authorities stripped out the racism from colonial slum discourse, but strengthened the emphasis upon the backwardness, disruptiveness, costliness and subhuman conditions of slums as they embarked upon the economic development and unification of their nations.

The Gold Coast, Britain's former and much prized colony, exemplified these trends. The Gold Coast was in the vanguard of the independence movement and in 1957 became the new nation of Ghana. Its leader, Kwame Nkrumah, sought popular support by contrasting the dependence and exploitation that had characterized colonialism with the modernizing aspirations of his national government. Nkrumah used 'slum' to epitomize a past and discredited order of things. By contrast, slum clearance, rehousing programmes and investment in the infrastructure needed for sustained economic development expressed Nkrumah's new way forward.[3] Although his increasingly autocratic regime was overthrown by a military coup in 1966, Ghana's slum-focused approach to urban development persisted for the remainder of the century.

Other former colonies in Africa followed Ghana's example. Uganda, which Milton Obote led to independence in 1962, announced grand plans for economic modernization and the better housing of its citizens. The new municipal leaders of Jinja, the nation's second largest city, in 1965 slammed the colonial-era model housing estate of Walukuba as 'rapidly becoming an unhealthy and increasingly lawless slum'.[4] Kenya, created in 1963, also launched a post-independence development plan, as a result of which the

> government considered slums an 'eyesore' and an indication
> of government failure. As a result, it first introduced control
> measures to reduce population movement into the city and
> then, under the pretext of 'maintaining law and order', adopted
> the more radical measure of slum clearance.[5]

Likewise in Singapore, Britain's 'Gibraltar of the East', which achieved limited self-rule in 1955, Chief Minister Lim Yew Hock proposed a modernizing agenda and deplored the 'congested areas of wooden houses which are a symbol of the old Singapore, which we are striving to replace'.[6] When Britain conceded full internal self-government to Singapore in 1959, the opposition People's Action Party (PAP) was elected to government and its leader Lee Kuan Yew became Singapore's first prime minister. Singapore initially joined the Federation of Malaysia, but withdrew in 1965 to become the fully independent Republic of Singapore. Lee Kuan Yew, who remained in office until 1990, single-mindedly set about building a new nation with a loyal and unified citizenry, and he publicized Singapore as a model for other postcolonial nations 'seeking to transform old-fashioned communities into modern industrialized and affluent societies'.[7] Slum deceits suited the PAP's agenda. They decried colonial Singapore's 'Overcrowded slums and squatter settlements that lacked proper sanitation, water or basic facilities, [and] were homes to more than half a million people'.[8] At the same time they embarked on a massive clearance and rehousing programme designed to relocate Singapore's population to modern public housing estates on the city's periphery.

The PAP used housing policy in Singapore as 'a vehicle for nation building' as it sought 'to build a nation from . . . disparate cultures and ethnic groups'.[9] In so doing, it ensured 'the continuity in the aims and methods of kampong clearance between the British colonial and PAP periods'.[10] Singapore's pre-independence Improvement Board was replaced in 1960 by a Housing and Development Board that began a massive drive to rehouse inhabitants of colonial 'slums' in government high-rise flats. An Urban Renewal Department was established in 1966 to coordinate slum clearance and this was reconstituted as a more powerful Urban Renewal Authority in 1974 with the objective 'to clear the slums in the city centre, thus freeing valuable land for urban redevelopment schemes'.[11]

In Latin America different languages and a different colonial legacy nonetheless set the context for similar outcomes during the second half of the twentieth century. In Latin America the Spanish and Portuguese conquerors had settled and integrated with the indigenous peoples, creating ruling elites that achieved independence from their colonial rulers early in the nineteenth century. These new nations continued to experience substantial European migration after independence. Different historical circumstances nevertheless created the conditions for a remarkable convergence with the former colonies of the English-speaking world. The ruling elites in Latin America denigrated the urban poor and used concocted traits of 'marginality' to describe them and the illegal settlements where they lived.[12]

Thus, notwithstanding the rhetoric of forward-looking postcolonial modernization, urban planning in the developing world during the second half of the twentieth century actually perpetuated many of the preoccupations that had influenced the thinking of colonial officials. Planning was conditioned in part by anxiety that urban growth was spiralling out of control as a result of accelerating migration from rural to urban areas. Demographically, an 'urban explosion' certainly took place in the developing world after the Second World War, the result partly of national development planning that prioritized industrialization. Significantly, much of this population increase was housed in informal settlements. In Nigeria, which became independent in 1960, rapid urbanization intensified in the 1970s as a result of booming oil exports. The nation's urban dwellers increased from about 10 per cent of Nigeria's population during the early 1950s to almost 30 per cent by 1980. Although the relative proportions in postcolonial India seemed less remarkable (the proportion of urban dwellers increased from 17 per cent of the total in 1951 to 22 per cent in 1981), the increase in the actual numbers of urban dwellers was staggering: the census listed 63 million urban dwellers in 1951, rising to 109 million in 1971. As the Government of India (GOI) remarked in 1981, launching India's Sixth Five Year Plan,

> The urban population of India is small as a proportion of the total population of the country, estimated to be only about 21.8 per cent of the total in 1980. However, the absolute size of more than 109 million people (in 1971) living in urban areas is large by any standards.[13]

In New Delhi, the national capital, population in the metropolitan region rose from under a million in 1941 to almost 1.5 million a decade later, then increased by almost another million by 1961 and topped five million by the late 1970s.

Politicians and planners fretted about how to maintain order amid such rapid growth. In Singapore, officials expressed alarm that the flow of immigrants into the city resulted in unauthorized wooden housing being erected overnight 'on hilly or swampy areas, unused burial grounds or areas adjacent to incinerators or sewage works at the urban periphery'.[14] By 1961, a quarter of Singapore's population was estimated to be living in such kampongs. These new concentrations of population were deemed to compromise public health and to invite other disasters. Outbreaks of fire in Singapore's squatter districts during the 1950s culminated in the Kampong Bukit Ho Swee fire of 1961, which devastated what the PAP government regarded as 'one of the most congested slums in Singapore' and left over 15,000 people homeless.[15] Such 'slums' were also accused of fomenting social and political disorder. Lee Kuan Yew's ever more authoritarian government characterized 'slums' as centres of Communist disaffection, and blamed these seemingly anarchic places for igniting the ugly Chinese–Malay race riots of 1964.

This post-independence perpetuation of slum stereotypes was influenced in part by the ongoing legacy of well-established colonial bureaucratic structures, processes and reference points. In Madras, for example, Britain's colonial bureaucracy had 'not only served their purposes fairly effectively but also survived the transition to Indian independence without radical reorganization'.[16] Bangalore's Improvement Trust Board, established in 1945, continued to operate after independence and became the Bangalore Development Authority in 1976. In Bombay, post-independence urban planning continued to be based on the old Bombay Town Planning Act of 1915. The slum clearance activities of Bombay's Improvement Trust, which after independence was merged with the Bombay Municipal Corporation, were strengthened in 1954 by a new Municipal Act whose slum clearance provisions were based on the English Housing Act of 1936. When the national government enacted its pivotal Slum Areas (Improvement and Clearance) Act in 1956, it perpetuated the old British regulatory phrase 'unfit for human habitation' as the benchmark for slum clearance, declaring that the 'powers available to Local Bodies for the declaration of slum-sites as "unfit for human habitation" will be exercised with vigour'.[17] In Singapore, Lee Kuan Yew's incoming government in 1959 similarly 'inherited the colonial mantle and methods of kampong clearance and resettlement'.[18] In sub-Saharan Africa today,

> Colonial-planning regulations still form the basis for urban development in many former British colonies, and as such, similar attitudes towards slums exist in varying degrees. This is evident in the continuous demolition of slums and squatter settlements in countries such as Kenya, Nigeria, Zambia and Zimbabwe.[19]

When the Kampala Capital City Authority began a new demolition drive against low-income housing during the early twenty-first century its first step was to declare the houses 'unfit for human habitation'.[20]

The continuing use of colonial models and concepts, notwithstanding the rhetoric of postcolonial modernization, was also conditioned by the immersion of the post-independence elites in British-based education and administration. Goh Keng Swee, for example, who became minister of finance in Lee Kuan Yew's first government of independent Singapore and subsequently deputy prime minister from 1973 to 1984, had studied at the London School of Economics before joining the colonial civil service. He had directed social and economic research, and was responsible for much of the analysis that underpinned colonial housing policy. Lee Kuan Yew and Nehru were both Cambridge graduates (by contrast, Kwame Nkrumah studied in the United States). P. R. Nayak, who advised Nehru on slum policy, had studied in Glasgow before joining the colonial Indian Civil Service. After independence he became commissioner for the Bombay Municipal Corporation in 1952, and in 1957 was appointed commissioner of the new Municipal Corporation of Delhi. Nayak devised a definition of 'slum' for independent India that was firmly based on the old British phrase 'unfit for human habitation'.[21] In 1962 V.S.C. Bonarjee, chairman of the Improvement Trust in Howrah (Calcutta's twin city in West Bengal) and later chairman of the Calcutta Improvement Trust, was still perpetuating the linguistic impositions of his British predecessors, referring to 'slum or "bustee" dwellers'.[22]

This continuation of pre-independence slum mindsets was further encouraged by the advice received from international development agencies. Progressive American thinking thus paradoxically reinforced the legacy of British colonialism. Charles Abrams, the widely respected New York housing expert, reaffirmed slum concepts even as he opposed the 'almost complete agreement on the need for tearing down slums' in the cities of the developing world.[23] He led the United Nations' Housing Missions to Ghana in 1956 and Singapore in 1963, the recommendations of which helped to reshape post-independence urban renewal and housing programmes. Abrams also participated in United Nations missions to Kenya, Pakistan, Jamaica and India.

Albert Mayer, a New York architect and New Deal housing planner for President Franklin D. Roosevelt, also played an influential advisory role in India. After the Second World War, he was invited by Nehru to assist Indian rural community development and urban planning. He contributed to Bombay's Master Plan during the late 1940s, introducing the city's chief engineer to American thinking on 'blight' and slum clearance. In 1952, when the Ford Foundation chose New Delhi for its first international field office, Mayer headed the initiative. He and his American team advised Nehru on Delhi's 'slum' problem and helped to prepare the 1961 Master Plan for the New Delhi region. Mayer warned Nehru of the likely proliferation of new slums on the periphery of New Delhi as population growth accelerated, and in 1959 he supported a proposal by the University of California to sponsor a conference in Berkeley 'with a few key Indian officials to discuss the problem of

Indian Urbanisation which is fast becoming critical'.[24] Mayer's suggestion that state authorities fund public housing by buying, developing and reselling land for profit prompted A. V. Venkatasubban, a senior bureaucrat in the Ministry of Home Affairs, to recall that

> The late Delhi Improvement Trust was more or less founded on this principle. It wanted to finance slum clearance schemes from out of the profits derived from lands sold at higher prices in the open market.[25]

However, it was another New Yorker, the anthropologist Oscar Lewis, who arguably did more than the development experts Abrams and Mayer to shape the thinking of international financial agencies and the United Nations regarding 'slums' as well as that of researchers and policy-makers in the postcolonial world. Lewis's fieldwork in post-war Mexico resulted in a string of publications during the 1950s and '60s that powerfully restated slum stereotypes and popularized the concept of a 'culture of poverty'.

International development policy was more fundamentally shaped by the Bretton Woods agreement in 1944. This established a global post-war framework for economic cooperation and influenced international economic planning until the oil crisis of the early 1970s. One immediate product of the Bretton Woods agreement was the International Monetary Fund (IMF) which was formally established in Washington, DC, in 1945 and began operations in 1947. The IMF expanded during the 1950s and '60s as former colonies became independent nations and sought membership. Another product of the Bretton Woods agreement was the World Bank. Created in 1944 and based in Washington, DC, from 1946, the World Bank initially focused on rebuilding war-devastated Europe but gradually widened its activities to include infrastructure and rural development in the postcolonial world. Its first loans outside Europe were allocated in Latin America during 1948, and loans were granted to India from 1949 and to African countries from 1950 (Uganda received support from 1959, and Kenya from 1960). During the 1970s the World Bank became concerned to widen the scope of its community development projects, and as a result the bank began to fund 'slum' improvement programmes in the 1970s and '80s.

POSTCOLONIAL TRENDS and paradoxes were most evident in India, which was by far the largest member of the newly formed Commonwealth of Nations and which also, under Nehru's leadership, became a role model for the broader non-aligned movement of independent nations.

Indian opinion-makers in the second half of the twentieth century reignited the slum deceits current in English-speaking nations since the nineteenth century. Commentators embellished upon the old slummer assertion of parallel yet juxtaposed worlds:

> Posh tourist hotels are rapidly coming up in our metropolises, airports are beautified, the latest Jumbo jets are bought, while just a few minutes drive to the outskirts of any city will show you clusters of hutments where people are forced to live in sub-human conditions without water taps or lavatories.[26]

They perpetuated the old theatrical device of attraction by repulsion. Bombay High Court judge S. B. Bhasme described the city's chawls in the mid-1970s in much the same way as British slummers had characterized poor neighbourhoods in British cities a century earlier. Bhasme declared that the chawls he visited 'present an appearance of slums':

> Young couples, adults, old men and women and children are huddled together like cattle. There are common latrines and bath-rooms . . . Everything is stinking and there is dirt and filth everywhere. There is a glaring absence of sanitation and hygiene. The density of population coupled with the unhygienic conditions make the lives of these working class folk miserable. They quarrel for petty reasons and brawls and street fights go on everywhere at all times of day and night. As if this is not sufficient, anti-social elements thrive on gambling, illicit liquor trade and matka dens. All these conditions have furnished a fertile breeding ground where seeds of communal hatred could be sown in no time.[27]

In Madras, the Slum Clearance Board warned in 1975 that 'Crimes are predominantly rampant in slums' and observed that 'Gambling, drinking, loafing about, cinema-going and smoking are a few of the leisure time activities of the slum dwellers.'[28]

This revulsion was used in part, as Nehru was doing, to express paternalistic compassion and to advocate humanitarian reform. Thus India's First Five Year Plan cautioned in 1953 that modernization

> has led to the overcrowding of industrial centres and large sections of their populations have had to live in slums, huddled together in jerry-built houses or mud-huts, without water and electricity.[29]

However India's expanding middle classes saw these consequences as a justification for contemptuous indifference towards, or even the coercion of, the massed urban poor. They shared Nehru's feeling of repulsion but not his reform agenda. They opposed the cost of large-scale public housing programmes yet they worried about being engulfed by slumland. Official statistics indicated that not only was urbanization accelerating but slums were growing even faster than the cities that hosted them. Government planners warned in 1959 that 'urbanisation is taking place at a very gigantic pace' and that without intervention 'the existing towns and cities will grow into enormous conurbations harbouring slums and making urban life almost intolerage [sic].'[30]

Anxieties initially focused on the nation's largest metropolises, but as the century progressed they extended to a broadening band of second-tier cities. A study of Calcutta's 'slums' concluded in 1969 that 'Almost half the Calcutta Metropolitan area consists of slums of one kind or another.'[31] Studies in India's other major cities drew similar conclusions. Half of Hyderabad's population was estimated to be living in slums in 1972.[32] In Bombay it was estimated during the mid-1970s that 40 per cent of the metropolitan population (and in some districts over 50 per cent of the inhabitants) lived in slums.[33] In Madras, it was calculated at the same period that over a third of the city's inhabitants lived in slums.[34] Planners also began to identify a worrying trend in the proliferation of second-tier cities (with populations over 100,000) during the 1950s, '60s and '70s, and to warn that within this band of cities population growth was the most rapid, and regulatory controls least effective.

After independence, India's urban policy was fundamentally shaped by the trauma of partition. The refugee catastrophe that unfolded as Muslims and Hindus sought to realign themselves within the new nation states of India and Pakistan would dominate urban research and policy over the next half-century. It seemed that cities were doomed to be swamped by slums, as refugees and the rural poor surged into them. When India's Planning Commission released its First Five Year Plan in 1953, it estimated that some 2.5 million displaced persons from West Pakistan had moved to Indian cities.[35] The Ministry of Home Affairs conceded that the 'problem of slums has assumed gigantic proportions after partition'.[36] The resultant pressure on urban housing, infrastructure and services was especially severe in Delhi, which absorbed much of the refugee flow from West Pakistan, and Calcutta, the destination for most of the refugees from East Pakistan. Partition overwhelmed the Calcutta Improvement Trust, whose existing redevelopment projects were swamped by 'refugee trespassers'.[37] However, it was in Delhi, where the refugee crisis unfolded alongside the formation of a new national government, that postcolonial slum anxieties most influenced the making of national urban policy.

India's minister for rehabilitation, Mehr Chand Khanna, remarked that when the ministry was established in Delhi during 1949 it was 'faced with the immediate task of [providing] accommodation [for] thousands of refugee families who were squatting on roads and public thoroughfares'.[38] The capital's refugee housing crisis remained acute throughout the next decade, and was compounded by the growing flow of migrant labourers into the city's booming construction industry as India's national bureaucracy rapidly expanded. Moreover, the establishment of large residential colonies for the civil service spawned the parallel development of adjoining squatter settlements comprising house servants, laundry workers, sweepers, traders and shop assistants to service them. One senior bureaucrat noted ruefully, 'As there is great employment potential in Delhi, people are coming from all over India into this city and thereby increasing the number of slum dwellers.'[39] The Delhi Development Authority (DDA, which was established in 1957, absorbing the Improvement Trust) acknowledged in 1958 that

> the problem of slum clearance and rehousing in Delhi has become very acute and extremely urgent as a result of the influx of refugees and the phenomenal expansion of Delhi as the Capital of free India.[40]

The social effects of partition upon Delhi were twofold. First, within the walls of Old Delhi the density of population and the pressure to find shelter became extreme. Bharat Sevak Samaj, a national development agency established by Nehru in 1952 and sponsored by the Indian Planning Commission, began a social survey of Old Delhi in 1956 and concluded in 1958 that 'the whole city is now a vast slum.'[41] It estimated that over 200,000 slum-dwellers existed in some 1,500 slum pockets within the city walls. The Samaj's opinion was endorsed by the DDA, which declared in 1959 that 'Slum conditions exist almost all over the old city of Delhi. The rapid growth of population especially within the past two and a half decades has turned the old city of Delhi into a slum.'[42]

Second, unauthorized squatter settlements (called *jhuggi jhompri* or *jhuggi-jhonpri* clusters) simultaneously spilled out beyond the old city, jostling for living space with the planned encampments for refugees and residential enclaves for government employees that the GOI was building throughout the New Delhi region. The increasing momentum with which these unplanned settlements sprang up seemed unstoppable. The Ministry of Home Affairs reported in 1977 that

> The jhuggi-jhonpri clusters are conglomerations of huts and hut-like tenements constructed out of mud, bricks, straw, bamboos, wood and such other sundry material. Their residents are basically rural migrants with very low income. They are rank squatters on public land.[43]

Initially, owing to 'the peculiar circumstances of partition, no notice was taken of these encroachments' during the late 1940s.[44] By the early 1950s, as Delhi's administrators realized that the proliferation of unauthorized huts and settlements was getting out of hand, they warned that 'any person occupying land without authority will not only be removed from that land but will also not be provided any alternative accommodation.'[45] However, populist politicians (most notably the independence movement activist Narhar Vishnu Gadgil, who became a minister in Nehru's cabinet between 1947 and 1952) nonetheless promised that squatters would not be evicted until alternative accommodation could be provided. In this policy stalemate, squatter settlements proliferated during the mid- and late 1950s. Bharat Sevak Samaj warned the minister of home affairs in 1957 that

> There has been an alarming increase in unauthorised huts being put up here and there by people. These bastis present

unseemly appearance and there are no suitable arrangements for sanitation etc. in these places. This practice on behalf of the people needs to be checked.[46]

Responsibility for clearing such settlements and relocating their inhabitants rested with Delhi's local authorities. The Improvement Trust and the Delhi Municipality, colonial creations which continued to operate after independence, were overwhelmed by the refugee influx, and in 1955 the central government merged them into the Delhi Development Provisional Authority (subsequently the DDA). The Delhi Municipal Corporation was established in 1957, and in 1960 responsibility for slum clearance was transferred to it. However, the activities of all these local agencies took place under the increasingly watchful eye of the GOI, which in 1956 abolished the short-lived state government of the Delhi region. The central government emphasized not only the 'utmost importance to all of us to see that slum work gets top priority in Delhi', but also its concern that 'Very little, however, is so far achieved and much more is to be done.'[47] Nehru expressed particular frustration that 'in practice very little control is exercised . . . over unauthorised construction in Delhi' by any of the local author-ities, and they were informed that the prime minister 'feels that it is necessary that fresh thought should be given to this problem'.[48] It was ultimately Nehru and the central government bureaucracy that devised a slum programme to address Delhi's housing emergency, and this response to the effects of partition in the national capital became the foundation from which a broader Indian slum war was launched in the new nation.

It was Nehru who reasserted both 'slum' and 'slumming' in the thinking of policy-makers in post-independence India. Deeply shocked by the effects of partition that he saw first-hand in the national capital, Nehru remarked in 1958 that

> For the last few years I have been deeply interested in the slums of Delhi. Every time I have visited them, I return with a certain feeling of numbness and an urgent desire to have something done to remove these slums.[49]

Encouraged by Nehru, Bharat Sevak Samaj had from its inception probed 'the question of slums in Delhi'.[50] Its slum survey of Old Delhi, which was funded by the prime minister, began as Booth's investigation of London had half a century earlier with

> visit[s to] the slum areas in order to gain further insight and understand all the numerous problems of the slums . . . Accordingly the Convenor undertook an extensive walking tour through the whole of the Delhi Municipal Committee in which he visited as many as 1462 places (including bustis and katras) spread over 18 wards of the Delhi Municipal Committee. The tour revealed the stupendous magnitude of the problem.[51]

The Samaj also organized slum tours for government ministers and officials, but its ultimate slummer tour involved the prime minister himself:

> All along the Samaj has enjoyed the privilege of drawing inspiration and encouragement from our Prime Minister, whose visit of April 1, 1956 to the different slum areas of Delhi arranged by the Samaj brought the whole question to the forefront and helped very much to activise official agencies concerned.[52]

At a subsequent meeting of key agency officials in the prime minister's office in May 1956 it was decided that the new Delhi Development Provisional Authority should be made responsible for carrying out slum clearance and improvement, but that its activities were to be directed by the central Ministry of Health. Nehru intervened again in the following year, establishing and chairing a Committee of the Cabinet 'to deal with the problems of planning, housing and slum clearance etc in respect of Delhi'.[53] Once key decisions about policy direction had been made to Nehru's satisfaction, the prime minister appointed an Advisory Committee on Slum Clearance in 1958 to oversee the start of these operations.

Three strategies were decided upon. In large part they echoed proposals made by the Nehru-backed Bharat Sevak Samaj.[54] The first task was to stop further squatting. Nehru put pressure on both the Ministry of Health and the DDA to act decisively, and at a secret cabinet meeting in April 1957 he brought together representatives from

Delhi's local authorities and central government ministries to resolve the issue. It was decided that the Ministry of Home Affairs would establish 'mobile squadrons' to demolish unauthorized structures and evict their inhabitants, tasks that were devolved to the new Delhi Municipal Corporation.[55] The evicted squatters were to be moved to decentralized resettlement colonies under a Jhuggi Jhompri Removal Scheme which the central government announced in 1958 and which was launched by the corporation in 1960.

Nehru's second strategy began as a simple holding action, intended to provide basic amenities for existing slum neighbourhoods until they could be redeveloped. As Nehru explained in 1958, until a carefully thought-out and long-term programme could be put in place for 'the clearing of slum areas from Delhi and providing better alternative accommodation for those who live there . . . something has to be done meanwhile to improve conditions'.[56] Pilot funding was given to the Improvement Trust, the Delhi Municipality and the Bharat Sevak Samaj to provide basic amenities (such as paved courtyards, drains, latrines, water, electricity and minor building repairs) in Old Delhi's neighbourhoods.

The third strategy was comprehensive slum clearance and the resettlement of their inhabitants to Delhi's periphery. The Improvement Trust had continued its slum clearance projects immediately after independence. The largest of these, the Ajmere Gate Slum Clearance Scheme, was estimated in 1957 to have moved over 700 families.[57] However such projects seemed to Nehru to be totally inadequate, and he looked instead to the DDA to prepare a comprehensive Delhi Master Plan (ultimately released in 1962) which would include slum clearance, decentralized resettlement and orderly planned development. In the meantime, however, the central government sought to address Old Delhi's pressing slum problem by passing the pivotal Slum Areas (Improvement and Clearance) Act of 1956. It became the basis for legislation and schemes rolled out throughout India from the 1950s to the 1970s.

The slum made real

India's Slum Areas (Improvement and Clearance) Act of 1956 was a global game-changer. It sought 'to wipe off the evil of slums by improving and clearing them'.[58] In some respects this statute expressed continuities rather than radical change. Notwithstanding Indian independence, the 1956 Act, which was amended in 1960, 1964 and 1973, was anchored in British legislative precedent. It empowered local authorities in union territories to take action against any buildings deemed to be 'in any respect unfit for human habitation' and to repossess entire areas for the purposes of slum clearance and redevelopment.[59] The Act, complemented by the GOI's five-year national development plans and financial grants in aid, became a blueprint for similar legislation and action throughout India over the next twenty years.

However, the 1956 statute and the subsequent legislation that copied and consolidated it differed in one important way from British precedent. While legislation in the English-speaking world had never used the word 'slum' to enable regulatory action, this seminal Indian law included 'slum' in its title, defined the term and incorporated it in the legal process required to define clearance areas. As Nayak explained in 1957, although the idea of slum clearance had originated in British India, it had hitherto been applied only indirectly through the use of regulations against 'unfit' buildings and areas, with the result that 'a legal conception of slums has only lately been emerging.'[60] In India, for the first time anywhere in the world, the statute book made an abstraction real; the term 'slum' now possessed 'a definite legal and socio-economic connotation'.[61] As a result, 'the term "slum" is [now] a formally defined settlement category in India.'[62] India's Second Five Year Plan (1956–61) used 'slum' as a tangible and quantifiable entity in urban redevelopment planning, and state governments were asked to undertake social surveys 'of their worst slum areas' in order to tabulate them and plan for their comprehensive removal.[63]

In pioneering a 'legal conception of slums' Indian lawmakers were guided in part by the United Nations, which in 1951 had defined 'slum' as

> a building, group of buildings or area characterised by over-crowding, deterioration in insanitary conditions or absence of facilities or amenities which because of these conditions or any of them endanger the health, safety or morals of its inhabitants or the community.[64]

Indian government officials and researchers referred to this definition throughout the twentieth century, the Ministry of Home Affairs acknowledging that the wording of the 1956 Act 'was analogous to this description'.[65] UN officials encouraged India's efforts, and agencies such as the United Nations Children's Fund (UNICEF), established in 1946, and the UN Development Programme (UNDP), founded in 1965–6, became active collaborators with central, state and municipal government efforts to eliminate 'slums'.

India's policy direction was also influenced by trends in American urban sociology and anthropology. American concepts were introduced in part through the Ford Foundation. Mayer's close ties with Nehru, senior ministers and bureaucrats have already been noted. The sociologist Marshall B. Clinard, likewise, whose doctorate in the early 1940s had focused on Chicago's 'slums', worked as a Ford Foundation consultant in India in the late 1950s and early 1960s. His starting point was that slums constituted 'a concrete problem' that urban planners should not ignore, and that 'the slums of India are generally considered among the worst and the slum dwellers among the poorest and most apathetic of any major country in the world.'[66] Clinard argued that 'Slums constitute the most important and persistent problem of urban life; they are the chief sources of crime and delinquency, of illness and death from disease.' Drawing upon the work of the anthropologist Oscar Lewis, he asserted that 'The slum has a culture of its own,' constituting 'a way of life, a subculture with a set of norms and values, which is reflected in poor sanitation and health practices, deviant behavior, and characteristic attributes of apathy and social isolation.'[67]

However, the transmission and legitimization of concepts and policy recommendations from the United States and the United Nations were increasingly sustained by Indian social scientists and public administrators. Like Nehru, the academic and professional elite expressed an abstract sympathy for the urban poor. In his inaugural address at the 1957 Seminar on Slum Clearance, the governor of Bombay cautioned that slum clearance should not become a one-sided process of demolition and eviction, because slums were 'formed by various humble folk who congregate in cities to supply the needs of the well-to-do'.[68] The Marxist sociologists Akshay Ramanlal Desai and Devadas Pillai were especially influential during the 1960s and '70s in highlighting urban inequality in India and using European slum analysis to assist in explaining it. Their study of Bombay slum life during the late 1960s, which was funded by the Indian Planning Commission and the Indian Council of Social Science Research, was comprehensively informed by British and American sources. Their starting point, like Clinard's, was the premise that 'poverty [is] seen in its most concrete form in slums, shanty-towns, shack-towns and squatters' colonies,' and they affirmed that in slums 'sub-human conditions have reached a new low.' Desai and Pillai 'said without fear of contradiction that almost all Indian cities have slums or slum-like conditions'.[69] They also edited a large and comprehensive compilation of academic research, *Slums and Urbanization* (1970), which combined European, Asian and Latin American studies.

Whereas Desai and Pillai showed a deep, if patronizing, sympathy for the urban poor, most Indian academics, complacent in their privileged class and caste positions, echoed the Dickensian 'attraction of repulsion' and borrowed freely from Oscar Lewis's arguments about a 'culture of poverty'. A study undertaken in Mysore (in the southern state of Karnataka) during the mid-1960s, for example, concluded that the inhabitants of the two slum study areas were 'socially maladjusted and poor', and that this resulted in 'delinquency, crime and vice in abundance'. The investigators noted with horror that the 'Streets are full of filth with pieces of bones, human excreta and stagnant water. Swarms of flies make the area all the more nauseating.'[70] The ill effects of this slum environment seemed clear:

> family disorganisation, and even disintegration, neglect of the child, sexual indecency, the rise of prostitution, crime, gambling and gangsterism, the juvenile inactivity, the development of work-shyness, lethargy and manual inefficiency, anti-social outlook etc. Sociologists have summed up these consequences as the emergence of 'slum mentality'.[71]

The sociologist Noor Mohammad, likewise, in his 1983 study of slums in Kanpur (in Uttar Pradesh), asserted that they 'reflect the other side of our civilization and the wretched aspect or the sore spots of our cities', constituting 'a sub-culture with its own set of norms and values'.[72] His study was predicated upon 'the assumption, that slum culture generates vice and crime, and is correlated with the variables of run-down housing, overcrowding, poverty, illiteracy, and a bad social life'.[73]

Such knowledge-building was skewed in part by the Western education, training and continuing international collaborations of India's academic and professional elite:

Instead of letting the people concerned decide what type of shelter they need and can afford, the experts go about prescribing high physical standards, giving statutory force to them, and deciding where and in what type of house the poor must live, regardless of whether the intended beneficiary would be able to afford it at all. The idealistic attempt to give the migrant a better house has actually resulted in denying him any shelter at all. Refusal to let him build a shelter for himself has forced him to exist in illegally and furtively constructed shacks in areas generally devoid of and far from civic services.[74]

In still greater part, these attitudes reflected the disdain and self-interest of India's rapidly expanding middle class. Bombay, the city that had hosted the pivotal slum seminar in 1957, exemplified this trend. India's post-independence 'cosmopolis of commerce' increasingly revealed itself during the 1960s and '70s as 'a malignant city': 'Jobs became harder to get. More rural arrivals in the city found themselves economic refugees. Slums and shacks began to proliferate. The wealthy began to get nervous.'[75] Middle-class professionals and academics recycled the slum deceits of the colonial era into self-justifying characterizations of the 'new slums' in independent India that they saw as standing in the way of democratic modernization.

THE 1956 SLUM AREAS (Improvement and Clearance) Act, together with the launching in the same year of India's Second Five Year Plan, provided the basis for a new slum war in postcolonial India that was larger than had previously been attempted in Britain some twenty years earlier.

The first skirmishes in India's slum war had begun with its First Five Year Plan, released in 1953, which recommended that 'Slum clearance should be considered an essential part of the housing policy and should proceed apace.'[76] However, the plan's main purpose was to stimulate the national economy by boosting agricultural productivity and developing heavy industry, and little was done to address the 'new slums' that resulted from this priority. The Planning Commission conceded when it released the Second Five Year Plan in 1956 that 'on the whole the slum problem continues much as it was,'[77] and the new plan therefore proposed a dedicated national slum programme. The

1956 Act provided a legislative model to underpin this programme, and in order to give it momentum the plan provided subsidies for slum clearance projects in the nation's six largest cities, Calcutta, Bombay, Madras, Delhi, Kanpur and Ahmedabad. By the end of the Second Five Year Plan in 1960, over 200 slum redevelopment projects had been launched. India's Third Five Year Plan, released in 1961, extended subsidies for such redevelopments to all cities with populations over 100,000 people.

In Bombay, the municipal corporation

> began carrying out slum clearance with a heavy hand in the mid-1950s. Although the practice of slum clearance had been used periodically since the late nineteenth century, eviction became the primary mode of government intervention in slums in this period.[78]

This approach was reinforced by the Maharashtra Slum Areas Improvement, Clearance and Redevelopment Act of 1971. In the national capital, the launch of Delhi's Master Plan in 1962, the first such planning instrument in India, brought in its wake ambitious slum clearance and rehousing projects that shifted enormous numbers of squatters to poorly serviced resettlement colonies. Many of these began to be characterized as new slums by the 1970s. Tamil Nadu's Slum Clearance Board was established in 1970, its specific goal being 'to clear the slums of Madras city on a massive scale within a period of 7 years'.[79] Gujarat's Slum Clearance Board was established in 1972, its prime task seen as being to root out the 'slums' of Ahmedabad.

Intrusive neighbourhood clearances and arbitrary relocations sparked anger and protest. GOI officials had known about local resentments ever since Delhi's post-partition refugee and squatting crisis during the 1950s, but it was a feature of the prevailing assumptions about slums that the protests of residents be ignored or repressed. When the GOI attempted to halt Delhi's squatter settlements the Ministry of Health warned that 'a considerable number of the squatters will resist moving to the new quarters and a degree of compulsion may have to be resorted to.' The ministry privately admitted that the squatters 'have built up some sort of structures which they have come to regard as their own':

Most of the squatting is within the heart of the city and any alternative accommodation will have to be somewhere outside the urban areas, as a result, they will find it not only expensive but also difficult to come to their places of business.[80]

The chairman of Delhi's Improvement Trust likewise acknowledged in 1957,

Some of these slums have existed for decades and are a part and parcel of the old way of living in the congested parts of the city. With our modern notions of hygiene and higher standards of living we consider these slums to be hopeless, but it is somewhat of a paradox that the residents therein do not appear to be so acutely aware of the deficiencies they suffer from. This creates reluctance on their part to move to new localities and gives a rather bad start to the authorities concerned with slum rehousing and slum clearance.[81]

In Calcutta, where the effects of partition and relocation were also severe, the residents of illegal squatter settlements formed local associations to negotiate for services and security of tenure. In 1965, when railway authorities attempted to clear one such settlement that had grown up since partition along the railway lines, residents formed a 'human wall' to resist the evictions.[82]

India's Planning Commission began to recognize in its second and third plans that some residents in slum clearance areas might have sensible and legitimate reasons for protest. However, the commission also drew attention to the huge cost to taxpayers of tearing down slums and rehousing their inhabitants. India's Third Five Year Plan noted in 1961 that although the impact of slum clearance and rehousing schemes 'so far has been negligible', it was 'obviously not possible to tackle this problem through public investment alone'.[83] It was the financial cost of slum clearance, not the social cost, that India's expanding middle class responded to. Middle-class resentment at the expense of the slum war was especially evident in Delhi, where illegal settlements snowballed during the 1960s and early 1970s notwithstanding a large public expenditure to eliminate them. Commentators objected that

The sheer magnitude of the problem is such that no amount
of public finance that a developing country could be expected
to set aside for the purpose, would prove adequate to meet its
needs of housing for the urban poor.[84]

POLICY-MAKERS RESPONDED to these tensions by shifting the slum war's
emphasis from demolition to 'improvement'. India's slum war thus
came in another key respect to echo the evolving strategies of Britain's
slum war from the 1930s to the 1970s. 'Slum improvement' in India was
initially devised during the 1950s as a temporary holding operation until
sufficient resources could be mobilized for the 'Permanent Solution' of
comprehensive clearance and rehousing.[85] This strategy was first evident
in Delhi during the 1950s and was most fully expressed in Calcutta's
'environmental improvement in slums' programme that began in the
mid-1960s. However, alongside these short-term measures, a more
radical community development approach to slum improvement also
developed, initially in Delhi and later in Hyderabad. This approach
emphasized community participation, and improvements not only to
the local 'slum' environment but also to the livelihoods that could be
pursued within it. This well-intentioned experiment was attractive to
international development agencies and charities, but did not convince
the bulk of Indian policy-makers and taxpayers. Increasingly, Calcutta's
pragmatic two-pronged approach of modest short-term improvements
and longer-term redevelopment was adopted as the national model. As
this became entrenched during the 1970s, the focus of 'slum improvement' narrowed to low-cost environmental upgrades rather than the
costly complexities of community development. Slum deceits prevailed
over social justice: socially disadvantaged communities were excluded
from the planning of sustainable neighbourhoods and livelihoods, and
politicians, planners and taxpayers made plain that they would not
countenance anything beyond low-cost holding operations until a
decisive victory could be won against the slum.

Slum improvement in India had begun as a result of Nehru's interventions during the 1950s to overcome Delhi's squatting emergency. As
the Delhi Development Authority observed,

Up to 1956, stress was laid only on slum clearance, and slum
improvement was entirely ignored. However, as a result of

personal interest taken by the Prime Minister in May 1956, the importance of slum improvement was recognized.[86]

This change in emphasis was initially intended as 'a temporary measure to tide over the next few years' until the housing crisis could be permanently resolved.[87] Explaining the phrase 'slum improvement', Nehru said at that time that 'Improving them means better water supply, lighting, latrines, drains and generally greater cleanliness.'[88]

Slum improvement was simultaneously proposed on a national scale by the Delhi-based Indian Planning Commission, which argued in India's Second Five Year Plan that

> While action is taken to prevent the development of slums in the future, it is also essential to tackle the problems of existing slums. To a large extent there is no alternative to their demolition and clearance, but there may be cases where measures for improvement are feasible.[89]

Commissioner P. P. Agarwal restated this point of view at the Bombay slum seminar in 1957, and Nehru's Advisory Committee on Slum Clearance also supported it. The Planning Commission reiterated this two-tier strategy in 1961 when it launched India's Third Five Year Plan, urging that the long-term objective of slum clearance needed to be complemented by short-term measures to relieve distress by providing 'minimum amenities like sanitary latrines, proper drainage, uncontaminated water supply, moderately good approach roads, paved streets, and proper lighting'.[90]

Slum improvement was given still more emphasis by the Planning Commission's Fourth Five Year Plan in 1970, which started to redirect attention away from slum clearance in favour of improvement as a long-term rather than a temporary strategy. The commission cautioned that 'Slum clearance schemes often lead to creation of new slums or deterioration of conditions in some of the older slums,' and – echoing British precedent – recommended the 'reconditioning of slums' rather than their costly demolition in order 'to try to ameliorate the living conditions of dwellers in slums as an immediate measure'.[91] The fifth, sixth and seventh national development plans continued to advocate this change of emphasis during the 1970s and into the 1980s. As the Planning Commission announced in India's Sixth Plan (1981),

It is proposed that the strategy of attempting massive relocation of slums in urban areas should be given up in the future.
Such relocation not only involves substantial hardship to those
affected in terms of loss of easy access to employment centres
and other amenities, but results in unnecessary destruction of
existing housing capital, however sub-standard it may be. It is,
therefore, important that substantially increased investments
be made in the environmental improvement of slum areas.
Low cost sanitation and drainage are key areas of much needed
investment in the slums of our cities.[92]

This switch in emphasis from slum improvement as a short-term
expedient to a long-term planning strategy was influenced in part by
the wider-ranging goal of urban community development that first
emerged in Delhi during the 1950s and was elaborated in Hyderabad
during the 1960s and '70s. During Delhi's post-partition housing crisis,
Nehru had cautioned in 1958 that 'slum' improvements

can only be achieved with the co-operation of the people concerned. This means that every attempt should be made to
interest these people, to educate them and to rely upon their
help. To some extent, the approach has to be on the lines of
the Community Development Schemes in rural areas.[93]

The prime minister's suggestion was thus a spin-off from his broader
Gandhian commitment to rural community development as a central
plank in post-independence social planning. Another of Gandhi's former
associates in the independence movement, Brij Krishna Chandiwala,
became president of Bharat Sevak Samaj, and at Nehru's slum crisis
meeting in 1956 he advocated improvement measures using a 'human
approach' that 'should involve no harassment, no coercion and no
adverse effect on the socio-economic condition of the slum dwellers'.[94]
Bharat Sevak Samaj's subsequent pilot project to test this approach,
funded by Nehru, sought

to enlist public cooperation and participation in [Delhi's] planning programme in general and in slum clearance and urban
development programmes in particular, through a chain of
centres located in the slum area of Delhi.

These centres were intended to operate on essentially the same lines as the philanthropic housing associations and university settlements that had begun in London three-quarters of a century earlier. They offered help with sanitation, education and 'cultural regeneration' and encouraged 'local leadership and organisation for active participation in planning processes'.[95]

The Samaj's pilot programme was overshadowed in 1958 by the Ford Foundation, which announced seed funding for 'framing detailed proposals for a programme of urban community development' in Delhi's slums.[96] Follow-up funding from the Ford Foundation, awarded to the Delhi Municipal Corporation between the late 1950s and early 1960s,

> was designed to stimulate citizen participation and self-help activities in coping with slum conditions and preventing further deterioration in the city, as well as in developing a sense of civic consciousness.[97]

By 1965, neighbourhood councils representing some 150,000 people had been established. They carried out community self-help environmental improvements, public health, educational and recreational activities and income-generation projects. Marshall Clinard, who worked for the Ford Foundation in India, called the Delhi project a world first in urban community development. He argued that

> To the slum dweller, this [project] represented perhaps the first time he had been asked how *he* felt about the problems of his area and what *he* thought the people *themselves* could do to solve them.[98]

A similar Ford Foundation scheme began in Ahmedabad in 1962. Its initiatives influenced the GOI to begin a national urban community development programme from the mid-1960s.

One of its outcomes was the Hyderabad community development programme which, begun by the municipal corporation in 1967, expanded to include the entire city during the 1970s, '80s and '90s. It was widely regarded as the most successful urban community development project in the nation because it seemingly proved that 'any neighbourhood, no matter how poor, can do something to improve itself by its own efforts [through] a gradual process of education, community action and self help.'[99] The Hyderabad programme attracted financial support from UNICEF during the late 1960s and '70s, and from Britain during the 1980s and '90s. The corporation collaborated with local community committees, working initially to provide environmental improvements such as water supply, public toilets, and street maintenance, drainage and lighting. Efforts then broadened to include social and economic improvements such as family health and welfare, education and recreation for children, community halls, employment training and work-related loans assistance, and help to achieve land security, obtain housing loans, plan and build.

These community development approaches to 'slum improvement' were certainly well intentioned, but their potential to engage effectively with local community aspirations was undermined by an underlying paternalism. The planners' talk about encouraging community participation was not matched by decisive action. Instead, the prevailing slum stereotypes made it seem that purposeful community organization and common-sense ideas had to be introduced to these places before local self-help could begin. Delhi's trailblazing project in collaboration with the Ford Foundation appointed neighbourhood facilitators who were 'educated and middle-class' and whose task was 'to create communities' and 'develop . . . a sense of civic consciousness'.[100] It was inconceivable that such things could already exist in 'slums'. Hyderabad's community development programme likewise set about 'organizing the local community' by manufacturing 'a change in the personality and outlook of the individual', with the hope of starting 'a gradual process of education, community action and self help'.[101] Whenever the Hyderabad programme was widened to include additional neighbourhoods, it was emphasized that 'The first step of the project staff was . . . to build awareness and motivation among the community.'[102]

As other cities imitated the Hyderabad experiment they reinforced the assumption that for 'slum improvement' projects to be successful it was 'necessary to develop local community feeling and to prepare the citizens to become aware of their civic responsibilities'.[103] Community development planners were not only blind to grass-roots organization and energy; they were also unaware of the subtle divisions of responsibility across gender lines. Delhi's Ford Foundation project initially worked primarily through male community representatives and only belatedly recognized that 'slum women were more likely to work for social change than were the men.'[104] However, as community development programmes spread to other cities, they were accused of continuing to pursue 'gender-blind policy approaches' that were further distorted by the 'frequently discriminatory attitudes of male project staff'.[105] Paul Wiebe's magisterial *Social Life in an Indian Slum* (1975) reproached India for its 'paternalistic approaches to slum clearance and slum improvement – where things are done "to" rather than "with" slum dwellers', out of the 'arrogance of knowing about what the poor need, want, and suffer from without the poor themselves having had the chance to participate in the development of the definitions'.[106] Moreover as urban community development initiatives were grafted on to an evolving national strategy for winning the slum war, their purpose was further narrowed to undertaking one-off environmental improvements rather than fostering the community participation that was necessary for their long-term success. It was cheaper and easier to build a standard-plan toilet block or install community water taps, for example, than it was to investigate each community's particular requirements, and to maintain long-term help with housing security, health services, education, training and income enhancement.

This overshadowing of community development by 'environmental improvement' in India's slum war was showcased by the Calcutta Metropolitan Development Authority. Initially through its Basic Development Plan of 1966, and subsequently through the 1970s and into the 1980s by its Bustee Improvement Programme, the authority provided water supply, drainage, road access, waste disposal and recreational facilities in designated 'slum' areas:

> This programme, as in the case of clearance and rehousing schemes, was conceived and implemented as a sanitation and clean environment drive, rather than being seen as an entry point for social and economic uplift leading to the integration of marginalized communities.

Rather than being encouraged to participate in planning, implementing and maintaining the environmental improvements, 'residents were grudgingly seen more as objects or targets who derived free benefits.'[107]

Calcutta's environmental improvement initiative won central government recognition and funding support in 1971, and in the following year the GOI used Calcutta's model to fund (with World Bank assistance) a programme of Environmental Improvement in Slum Areas in the nation's eleven largest metropolitan areas. The new programme provided momentum for other local 'environmental improvement' initiatives. In Bombay, the city corporation had begun to dabble in slum improvement works from 1969, and the new Maharashtra Slum Improvement Board undertook this work on a firmer basis from the early 1970s. In Delhi, a Scheme for the Environmental Improvement of Slums began in 1973. Funding for the 'environmental improvement in slums' was subsequently extended by the GOI to the nation's largest twenty cities, and was further enlarged by the Fifth Five Year Plan (1974–9) as part of the national Minimal Needs Programme, with the aim of including all of India's 'slums'. The 'environmental improvement in slums' programme was continued under various names in later five-year plans to the end of the century.

The shift in emphasis from slum clearance to slum improvement, and from Nehru's participatory community development approach to technocrat-driven environmental improvement, was influenced by pragmatic considerations that were fundamentally shaped in turn by the ongoing slum deceits that prevailed among India's ruling and middle classes. As the director of the National Institute of Urban Affairs explained in 1979,

> The problem became so overwhelming and the resources so limited that it was decided at a high level meeting in 1969 to resort to slum improvement rather than wholesale clearance of slums. The Planning Commission reiterated this approach in the guidelines circulated for the formulation of annual plan programmes for 1970–71.[108]

Environmental improvements were much cheaper than outright clearance and rehousing. Moreover, they left open the possibility of more profitable redevelopment than low-cost housing would allow:

> All lands in the central city area have enormous economic potential if they are used for commercial enterprise and can prove to be a permanent source of income to the city.[109]

As another public policy expert commented in 1979 on 'the recent switch-over from "slum clearance" to "slum improvement"', urban social programmes had to be considered alongside other national investment priorities. He reasoned, 'The idea is not to launch a full-scale attack on slum problems, but to see that the problems do not assume an alarming proportion and get completely out of hand.'[110]

Indian public opinion remained repelled by, but complacently indifferent towards, the widespread poverty and environmental deterioration that characterized the nation's cities. Astute policy observers, however, began to speak about 'the utter failure of slum improvement activities' in India.[111]

THE CONTINUING PREVALENCE of slum deceits in postcolonial India and their negative effect upon urban social policy were highlighted during the state of national emergency which Prime Minister Indira Gandhi declared between 1975 and 1977 in order to suspend democracy and shore up her authoritarian rule. Nehru, her father, had died in office during 1964, and after a nineteen-month interregnum Indira had become India's third prime minister in 1966. During the Emergency, slum policy in India was again shaped by developments in the national capital, and, for the first time since independence, these developments could be undertaken without immediate regard to electoral opinion. Gandhi oversaw a 'phenomenal increase' in slum demolitions across the Delhi region and 'did not pay much heed to the criticism of the demolition operations'.[112] Her hard-line approach was reinforced by her son and adviser, Sanjay Gandhi, who entrusted Jagmohan Malhotra, vice chairman of the Delhi Development Authority, with the task of overseeing Delhi's accelerated slum clearance drive. Jagmohan asserted that his objective was

> to make Delhi an ideal city, a model for other cities to follow . . . if Baron Haussman . . . had not cleared the slums . . . and not built the great highways . . . Paris would have been today an ugly and despicable town.[113]

Delhi's renewed slum clearance drive was replicated in cities across India. Another wave of evictions was attempted in Calcutta's squatter settlements, resulting in renewed protests, community mobilization and deal-making with the contending political parties. In Bombay, where city and state authorities strongly backed the prime minister, the city corporation established a demolition squad to destroy informal housing clusters. It has been estimated that some 72,000 people in Bombay were evicted during the Emergency, as the result of slum clearance schemes that were funded in part by the GOI and the World Bank.[114] The Bombay evictions sparked mass demonstrations, and in the aftermath of their failure the National Slum Dwellers' Federation was established to represent the interests of low-income communities more effectively. Activist Jockin Arputham recalls dumping rubbish in front of Bombay's municipal offices as the new federation sought to draw attention to its grievances.[115] However, world attention was drawn to India's new slum war not so much because of events in Bombay but because of those unfolding in the national capital. In April 1976, police in Old Delhi used tear gas, batons and lethal gunfire to scatter stone-throwing residents from a clearance area near Turkman Gate. Ironically, this atrocity occurred in a neighbourhood that had first been targeted by the colonial Improvement Trust's Ajmeri Gate Slum Clearance Scheme during the late 1930s.

In the national election called by Gandhi in 1977, she lost by a landslide to the Janata Party opposition. She returned to office in 1980 but was assassinated in 1984. Her reignition of the slum war during the 1970s reinforced on a massive scale the trend for slum clearance schemes to redevelop potentially lucrative inner-city land and to relocate residents to cheaper land on the urban periphery. Pillai, writing about slum clearance schemes in Bombay during the 1980s, argued that the Turkman Gate's 'style of aggression and conflict has almost come to stay after the Emergency'.[116] The other effect of Gandhi's intensified slum war was to entrench the prevailing negative characterizations of slums and slum-dwellers and thus to deny local people any chance of a meaningful voice in forward planning. Not only were low-income neighbourhoods patronized by environmental improvement programmes, but they were repressed when they protested against the destruction of their homes. These trends persisted for the remainder of the century:

> Since the mid-seventies a great deal of attention has been focussed on urban slums. This began with the massive slum clearance programme. At regular intervals under such pretexts as environmental protection, urban development and beautification, the slum dwellers are being consistently and ruthlessly thrown out of their meagre shelters and driven out

to areas far from the sources of earning a living, without proper arrangements for their shelter and livelihood.[117]

THE ENTRENCHING OF SLUM stereotypes in India between the 1950s and 1970s exemplified trends elsewhere in the British Commonwealth and the wider developing world. In the Philippines, which became independent of the United States in 1946, a Presidential Slum Clearance Committee was established in 1950, its name indicating how the government viewed squatter settlements and how it intended to deal with them. In December 1963 over 22,000 squatters were evicted from the Intramuros area in Manila. Government policy-making in the Philippines had been shaped by the English-language constructions of American colonialism for almost half a century and previously by Spanish colonialism for over three centuries. By contrast, Thailand had remained independent of European colonization, but it was nonetheless greatly influenced by the United States during the Cold War, and in 1960 the American architects Litchfield, Whiting, Browne & Associates were commissioned to prepare Bangkok's first city plan. The consultants reported that almost half the population of Bangkok lived in substandard housing and the government responded with the Slum Clearance Act of 1960. By the early 1970s the inattention to urban disadvantage that had hitherto characterized many countries of the developing world was likewise giving way to interventions against 'slums'. In Africa a wave of evictions took place during the 1970s and early 1980s. In Latin America, over 100,000 people were evicted from squatter settlements (called *favelas*, a term for 'aberration' that entered the official lexicon during the 1930s) in Rio de Janeiro alone during the early 1970s.[118]

Post-war Latin America had been shaped by a different colonial chronology from that of English-speaking colonization and had been moulded by non-English conventions in language, culture and governance. Latin American nations were sympathetic towards, but mostly not formal members of, the post-war non-aligned movement that India strove to establish during the 1950s and '60s. Yet slum concepts were evident in Latin America as well. Here they were anchored in class divisions (ruling-class opinion was 'offended by the favelados' supposed non-conformism with middle-class norms'),[119] and influenced as well by the viewpoints expressed at international forums by representatives of the former colonies of the English-speaking world. Furthermore, in a parallel process of word association and substitution, English-speaking academics (led by Oscar Lewis, whose influential publications during the late 1950s and the 1960s on a culture of poverty were based on Mexican research), development experts and journalistic slummers equated socially disadvantaged areas in Latin American cities with 'slum'. English, which was increasingly becoming the intermediary language for international communication, subsumed Latin America's clichés about the urban poor into the slum deceits of the English-speaking world.

Rapid urbanization in Latin America after the Second World War created some of the world's largest metropolitan areas: Mexico City, São Paulo (Brazil), Buenos Aires (Argentina), Rio de Janeiro (Brazil), Lima (Peru), Bogotá (Colombia) and Santiago (Chile). It also created some of the world's most grotesque juxtapositions of wealth and poverty. In Lima, for example, most of the city's massive growth during the 1950s and '60s was absorbed by informal settlements (*barriadas*). Rio de Janeiro, Brazil's second-largest city and its federal capital until 1960, and Argentina's capital city, Buenos Aires, are good examples of these trends. Government regulators and social reformers in both cities had since the late nineteenth century characterized inner-city tenement housing and shanty towns on the city periphery as sites of disease and moral decay. As population growth accelerated from the late 1930s informal housing proliferated, creating the massed *villas miserias* of Buenos Aires and the favelas that sprang up around the hills of Rio de Janeiro. By the late 1950s a million people lived in Rio's 'marginal housing' areas.[120] Heavy-handed state programmes of demolition and mass displacement were enforced in Brazil and Argentina from the 1930s under the populist regimes of Getúlio Vargas (president of Brazil, 1930–45 and 1951–4) and Juan Domingo Perón (president of Argentina, 1946–55 and 1973–4). This activity intensified in both nations during the periods of military rule (1964–85 in Brazil, 1966–73 and 1976–83 in Argentina). By the 1970s, Rio's favelas were widely regarded as 'syphilitic sores on the beautiful body of the city, dens of crime, and breeding grounds of violence, prostitution, family breakdown, and social disorganization'.[121]

As Latin America and India highlight, growing international concerns about 'slums' during the 1970s were largely a response to rapid post-war urbanization and the proliferation of unplanned squatter settlements in the cities of the developing world. The 'slum' was now equated entirely with the 'developing' rather than the 'advanced' world, and – as in New Delhi – its perceived problems were mostly associated with 'new slums' built by squatters around the margins of cities rather than with the 'old slums' that had historically existed in the inner cities. In part, the obsession with slums old and new was also the result of booming property markets and speculative redevelopment of urban land by private enterprise. Thus, from 'the mid-1970s, evictions all over Asia were on the rise as city developers and private builders found the land on which slum settlements existed to be prime real estate'.[122] In part, too, the redevelopment of 'slum' areas was encouraged and financed by international development agencies such as the United Nations and the World Bank, as well as newer organizations such as the Inter-American Development Bank in Latin America and the Caribbean (established in 1959), the African Development Bank (established in 1963) and the Asian Development Bank (established in 1966).

Anxiety concerning accelerating city growth in the developing world did not, however, result only in the heavy-handed 'slum' clearances and forced relocations that characterized much of India's slum war. India's dabbling in radical community development through 'slum improvement' was also widely imitated, and gained momentum from the late 1970s. Singapore, for example, with encouragement from the World Bank, experimented from the late 1970s with slum 'upgrading', conserving the historical character of distinctive 'slum' districts such as Chinatown and giving some scope for local citizen participation. Latin American experiments with what English-speakers called 'slum upgrading' had begun in the early 1960s. Municipal governments in Rio de Janeiro and Buenos Aires, supported by state and federal governments, attempted a three-tier programme of 'slum' improvement, clearance and relocation to public housing estates. The initiatives were influenced by recent American sociology and anthropology and funded by the Democratic Kennedy and Johnson administrations as part of America's Cold War pre-emptive response to communism in Latin America. However, the initial gestures of collaboration with shantytown residents were quickly followed by bulldozers and police. It was only when Brazilian military rule started to weaken in the mid-1970s that the removal of favelas slowed and community organizations could lobby more successfully for secure land tenure and improvements to infrastructure and services. This softening approach became most

evident in the provincial state capital of Belo Horizonte, where participatory projects of slum upgrading continued into the 1980s and '90s
with funding assistance from Germany and Italy. In Rio de Janeiro, too,
after the restoration of democracy, upgrading projects received greater
emphasis because almost a third of the electorate lived in informal
housing settlements.

In the 1970s and '80s the United Nations, drawing upon experiences
in Latin America and India, gradually reconfigured the contradictory
elements of 'slum' clearance and upgrading programmes into a more
coherent and socially progressive approach. India especially informed
UN policy, not only because UN agencies were actively involved in urban
community development there, but also because of the respect accorded
to Indian participants in international forums as a result of India's leading role in the non-aligned movement. United Nations resolutions
in 1967 and 1972, outlining the basic needs of squatter settlements,
echoed the 'minimum needs' approach to service provision in 'slums'
that was developing in India. India's example was also influential in
1976 at the World Employment Conference in Geneva, at which the
United Nations' International Labour Organization (ILO) proposed
a comprehensive basic needs strategy for the developing world that
incorporated benchmarks for food, clothing, shelter, education, trans-
portation and also participatory decision-making in implementing the
strategy. The ILO's basic needs development approach was endorsed by
other UN agencies and the World Bank, and by the 1980s had become
widely accepted as a community development framework.

United Nations concerns about rapid and uncontrolled urbanization, and the need to impose upon it 'progressive minimum standards
for an acceptable quality of life',[123] led to the convening of a United
Nations Conference on Human Settlements (HABITAT I) in Vancouver,
Canada, in 1976. The resulting Vancouver Declaration on Human
Settlements was endorsed by the UN General Assembly in 1977. It
was a bold and visionary document, espousing social justice and
democratic inclusion. The word 'slum' did not appear, and in the
immediate aftermath of HABITAT I it seemed that slum deceits might
at last be stripped out of progressive urban planning. The Declaration
announced that 'the circumstances of life for vast numbers of people
in human settlements are unacceptable, particularly in developing
countries', and affirmed that

Adequate shelter and services are a basic human right which places an obligation on Governments to ensure their attainment by all people, beginning with direct assistance to the least advantaged through guided programmes of self-help and community action.[124]

The UN General Assembly agreed to establish a Centre for Human Settlements to help to realize this goal and the resulting UNCHS (Habitat), based in Nairobi, was established in 1979. A refreshingly new approach to human settlement planning in an increasingly urban world seemed about to dawn.

SIX

LITTLE PALACES

When New Delhi's Yamuna Pushta squatter district was demolished in 2004, dislocating some 150,000 people, an evicted resident asked bitterly, 'Why let us build our homes and dreams, if you are going to bulldoze them to the ground after twenty or thirty years?'[1] Some thirty years earlier, as a former resident of Rio de Janeiro's Catacumba favela recalls, 'We were given 24 hours' notice . . . the rain soaked right through our mattress. I had been paying for that mattress for over a year in monthly installments and it was ruined.'[2] Throughout the nineteenth and twentieth centuries, and now in the twenty-first, residents in disadvantaged neighbourhoods throughout the world have reacted with similar bewilderment and anger when outsiders labelled their homes and communities 'slums' and attempted to destroy and remake them according to an imposed foreign logic.

Residents of Manchester's infamous Ancoats district (infamous, that is, to outsiders who scarcely knew it) told investigators in 1930 that they 'liked the neighbourhood', and one man announced defiantly that 'he "would not move for the Town Hall clock".'[3] In Bristol, residents of Barton Hill had by the 1950s accumulated enough savings to buy and renovate their hitherto rented homes. As one woman explained, 'My husband and I have given up our holiday and redecorated all through.'[4] Such plans were undone when the city council declared their neighbourhood a slum and embarked upon a clearance scheme to redevelop it. When Glasgow's Maryhill neighbourhood was designated a slum clearance area in the early 1970s, residents were uncomprehending. As one of them recollects,

> We were very happy there and people couldn't believe that
> they were taking the place apart . . . To me it was like a wee
> village and everybody knew what was happening to people
> and everybody was interested in each other. It was like a death
> sentence that kind of thing coming to us.[5]

Latiefa and her husband Ameer were among the last to leave when
South Africa's apartheid regime tore down District Six, a mixed-race
working-class community in Cape Town, and forced its residents
to relocate to the distant Cape Flats. Their house was bulldozed in
1982. Visiting their former community a year later, Latiefa and Ameer
returned to nothing. Only the roads remained, and forlornly – amid
the emptiness – a boarded-up mosque. 'It's only the sand that you see,'
said Ameer bitterly. While their three children improvise a racetrack
down a sloping street, using old plastic milk crates on which to slide
at breakneck speed, the parents point out traces of their former home:
'Here was the kitchen'; 'There was your room.' 'My mother was born
here,' reflects Ameer. He muses further: 'I used to play here all the
time – rugby, cricket, soccer. But it's all gone now. It's gone with the
wind. It makes me feel sick.'[6]

There is a common pattern here. The inhabitants of poor neighbourhoods from Ancoats to Yamuna Pushta all experienced – through
police harassment, municipal inattention to local services, cynical
manipulation by mainstream political parties and business interests,
petty corruption by local officials, marginalization from the design
and implementation of redevelopment projects, and denigration by
the mainstream media – what Patrick McAuslan called the 'pejorative'
effect of slum deceits, 'which assume that in some way the urban poor
are an aberration, the departure from the norm'.[7]

These negative characterizations of slumland climaxed during
the second half of the twentieth century in the developing
world. When Prime Minister Indira Gandhi chaired the Seventh
Commonwealth Heads of Government Meeting in New Delhi
in 1983, every potentially embarrassing 'slum' that might be seen
between the airport and the city centre was 'fenced off out of sight
of the visiting dignitaries'.[8] Assaults on disadvantaged city communities, carried out in the name of a war against slums, also climaxed
in the developing world. It is here that the world's largest-ever
cities and the highest proportions of urban social disadvantage are

concentrated. By 1990, 45 per cent of the world's urban population lived in the Asian region alone, and in cities there it was routinely estimated that at least half the population lived in unplanned and ill-serviced squatter settlements. Governments entrusted with protecting their people carried out massive clearances and evictions instead, probably the largest of which took place in Seoul, South Korea, where some 720,000 people were evicted in the lead-up to the 1988 Olympic Games.[9] The United Nations estimated in 1996 that throughout the developing world,

> Several million urban dwellers are forcibly evicted from their homes and neighbourhoods each year, as a result of public works or government-approved redevelopment programmes. They are usually evicted without compensation [or] relocation schemes that are acceptable to those relocated.[10]

These slum wars peaked in the developing world not only because of the unprecedented aggregation of city populations but because it was here that, during the second half of the twentieth century, a majority of the world's poor people took the initiative and built their own homes and communities. They did so in the unplanned squatter areas that ringed the world's largest cities, because neither the public nor the private sector provided them with affordable housing. It was their makeshift creations that outsiders derided as slums. Yet, notwithstanding this scorn, their activities highlight grass-roots precedents that can be traced back to the nineteenth century.

Slum stereotypes have disguised the fundamental normalcy of the places that outsiders marginalize as 'slums'. They deny the aspirations, decision-making and orderly incremental achievements of 'slum-minded' people. Some people have always resisted these deceits. As the American housing and urban development expert Charles Abrams suggested, drawing on his experiences both in the United States and the developing world during the 1950s and '60s, 'Slum life is not always the symbol of retrogression. It may in fact be the first advance from homelessness into shelter, or the way station on the road from abject poverty to hope.'[11] The English writer Jeremy Seabrook, who studied Bombay's poorest neighbourhoods in the 1980s, concluded that the city's 'slums are far from being the depressing places they may appear; they seethe with vitality and hope'.[12]

Stan Hall had grown up amid such surroundings, not in late twentieth-century Bombay but in early twentieth-century York. He lived in the city's disadvantaged Hungate district until it was demolished during the early 1930s, and remembers:

> There was seven of us children and we had to go outside to our toilet . . . For all them little houses were small, some of them were little palaces. Brass fenders, brass spittoons, everything brass.[13]

This idiomatic sense of fashioning 'little palaces', expressed in ignorance, and then defiance, of outsiders' talk of 'slums', has both potency and longevity. In Melbourne in 1957, the state minister for housing conceded when he visited the inner suburb of Carlton that the condemned 'slum' housing he inspected was in fact being maintained like 'little palaces' by its Italian immigrant occupants.[14] It was because Yamuna Pushta's little palaces, and those in Ancoats, Maryhill, Catacumba, District Six and countless other places, built up painstakingly over many years, were so arbitrarily torn down that the residents bewailed their ruined dreams.

These ruined hopes, and the shattered stability of the neighbourhoods that had sustained them, do not necessarily mimic mainstream expectations about sensible life choices and tolerable living conditions. The 'little palaces' are not simply a debased approximation to universal norms and minimum standards; the lifestyles within them might modify, contradict and even defy society's expectations. In such neighbourhoods,

> Many of the so-called lacks – of amenities, infrastructure, livelihood, markets, and governance – become occasions for residents to assemble ways of working together that otherwise would not be possible given existing cultural norms, political practices, and urban experiences.[15]

They might enable

> an alternative lifestyle. This is a lifestyle which is not hampered by petty regulation, where one can live in a semi-rural style, but still within the city. This includes the opportunity to

keep livestock, practice trades and commerce with a minimum
of official interference, and construct affordable houses from
traditional materials.[16]

Such lifestyles, argued a recent study in São Paulo, Brazil, constitute
a form of 'insurgent citizenship'.[17]

YES, UNAMBIGUOUSLY, the majority of these 'slum' people are poor, and
the United Nations' Millennium Development Goals, set at the end of
the twentieth century, were right to attempt to slash entrenched social
disadvantage. In both the past and in the present day, poor people's life
choices have been constrained by the workings of labour and housing
markets, and market-driven property redevelopment; they have been
victimized by law enforcement agencies and short-changed by service
providers. These people cannot be dismissed as a marginal underclass:
the World Bank estimated that in 2005 1.4 billion people, or about a
quarter of the population of the developing world, were living below
the U.S.$1.25 a day benchmark that the bank used to calculate extreme
poverty.[18] There is little romance in attempting to make do on a little
more than a dollar a day when, as in Bombay's infamous Dharavi
district, one's little palace is invaded by 'gutter water . . . even sewage
– the house stinks. We face difficulty for everything. One day we eat,
other days we sleep hungry.'[19]

Yes, undeniably, in even the best of weather these 'little palaces' are
cramped and structurally deficient, and the possessions within them
are meagre. Michael Young and Peter Willmott's pioneering insider's
view of London's notorious Bethnal Green during the 1950s remarked
that the structural condition of the houses was indeed 'deplorable'.[20]
Little had changed in the conditions of English working-class life by
1969, when a survey of disadvantaged households in Liverpool found
that almost three-quarters lacked at least one basic amenity (a bath or
shower, basin and sink, internal toilet, hot and cold water).[21] These
conditions remained entrenched in the developing world during the
late twentieth and early twenty-first centuries. In the squatter districts
surrounding India's booming high-tech capital of Bangalore, 'Except
for some kitchen utensils, [the] houses are completely empty.'[22] In
Kibera in Nairobi, Kenya, the most iconic 'slum' in sub-Saharan Africa,
the shacks contain just one room, on average 3 m (10 ft) square, with

wattle-and-daub walls and corrugated iron roofs, lit by kerosene lamps, and drained by open ditches and pit latrines.

Yes, these neighbourhoods have usually grown without officially sanctioned plans, are starved of municipal services and are insanitary. Kibera has no electricity and no regular piped water, and sits upon red dirt that turns to gluey mud whenever it rains. There are no paved roads, and the railway track that runs through the township is used as the main walkway. In India's capital, New Delhi, a study of squatter settlements calculated that there were on average 130 users per lavatory and one water tap serving 400 people.[23] Another study, set in the southern metropolis of Hyderabad, found that water was provided to the poorest districts by a meagre scatter of public taps, bores and open wells, the supply being available for at best several hours per day. Only 28 per cent of the inhabitants had a secure water supply, 27 per cent had their own latrine and just 51 per cent had electricity.[24] These conditions recur throughout the developing world. In the district of Sujatnagar Bastee in Dhaka, Bangladesh, there is neither sewerage nor drainage, and residents form long lines for water from the public taps whenever the supply is available.[25]

Yes, there are claims of neurological damage from adverse living and working environments, resulting in so-called 'slum-minded' behaviour. Historian Jerry White, a deeply sympathetic and astute interpreter of England's working class, concluded that life in London's poorest neighbourhoods during the 1920s and '30s 'took a psychological toll . . . unfitting men and women for regular work through various forms of nervous exhaustion or depression, and contributing to widespread alcohol abuse'.[26] Economist Joseph Stiglitz argues that in more recent times the psychological cost of striving to make ends meet 'may actually impair the ability to take decisions that would help alleviate the situation'.[27]

Yes, the inhabitants themselves have mixed feelings about their neighbourhoods. The long queues for scarce water supplies in many poor urban areas of the developing world often lead to quarrels and fights, and inadequate toilet facilities force residents to use open land, a practice which, especially for women, can result in embarrassment and harassment. Differences in behaviour can generate frictions within poor communities. These include gender abuse, child abuse and elder abuse; conflicts over social status, religion and ethnicity; and tensions fuelled by addiction to alcohol and drugs. So it was historically: White's study of the Campbell Bunk district in London, which was torn down during the 1950s, concluded that the collective experience of its inhabitants was 'deeply fractured and contradictory'.[28] So it remains in the present day: AbdouMaliq Simone concedes that in Jakarta's squatter districts, although 'generosity and reciprocity remain strong in most neighborhoods, alliances and affiliations among neighbors may be volatile'.[29] Asked why she lived in the Gobindapur Rail Colony Gate No. 1 squatter settlement in Calcutta, Dhiren Manna replied with passion:

> It is an economic compulsion! The children have to grow up in an unhealthy atmosphere. We live amidst unceasing quarrel, words of abuse and trouble. It would be better to live in rural surroundings in one's native place.[30]

Like Dhiren Manna, many residents are keen to move on from these homes and neighbourhoods, though they do not necessarily comprise a majority of the community. In 1930, residents of Ancoats

> complained of the impossibility of keeping their houses clean owing to their dilapidated condition, lack of conveniences, and the dirt of the district; as one woman said, 'When you've finished cleaning through to the back, you can write your name on the things in the front.'[31]

Some 49 per cent of the Ancoats sample were recorded as being willing to move; 51 per cent were not, citing its convenience to their workplaces. Ajay Mehra's 1991 study of Old Delhi similarly found that 47 per cent of respondents were prepared to move if basic alternative accommodation was provided near their workplaces, with good access to shopping and public transport; the other 53 per cent were opposed to moving, not so much because of sentimental attachments but because they did not believe that such concessions would ever be forthcoming.[32] A parallel survey in Hyderabad reported that

> Two out of every three slum dwellers claimed that they had stayed on in the slum because they were happy with the houses they were in . . . while a little less than a quarter (20 per cent) stayed on because the slum was near their place of work or

provided them access to other facilities. Only about 1.5 per cent claimed that they had no other alternative, and about 5 per cent did not really want to stay in the slums.[33]

Yes, there are also mixed reactions to the word 'slum' by inhabitants of neighbourhoods thus described. Some are offended by it and deny its applicability to their communities – although they may apply it to others. Talk to Tank Ranchhod Savdas, a potter in Dharavi, about 'a slum-free Dharavi' and he will 'shake with anger. How dare anyone claim [that it] is "a slum" in need of rehabilitation!'[34] Other residents embrace the word. Jockin Arputham, the spokesperson for India's National Slum Dwellers' Federation and for the international umbrella organization that developed from it, declares 'I am very proud to be a slum dweller.'[35] This tongue-in-cheek acceptance of 'slum' is often used to subvert dominant usage, to mobilize neighbourhoods to negotiate for better arrangements and to resist arbitrary intervention. Arjun Appadurai argues that phrases such as '"pavement dwellers" and "slum dwellers" are no longer external labels but have become self-organizing, empowering labels for large parts of the urban poor'.[36]

Yes, some outsiders' well-intentioned efforts to publicize urban inequalities can pile deceits upon deceits, further obscuring insiders' aspirations and achievements. In India, many researchers have cautioned against 'presenting the ingenuity of the poor in a way that may romanticize poverty, because this may obscure the true misery and hardship of life in these communities'.[37] However, Owen Lynch derided these arguments, calling them a '"sob sister" approach to slums and squatter areas. In this approach . . . there is nothing like a social life for the living dead, squatters are seen as listless, apathetic and without hope.'[38] White noted drily that there are 'many reasons to romanticise, excuse, embroider, and lie' about the internal dynamics of marginalized neighbourhoods.[39]

However, none of the above concessions legitimizes the continuing currency of slum concepts and the warped 'reform' agendas that result from them. They are limited in large part to what Henri Lefebvre calls 'the abstract space of the experts', which he warned can all too easily become 'the tool of domination'.[40] In this chapter I attempt to move beyond that abstract space to probe the actual living environments of poor households and communities. In the early 1950s, as compulsory land acquisition by the federal government spelt the end of Australia's most notorious slum, Melbourne's 'Little Lon', the *Herald* newspaper told its readers to 'look for beauty . . . in unexpected places'. One of these places, the *Herald* suggested, was a tiny 'slum' cottage in Little Lon occupied by Mary Hayes and her sister Tess. The cottage in which Mary and Tess

> have lived since they were born more than 70 years ago is not easy to find among the little factories and workshops of the north-east corner of Melbourne city. It is in Cumberland Place, a path-wide lane off McCormac Place, which is off Little Lonsdale Street.
>
> The little weatherboard house has stood unchanged well over 100 years. John Hayes and his wife had their eight children there when it was already 40 years old, or more . . .
>
> Now the Commonwealth Government has acquired the whole block . . . It proposes ultimately to pull down all the factories and workshops, the Chinese quarters, and church missions, and the Hayes sisters' home. In their place it will build grand Federal offices . . .
>
> 'This area used to have a bad name', the gentle Tess will tell you. 'Some of these streets were not pleasant, but everyone has always been kind to us. No one ever molested us, or even made us afraid' . . .
>
> 'I hope they won't have to put us out; but if they do, I am sure they'll look after us.'[41]

To look for beauty in unexpected places? Brass fenders in little palaces? As Lefebvre pointed out,

> The vast shanty towns of Latin America (*favelas, barrios, ranchos*) manifest a social life far more intense than the bourgeois districts of the cities . . . Their poverty notwithstanding, these districts sometimes so effectively order their space – houses, walls, public spaces – as to elicit a nervous admiration.[42]

British architect John F. C. Turner, who exhaustively studied the shanty towns of Lima in Peru from the late 1950s, sought to convince international opinion during the 1970s and '80s that any interventions in such places should 'concentrat[e] attention on the human resources of the poor, rather than on their often appalling conditions', and aim to bolster those grass-roots resources rather than condemning the living conditions that had been fashioned from them.[43] He argued against those who 'regarded urban settlements built by low income people as "slums", "eyesores", "cancers" and so on', and who bemoaned the 'substandard' material forms of such places and the 'irrational' life-styles that sustained them.[44] Turner directed attention instead to the vernacular logic which underpinned the arrangement of homes and neighbourhoods and which expressed the livelihood opportunities available to poor communities. Here, he said, could be found the best opportunities for constructive interventions to assist the urban poor.

Turner's influence on international development agencies in the late twentieth century was immense. There was an enormous impediment, however, to implementing his advice, as there is in writing this chapter. The viewpoints of poor people, and particulars about their homes, communities and livelihoods, are elusive. Where is the 'evidence' about them to counteract 200 years of slum deceits? The urban redevelopment programmes recorded in libraries and archives 'all just gave outsiders' views'.[45] As for the programmes that are unfolding today, one Indian critic observed that their 'definitions do not reveal concern for the inhabitants of slums. They describe and define them. The upper class bias is inbuilt in the acts and rules.'[46] Another researcher recently acknowledged that even now 'Little is known on how slum dwellers themselves look at their problems and how they perceive their living conditions and their future prospects.'[47] He had not cracked the slum deceits, but he did discern their basic problem.

Chaos

From the early nineteenth to the early twenty-first century, well-intentioned reformers set out to 'order the disordered world' of slums.[48] In the early twentieth century, British urban planning advocate John Nettlefold remonstrated with working-class hecklers during local elections in Birmingham that housing reform 'is a very serious matter for you chaps. It is a marvel to me how you men live here at all. The conditions of living are not liveable now. We are trying to make them liveable.'[49] A century later Óscar Arias (a Nobel Prize winner and Costa Rican president in 1986–90 and 2006–10) urged that 'Latin America's slums' be replaced by planned settlements or a new generation would grow up 'without faith in democratic institutions, and without hope for the future'.[50] Arias's comments seemed especially appropriate for the times, because by the early twenty-first century slum representations focused entirely on the informal settlements of the developing world. Once-notorious names such as Birmingham's St Mary's district, London's Bethnal Green and New York's Five Points were overshadowed by newly infamous places such as Rocinha, Rio de Janeiro's largest favela, crammed onto the hills above the city's most chic and sought-after beaches; Dharavi in Bombay (in 1995 renamed Mumbai), the so-called 'greatest slum of Asia',[51] which is paradoxically overlooked by the tower-block residence of India's richest man; and Kibera, 'Africa's so-called largest "slum"',[52] hemmed in between Nairobi's central business district and affluent middle-class suburbs.

Characterizations of such iconically bad places in the late twentieth and early twenty-first centuries reinforce core elements of the slum stereotypes that had prevailed since the nineteenth century: chaotic physical environments and the dysfunctional economic and social life within them. These deceits rationalized slum clearance interventions and private enterprise redevelopments, but equally importantly they justified the social mainstream in turning a blind eye to urban social disadvantage. As a former head of the Delhi-based NGO the Ankur Society for Alternatives in Education reflected in the aftermath of the Yamuna Pushta evictions, India's expanding middle class

> would like to wish them away. Slums are considered to be a blot, where the common perception is that criminal groups and diseases flourish. These notions and myths are further perpetuated by the media and by the so-called educated . . . We want all their services; we want our drivers, we want our *aayas* (maids), we want the rickshaw drivers, the taxi drivers, the rag pickers to clean our city; we want everyone to work for us, but we do not want to see and know, how they exist.[53]

EXTREME ENVIRONMENTAL CHAOS is said to characterize all slums. This cliché, prevalent during the nineteenth century and the first half of the next, was strongly reasserted after the Second World War. The head of Chicago's South Side Planning Board declared in 1947 that the district's vista 'of destroyed buildings and homes is worse than any

Little Palaces

picture of London destruction by the German Air Raids of the last war'.[54] Thirty years later, similar comments were being made about the impacts on both sides of the Atlantic of global economic adjustments upon the core cities of the first urban revolution. The Liverpool Inner Area Study concluded in 1977 that the 'impact of abandoned docks, empty warehouses, crumbling factories and mills and acres of derelict land add up to a form of environmental anarchy'.[55] By the late twentieth century such depictions of environmental anarchy were being used chiefly to describe the 'slums' of the developing world. Kibera exemplified the apparent chaos of the informal settlements that seemed to be choking the orderly growth of cities in the developing world. It had apparently been built without overall plan: 'structures have been built randomly and are crammed together wherever there was space available.' Its massed housing existed, perplexingly, without any of the orthodox markers of stable homes and neighbourhoods: 'few have post box number, no formal addresses.'[56]

These characterizations were inherited from British colonialism. In Egypt, which the British controlled from the early 1880s until the early 1950s, the concept of 'slum' was captured by the local word *Ashwa'iyyat*, meaning disordered, haphazard.[57] In Singapore, the Improvement Trust complained in 1953 that the territory's kampongs formed 'a maze of temporary buildings interpenetrated with pathways, the development being dense and chaotic'.[58] This point of view strengthened after independence as Lee Kuan Yew embarked upon an ambitious programme of modernization and nation-building. Thus as colonialism receded in the developing world during the 1950s and '60s, the modernization agendas pursued by the new nation states reinforced the old stereotypes about slumland chaos. European consultants were commissioned to draw up city master plans that 'look[ed] forward to a millennium where all squatter huts will be eliminated and replaced by regularly laid out housing in the image of the Western city'.[59] It seemed to them that the unplanned growth of cities in the developing world was 'too chaotic to permit of their easy rationalization'. They lambasted

> the poor design and layout both of the individual dwelling and of the community as a whole when constructed almost wholly by unskilled and often ignorant workers who, if not direct migrants, may be only a few years removed from rural hinterlands. At the level of the individual dwelling there is usually

203

a marked tendency to produce already known but basically unsatisfactory forms, either those of the houses of the poor in the countryside or those of the urban slum near the city centre.[60]

Charles Stokes's widely cited 'A Theory of Slums' (1962) was grounded on the proposition that 'Slums appear to be planless and even antiplan.'[61]

United Nations agencies, development banks and international aid organizations reinforced these opinions. The World Bank, assessing the effects of informal urban development in Latin America, concluded in 2003 that

> The 'spontaneous' or 'unplanned' pattern of land occupation of squatter settlements is characterized by narrow and tortuous access routes, occupation of areas of risk (e.g., landslide or flood-prone areas) and, perhaps most of all, by the lack of a precise definition of public and private spaces. In a typical squatter settlement, such as those in Rio's Favela-Bairro or São Paulo's Guarapiranga, many plots lack direct access to a street or lane, forcing people to cross other plots to get to their own.[62]

In 2004 UN officials lamented that in Ghana's capital, Accra, 'Unplanned, haphazard, uncontrolled and non-conforming development is . . . making nonsense of . . . the statutory provisions governing planning and development control.'[63]

India, the leader of the non-aligned movement in the developing world, exemplified these trends. The director of Bombay's influential 1957 slum seminar had declared that

> A slum may be described as a chaotically occupied, unsystematically developed and generally neglected area which is over-populated by persons and over-crowded with ill-repaired and neglected structures. The area has insufficient communications, indifferent sanitary arrangements, and inadequate amenities necessary for the maintenance of physical and social health and the minimum needs and comforts of human beings and the community. There is a general absence of social services and welfare agencies to deal with the major social problems of persons and families, in respect of sub-standard health, inadequate income and low standard of living.[64]

This definition was still being used by academic and professional experts at the end of the twentieth century. It was built into urban planning regulations. In Madras, for example, the city corporation declared in 1961 that

> a slum is taken to mean hutting areas with squalid surroundings. In such areas huts are erected in a haphazard manner without proper access. Minimum basic amenities are lacking in these areas.[65]

The Bombay municipal corporation was still defining 'slum' during the 1980s as

> an area consisting of buildings which are by reasons of disrepair, or sanitary defects and inadequacy thereof or by reason of bad arrangement or narrowness of the rooms or buildings or bad arrangements of streets, are dangerous or injurious to the inhabitants of the locality.[66]

These viewpoints were endorsed by international community development experts working in India. Marshall Clinard announced in 1966 that

> Delhi's huge and dense slum population lives among a squalid chaos of tenements, hovels, shacks, and bazaar stalls scattered through narrow congested streets, alleys and lanes, where open drains are often blocked with refuse, garbage, and excreta.[67]

A later generation of Indian experts perpetuated these assumptions through the 1970s, '80s and '90s. A 'slum' study in Mysore concluded that

> Huts have come up like mushrooms, anywhere and everywhere without proper perspective. Garbage is dumped right in front of the houses. People have no civic sense whatsoever. They spit in front of their own house. Flies are found everywhere.[68]

The 'slums' of Allahabad in the northern state of Uttar Pradesh were allegedly prey to 'chaotic conditions of over-crowding and insanitation'.[69] Another study from Uttar Pradesh, set in Kanpur, drew attention to the 'poorly arranged and badly designed housing' which seemed to be becoming ever more 'run-down' rather than evolving and improving.[70] Researchers in the central Indian state of Madhya Pradesh claimed in the early 1990s that

> the quality of the shelter is so poor that it is neither possible to maintain it, nor is there any incentive or sense of civic pride which would drive the dweller to keep his little shelter in good condition.[71]

At Aurangabad (in Maharashtra state) it was reported that 'The huts are constructed mostly without any plan consciously drawn.'[72] Likewise in Calcutta, it seemed that 'The huts are built in a haphazard manner without any plan.'[73] Vandana Desai, writing about Dharavi, asserted in 1988 that 'the slums of Bombay . . . form a mosaic of hutments, huddled together without any order or basic civic amenity and without even the rudiments of streets.'[74] Hyderabad's long-running and influential community development programme was based on the premise that slum 'communities . . . live under conditions which cannot be termed "human"', and a review in 1996 applauded the 'programme [for having] converted the unplanned hazardous slum localities into planned colonies'.[75]

THE SLUM'S ENVIRONMENTAL chaos was seemingly intensified by profound economic instability and social maladjustment. In descriptions of both the old slums of the developed world and the new slums of the developing world, low-income areas were characterized as suffering not just economic disadvantage but crushing and unrelenting pressures that buffeted and pummelled resourceful human beings into mere pawns. Residents became disorganized, apathetic and inactive. The resulting social anarchy compounded the economic and environmental chaos of slums. A local church worker in Kibera remarked in 2005 that its inhabitants 'live every day in an environment whose conditions are degrading and dehumanising, where corruption and violence are commonplace. They are ignored and forgotten by society.'[76] In Bangkok, an American missionary reported that

Violence is a way of life. You just walk with your head down
and don't look people in the eye. If someone talks to you, you
hurry on by without answering, and if it's a curt remark or a
curse, you step up your pace without a peep.

He speculated that because violence had escalated in the early
twenty-first century as local gangs struggled to control the drug
trade, neighbourhood cohesion eroded and the old 'codes [of social
behaviour] are in disarray'.[77] Social disintegration seemingly threatened to engulf iconic cities. Commentators in New York worried
during the late 1980s and early 1990s that epidemics of gun violence
and crack-cocaine addiction were 'devastating entire inner-city neighborhoods'.[78] Incoming city mayor David Dinkins declared in 1989 that
New York was 'a city under siege':

> Whole neighborhoods are fast becoming free-fire zones. Some
> of our housing projects have become base camps for armies of
> drug dealers. And too often we hear of roving gangs raining
> terror on our subways, on our streets and in our parks.[79]

The *New York Times* characterized the social disintegration intertwined
with 'Crack, AIDS and homelessness [as] the new urban plagues'.[80]

In India, preoccupation with slumland economic and social chaos
dates back to the refugee crisis that unfolded after partition. Describing
the squatter settlements that sprang up around Delhi, Bharat Sevak
Samaj cautioned Nehru in 1956 that 'the miserable environment
in which they live breeds despair and a fatalistic approach to life.'[81]
Participants at Bombay's slum clearance seminar in 1957 also worried about the social effects of 'minds . . . dominated by anxiety and
insecurity', and pointed to evidence of

> the emergence of [a] 'slum mentality' . . . blunting community
> consciousness and aesthetic sense; [creating] bad neighbour-
> liness and aggression in some and fear, submissiveness and
> cowardice in others.[82]

The seminar identified disturbing social markers of this slum mentality, such as psychological maladjustment, family disorganization,
social disorganization and an unravelling of the 'status and dignity of

the woman'.[83] Over subsequent decades, as Indian experts elaborated upon the apparent association between chaotic living and working conditions on the one hand and social disorganization on the other, they reinforced one of the enduring original deceits that as slum-dwellers 'pick up bad habits' a collective slum mentality emerged that was manifested in a very high birth rate, drunkenness, wife beating, rape, across-the-board assaults,

> family disorganisation, and even disintegration, neglect of the child, sexual indecency, the rise of prostitution, crime, gambling and gangsterism, the juvenile inactivity, the development of work-shyness, lethargy and manual inefficiency, anti-social outlook etc.[84]

It became generally accepted by Indian experts during the late twentieth century that, as a result of this debilitating slum mentality,

> slum-dwellers do not take part in community activities. Leisure is expended in loafing around in the neighbourhood . . . They are physically weak, mentally sub-normal and inefficient and morally wrecks.[85]

In such communities, supposedly, 'slum dwellers are highly suspicious of each other and nobody would contribute voluntarily towards the maintenance of the infrastructure.'[86] Thus, it was contended, 'lack of real community feeling is one of the major characteristics of slum culture.'[87] There were two key consequences. First, it was asserted that most slum-dwellers were apathetic, helpless and politically subservient. A Dutch researcher concluded from fieldwork in Bangalore that the inhabitants of one such 'slum' showed

> absolute indifference to everything including towards issues that directly affected their lives . . . The people showed a fatalistic attitude: 'We were born as poor coolies and will remain so for the rest of our days'.[88]

Second, this apathy supposedly provided an opening for 'those who are manipulative, clever and can make their voices hear[d]'.[89] It was claimed that these opportunists cynically asserted themselves as local community leaders when participatory community development and 'slum improvement' schemes developed momentum in India. In 2008 the multi-award-winning movie *Slumdog Millionaire* pictured Dharavi as 'a feral wasteland, with little evidence of order, community or compassion . . . This is a place of evil and decay, of a raw, chaotic tribalism.'[90]

AT LEAST, that is how many well-to-do Indians imagined places such as Dharavi, and how they reacted to *Slumdog Millionaire*. The movie won eight Oscars, but

> angered many Indians because it tarnishes the perception of their country as a rising economic power and a beacon of democracy. India's English-language papers, read mainly by its middle class, have carried many bristling reviews of the film that convey an acute sense of wounded national pride.[91]

However, there was another response to *Slumdog Millionaire*. Some people, echoing Turner's arguments of the 1970s and '80s, suggested that the movie's bedrock was the 'theme of bottomless optimism amid-adversity'.[92] Interest stirred that there might be another side to conventional representations of slums. Was slumland chaos axiomatically bad? As *The Hindu* newspaper pointed out,

> 'Slum' is an evocative word that goes to the heart of the con-tradictions within India and [is] inarguably part of the movie's draw. It is not, however, Hollywood's highly romanticised ver-sion of gutters and swine. [Director Danny] Boyle wants us to visualise it differently: 'They are just places where people live. They are not wealthy people, but quite resourceful people. They are not provided [for] by the state. The sewage system doesn't work, but the homes are clean. They are very generous. They were very keen that we didn't just say they were poor.'[93]

Boyle 'described Dharavi as an "amazing" place, both self-reliant and self-sufficient, and he has been keen to make clear that he was not interested in producing a film that was "poverty porn"'.[94]

A similar rethinking about 'slums' was simultaneously taking place throughout the developing world. Jonas Bendiksen, for example, argued in *The Places We Live* (2008), a photographic essay set in Nairobi, Mumbai, Jakarta and Caracas, that

> The common perception of slums as locations of poverty, squalor, destitution, insecurity, and danger tells one part of the story – but there are also stories of enterprising, hardworking slum denizens.[95]

Such arguments gained considerable currency during the late twentieth and early twenty-first centuries (in part, as we shall see, because they suited the dominating neoliberal policy framework of the period), but they had a much longer history than either *Slumdog Millionaire* or John F. C. Turner. Charles Abrams knew both sides of the 'slum' argument because he had been both an insider and an outsider. Abrams worked for New York mayor Fiorello La Guardia during the 1930s and '40s, and was a United Nations expert consultant throughout the developing world during the 1950s, '60s and '70s. He had been born in Poland in 1902 and his family emigrated shortly afterwards to the United States, where they settled in Brooklyn, New York. Many years later,

> when Abrams worked on a housing code for the La Guardia administration, he was amazed to find that, according to all physical standards, he had grown up in a slum. But since nobody then realized it, it wasn't – except statistically. Williamsburgh was a hard-working, lively, close-knit community, as was the Abrams family, and young Charles was happy in both. It instilled in him a sensitivity to the important role of neighborhoods in people's lives.[96]

Since the nineteenth century outside observers had acknowledged to some degree the attachment felt by local communities, however poor, to their neighbourhoods, and the resulting hostility shown by many of them towards officials and developers who disrupted their neighbourhoods. In the developed world, this realization contributed during the 1960s and '70s to the gradual erosion of domestic slum stereotypes (see Chapter Three). As British government investigators in Oldham reported in 1962, many slum-dwellers 'have an extremely strong attachment to their locality'.[97] Sociologist Norman Dennis, in his studies of the northeast English town of Sunderland during the 1960s, was told by the resident of one house that had been scheduled for slum clearance: 'It's been a happy home. That's the beauty. When you've lived in a house all your life since you've married you dinnit want to move.'[98] By the late twentieth century, such local loyalties were also becoming more widely recognized by observers of the squatter settlements of the developing world. It was pointed out that in Kibera residents liked the place because it was close to their jobs and food was cheap. One resident explained, 'I am here because the houses are nice, you don't have to stoop to enter the room and you can stand up inside.'[99]

Usually such attachments were explained away as shallow sentimentality. In 1979, for example, a former engineer for Bangalore's City Improvement Trust Board (which had recently been reconstituted as the Bangalore Development Authority) asserted smugly that the 'excuse for [residents] not moving out is often said to be sentimental attachment, but the fact is that they have developed a "slum mentality" and do not like to change'.[100] Occasionally, more astute observers acknowledged that neighbourhood attachments were anchored in sensible, although constrained, economic choices that sought to balance place of residence, work and affordable shopping. As the Calcutta Improvement Trust had conceded far back in the mid-1920s, 'Generally speaking, the working classes prefer the independence of bustee life to the better sanitation of a "chawl".'[101]

However, all such acknowledgements are overshadowed by the prevailing assumptions about slums. Even sympathetic observers can do no more than say low-income people tolerate slumland chaos because of their compromised livelihood choices: it is the best they can achieve in an unequal world. Father Joe Maier, an American missionary in Bangkok, explained in 2005:

> You have to understand something about the slums: they are not always places people want to leave. Given a choice between living in Tap Gaew or in one of the nice 'uptown' neighborhoods, there is no question. But it's not a question of choice. Slum people get used to their own community. They form established neighborhoods that have a cohesive integrity. Some slums in Bangkok have been home to families for three consecutive generations, and more or less happily.[102]

Likewise in Africa, progressive researchers allow that 'informal settle-ments are made tolerable by those who inhabit them.'[103] Meanwhile, in Calcutta's Gobindapur Rail Colony Gate No. 1 squatter settlement, Badal Das, a skilled mechanic, tells his interviewer (who controls the interview process with his questions, and selects which answers to include in his report): '*I am used to this place*. I find it so convenient and congenial.'[104]

We can go deeper than this, however, notwithstanding the diffi-culties of penetrating slum stereotypes in order to connect with actual communities. Beyond outsiders' talk of shallow nostalgia and restricted life choices, there lies a largely ignored vernacular material order and a guiding idiomatic logic to the homes and neighbourhoods of dis-advantaged communities. The value of studying these positive aspects of disadvantaged communities was suggested in part by sociological research in the developed world. As Gerald Suttles observed after living in the Addams area of the Near West Side of Chicago in the mid- to late 1960s, the neighbourhood had been generally regarded as 'one of the oldest slums in Chicago', but 'Seen from the inside, however, the Addams area is intricately organized according to its own stand-ards.' Suttles speculated that it was 'possible for slum neighborhoods to work out a moral order that includes most of their residents'.[105] Such approaches were corroborated by parallel studies in the developing world. Turner's fieldwork in Peru between 1957 and 1965 is the best known. Marshall Clinard also realized from his experiences in India during the 1960s that 'Rather than being "disorganised", the slum often simply has developed its own organization, a type of organiza-tion usually regarded as unconventional by the middle class.'[106] Janice Perlman's *The Myth of Marginality* (1976), based upon research in Rio de Janeiro during the late 1960s and early 1970s, tackled the slum deceits head-on. Perlman acknowledged that 'From the outside, the typical favela seems a filthy, congested human antheap,' but went on to argue that

> Behind the apparent squalor is a community characterized
> by careful planning in the use of limited housing space and
> innovative construction techniques on hillsides considered
> too steep for building by urban developers. Dotting the area
> are permanent brick structures that represent the accumulated
> savings of families who have been building them little by little,

brick by brick. The sign of the local athletic club is newly painted, and the two men in front of it are neatly dressed in middle-class styles acceptable anywhere in the world. They are both wearing leather shoes and wrist watches, symbols of their achievement in the urban environment.[107]

Perlman used bourgeois symbols such as shoes and watches to symbolize achievement. This carries the risk of seeming to normalize inequality by redefining the 'slum-minded' as being much the same as 'normal' folk after all. There is, for example, a tendency amongst archaeologists to interpret domestic chinaware recovered from working-class housing sites within former 'slums' as evidence of quasi-bourgeois respectability, and to conclude that poor people were simply on the bottom step of an escalator ride into increasing well-being. Achievement in disadvantaged communities need not mimic mainstream expectations. Marie Huchzermeyer, drawing upon recent research in Africa, argues that

> It would be incorrect to portray informal settlement residents as merely passive victims of . . . hidden forces. While the real lack of options must be acknowledged, informal settlements would not exist without the will or resolve of thousands of households or individual men and women, who assess their situation and decide actively to connect their lives to the city or its fringes through a particular informal settlement, and by consciously navigating among (and at times resisting or defying) players whom they know exploit their existence. Collectively and individually, the residents of informal settlements create and shape urban space (even as tenants), often against the odds. It is important to recognise the personal endeavour, ingenuity, intimacy, complexity, human scale, political action, small-scale market activity and cultural and artistic expression in these settlements.[108]

Homes

The 'little palaces' in low-income neighbourhoods are a key example of purposeful energy and achievement within 'slums'. Historians of Victorian and Edwardian England have probed the rational realignment

of space and function within the low-income rental housing of the
urban working classes, undertaken by tenants to suit their needs and
aspirations.[109] White argued that in even the most menacing neighbourhoods of London's East End, houses were scrubbed 'fanatically
clean' and kept 'spotless', and were often decorated with window boxes
as 'symbols of [a] careful, bright home'.[110] Similar behaviour can also
be found in the poorest city neighbourhoods of the developing world
today. This is not purely decorative and functionally irrelevant. Nor
does it merely attempt to approximate mainstream norms. It expresses
idiomatically what outsiders allege is lacking in slumland: good order
and strategic direction.

Low-income homemaking aims in part simply to make unpleas-
ant surroundings more tolerable. However, it also seeks to tame and
possess those surroundings: to make them intimate and personal.
Historical archaeologists have found nineteenth-century evidence of
these attempts in domestic ornaments recovered from 'slum' sites in
cities such as Boston, New York, San Francisco, Sydney, Melbourne
and Cape Town.[111] Since the early twentieth century, social workers
in Britain had also begun to draw attention to sensible patterns in
low-income domestic behaviour. Manchester University Settlement's
studies of Ancoats during the 1930s drew attention to 'the people's
pride in their homes', which was expressed, for example, in the application of 'fresh paint to decayed woodwork and new paper to walls whose
crumbling plaster would hardly hold it'.[112] The investigators marvelled
at 'how clean many of the houses are and what infinite trouble is taken
to "beautify" crumbling walls and defective woodwork':[113]

'Stoning' [polishing with a stone] the window-sills and the strip
of pavement in front of the house as well as the doorsteps is
still practically universal and the investigators noted with interest that most of the women chose bright coloured casement
cloth for their curtains. A good strong blue predominated
with golden brown as second favourite. Ragged lace curtains,
such as would be seen in a slum district in London, do not
appear in Ancoats.[114]

In Bristol, as the Barton Hill slum clearance scheme unfolded during
the 1950s and '60s,

Even the inhabitants of solitary houses marooned in streets which were mainly boarded-up continued to sweep the pavement and keep the customary vase of flowers or china ornament in the front window.[115]

Similar findings were reported in other British cities in the 1970s. In Liverpool, even 'among the smallest houses, there are polished knockers and often bright front doors painted in a variety of colours,'[116] and 'Three-piece suites and colour television sets vie with smart prams and chopper bikes, in rooms which open straight onto the street.'[117] In Glasgow, a social worker at the Maryhill slum clearance area remarked that the condemned tenement buildings were 'brightly decorated and furnished', and kept 'spotlessly clean'.[118]

Homeliness and the accumulation of domestic possessions are also noted by slummers in the developing world. In Kibera, local resident Charles Arori showed Bendiksen around his home, explaining: 'I put these newspapers up to decorate my house – for their beauty. It makes the house look beautiful, and it allows you to see everything, like cockroaches.'[119] Robert Neuwirth, a twenty-first-century slummer who lived for a time in Kibera, remarked that its residents 'routinely give their mud huts little homely touches'.[120] In Cape Town's massive Khayelitsha settlement, one-room shacks are 'meticulously maintained in the midst of overflowing refuse'.[121] In the Bhaskara Rao Peta 'slum', located in Vijayawada, the regional capital of coastal Andhra Pradesh, 'Although people live in huts, the walls and floors are plastered with cowdung which is a free disinfectant. They keep the surroundings . . . clean.'[122] In Mumbai, 'plants and flowers are planted in front of the houses in improvised pots – cans and vehicle tyres.'[123] Neuwirth, who lived for a time in Dharavi, commented that Mumbai's slum homes were kept 'amazingly clean inside'.[124] In Mysore's hutments,

There are very few houses which do not possess photos. The most common portraits selected by these slum-dwellers are those of Lord Venkateswara of Tirumalai, Sri Ranganatha and Sri Saibaba. The portrait of Lord Sri Rama is also found in a number of houses.[125]

A study of one low-income community in southern Delhi calculated that although 93 per cent of its inhabitants lived in one-room houses,

76 per cent of them had access to television.[126] In 2012, it was estimated that two-thirds of the inhabitants of Bangkok's 'slums', which housed over one million people, owned a CD player, a mobile phone and a washing machine.[127] In Kibera, resident Andrew Dirango remarked to Bendiksen,

> I don't know how you see my house, but to me it's beautiful. I appreciate it even if it is small. I have my bed here – it's comfortable. I have my seats, the sofa, I have my little kitchen, and I can put my television and CD player there, my speakers there, my aquarium there.[128]

Homemaking like this not only attempts to establish internal order within low-income households; it aims to create an external order by positioning them relative to their neighbours. Social worker Sidney Jacobs, working in the Maryhill slum clearance area in Glasgow in the early 1970s, learned that the district comprised a mosaic of 'roughs' and 'respectables'.[129] People's homemaking skills made explicit each household's place within this social mosaic. Suttles argued that in Chicago's Addams district, orderly homes – in which the 'curtains are of lace, the bedspreads are chenille, the furniture elaborate with design and doilies, the colors light and delicate' – were intended by their occupants to act as 'a "show place" to demonstrate the housewife's diligence and domestic skills'.[130] Liverpool's Inner Area Study likewise identified 'a hierarchy of status' within and between low-income neighbourhoods, which was explicitly demonstrated by home decoration:

> Outward appearances are staunchly maintained. Front steps, window sills, stretches of front pavement and even back lanes are regularly scrubbed. Neat lace curtains, washed every few weeks, are discreetly pulled back to reveal brass ornaments proudly displayed or football rosettes pinned up. Rooms are still wallpapered annually, partly against damp, and house fronts regularly painted and rendered by those who have bought their houses.[131]

In Dharavi, too, some astute observers noted a complicated local social hierarchy that was reflected in distinctions between simple shelters made from tarpaulin and bamboo poles; huts with walls of planks, sacking or flattened tins, roofs of coconut leaves, thatch, tin, and mud floors smeared with cow dung; and small 'pukka' dwellings with brick or mud walls, cement or stone slab floors, and asbestos sheets or tiles for roofing.[132] In Kibera, Charles Arori said proudly of his small home (which boasted a television set), 'Our neighbors regard me as "first class" within the slums.'[133]

THE MOST STRIKING EXPRESSION of the strategic purpose behind low-income homemaking is self-help home improvement. Evidence of small-scale but accumulating home improvements exists from the late nineteenth and early twentieth centuries. Manchester University Settlement's Ancoats study found that

> Quite a number of the tenants had had electric lighting installed at their own expense, through the Corporation's assisted wiring scheme; others had put in improved gas lighting with switches at the doors.[134]

A generational shift was simultaneously occurring as working-class families fanned out from rental accommodation in the inner cities to owner-occupied houses in the suburbs. This trend was especially evident in Australia and North America. However, the most dramatic evidence of self-help home improvement is to be found in the initial construction and subsequent consolidation of low-income housing in the developing world since the mid-twentieth century. Scholars have called this incremental process 'urban informality'. Explaining the term, the geographer Alan Gilbert remarked, 'Informality is the process whereby people engage in painstaking effort to construct dwellings often years before services reach them.'[135] Gilbert's research focus, like Turner's, is Latin America, and it is here and in the neighbouring Caribbean that vernacular housing has received the greatest attention. Florian Urban, for example, has showcased the accumulating effects of informal homemaking in Puerto Rico's La Perla district, which Oscar Lewis had characterized in the 1960s as a slum irrevocably caught in a culture of poverty.[136] However, it has been suggested that the urban poor in South Asia and Africa, similarly, in taking the initiative through squatter housing to address 'their need for shelter, have demonstrated extraordinary ingenuity'.[137]

Turner called such self-help housing 'architecture that worked', and concluded that 'Some of the poorest dwellings, materially speaking, were clearly the best, socially speaking.' He praised 'The initiative, ingenuity, perseverance, and hope so evident' in squatter settlements.[138] A resident of the Los Barrios favela in Caracas, Venezuela's capital city, described how

> When we arrived here, this was just mountainside – it was wild . . . What you see was constructed little by little, with sacrifice. It wasn't like this before. This used to be a shanty with four cardboard walls . . . We've added a lot. My wife loves painting ceramics, decorating it this way, and maintaining the home where we have formed our family. I wouldn't think of moving from here . . . No, it has not been easy at all, but we've done it. We have been making sacrifices and, gradually, we've come out ahead.[139]

In the favelas of Rio de Janeiro, likewise, 'The shacks became houses, built up with more solid materials, painted anew; sometimes it gained another floor.'[140] Perlman argued that the

> Houses are built with a keen eye to comfort and efficiency, given the climate and building materials. Much care is evident in the arrangement of furniture and the neat cleanliness of each room. Houses often boast colourfully painted doors and shutters, and flowers or plants on the window sill. Cherished objects are displayed with love and pride.[141]

Neuwirth, who lived for a time in Rio's notorious Rocinha favela, remarked that from 'a distance there seemed to be no roads, no yards, no restful space of any kind. Just a beehive of human habitations,' but the district in fact exhibited a 'dynamic' and 'organic' coherence that was best expressed in its evolving self-help housing: 'a mud or cardboard hut gives way to wood, and wood gives way to brick, and brick to reinforced concrete.'[142] In the Brazilian city of Recife, likewise, where over half the population was by the late twentieth century living in squatter settlements,

> At first, shacks tend to be erected out of wood, plastic and cardboard and have soil floors. At a later stage they can be

strengthened and improved with bricks and a variety of other materials, such as cement, concrete or tiles. Most shacks have a television, radio, an old refrigerator, a stove and a bed. Many people sleep together in the same room or in the same bed. The shacks are built next to each other, with thin walls.[143]

In India the grass-roots activist Jockin Arputham noted that Dharavi's inhabitants

> will make use of anything – gunny [sack], posters, plastic sheets, bamboo, palm leaves, packing cases. They always start with cheap and fragile materials. Once they feel secure and know their house won't be demolished, they'll improve it – buying one sheet of tin at a time, until a whole wall is replaced; then a wooden door-frame; then maybe a brick or cement wall, and Bangalore tiles for the roof. Then, if they prosper, they'll build a second storey, cement or tile the roof.
>
> On the pavements, it's different. There is no security, so you don't build with the same care. Even so, very cramped dwellings are organized with great economy and foresight. They are always kept clean inside, however great the squalor of the surroundings. Demolition has become routine for the pavement dwellers of Bombay. They are very fatalistic. Demolish today, I'll be back tomorrow.[144]

Sometimes the improvements made are so subtle as to be easily overlooked by outsiders: in Calcutta, shacks crammed alongside the railway lines have creepers and vines with pumpkins and bottle-gourds cultivated so as to grow over their roofs, and herbs being tended alongside.[145] Yet as Jeremy Seabrook observed,

> in spite of the ramshackle quality of these living places, it is wrong to judge by appearances. What these self-built shanties speak of is not squalor and degradation, but of the ingenuity and inventiveness of people who have nothing but who nonetheless provide themselves and their families with adequate shelter and a life of dignity.[146]

Communities

Although outsiders have periodically acknowledged self-help initiatives by individual households in slumland, the usual assumption is that these efforts are random, unsynchronized with others and therefore unsustainable in the long term. They are seen as yet another example of the disorganized chaos of slums. However, vernacular house building and home improvement are often undertaken cooperatively, and their cumulative effects can benefit whole neighbourhoods and districts. Collective action is often generated by dire necessity. As a resident in Nairobi's Mukuru district explained,

> We are about fifteen families on this one plot owned by one landlord . . . All fifteen families on this plot use the one pit latrine which you can see outside there. There is also one common bathroom which is adjacent to it and whose entry is covered by a polythene bag . . . Because we are many, we have to organize, throughout the day, on how to use the pit latrine and particularly the bathroom.[147]

However, such collaboration can open up further opportunities for mutual improvement that gradually enhance community life. Geddes, writing in India in 1915, was ahead of his time when he applauded the benefits that flowed from 'these . . . ties of attachment between place and people, this web of social solidarity, this estimable civic unit!'[148] Early in the twenty-first century the head of the United Nations Human Settlements Programme, based in Nairobi, allowed that through such collaborations and 'Against all odds, slum dwellers have developed economically rational and innovative shelter solutions for themselves.'[149] As an American researcher said of the Lang Wat Pathum Wanaram 'slum' district in Bangkok in 2009,

> it is a place of vitality and dynamism, not desperation. The basic amenities are present, food is plentiful, the prosperity of economic growth over the last four decades has trickled into the slum in the form of motorcycles, televisions, refrigerators, and the ubiquitous cell phone.[150]

IN THESE OBSERVATIONS, the aspect of life most remarked upon is that notwithstanding economic disadvantage these places hum with economic life. Their inhabitants are not paralysed by disadvantage and exploitation; they devise strategies to counteract and overcome them. As Wiebe emphasized in his *Social Life in an Indian Slum*,

> The people of Chennanagar are very poor, yet they do make ends meet in relation to the possibilities their environment provides and in relation to their own ingenious ways of finding work, gaining little bits of added income and helping each other out.[151]

Historians have provided glimpses of the resilient local economies of working-class communities in late nineteenth- and early twentieth-century cities. In London, for example,

> The local network played a central part in day-to-day survival when times were difficult. You knew or would quickly hear on the grapevine where to go for cheap or free food and fuel, who would give you credit, where there might be homework given out or a child wanted for errands or child care, what firm was taking on hands, how to get a reference or charitable help.[152]

Studies by social workers and sociologists since the mid-twentieth century add to this picture. Manchester University Settlement's social surveys during the 1930s concluded emphatically that 'Ancoats people are not a derelict population.'[153] However, two other developments were more significant in directing attention to purposeful economic activity in disadvantaged city communities, especially in the developing world. The first was the growing influence from the 1980s of neo-liberal ideas upon opinion- and policy-makers. Neoliberals applauded any suggestion that grass-roots entrepreneurialism and self-help might endure notwithstanding the chaos of slums. Second, social science researchers during the late twentieth and early twenty-first centuries created 'informality' and the 'Global South' as a major new study area. It was in these contexts that Seabrook's *Life and Labour in a Bombay Slum* argued that 'Almost everyone in the slum is engaged on some vital economic purpose, however chaotic and unco-ordinated it may appear.'[154]

Neoliberals delighted in providing commentaries on 'slums' such as Dharavi and Kibera, because they showed that local entrepreneurialism could seemingly flourish notwithstanding the surrounding chaos and the ineffectiveness of government interventions. Neoliberalism (which is discussed further in Chapter Seven) celebrates stories about successful small business activities. It gives publicity to the efforts by micro-credit advocates such as the Self-Employed Women's Association in India (which established the SEWA Bank in 1974) and Muhammad Yunus (founder of the Grameen Bank in 1983) to encourage the pooling and effective use of local savings. It endorses Turner's advocacy of self-help housing as a preferable alternative to costly government housing programmes. It is especially appreciative of small-scale family businesses and unregulated competitive markets. Dharavi became the world's best-known 'slum' because it most obviously expressed these principles. It featured on the cover of *National Geographic* in 2007,[155] and was also profiled by the *Observer* newspaper:

> Mumbai's labyrinthine Dharavi slum. A 175 ha maze of dark alleys and corrugated shacks, Dharavi swarms with more than a million residents.
>
> But if you have the patience to look closer, you will find here one of the most inspiring economic models in Asia. Dharavi may be one of the world's largest slums, but it is by far its most prosperous – a thriving business centre propelled by thousands of micro-entrepreneurs . . . A new estimate by economists of the output of the slum is as impressive as it seems improbable: $1.4bn a year.[156]

During the furore occasioned by *Slumdog Millionaire*'s release in 2009, one commentator reflected that

> Dharavi teems with dynamism, creativity and entrepreneurship, in industries such as garment manufacturing, embroidery, pottery, leather, plastics and food processing. It is estimated that the annual turnover from Dharavi's small businesses is between $50 and $100 million. Dharavi's lanes are lined with cellphone retailers and cybercafes, and according to surveys by Microsoft Research India, the slum's residents exhibit a remarkably high absorption of new technologies.[157]

Meanwhile contemporary social science has begun to draw attention to the 'informal city' of the Global South. Realization stirs that informal and largely unregulated economic activities dominate the livelihoods of most of the world's urban dwellers. However, the persistence of slum deceits means that most analysts still consider these activities as 'located within the "informal" and/or "unorganized" sector' of the economy.[158] It is calculated that in African cities on average 75 per cent of basic human needs are provided through the informal sector; in some cities up to 90 per cent of new housing is built informally and over half their adult populations are engaged in unregistered employment. In Kibera, the conventional measuring stick for such calculations in Africa, it is said that

> The informal sector economy is vibrant . . . and is seen in the hundreds of kiosks throughout the entire settlement. Virtually anything needed for daily life is available including food, household goods, charcoal, clothes, beds, car parts, and even coffins. There are also stalls where carpenters, tailors, shoemakers, and metal welders advertise their services as well as photograph shops, repair kiosks and barbershops. Many people sell meat and fish. Very few of these businesses have permanent structures or locations and most kiosks are located on the veranda of the owner's house or on the roadside.[159]

This emerging attention to neighbourhood 'micro'-enterprises is matched by interest in 'micro'-credit initiatives. The formal banking sector does not engage with 'slums', so savings and loans are arranged informally through relatives, friends, employers and private moneylenders. As researchers have come to recognize these dynamics, they have begun to question assumptions that the urban poor are economically disorganized and clueless. Social science researchers overlap with neoliberals in highlighting grass-roots organizations such as Mahila Milan (founded in 1986 in Bombay by poor women) and South Africa's Homeless People's Federation (established in 1995) that have successfully launched savings and credit schemes.

Observers of urban informality in the developing world also confirm a fact detected by historians in the nineteenth century: that slumland labour and entrepreneurialism not only give an internal economic order to working-class communities but also help to underpin the formal economies of their host cities. Scholars of Latin America have demonstrated how important even apparently marginal activities such as rag-picking and collecting bottles are to the formal economy.[160] In India, also, some researchers began to acknowledge in the late twentieth century the importance of 'slums' in providing cheap labour for manufacturing, construction work and retailing, and domestic help for middle-class residential areas. Rudolf Heredia said of the 'slums' in Bombay that 'without their labour power, the city would grind to a halt.'[161] When Yamuna Pushta was destroyed in 2004, one critic pointed out that the workforce housed in such areas had constructed

> the buildings, the monuments, the flyovers, the hospitals, the shopping malls, the commercial centres, the very homes you and I live in. More importantly, it is because of them, that our quality of life is so greatly enhanced. Our cooks, maids, drivers, peons, clerks, garbage and rag pickers, road sweepers, electricians, plumbers, and so many, from the work force, live in slums or resettlement colonies or inhabit those localities.[162]

THERE IS ALSO, periodically, recognition that a well-developed social life exists within disadvantaged city neighbourhoods. Notwithstanding the prevailing stereotypes of slums as a chaotic mess of short-term sojourners, historians have found significant continuities of residence within working-class communities during the nineteenth century, and contemporary sociological studies have identified similar patterns of residence from the early twentieth century. In Manchester's Ancoats district, surveyed in the late 1930s, 41 per cent of the sample had lived in the same house for over twenty years.[163] During the 1950s, likewise, Young and Willmott's study of Bethnal Green and Hilda Jennings's study of Barton Hill found that 'long-standing residence is the usual thing.'[164] Surveys of disadvantaged city communities in India in the late twentieth century repeatedly found that half or more of their sample had lived there for at least five, and often twenty years and more.

There is also compelling evidence of social consensus and stability within these neighbourhoods, notwithstanding slum stereotypes of antisocial behaviour and communal violence. Historians sometimes glimpse these overlooked local dynamics. Former residents of the

Rothschild Buildings tenement block in London's East End told White that 'The community was very close . . . You had that sense of warmth, of friendliness among the people.' One of them recalled,

> We'd all rejoice in one another's weddings and all mourned each other's tragedies. That was a wonderful thing. There's no such thing any more. If anybody died, everybody mourned with them, like one big family.[165]

There were local rules of behaviour to underpin such activities: as one London clergyman noted early in the twentieth century, 'These people have their own code. It differs largely from ours, but it is a code, and infractions of it were intensely resented by the people themselves.'[166]

Social workers and sociologists confirm such findings in the present day. Suttles's suggestion that a 'slum' might well be 'intricately organized according to its own standards' has been influential throughout the world.[167] His findings reinforced earlier studies, such as those of Herbert Gans, who concluded from his fieldwork in Boston's West End during the late 1950s that

> the highly developed system of informal social control in the West End makes it possible for people with different standards of living and ethnic backgrounds to live together peaceably, tolerant of those with problems.[168]

In Britain, a resident of Bethnal Green told Young and Willmott, 'I suppose people who come here from outside think it's an awful place, but us established ones like it. Here you can just open the door and say hello to everybody.'[169] Jennings, in her Bristol study, argued that residents in the Barton Hill district had developed 'a recognized minimum standard below which few were willing to be seen to fall'. She relayed the local shopkeepers' consensus that at 'Barton Hill people are so friendly and neighbourly', and she commented that there 'was no street . . . the inhabitants of which individually and together did not claim that they were "like one big family" or "one happy family"'.[170] Such internal cohesion could flourish alongside the violence that outsiders drew attention to. Residents in Salford, Greater Manchester, which had featured in world news reports during the wave of anti-police rioting in English cities during 1992, assured a researcher that 'It's safe for locals but not strangers in the area' and explained 'you are required to obey certain rules as well as to simply "be known".'[171]

In the developing world since the 1960s, an undercurrent of sociological research has rejected Oscar Lewis's suggestions of a divergent slumland culture of poverty, and instead supported Suttles's concept of a 'moral order' within low-income communities. Siddiqui and Hossain's *Life in the Slums of Calcutta* (1969) argued that 'Despite the insanitary conditions and crowding in these "bustees", life in them is generally well-organised, relatively free of serious crime, and co-operative.'[172] Sociological fieldwork in Calcutta during the 1980s supported their findings, and emphasized the

> close community life which the slum dwellers adhere to. The BASTI people know each other very well, their children play together, there is a relationship of mutual help which often crosses the religious boundary, they take part in many collective activities such as in social and religious functions, in development programmes, in trade union and party activities and so on. One can often notice the people playing cards or just chatting and . . . joking with each other while standing at a street corner. The exchange of social visits among the neighbours was also very frequent. It can also be observed that the social groups and institutions such as family, marriage, kinship, and religion are as functional as in any cross-section of Indian population.[173]

Wiebe's influential 1975 study of the Chennanagar district in Madras likewise contended that its inhabitants were 'not simply an aggregate of disorganized peoples'.[174] Wiebe agreed that such communities needed external assistance to provide services, better health and education, but he argued that the success of such interventions hinged upon local residents being 'recognized as able to understand their own needs and expectations'. Wiebe demonstrated that notwithstanding Chennanagar's informality, its residents had a strongly developed sense of family, caste, and political organization. They prioritized homeliness: 'almost all the people . . . have invested what are to them considerable sums of money in their households.' They put value upon orderly community life: there were shopping areas and temples, and residents shared in the major festivals of each year.[175] In Delhi, a study of Dalit community life noted that

Very often, slums are projected in a negative manner and are blamed for all the ills of the city that include pollution, lawlessness and overcrowding. Little appreciation is given to the fact that these micro-units of community life are constituted by individuals capable of making rational choices, the victims of circumstances, who are constantly striving for a better life in the face of deprivation and hostility.[176]

Even in notorious Dharavi, regarded by many as the vortex of slumland chaos, researchers demonstrated that the district's actual internal dynamics are 'entirely different', with close-knit networks organized according to place of origin, language, religion, caste and occupation.[177] *The Times* recorded similar findings anecdotally in Nairobi, where Africa's slumland woes were supposedly most concentrated, citing no less an authority than u.s. president Barack Obama's younger brother, a Nairobi 'slum' dweller, as saying 'Here I am surrounded by friends and family and feel safe and secure.'[178]

Idiomatic codes of behaviour and unwritten rules prevail in even the seemingly most disadvantaged and vicious of places. In the Slaughterhouse neighbourhood of Bangkok's Klong Toey district, for example, 'the Slaughterhouse lives day to day and survives on the unwritten laws. Laws that no one uptown really knows about or wants to know about.'[179] As a woman living in Caracas's Los Barrios favela remarked,

> If those guys from up there are going to shoot it out with the guys from down here, you close the door and hide – you're fine. They don't get involved with you. They don't go into your house. The problem is between them, thug-to-thug, as my grandson says.[180]

Explaining the local rules and benefits of these gang confrontations, a barrio resident in the Nicaraguan capital of Managua said,

> the gang looks after the neighbourhood and screws others; it protects us and allows us to feel a little bit safer, to live our lives a little bit more easily . . . Without them, things would be much worse for us.[181]

The informal codes that bind communities together are most visible when channelled through local organizations. Studies of social life in the informal settlements of the developing world have increasingly drawn attention to the role of residents' associations in mediating local disputes, lobbying state agencies and politicians, attracting sympathetic media coverage, partnering with NGOs, and organizing recreational events, welfare activities, micro-credit self-help and environmental improvements. As one analyst remarked, low-income communities are 'beehives of activity, movement and group life . . . Slums abound in "committees".'[182] Acknowledging this tendency for locals to band together for mutual benefit, the United Nations in 1996 drew attention to the rich 'social economy' of low-income neighbourhoods.[183] This is evident in organizations such as the Urban Poor Consortium in Jakarta, and Muungano Wa Wanavijiji in Nairobi which grew out of the anti-evictions protests in Kenya during the late 1990s and early 2000s. In India, neighbourhood organizations are supported by national umbrella associations like Mahila Milan and the National Slum Dwellers' Federation. The latter, which grew out of anti-eviction protests in Bombay during the 1970s, played a leading role during the 1990s in launching an international federation, Shack/Slum Dwellers International. Until the evictions and demolitions of 2004 in New Delhi,

A world within a world existed in Yamuna Pushta. Schools, medical and healthcare centres, self-help groups, shops, restaurants, crèches, small businesses and various social organizations, worked closely with the community, bringing about immense positive change in the lives of the residents.[184]

THE HARDEST THING to grasp in attempting to think beyond slum deceits is that the seemingly chaotic layouts of disadvantaged city districts actually display a quirky spatial logic. They have been fashioned by the people who live in them into what Gans called 'an effective environment'.[185] The concessions periodically made regarding economic and social organization within low-income districts all leave the assumed fundamental reality of slums unchallenged. The observers who make these concessions still call these districts 'slums', and characterize their residents as battling towards normalcy, earning our respect by doing so and deserving our support to become more like us. What has never been accepted is that these disadvantaged environments – notwithstanding their many deficiencies – might yet embody effective vernacular arrangements that have been designed by their inhabitants to maximize their opportunities for enhancing economic and social life. To admit this would be to give up the word 'slum' and the deceits that it perpetuates.

The vernacular logic of self-built housing was highlighted by Turner in the 1970s and '80s and has met with guarded approval by governments, the United Nations and international development organizations, in large part because it accords well with neoliberal thinking and can be subsumed within conventional wisdom about slums and appropriate programmes to 'improve' them. However Turner's advocacy of local self-help was not limited to individual homes or even clusters of homes: he was thinking about broader neighbourhoods and communities. In reference to the International Year of Shelter for the Homeless in 1987, Turner pointed out that low-income people were responsible for 'actually building most homes and neighbourhoods in many Third World cities'.[186] Indian researcher Ashok Ranjan Basu drew a similar conclusion after studying squatter housing in New Delhi during the late 1980s: 'the vast majority of Third World housing is built in small increments over long periods, and communities take shape slowly over time as needs are felt and money becomes available.'[187]

Basu added that vernacular fashioning of homes and communities 'has failed to win wide acceptance as a solution to housing problems as it does not conform to elitist values'.[188] Sporadically it is realized that low-income environments have been purposefully shaped by their inhabitants, with the caveat that their activities are constrained by limited knowledge and restricted opportunities. Thus the 'slum' environment can be acknowledged as working, after a fashion, for its inhabitants' benefit, but it remains a 'slum' environment nonetheless. According to Patrick McAuslan in the mid-1980s,

> The true builders and planners of Third World cities are the urban poor. They build their houses and establish their settlements where they can, largely illegally: on unused land, on hills and over swamps. The land is illegally occupied or illegally subdivided; the houses ignore building and health codes; the settlements ignore zoning and subdivision regulations and the 'Master Plans' beloved of city planners.[189]

McAuslan's comment was bold for its times. However, we need to go further and conceive these places as living environments that are actually made to work socially, culturally and economically by their inhabitants. Effective living environments do not necessarily require the rectilinear street grids and formal civic centres favoured by mainstream urban planners, nor the allotment sizes offered by upmarket property developers. Neighbourhoods may place greater value on seemingly more mundane things, as Arputham noted when he explained the National Slum Dwellers' Federation's advocacy of toilet blocks for disadvantaged communities:

> In India, a public toilet is not simply a toilet. Public toilets are [a] community centre where people meet to exchange news about what is happening in the community, or in the family, or what happened the other day or last night. When you go to a public toilet, you get all the news about the settlement.[190]

It was Geddes, working in India in the early twentieth century, who was among the first outsiders to see through slum stereotypes and appreciate the functionality and even the aesthetics of neighbourhoods that were being targeted for slum clearance simply because 'we . . . do obeisance to the straight lines of the drawing board and the set square.'[191] Geddes championed vernacular spatial arrangements. He argued that 'in European cities, but far more obviously in Indian ones, the townsfolk are still very largely villagers' and as such their preferred spatial arrangements recreated a 'village-like layout' with trees, public spaces, narrow lanes for shade and quiet, and household gardens.[192] In the second half of the twentieth century the community activist Jane Jacobs and the historian Sam Bass Warner, Jr, argued much the same thing in relation to effective living environments in American cities.[193] The British geographer D. J. Dwyer also echoed Geddes when in 1979 he criticized the 'almost total dedication to what might be called "paper planning"' in the developing world and regretted that 'spontaneous settlement, being unplanned, unpretentious and apparently chaotic, is usually either totally neglected in the delineation of the image of the future or else condemned.'[194]

This line of thinking was reinforced during the 1970s and '80s by a series of publications by the American architect Amos Rapoport. He argued that apparently informal and spontaneous settlements, like all human environments, do not just happen; they are designed in the sense that purposeful changes are made to the physical environment through a series of choices among the alternatives available.[195]

He described them as a type of 'vernacular environment', which, despite the severe constraints upon those who fashioned them, was 'vastly superior' – socially, economically, culturally – to those designed by professional planners.[196] He recommended that

> Often one needs to learn to ignore building materials, garbage in spaces, and the like; one needs to become aware of relationships rather than only elements. Since the former are the more important, high-quality environments can be created from torn sacking, cardboard, rusty metal, bits of wood, and other such materials.[197]

Informal settlements provide effective living environments precisely because of the 'chaos' that is attributed to them: living and working conditions that appear chaotic to outsiders are, as Rapoport recognized, 'extremely open-ended'.[198] They evolve according to their users' direct needs and aspirations. Thus, railway tracks are appropriated as walkways by surrounding informal settlements; shared arrangements might be devised for cooking, bathing and toilet needs; work activities might encroach on households' sleeping areas and spill out into the streets. Perlman's studies of favela life in Rio de Janeiro during the late 1960s and early 1970s led her to conclude that

> because it is the outcome of many incremental decisions based on human needs, the favela is well-designed. Friends and families live close together; walkways are distributed where the need requires; public spaces emerge and recede according to use; and tacit agreements not to develop certain areas are obeyed.[199]

Neuwirth recognized in the early twenty-first century that Rio's Rocinha district, although illegal in a formal planning sense, had been fashioned by an informal planning process whereby 'Rocinha homeowners still negotiate with their neighbors if they want to add onto their homes and, usually, will not go ahead with a plan if anyone objects.'[200]

Vernacular design and usage – although they might transgress professional planning principles and municipal regulations, and also mainstream social conventions about desirable boundaries between shared and private use of space – maximize the functional use of available space, materials and services, and express a loose neighbourhood consensus about appropriate layout and activities. Studies of the Indian city of Indore during the 1980s drew attention to the development of

> a complex hierarchy of . . . house extensions: spaces in front
> of the home that are nominally a part of the public realm, but
> have acquired a private character through use, and through
> various physical modifications.[201]

The researchers also noted that 'in existing slums and unplanned settlements, trees are conspicuously planted, maintained and protected by the inhabitants', serving as neighbourhood reference points and providing shady substitutes 'for the arcades, porches and covered outdoor spaces that are a part of the *normal* urban fabric'.[202]

Through such common-sense practices, vernacular design choices carry with them the potential for incremental improvements over time as flimsy huts are refashioned into more durable dwellings, and residents' groups mould the local landscape, filling in swamps, making roads and pathways, building and cleaning out drains. Inhabitants also collaborate to obtain more reliable water supplies and electricity, create places for public meetings and sports, and establish schools and places of worship. In so doing, 'such settlements act as forward moving vehicles of social and economic change.'[203] Alan Gilbert observed that in Latin America

> Self-help housing has . . . helped to improve the housing stock.
> What begins as a shanty soon becomes a consolidated house.
> Gradually, electricity and water are installed in the neighbour-
> hood, the roads are paved, bus services begin operating, and
> schools are built . . . Service improvements have permitted vast
> areas of shanty towns to be transformed into proper suburbs.[204]

Dwyer noted that throughout the developing world

> a feature of every spontaneous settlement is initiative; and
> many settlements also demonstrate the ability of substantial

segments of the urban poor to mobilize resources of incremental capital for the piecemeal purchase of building materials, impressive resources of construction skills and, at the most elemental level, impressive resources of simple human energy for building purposes.[205]

Such mobilization transcends basic survival needs and household-centred incremental improvements: in Rio de Janeiro's Vidigal favela, for example, the community has transformed a rubbish dump into a public garden:

> Now the garden is a thriving community hub, where residents can meet to celebrate, exercise, learn and create. Local artists have contributed vibrant murals and sculptures to the landscape, recycling any remaining pieces of metal, timber and plastic left over from the garden's rubbish dump days into colourful creations.

Vidigal exemplifies the aspirations, skills and gritty achievements from which 'little palaces' are made and stable communities sustained. But at Vidigal, nonetheless, the 'future of the park . . . is unclear, with rapid gentrification in the area threatening to see the neighbourhood transformed into hotels and shops'.[206] Similar aspirations, skills and achievements were evident at Yamuna Pushta; they were evident at District Six. Then the demolition crews arrived.

SEVEN

BUILDING COMMUNITIES?

The United Nations estimated that in 1990 'almost half the urban population in developing regions were living in slums.' That equated to 689 million people.[1] During the late twentieth century, however, there were signs that governments, development agencies and private developers might at last begin to collaborate effectively with low-income communities in the developing world to upgrade slumland's 'little palaces' and enhance the livelihoods of their inhabitants. Urban community development projects in India since the 1960s, and in Latin America since the 1970s, had been criticized as top-down experiments that attempted too little and were overshadowed by slum clearance. The mass evictions carried out in Indian cities during the state of emergency in the late 1970s supported this judgement. However, during the 1980s and '90s, self-help upgrading projects in disadvantaged city neighbourhoods expanded rapidly throughout the developing world, assisted by the United Nations and the World Bank, supported by all tiers of government, international development agencies and NGOs, and partnered by local community organizations. This trend seemed to have in common what had been lacking before in the slum wars: respect for vernacular housing and neighbourhood design, sensitivity to the broader strengths and aspirations of 'urban informality', and advocacy of community participation in designing and implementing self-help projects. These values were made explicit in Istanbul in 1996 when a second United Nations Conference on Human Settlements (HABITAT II), held twenty years after the first such meeting in Vancouver, issued an international plan of action called the Istanbul Declaration.

LOCAL PARTICIPATION was said to underpin these new possibilities, and 'slum' upgrading rather than heavy-handed clearance was espoused as the new goal. By ensuring the participation of low-income communities in slum upgrading projects, it seemed that the earlier limitations of Britain's reconditioning approach and of urban community development schemes in India and Latin America could be overcome. India continued to provide a leading example. Its Environmental Improvement of Urban Slums programme, begun during the 1970s, expanded during the 1980s as upgrading of low-income housing, rather than redevelopment and relocation, was increasingly built into the central government's five-year planning cycles. The Indian Planning Commission, releasing the Sixth Five Year Plan (1980–85),

> proposed that the strategy of attempting massive relocation of slums in urban areas should be given up in the future. Such relocation not only involves substantial hardship to those affected in terms of loss of easy access to employment centres and other amenities, but results in unnecessary destruction of existing housing capital, however sub-standard it may be. It is, therefore, important that substantially increased investments be made in the environmental improvement of slum areas. Low cost sanitation and drainage are key areas of much needed investment in the slums of our cities.[2]

The Urban Basic Services (later the Urban Basic Services for the Poor) Programme, begun in 1986 with UNICEF, state and central government funding, aimed to work with local communities to provide both environmental improvements (sanitation, community water taps, latrines) and community development initiatives aimed especially at women and children: health care and health education, nutrition, family planning, crèches, pre-schools and vocational training.

India's largest cities vied to implement the national programmes. Hyderabad's trailblazing community development project expanded during the 1980s and '90s with funding support from UNICEF and later from the British government, and was widely applauded for having 'evolved out of the felt needs, hopes and aspirations of the slum dwellers'.[3] Environmental improvements there included self-help housing, road upgrades, drainage, water supply, community lavatories, street lighting, parks and playgrounds. It was emphasized that 'Self-help is encouraged in these construction activities. Almost all slum dwellers are involved in the construction of their houses working whenever they get time during the nights.'[4] Community development and livelihood activities included health care, nutrition, education, employment training (such as sewing machine repair, typewriting and shorthand, auto-rickshaw driving), and recreational activities. The Hyderabad programme also arranged loans for local women to buy sewing machines in order to generate household income. In Madras, the Metropolitan Development Authority launched a similar self-help slum-upgrading programme in 1977 with co-funding from the World Bank. This collaboration continued for a decade – as a result of which Madras was claimed to be 'one of the few Indian cities which have attempted to enhance community participation in its low income housing policy'[5] – and was then extended by the World Bank to cities throughout Tamil Nadu. In Madras (which was renamed Chennai in 1996) the United Nations' new Sustainable Cities Programme provided support from 1995 for the continuation of environmental improvements in the poorer areas of the city. Bangalore's Urban Poverty Alleviation Programme, co-funded by the Dutch government from 1993, likewise emphasized community participation in slumland improvements.

Community participation in 'slum upgrading' also began to receive attention in urban community development programmes throughout the developing world. Indonesia's Kampung Improvement Programme, begun in the late 1960s and supported by the World Bank from the mid-1970s, was estimated by the turn of the century to have been implemented in 800 Indonesian cities and to have benefited almost thirty million people.[6] Sri Lanka's Million Houses Programme began in the mid-1980s. These initiatives were welcomed by the United Nations as representing a new 'bottom-up, decentralized and broad-based partnership approach to urban environmental management'.[7] Interest was especially drawn to Latin America, where international development agencies became involved during the 1980s and '90s in supporting self-help community development projects such as the favela upgrading activities in the Brazilian city of Belo Horizonte (undertaken with German and Italian financial support) and São Paulo's Guarapiranga district (backed by the World Bank), and Rio de Janeiro's massive Favela-Bairro 'slum to neighborhood' project that began in the mid-1990s with funding from the Inter-American Development Bank.

These efforts to engage with local communities were stimulated in large part by the proliferation of NGOs and community organizations. The UN Centre for Human Settlements (UNCHS) declared in 1996 that NGOs had become 'critical intermediary institutions supporting citizens' organizations' in negotiations with project officials.[8] The most effective of these NGOs, such as the Urban Poor Associates in Manila, the Urban Resource Centre in Karachi, the Society for the Promotion of Area Resource Centres (SPARC) in Mumbai and the Brazilian Movement for the Defence of Life in Rio de Janeiro, had emerged out of the opposition movement to the previous policies of forced 'slum' evictions. SPARC, for example, was established by social workers in Mumbai in 1984, and partnered with the National Slum Dwellers Federation and Mahila Milan to oppose slum clearances in Mumbai and propose an alternative 'People's Plan' for Dharavi's future. This grass-roots movement challenged official redevelopment planning, staging toilet festivals and housing exhibitions that 'enabled the poor, especially the women among them, to discuss and debate designs for housing that suit their own needs'.[9]

As Dharavi's people's plan illustrates, the bedrock for local engagement with the new community development policies was the neighbourhood associations and the federations that arose to give local opinions greater clout. A spokeswoman for the Zimbabwe Homeless People's Federation explained, 'Our message was simple – that we were slum dwellers but we were not hopeless. We wanted the government to change the policies that make it difficult for the poor to live decently in towns.'[10] Community organizations demanded their right 'to participate in development activities as partners rather than as beneficiaries'.[11] They represent the hitherto overlooked grass-roots initiatives to build 'little palaces' and secure livelihoods to sustain them. They represent community groups in neighbourhoods from Dharavi to Kibera, organizing workshops on 'house dreaming and design' and running savings schemes to help residents to realize their dreams.[12] The efforts of local organizations have been reinforced by metropolitan, national and international federations. Good examples of the former are the favela federations of São Paulo and Rio de Janeiro (the latter holding its first congress in 1957). A good example of the national is the Philippines Homeless People's Federation, which emerged during the mid-1990s to coordinate savings schemes and create 'a large, communal pool of knowledge which is available to everyone'.[13] In 1996, community organizations and NGOs throughout the developing world launched Shack/Slum Dwellers International.

There was, however, another key influence behind the late twentieth-century rhetoric about self-help slum upgrading: an emerging neoliberal public policy direction from the developed world that in 1989 was termed the 'Washington Consensus'. The term encapsulated the development policies being advocated by Washington-based organizations such as the World Bank, the IMF and some sections of the United Nations. Neoliberalism sought to energize communities by cutting back on the role of governments, unleashing local entrepreneurial talents and facilitating the free operation of global markets. Many governments in Latin America implemented neoliberal policies as the price for international monetary support when they sought to overcome the debilitating 1980s Latin American economic crisis. Neoliberalism also influenced the framing of India's National Housing Policy during the late 1980s and 1990s, which emphasized community self-help, private sector involvement and reduced state responsibilities. World Bank support for slum-upgrading projects throughout the world increasingly reflected neoliberal principles after the mid-1980s, and in 1991, after reviewing all its aid programmes, the bank collaborated with the United Nations Development Programme to produce an explicitly new development strategy that emphasized the harnessing of self-help neighbourhood upgrading to the activities of NGOs, international aid agencies and the private sector. Throughout the developing world, neoliberal suggestions that governments 'carry out structural adjustments' have gradually led to policy statements underlining the crucial role of slum dwellers themselves in improving their living conditions'.[14]

As the new policies for 'slum' upgrading gained momentum during the 1980s and '90s, Pakistani planners announced that they had so rethought their professional approach as now to 'follow the same procedure as the successful informal sector did'.[15] Neoliberals loved such endorsements of the 'wellsprings of entrepreneurial energy' that were seemingly being nurtured within the informal economies of low-income districts in the cities of the developing world.[16] The international development banks and the United Nations were especially attracted by Turner's criticisms of previous government public housing programmes in the developing world, and their selective reading of Turner's writings led them increasingly to advocate participatory 'slum' upgrading in preference to wholesale clearance and rehousing. Turner's growing influence was evident in Patrick McAuslan's review of housing programmes in the developing world, undertaken in preparation for the Helsinki meeting of the UN Commission on Human Settlements in 1983. McAuslan, a prominent legal scholar and adviser on human settlement and land reform in the developing world, urged that shelter policies revolve around

> participation by action: the harnessing of the creative energies of the urban majority to develop their own environments and build their own homes, as far as possible, in the places they have chosen. This means site-and-service and squatter upgrading programmes are preferable to massive public housing schemes.[17]

The UNCHS responded to Turner's lobbying in the lead-up to the International Year of Shelter for the Homeless in 1987 by likewise recommending that the year be marked by 'developing and demonstrating new approaches to assist directly in the current efforts of the homeless to secure their own shelter'.[18]

Commentators lauded the Latin American self-help initiatives that Turner's early work had highlighted, and suggested paternalistically that they provided a blueprint for the entire developing world:

> A chain reaction was unleashed by upgrading. The residents of the informal settlements began to feel like ordinary citizens. They have an address, a postman comes to their house, they receive bills for water and electricity. This normality increased the people's self-esteem and strengthened their sense of belonging to a physical and social environment. It also clearly stimulated residents' economic investment in their community.[19]

A neoliberal utopia seemingly beckoned, with shared values among 'ordinary citizens' that made it

> possible to realize equity in the distribution of income through market mechanisms and distributive government policies. In other words . . . market efficiency and equity can go hand in hand.[20]

The World Bank found in the UNCHS a willing global partner to implement this vision. The UNCHS had been established in 1978 following the United Nations' HABITAT I conference in Vancouver but initially struggled to identify a clear purpose and plan of action, and by the 1990s was determined to find ways of 'scaling up' its activities.[21] In December 1999 the two organizations met in Berlin to establish the Cities Alliance, a self-styled 'major global alliance of cities and their development partners'.[22] These partners initially comprised international aid agencies, who were soon joined by governments in Europe, North America and Japan, other UN agencies and the Asian Development Bank. The Cities Alliance formulated a Slum Upgrading Action Plan called 'Cities Without Slums' that aimed to 'improve the lives of 100 million slum dwellers by 2020'.[23] Nelson Mandela, president of the new South Africa (representing a region in which urban poverty was increasing faster than in any other in the world), became the alliance's patron, and India, where urban poverty seemed most entrenched, was used as the alliance's first case study. 'Cities Without Slums' became the alliance's ongoing signature line, and its greatest triumph was to insert its 2020 target into the United Nations' Millennium Development Goals at the turn of the century.

The Cities Alliance encapsulated neoliberal thinking about 'slum' upgrading. First, it advocated city-wide and even nationwide upgrading projects rather than unrelated neighbourhood-specific schemes. Second, it championed private enterprise 'buy-in' to finance these schemes, which often resulted in the redesign and reconstruction of entire areas rather than strategic improvements to them. Third, it suggested a revitalized role for city governments in partnership with private enterprise developers. Fourth, it echoed Turner's proposals for 'pro-poor' strategies that welcomed local communities, community organizations and NGOs as 'active partners in slum upgrading projects'.[24] Finally, it acknowledged something of the broader livelihood issues and objectives with which such communities grappled:

Today, emerging policy strategies to improve the lives of slum dwellers attempt, for the main part, to avoid working through projects that merely target the manifestations of urban poverty in slums. Instead, they are becoming more supportive of approaches that address the underlying causes of poverty, and that involve the people who live in poverty and their representative organizations.[25]

The alliance's 'Cities Without Slums' action plan dovetailed especially closely with the new strategic approach of its United Nations sponsor, the UNCHS (which was upgraded to the UN-Habitat programme in 2002). UN-Habitat's operations had spread to over 150 cities in 61 developing world nations by the early twenty-first century.

THIS SEEMINGLY NEW APPROACH to 'slum' upgrading was new in rhetoric rather than in its fundamentals. Clearance projects by private developers and public authorities continued to be undertaken on a large scale, notwithstanding talk about helping poor communities to help themselves. Moreover, the manner of implementing upgrading and redevelopment projects provided only limited opportunities for community participation. In India, it was estimated that during a five-month period in 1983 almost 10,000 'unauthorised hutments' were demolished in Bombay, and when the populist Marathi and Hindu fundamentalist Shiv Sena party won control of the city government for the first time in 1985 it launched an intensified clearance programme called 'Operation Slum-Wreck'.[26] In Bangalore, which vied with Bombay to be seen as the most modern city in India, 'slum' clearance was widely applied during the 1990s.[27] Wiebe had cautioned during the 1970s that notwithstanding the useful environmental effects that were being achieved by the alternative strategy of 'slum' upgrading, 'in general, slum peoples are still treated as "disorganized", burdened by "slum mentalities" and so on.'[28] However, after another twenty years of slum upgrading activities, a professor of planning in Delhi could still maintain that 'Slum dwellers need to be organised in order to solve their problems.'[29] Such paternalism typified the redesign of 'slums'. Hyderabad's much-applauded community development programme, for example, was initially based on the conventional planning assumption that slumland chaos had to be replaced with orderly layouts based upon 'straight' lines.[30] Little had changed when Hyderabad's programme was reviewed in the mid-1990s: it was praised for having 'converted the unplanned hazardous slum localities into planned colonies', and for so 'enlightening the community' that 'The hitherto hopeless slum dwellers have gained hope and confidence to improve their lives.'[31] The Bombay Urban Development Project, similarly, which began in 1985 in partnership with the World Bank, was lauded as 'the first significant attempt at facilitating self-help housing by public agencies'. However, sceptics queried whether its core objective was community self-help or commercial redevelopment:

> In most cases slum-dwellers have little control over the redevelopment process. Once they agree to leave the slum and allow the demolition of their old housing, the investors of capital dominate decision-making.[32]

Likewise in Latin America, the much-lauded favela upgrading programme in Belo Horizonte begun in the late 1970s was said by some observers to have left its inhabitants unimpressed. In Belo Horizonte's supposedly trailblazing programme 'the categories and concepts used in the planning process [were still] entirely based on the technical perspective, not on the inhabitants' knowledge and experience,' which resulted in a mere semblance of community participation through which 'people are allowed to take part in decision-making without being able to change its norms.'[33]

Community activists began to object that despite the rhetoric of community participation, slum upgrading was a sham. Jockin Arputham, spokesman for India's National Slum Dwellers Federation, cautioned that

> when the poor don't take responsibility for their lives, everyone from NGOs to the World Bank will take this responsibility away from them. They will tell you how to live, how to eat, how to dress, etc. They will even tell you how to use a toilet. What nonsense! I am an adult, why should anyone control my life?

Arputham objected that World Bank community development projects were failing because they did not really set out to involve the communities within which their projects were set: instead, experts had wasted years '"studying" Indian culture, Indian values, even Indian ways of shitting. Tell me, how can a consultant from Mexico or London know these things?'[34]

Some observers responded to grass-roots criticisms by blaming politicians for manipulating upgrading and redevelopment projects so as to win votes. Others blamed self-styled community leaders for being motivated 'more because of opportunities for personal gain than out of a concern that the slum-dwellers enjoy genuine representation',[35] or questioned how broadly representative local organizations really were; still others doubted the motives and inclusiveness of the NGOs that claimed to empower local communities. When Jeremy Seabrook returned to Mumbai to see how the upgrading schemes he had seen begun in the Indiranagar district were progressing, he found that a road was being driven through the area, causing the demolition of hundreds of huts. The inhabitants were confused and demoralized; their 'sense of security that had been created by the belief that the slum was now recognized [by the upgrading project] proved to be an illusion'.[36] A review of India's Environmental Improvement of Urban Slums programme concluded in 1994 that although three-fifths of respondents agreed that some improvements had been made to their living environments, under one-tenth of them had actually been consulted about the improvements that were made.[37] Assessing this disappointing record, Prodipto Roy, a former director of the Council for Social Development, remarked:

> There seems to be a hangover, that slums are the shame of a city. There is no doubt, that proud city fathers . . . are ashamed of their slums. Very few of our scholars, who come from the upper classes and upper castes, are comfortable sitting on a charpoy in a Jhuggi.[38]

Perlman experienced similar disappointments when she returned to Rio de Janeiro. At Favela-Bairro, for example, the city's most celebrated favela upgrading project that began in 1995, 'for the most part, I saw that the residents did not feel a sense of *ownership* over the improvements that had been made.' Perlman mused that even the

> best intentioned and most experienced professionals, nonprofit directors, or community leaders cannot speak for the residents, and unless the residents have an influential voice in the process and outcomes, they will remain 'clients' rather than 'players'.[39]

Perlman's experiences were echoed throughout the developing world, as the glowing talk about community participation and empowerment was everywhere contradicted by practices that were inimical to Turner's core proposition that 'people have a right to house themselves.'[40] Reviewing the totality of slum improvement activities since Turner had first sought to influence them in the 1960s, urban poverty reduction expert David Satterthwaite concluded sombrely in 2001 that

> Perhaps the single most important factor in the limited success or scope of so many housing and urban projects supported by governments and international agencies over the last 40 years is the lack of influence allowed groups of the urban poor in their conception, location, design, resource mobilization, financing, implementation and management, and evaluation ... The discourse about urban development (and within this the discourse about reducing urban poverty) is dominated by professionals – the staff of NGOs, government departments and international agencies.[41]

Anna Tibaijuka, head of the United Nations Human Settlements Programme (UN-Habitat), conceded in 2003 that slum improvement in the developing world, having gathered momentum during the 1970s, had peaked in the 1980s and during the 1990s had become 'feeble and incoherent'.[42] She argued that a revitalized approach to shelter provision and poverty reduction needed not only to reassert community participation in the environmental aspects of slum upgrading, but to take seriously the broader livelihood needs of disadvantaged communities.

IN THE CLOSING YEARS of the twentieth century there were encouraging signs that the accumulating weight of criticisms against 'slum wars' and 'slum upgrading' since the 1970s might finally be heeded. It seemed possible that a fresh approach might be devised that finally eschewed the old 'slum' mindset, and that counteracted the accelerating urbanization of global poverty by genuinely respecting and effectively harnessing local self-help activities. The decisive breakthrough seemed to be the United Nations' Habitat II conference in Istanbul in 1996. In preparation for the conference, the UNCHS released a global assessment of urban trends that cautioned conference participants 'how simplistic and often inaccurate it is to assume that most low-income groups lived in "slums" or "slums and squatter settlements"'.[43] The Istanbul Declaration, issued at the conference's conclusion, seemed to show learning from past mistakes, and committed participating nations and organizations to 'ensuring adequate shelter for all and making human settlements safer, healthier and more liveable, equitable, sustainable and productive'. The conference simultaneously proposed a detailed Habitat Agenda that fleshed out these aspirations, and a supplementary Global Plan of Action for their implementation. These resolutions were subsequently endorsed by the UN General Assembly.[44] In none of the policy documents that followed Habitat II was the word 'slum' used.

The progressive rethink that Habitat II represented was confirmed and extended at the beginning of the new century, when in September 2000

> the largest gathering of world leaders in history adopted the UN Millennium Declaration, committing their nations to a new global partnership to reduce poverty, improve health, and promote peace, human rights, gender equality, and environmental sustainability.[45]

Eight Millennium Development Goals (together with eighteen specific targets) were announced, designed to put the declaration's vision of 'a more peaceful, prosperous, and just world' into speedy and practical effect.[46] The first and most important of these goals was to eradicate extreme poverty and hunger, and the associated Target One aimed by 2015 to have halved the proportion of people across the world whose income was less than U.S.$1 per day.[47] Seemingly intended to complement these undertakings, the declaration also undertook by 2020 'to have achieved a significant improvement in the lives of at least 100 million slum dwellers as proposed in the "Cities Without Slums" initiative'.[48] This aspiration was spelled out in the Millennium Development Goals' Target 11.

It is unclear whose brain bubble it was to insert the neoliberal Cities Alliance's 1999 Action Plan for 'Cities Without Slums' into the new century's reform agenda for achieving a more just world. Celebrating its achievement, the alliance noted that the 'Cities Without Slums action plan has been endorsed at the highest political level internationally'.[49] What is clear is the effect of its inclusion: by inserting the word 'slum' and its embedded meanings into the Millennium Declaration, the United Nations had retreated from the reform agenda that had been endorsed after Habitat II and compromised another century of progressive social reform. The UNCHS led the way. Tibaijuka, who had been appointed its executive director in September 2000, at the same time as the Millennium Declaration, lobbied energetically for the centre to be upgraded into a full programme with core United Nations funding. This was agreed to late in 2001 and was formally approved in January 2002 by the General Assembly, which renamed UNCHS as the United Nations Human Settlements Programme (UN-Habitat). Tibaijuka declared that UN-Habitat would be

> the focal point, within the United Nations system, for the implementation of the Millennium Declaration target on slums, as well as for the global monitoring of progress towards this target.[50]

UN-Habitat's *The Challenge of Slums* (2003) reiterated the Cities Alliance action plan and announced that the purpose of the Human Settlements Programme was to 'achieve the goal of "cities without slums"'.[51]

Thus, at the very point in time when it seemed possible that two centuries of slum misrepresentation might finally be losing traction, the United Nations gave them renewed legitimacy. UN-Habitat's *Harmonious Cities* (2008) used the milestone of a dawning 'urban century' – as, for the first time, over half the world's population were classified as living in urban areas – to warn that 'One out of every three people living in cities of the developing world lives in a slum.'[52] UN-Habitat used both 'scientific' methods and sloppy generalizations to spread its message. On the one hand, it introduced 'a newly accepted operational definition of slums' that had been formulated by a UN Expert Group Meeting at Nairobi in October 2002,[53] which it used to generate supposedly irrefutable measurements of 'slums' (rather than of the specifics of actual social disadvantage) by means of maps, graphs and statistical tables. Booth's pioneering methods of the late nineteenth and early twentieth centuries were thus recycled a century later. On the other hand, in order to support its sensational assertions about slumland's rapid expansion, UN-Habitat decided that 'The terms "slum" and "informal settlement" will be used interchangeably.'[54] UN-Habitat and the Cities Alliance thereafter threw their weight behind 'slum' redevelopment projects as the best mechanism for implementing the poverty reduction objectives of the Millennium Development Goals, contending that 'Slum upgrading is widely seen as the most pro-active and effective way to achieve this target.'[55] Neoliberal plans for urban redevelopment on a global scale overwhelmed neighbourhood aspirations to build better communities.

A new slum war had begun. UN-Habitat's *The Challenge of Slums* urged, as slum crusaders had first done three-quarters of a century before, that poverty eradication required an 'attack on the slum problem'.[56] Notwithstanding the continuing talk about community participation, the partnerships forged with community organizations and NGOs, and the hesitant recognition afforded to spatial and social order within slumland, the Millennium Development Goals' 'Cities Without Slums' initiative gave renewed momentum to heavy-handed interventions in disadvantaged city districts that undermined the livelihoods of the world's poorest people.

EIGHT

SHADOW CITIES

News broadcasters and columnists throughout the world announced during 2007 that for the first time in history half of humanity lived in towns and cities. UN Secretary General Ban Ki-moon said that this demographic turning point marked the beginning of an 'urban century', and UN-Habitat announced that 'Humankind as a whole crossed the Rubicon to become a predominantly urban species.'[1] UN-Habitat's head, Anna Tibaijuka, also drew attention to an apparently parallel trend, contending that in 2007 the number of 'slum' dwellers topped one billion people – one in every six persons – and she warned of a pending global crisis as slums spread across the planet.[2] In doing so, she echoed Mike Davis's startling argument in the previous year that humankind was creating a 'Planet of Slums'.[3]

Urbanization is widely celebrated for driving economic growth and innovation, but it also highlights 'the strange logic' of global capital flows,[4] and the accumulating ill effects of the neoliberal globalization trends since the late twentieth century that are associated with the developmental policies of the World Bank and the International Monetary Fund. The United Nations cautioned in 2003 that notwithstanding the anticipated modernizing benefits of the new urban century,

Much of the economic and political environment in which globalization has accelerated over the last 20 years has been instituted under the guiding hand of a major change in economic paradigm – neo-liberalism, which is associated with the retreat of the national state, liberalization of trade, markets and financial systems and privatization of urban services. Globally, these neo-liberal policies have re-established a rather similar international regime to that which existed in the mercantilist period of the 19th century when economic booms and busts followed each other with monotonous regularity, when slums were at their worst in Western cities and colonialism held global sway.[5]

The global financial crisis of 2007–9 can 'be seen as the culmination of a pattern of financial crises that had become both more frequent and deeper over the years since the last big crisis of capitalism in the 1970s and early 1980s'.[6] In response, state power has again been used as it was during the worrying economic and urban transformations of the nineteenth century: to 'privatise profits and socialise risks'.[7] Thus the socially polarized cityscapes of nineteenth-century England are echoed today throughout the world.

Some of the accumulating ill effects of capitalist change since the financial crisis of 1973 have been acutely felt in the developed world. Intensifying 'urban marginality',[8] the end-effect of economic globalization and the population shifts that accompanied it, devastated neighbourhoods in Detroit, New York City and Boston, for example, as industries relocated to the developing world. In Los Angeles, the second largest city region in the United States, it has been estimated that as many as a third of homeowners have informal or insecure tenure over their homes, a phenomenon that is usually associated with the shanty towns of the developing world.[9] In northern England, manufacturing employment in the Tyneside industrial region almost halved between 1979 and 1997. Urban marginality took violent form in escalating neighbourhood violence and social collapse. It was expressed, as well, in the riots that ripped through disadvantaged communities during the late twentieth century in Lyon in 1990 and in Bristol, the British Midlands and Los Angeles in 1992, and which were amplified during the early twenty-first century in another wave of unrest in Paris and other French cities during 2005 and again in 2007. Mass rioting re-ignited in London, Bristol, Nottingham, Birmingham, Liverpool, Salford and Manchester during 2011. Prime Minister David Cameron called the rioting a symptom of a 'broken society'.[10]

However, commentators mostly draw attention to what they call the urbanization of poverty in the developing world. It is this alarming trend that the Millennium Development Goals (MDG) target of improving the lives of at least 100 million slum-dwellers was intended to overcome, with UN-Habitat, the Cities Alliance and the world development banks seeking to realize it through yet another campaign of 'slum' upgrades and redevelopment. Some critics spoke out against this new slum war. The one most noted was Robert Neuwirth, who published *Shadow Cities: A Billion Squatters, a New Urban World* in 2005. Neuwirth had gone 'slumming' among the informal settlements of Rio de Janeiro, Nairobi, Mumbai and Istanbul, and he echoed John F. C. Turner in celebrating the energy and self-reliance of their inhabitants in building and consolidating homes, communities and livelihoods. Although he expressed respect for UN-Habitat's 'undeniably good intentions', he asserted that among the neighbourhoods 'where the people Habitat wants to represent actually live, the agency has almost no relevance at all'. Neuwirth suggested that

> Habitat might want to rethink its emphasis. The true challenge is not to eradicate these communities but to stop treating them as slums – that is, as horrific, scary, and criminal – and start treating them as neighborhoods that can be improved.[11]

An urbanizing world

Over half the world had become urban dwellers by the early twenty-first century, and it is the developing world that is driving this urban growth. Almost all the world's largest city conglomerations are now located in Asia or Latin America: Tokyo is the largest of them all, followed by Delhi, Shanghai, Mexico City, Mumbai, São Paulo, Osaka, Beijing, New York–Newark and Cairo. Jakarta, Seoul, Manila, Karachi and Lagos are not far behind. This urban transformation has taken place against a backdrop of entrenched, albeit gradually declining, global poverty. Manifestly, urbanization, modernization and economic growth in the developing world are not readily translating into poverty reduction. The new urban century is not bringing with it a happy new dawn for humankind. In 2008 World Bank analysts recalculated global poverty trends since 1982, using as an international poverty line those people making do on less than U.S.$1.25 per day. They concluded that the number of people living below this poverty line in the developing world had declined from 1.9 billion in 1982 to 1.4 billion in 2005, but they pointed out that this meant that one-quarter of the population of the developing world was still living in extreme poverty.[12] Notwithstanding the dawning urban century, about three-quarters of this total live in rural areas.[13] Since the late 1990s, however, observers have increasingly spoken about the 'urbanization of poverty'.[14] UN-Habitat asserted repeatedly during the early twenty-first century that 'up to 1 billion people live in slums in the cities of the world – one sixth of humanity – and . . . the numbers are rising.'[15] This is shallow sensationalism. However, social inequality – the uneven distribution of resources within any given population – certainly has increased since the late twentieth century. Inequality was intensified in Asia by the financial crisis of 1997–8, and throughout the world by the global financial crisis of 2008–9, but the long-term trend of increasing global inequality is generally blamed on cities.

It is widely acknowledged that increasing social inequality is also a feature of cities in the developed world. A consensus prevails that cities in the United States and Britain are 'becoming increasingly diverse, fragmented and polarised'.[16] Oxfam suggested in 2013 that in Britain 'inequality is rapidly returning to levels not seen since the time of Charles Dickens.'[17] A booming restructured British economy since the 1980s, occurring alongside sustained neoliberal cuts to public spending, is creating

> a 'two-tier' workforce, in which millions of people are stuck in low-paid, part-time jobs, [creating] an ever-wider divide between people in low-skilled work and those in more stable, skilled, managerial and professional jobs.[18]

This divide is especially evident in the cities of the former manufacturing hubs of central Scotland, northern England, the Midlands and south Wales. Similar trends are evident in the United States. James J. Florio became governor of New Jersey in 1990 on the back of a Democrat election campaign that warned of economic restructuring that was creating 'two New Jerseys'. The city of Camden exemplified the social problems Florio had in mind: 'This once-powerful industrial city on the Delaware River has been so battered, drained and gutted that there is little left today except neighborhoods of the extraordinarily poor.'[19] Some twenty years later the national capital of the free world was said to comprise 'two Washington DCs. There is the DC of the White House and Congress . . . And there is the DC that is seldom heard or seen, the neighbourhoods that are among the poorest in America.'[20] The United Nations estimated that inequality ratios in American metropolises such as Washington, DC, New York City and Los Angeles were equivalent to those in Nairobi and Buenos Aires.[21]

The comparison is telling. Social inequality has become most evident in the new powerhouses of the dawning urban century, the cities of the developing world. Here, the formal centres of business and government, and elite residential neighbourhoods, contrast ever more dramatically with the informal settlements and informal economies that have absorbed most of the population growth. In Nairobi, for example, the population living in informal settlements increased from 100,000 in 1971 to over one million by 1995. In metropolitan Manila (generally known as Metro Manila), 35 per cent of the total population, or some four million people, were estimated to be living in informal settlements by the early 2000s. In India, informal settlements form 'a degenerated periphery' around those cities that in economists' eyes have most successfully integrated themselves into the global marketplace.[22] On the other hand, India's 'super-rich' have accumulated assets worth a trillion dollars. In one example, India's richest man, Mukesh Ambani, has built a U.S.$1 billion house in Mumbai, a 27-storey tower boasting helicopter pads, cinemas and a staff of over 600.[23] This extravagance overlooks Dharavi.

Kofi Annan, the UN's Secretary General between 1997 and 2006, drew attention in 2001 to the uneven distribution of globalization's supposed benefits:

> Cities present some of the starkest of these contrasts: homeless people living in cardboard boxes, next to skyscrapers occupied by corporations whose budgets exceed those of many countries; growing gaps between the salaries offered by labour markets and the housing costs determined by urban land markets; enormous levels of consumption alongside great pyramids of waste that threaten the environment and human health; and hitherto unseen patterns of segregation, with pockets of wealth at the centre and vast enclaves of poverty on the periphery.[24]

SUCH SOMBRE WORDS are nonetheless intermingled with messages of hope about the dawning urban century in the developing world. In the early twenty-first century, more than ever before, recognition stirs that notwithstanding entrenched urban inequality, disadvantaged communities display functional coherence and strongly assert their rights 'to have a home, a place, a location in the world'.[25] The United Nations' *Global Report on Human Settlements 2001* affirmed that

> The biggest investors in low-income housing are the poor themselves. With only limited assets, many of the urban poor find land in the city, invest in housing, negotiate for services and secure land tenure, often in that order. This is the reverse of the formal process of housing development.[26]

This new recognition is in small part a direct response to grass-roots mobilization within these communities to demand, as basic human rights, adequate shelter, secure livelihoods and an effective voice in decision-making. South Africa's townships revolt, which culminated in national democratic elections in 1994 and a redrawn constitution, gave such demands international recognition and contributed to a reawakening interest in what the French philosopher Henri Lefebvre had, during mass protests in Europe in 1968, called the people's 'right to the city'. In 2005 local filmmakers from Nairobi's Mathare district established 'Slum TV' to document 'the crooked labyrinth of iron-sided shacks, graffitied beer joints, rickety-stick markets and open sewers that is their home'.[27] The Internet now allows spokespeople from disadvantaged communities to speak directly to the world about their right to the city. In 2012 local youth from Mathare used YouTube to depict their community in 'Tour of Mathare Slum'.[28] The blog 'Life in Favela of Rocinha, Rio de Janeiro, Brazil' has been maintained since 2009 by a 'simple guy who is enjoying life' in both his native Brazil and the United States.[29] Grass-roots assertions of a right to the city were formally recognized by the UN Commission on Human Rights, which resolved in 1993 that the 'practice of forced eviction constitutes a gross violation of human rights, in particular the right to adequate housing'. The commission reaffirmed this principle in 2004, and it has been endorsed by all subsequent international meetings on community development.[30] Nelson Mandela urged in 2006, 'Overcoming poverty is not a gesture of charity. It is an act of justice. It is the protection of fundamental human rights.'[31]

To a much greater extent, it is external advocacy that has prompted international recognition of the positive energies and incremental improvements within the shadow cities of the developing world. John F. C. Turner's late twentieth-century championship of self-help housing and community development hugely influenced international shelter policies. These policies have also been shaped since the 1980s and '90s by Peruvian economist Hernando de Soto's neoliberal calculations of the reduction in global poverty that can be made by supporting the informal sector of the developing world. Small-scale entrepreneurialism is to be encouraged, and greater support for savings schemes in low-income communities is to be given by micro-finance housing and mortgage companies, governments and international development agencies. In 2006 Muhammad Yunus won the Nobel Peace Prize for the efforts of his Grameen Bank 'to lift millions out of poverty by lending tiny amounts of money directly to the neediest people on the planet'. Since its establishment in Bangladesh in 1983, the bank had lent U.S.\$5.7 billion to the poor; in 2006 it had 6.5 million borrowers in Bangladesh, 97 per cent of whom were women.[32] It has become a commonplace to applaud informal enterprise throughout the developing world whereby 'communities and individual families are showing the way forward, through the use of individual or collective savings and self help actions to improve their houses and local habitat.'[33] UN-Habitat, the World Bank and the Cities Alliance now champion collaboration with neighbourhood-based organizations such as Shack/Slum Dwellers International as being the essential precondition for undertaking successful community-based urban development projects. The World Bank badges this new approach as 'inclusive urbanism'.[34]

These partnerships are necessary, it is now said, because local self-help activities can transform the shadow cities by harnessing the positive energies of their inhabitants. In 2002 a BBC report on 'Africa's largest slum', Kibera, recounted the story of one resident, 22-year-old Elizabeth Wambui, who was studying commerce at Nairobi University:

'The teachers talk about Kibera like it's some sort of filthy jungle. Like no one intelligent could possibly live here. They're snobs. Sure, it's dirty. But we can still afford the basics.' Her parents built their brick house in the slum years ago [in 1987].
Over the years, they've built other wooden shacks nearby to rent out. They've also got the shop – and a water pipeline – half a mile of tubing which they've connected up to the city mains. The tap in the courtyard is a lucrative business . . . The

family got electricity installed in the house quite recently. The bill comes to a PO Box in town. 'Imagine a postman coming to Kibera,' Elizabeth laughs.[35]

The BBC discerns a similar storyline in the favelas of Rio de Janeiro:

Recent reports suggest 65% of favela residents are a part of Brazil's new middle classes. And despite these people's relatively low incomes, many of these communities are a long way from being 'slums' as they are often portrayed.[36]

THE BBC'S REPORTS on Rio and Kibera echoed prevailing neoliberal enthusiasm for evidence of entrepreneurialism and self-help in the shadow cities of the developing world. However, their allusion to slums hinted at the extent to which slum deceits continue, in the twenty-first century, to overshadow understanding of informal-sector livelihoods and shelter provision, and analysis of urbanization trends in the developing world. It has become a truism that 'Slum-led growth is how much of the developing world urbanizes.'[37] About half the urban growth of developing countries in the twenty-first century, it is said, is 'strongly associated with slum formation', and this trend is especially identified with urbanization in sub-Saharan Africa.[38] It is estimated that in Africa's largest city, Lagos, 70 per cent of the population (which is estimated variously at fifteen to twenty million) live in 'slums'. It has become routine to say that about 60 per cent of the inhabitants of sub-Saharan Africa's other 'shock city', Nairobi, live in 'slums'. In Latin America, which is often called the most urbanized and most socially unequal region on earth, policy-makers are preoccupied with slums, shanty towns and squatter settlements (and the words *favela*, *barriada*, *poblacione* and *villas miserias* are now firmly embedded in the new international circulation of slum stereotypes).[39] *The Guardian* commented in 2005 that in Rio de Janeiro 'nearly 20% of the population, a million people, now live in about 750 slums.' The BBC concurred in 2007 that 'More than one million people live in the city's sprawling slums.'[40] Brazilian authorities conceded in 2009 that 'Brazil's slums, the *favelas*, impress by their extent and presence throughout the country's cities: more than 12 million Brazilians are slum dwellers.'[41] However, it is generally agreed that long-term slum problems are most entrenched in Asia. Over 40 per cent of people in India's national capital, Delhi, are said to live in 'slums'. India's commercial hub, Mumbai, almost 60 per cent of whose enormous population are claimed to live in 'slums', is called 'the world capital of slums'.[42] It is said that the 'proliferation of slums and squatters in large Indian cities has become the central theme of discussion among policy-makers, public officials and academics'.[43] Launching the Jawaharlal Nehru National Urban Renewal Mission in 2005, Indian Prime Minister Manmohan Singh declared:

> Rapid urbanization has not only outpaced infrastructure development, but has also brought in its train a terrible downside – the downside of proliferating slums, the downside of increasing homelessness, the downside of growing urban poverty and crime, of [the] relentless march of pollution and ecological damage.[44]

The overshadowing by slum stereotypes of legitimate concerns about intensifying urban inequality is largely the paradoxical result of the well-intentioned Millennium Development Goals, and the United Nations' willingness to measure success in reducing global poverty according to its spurious aspiration to 'achieve the goal of "cities without slums"'.[45] This target has been single-mindedly pursued by UN-Habitat. The change away from United Nations thinking at the Habitat II conference in Istanbul in 1996, when progressives rejoiced that slum stereotypes had been consigned to the dustbin of history, became evident in UN-Habitat's *The Challenge of Slums* (2003). Kofi Annan announced in the report's foreword that almost one billion people were living in 'slums', and this sensational benchmark figure was thereafter often repeated by the United Nations in the lead-up to the supposed reaching of this grim threshold in 2007.[46] In the following year, it became apparent that slum deceits now totally dominated United Nations thinking when UN-Habitat released its *Harmonious Cities* report on the health of the world's cities. 'Slum' had now become a central and supposedly measurable element for assessing city well-being; it could be made explicit by maps, graphs and exact percentages. The results made for sombre reading. First, the global 'proliferation of urban slums' meant that 'One out of every three people living in cities of the developing world lives in a slum.'[47] Second, the intensification of slum conditions within these cities meant that for the first time in human history slum problems could no longer be largely contained within discrete neighbourhoods or districts, but spilled out across 'entire "slum cities"'.[48] The United Nations warned of 'burgeoning slum populations' throughout the developing world because 'urbanization is outpacing slum improvements.'[49]

The United Nations and its collaborators reasserted the old slum deceit that in these newly emerging slum cities inhabitants were pawns in the playing-out of large and irresistible forces:

> slums are the products of failed policies, bad governance, corruption, inappropriate regulation, dysfunctional land markets, unresponsive financial systems and a fundamental lack of political will.[50]

The late twentieth-century champions of local self-help would have winced. Still more insidiously, the United Nations also reinserted the old slum deceit of slumland villainy, warning of the likelihood that 'slums become the sites of riots and violent protests.'[51] This warning drew in large part on news reports and research in the developing world. In 2007–8 the world media reported widespread ethnic violence in Mathare, Kibera and other Nairobi 'slums' as a result of disputed presidential elections. It also seemed from news reports that in Latin American cities the poorest districts were being torn apart as criminal gangs battled one another, the police and the security forces to win control of the lucrative drug supply chains into North America and Europe.

The escalation in 'slum violence' in Latin American cities was called '*the* defining feature of life in such settlements at the beginning of the 21st century'.[52] In Managua, the capital of Nicaragua, the drug trade transformed local gangs: 'What had been solidaristic social institutions had become intensely predatory, viciously attacking the populations of their local neighbourhoods instead of providing them with pro-tection.'[53] Veteran researcher Janice Perlman judged that the intense struggle since the mid-1980s between criminal gangs in the favelas of Rio de Janeiro to control the booming drug trade had 'weakened the trust and solidarity that has held the community together':

> When I lived in the favelas in 1968–69, I felt safe and protected, while everyone from elites to taxi drivers to leftist students

foolishly perceived these settlements as dangerous. The community was poor, but people mobilized to demand improved urban services, worked hard, had fun, and had hope. They watched out for each other, and daily life had a calm convivial rhythm. When I returned in 1999, the physical infrastructure and household amenities were greatly improved. But where there had been hope, now there were fear and uncertainty. People were afraid of getting killed in the cross fire during a drug war between competing gangs, afraid that their children would not return alive after school, or that a stray bullet would kill their toddlers playing on their verandas. They felt more marginalized than ever.[54]

Perlman suggested that this 'marginalization of Rio's poor is so extreme as to exclude them from the category of personhood'.[55] This is a recantation indeed from her pre-drug-war classic *The Myth of Marginality* (1976). It seemed that not only were the favela communities disintegrating; cities themselves polarized as the well-to-do and the middle classes retreated into 'safe havens', leaving the police 'to contain [violence] in the slums and shantytowns of Latin American cities in order to allow urban elites to live in comfortable and "splendid segregation"'.[56]

Stereotypes of slumland chaos have proliferated around the world. The 'hellish life' that is said to characterize developing-world slums is regularly juxtaposed with what are called modernizing and normalizing trends.[57] The *Jakarta Globe* remarked in 2010,

> It is impossible for any middle-class resident of Jakarta or any other big city in Indonesia not to notice the sprawling slums that exist in their midst. Even in up-market areas such as Ancol, million dollar homes sit side-by-side with hovels, the two sides of a coin that defines most developing countries.[58]

The names of a handful of these slums have become household words throughout the world. Dharavi, 'Asia's largest', is named to encapsulate the horrors of Asian slums.[59] Rocinha in Rio de Janeiro is regarded as 'the largest slum in all of South America',[60] and Kibera is called 'the biggest, poorest slum in Africa'.[61] It is said that 'At least half the population of Nairobi live in Kibera and other nearby slums – hidden away like a dirty secret along railway embankments, and beside rubbish dumps.'[62] In descriptions of these places, Charles Dickens's concept of the 'attraction of repulsion' remains powerfully alive in the twenty-first century. As Charles Kenny observed,

> There is something viscerally repulsive about urban poverty: the stench of open sewers, the choking smoke of smoldering trash heaps, the pools of fetid drinking water filmed with the rainbow color of chemical spills. It makes poverty in the countryside seem almost Arcadian by comparison.[63]

The reputation of these places has triggered a new wave of slummer tourism.[64] UN Secretary General Ban Ki-moon was guided through Kibera in 2007 by UN-Habitat chief Anna Tibaijuka. However, YouTube enables anyone with Internet access to go slumming in Kibera and other iconic 'slums'.[65] These virtual reality experiences are given depth by documentary films such as *Urbanized* (2011) and books such as Katherine Boo's *Behind the Beautiful Forevers: Life, Death and Hope in a Mumbai Undercity* (2012). Organized face-to-face 'slum' tours in Cape Town, Johannesburg and Rio de Janeiro have also become popular with international tourists since the early 1990s, and have taken off in many other developing-world cities during the early twenty-first century. A new generation of slummers now 'associate sordidness and poverty, as well as violence and crime with the terms, township, favela or slum'.[66] As a tour operator in Dharavi explains:

> Basically what happens when you say: the 'slum', that name gives all the negative images: that people are just poor or doing nothing, that they are sitting around, that there is a high crime rate, that children don't go to school and this kind of stuff.[67]

Some tourism operators seek to challenge these stereotypes and support community development projects. In Venezuela, 'a wave of backpackers, artists, academics and politicians' toured Caracas's La Planicie and other 'slums' to see for themselves the positive social effects of President Hugo Chávez's socialist revolution (1999–2013).[68] One tour operator in Mumbai likewise aims to demonstrate that

> life in informal settlements is not exclusively characterised by poverty, misery and suffering. Rather, the inhabitants' creative

engagement with the precarious living and working conditions is presented. The aim is to display that the so-called poor quarters are not ruled by apathy, fatalistic lack of perspective and socio-economic exclusion. Even though life there is presented as hard, nonetheless, positive impulses of development, success and *normality* of the situations of those living there are focused upon.[69]

Such aspirations fly in the face of entrenched slum stereotypes. In the early twenty-first century, 'slum' evokes throughout the world much the same repulsion that it first triggered in England during the early nineteenth century. Then, as now, the response is a mixture of anxiety, contempt, intolerance, self-interest and paternalistic sympathy. Now, as then, the playing out of these mixed responses has conditioned and constrained the interventions in disadvantaged city communities by both the public and private sectors in the name of the United Nations' goal of 'Cities Without Slums'.

Making slums history

A global anti-poverty campaign to 'Make Poverty History' has since 2005 sought to complement the United Nations Millennium Development Goals. It expresses a broad consensus that the developing world can be assisted to implement investment and planning strategies for 'achieving sustainable development' that will increase the efficiency of cities as 'the world's economic engines'.[70] It is predicted that doing so would 'cut world poverty by half. Billions more people could enjoy the fruits of the global economy. Tens of millions of lives can be saved.'[71] Slums are seen as forming a major developmental challenge to these aspirations. Hence the widespread commitment by progressives as well as neoliberals to 'Making Slums History'.[72] The means to this end that has been favoured by UN-Habitat, the World Bank and their joint creation the Cities Alliance (which until 2013 was based in the World Bank's Washington, DC, headquarters) is the participatory community development style of 'slum upgrading' that had been trialled in the developing world during the late twentieth century. The three organizations forged partnerships with city, regional and national governments, non-governmental organizations (NGOs) and community organizations to implement 'Cities Without Slums' programmes. Project officials spoke not only of environmental improvements but of expanded livelihoods and women's rights. However, the shortcomings of previous 'slum'-centred reform endeavours again became widely evident. 'Upgrading' was subsumed within marketplace-driven urban redevelopment planning, and socially disruptive 'slum' clearance' programmes have intensified.

THE EFFECT OF THE Millennium Development Goals' 'Cities Without Slums' initiative has been powerfully to restate the old and hitherto tarnished goal of 'slum' improvement through neighbourhood environmental upgrading and community development activities. The twenty-first century's 'slum' triumvirate – UN-Habitat, the World Bank and the Cities Alliance – advocated 'Slum upgrading . . . as the most proactive and effective way to achieve this target'.[73] It was predicted that their new campaign of 'slum' upgrading would at last deliver 'pro-poor' results because it recruited 'slum'-dwellers as 'active partners in slum upgrading projects'.[74] Seemingly, the energies and strategies of disadvantaged communities were finally being recognized. In its first annual report the Cities Alliance, echoing Turner, noted that

> the urban poor . . . have demonstrated enormous resilience and ingenuity in mobilising and organising themselves when formal institutions have failed to serve them, and are increasingly positioning themselves . . . as active participants in development.[75]

The Cities Alliance partnered with Shack/Slum Dwellers International in order to start 'Learning from Slum-Dwellers'.[76] A pilot for the new approach was agreed upon late in 2000 and formally launched four years later. It was called the Kenya Slum Upgrading Project, and was centred in Nairobi, where UN-Habitat was headquartered. UN-Habitat explained that 'Kenya's capital Nairobi has some of the most dense, unsanitary and insecure slums in the world. Almost half of the city's population lives in over 100 slums and squatter settlements.'[77] Kibera was chosen as the starting point because of its reputation as 'the most difficult and notorious of Kenya's slums'.[78] The project was jointly funded by UN-Habitat and the World Bank, the Cities Alliance and the Government of Kenya, and was intended to include local community groups and the private sector as 'equal partners in the programme'. It sought to provide basic infrastructure such as water and sanitation. These improvements were to be accompanied by initiatives aimed at 'capacity-building' and 'improving livelihoods'.[79] The project funded community training courses and encouraged savings schemes and cooperative housing endeavours, on the grounds that 'participation in cooperative saving schemes brings the community together as it works towards a common goal, and thus contributes to social integration and cohesiveness'.[80] Applying similar principles over a broader scale, in 2004 UN-Habitat established within its organizational structure a Slum Upgrading Facility to assist other pilot 'slum' upgrading projects in Ghana, Tanzania, Indonesia and Sri Lanka. The World Bank worked in parallel, the results of which were especially evident in Brazil, which became the World Bank's biggest borrower for urban development. One of their best-known collaborations was the 'slum' upgrading project undertaken in the city of Recife (the fourth largest in Brazil), which was agreed to by the World Bank, state and municipal governments in 2003 and begun in 2007.[81] It is the World Bank's largest slum upgrading project in Latin America, and ranks alongside the earlier Belo Horizonte project, São Paulo's Guarapiranga project and the Favela-Bairro project in Rio de Janeiro.

All these pilot projects had in common an appreciation that improvements needed to go beyond environmental upgrades and address the underlying causes of discrimination and disadvantage. UN-Habitat emphasized support for livelihoods:

> Many past responses to the problem of urban slums have been based on the erroneous belief that provision of improved housing and related services (through slum upgrading) and physical eradication of slums will, on their own, solve the slum problem. Solutions based on this premise have failed to address the main underlying causes of slums, of which poverty is the most significant. [UN-Habitat] therefore emphasizes the need for future policies to support the livelihoods of the urban poor by enabling urban informal-sector activities to flourish and develop.[82]

The Asian Development Bank, similarly, released a Poverty Reduction Strategy in 1999 which was intended to guide its funding allocations, and which was subsequently revised in order to align with the

Millennium Development Goals so that the strategy was explicitly based 'on three mutually reinforcing pillars of pro-poor, sustainable economic growth; inclusive social development; and good governance'.[83] 'Slum' upgrading projects, influenced by the broad social justice objectives of the Millennium Development Goals, also seriously began to address gender discrimination, abuse and women's basic rights. As a result of this new, kinder slum war, Ban Ki-moon could report triumphantly in 2012 that 'Conditions for more than 200 million people living in slums have been ameliorated – double the 2020 target.'[84]

Behind such talk, problems quickly became evident with the new wave of 'slum' upgrading projects undertaken in support of the Millennium Development Goals. Some observers have noted that the pilot projects, notwithstanding the fanfare with which they are launched, 'rarely lead to large-scale, long-term programmes capable of reversing the growth of slum settlements'.[85] The United Nations acknowledged that notwithstanding a reduction in the proportion of poor people living in developing-world cities, the actual number of dwellers in 'slums' had increased from 792 million in 2000 to over 880 million in 2014.[86] More fundamentally, the 'upgrading' projects often did not sympathetically partner local self-help initiatives, but imposed externally prepared redevelopment plans on local communities. Notwithstanding the new rhetoric of pro-poor goals and practices, the paternalism associated with slum concepts has persisted into the twenty-first century. In Kenya, which UN-Habitat represented as a best-case model for 'Making Slums History', Amnesty International judged that 'No government . . . has consulted people living in informal settlements and slums.'[87]

These inconsistencies are clearly evident in the Latin American scheme at Recife. Project officials treated residents 'as children that had to be educated' rather than as self-help activists whose achievements were to be heeded and assisted.[88] As a result, upgrading in Recife 'bears amazingly little relation to the lived reality of the slum dwellers'.[89] Residents quickly 'developed a sensible scepticism' about the upgrading process, recognizing that their 'opinions . . . were completely ignored':

> The population regularly referred to the participatory discourse used by the officials as *enrolação*, which means beguilement and in daily speech is used to refer to persuading with the use of beautiful words or plain cheating.[90]

Supposedly participatory planning was really a one-way 'channel to inform the people and a legitimization for intervention rather than a means to incorporate the interests and views of the subject population'.[91] The vernacular logic of neighbourhood spatial arrangements, designed by residents to maximize livelihood opportunities, was entirely ignored. Supposedly more-appropriate housing estates were substituted, and

> the people were told how they ought to maintain their new house, how they were expected to take care of the environment and trees, how they should separate their garbage, what agencies they had to address with their problems, how they were supposed to raise their children, and what they should do to improve their lives. In other words, they were instructed about their rights, but more especially their duties, as decent citizens. Helping the poor in the project was aimed at changing them from marginal, criminal subjects into lawful, self-helping citizens.[92]

Even in Bolivia, where statutory recognition of grass-roots rights is more fully developed, it has been said that, in reality, participatory planning for 'slum' upgrading 'almost doesn't exist'.[93] Throughout Latin America, disadvantaged communities responded with anger or retreated into apathy, while project officials say dismissively of them that notwithstanding the upgrades 'they kept the slum inside their heads.'[94]

Similar outcomes are evident throughout the developing world. There is a further twist: whereas 'slum' interventions had been imposed on poor communities 'in a simply authoritarian fashion' during the nineteenth and twentieth centuries, in the twenty-first century, encouraged by the Millennium Development Goals, 'slum dwellers themselves have negotiated and facilitated elite-biased redevelopment interventions.'[95] In 2001, for example, Shack/Slum Dwellers International collaborated with the World Bank, UN-Habitat and the Cities Alliance to launch the Three Cities Project, which was to be undertaken in Durban, Manila and Mumbai 'by [the] slum dwellers themselves'.[96]

Disenchantment among many residents at the unfulfilled promises of 'slum' upgrading projects is intensified by the trend for neighbourhood improvements to morph into their comprehensive redesign in accordance with the priorities of politicians and private investors rather than those of the local communities. India's Common Minimum Programme, for example, announced by the Congress-led coalition that won national government in 2004, pledged that 'forced evictions and demolitions of slums will be stopped,' but it undertook instead merely to ensure that 'care will be taken to see that the urban poor are provided housing near their place of occupation.'[97] Local environmental improvement works and community development programmes are often regarded as providing 'only . . . an interim solution'.[98] They pave the way for subsequent 'in situ slum rehabilitation projects' whereby residents are removed to holding camps while multi-storey apartment blocks are built over part of their former community and the remainder is opened up for recreation and other activities 'including commercial development'.[99] Mumbai exemplifies this approach.[100] Redevelopment plans for Delhi's famous Kathputli Colony likewise propose 'to flatten its 3,000 homes and build a 54-storey tower block with a mall and luxury flats'. Residents declare, 'We will fight the bulldozers.'[101] When the Kenya Slum Upgrading Project began in Kibera in 2004, some 25,000 inhabitants were temporarily relocated while new housing was built, but the residents complained that they had not been adequately consulted.[102] In Latin America, when the first 'slum' neighbourhood was pulled down in Recife in 2007 to make way for new housing,

> This demolition was an emotional event for the inhabitants. Many people sat down crying on the place where their house had been taken down. Others regularly returned to the area and to the place where their shacks had been.[103]

Whereas residents often expressed anger and despair, governments and mainstream society declare relief at the upgrades and redevelopments. Most people regard 'slums' as eyesores, embarrassments, as menacing centres of violence and criminality. Brazil's Recife slum-upgrading project was intended to be a forerunner for others that would remove or 'give . . . a face lift' to the nation's worst slums before the 2014 Fédération Internationale de Football Association (FIFA) World Cup and the 2016 Olympic Games.[104] An estimated 170,000 favela dwellers were moved in preparation for the Olympics.[105] An earlier spate of favela clearances took place in Rio de Janeiro in preparation for its hosting of the Pan American Games in 2007, and at one stage the authorities contemplated building a high wall around the favelas to separate them from international visitors. With world attention directed at Brazil in the lead-up to the World Cup and Olympic Games, the nation's elite and expanding middle class were determined that 'slums' should not dent Brazil's reputation as an emerging world power. The mayor of Rio de Janeiro released a ten-year plan in 2010 for the 'Slums in Rio de Janeiro . . . to be cleared and cleaned up as part of a major rebuilding plan ahead of the 2016 Olympic Games'.[106] In 2011, after city officials complained that Google Maps 'gave too much prominence to favelas', Google responded that 'the company had never intended to "defame Rio"' and that its map labelling would be changed.[107] Environmental improvement programmes inched ever closer to becoming out-and-out slum clearance programmes as Rio sought to spruce itself up for the World Cup and the Olympics. The inevitable consequence is 'involuntary resettlement':[108]

Berenice Maria da Neve is beside herself with grief and rage. As we stand beside a busy highway on the outskirts of Rio de Janeiro, she points furiously at a pile of rubble.

'Look at that,' she says. 'That's where my house used to be. That's where I lived with my children and grand-children.

'Then they came and knocked it down – they destroyed everything, my table, my sofa, even a wardrobe with all my clothes inside'.

Berenice's misfortune was to live in one of Rio's slums being levelled ahead of the 2016 Olympic Games, as Brazil works to improve its infrastructure.

She is – or rather was – one of millions of people living in illegally-built favelas or shanty towns. She ekes out a precarious living by selling food to labourers on construction sites.

In the little community where she has lived for the past eight years, about 1,000 people have already seen their homes destroyed to make way for a new, improved highway, which the authorities say is part of their preparations to host the 2016 Olympic Games.[109]

In a further twist, the covert war on slums began to overlap with the explicit war waged against the drug trade. In 2007 the governor of Rio de Janeiro announced that the state was 'at war with crime' as troops entered the favelas to confront the drug gangs.[110] In 2010 security forces launched another 'assault' on Rio's drug traffic strongholds as '2,600 police and troops, backed by armoured vehicles and helicopters, moved into the Alemão complex of slums' in order 'to make the city safer ahead of the World Cup in 2014 and Olympic Games in 2016'.[111] Thereafter the army was deployed 'to take on peacekeeping duties in the poor areas of Rio de Janeiro'.[112] In 2011 world news reports announced that, again,

> Brazilian security forces have occupied one of Rio de Janeiro's biggest slums as part of a major crackdown ahead of the 2014 World Cup and 2016 Olympics.
>
> Some 800 police and special forces moved into the Mangueira shantytown, without needing to fire a shot, having announced the raid in advance.
>
> The slum – or favela – is close to Rio's famous Maracana stadium, where the World Cup final will be played.
>
> The pre-dawn operation involved armoured vehicles and helicopters.[113]

Later in the year the slum war moved to notorious Rocinha:

> More than 3,000 troops launched a pre-dawn assault on Brazil's largest shantytown, driving heavily armed gang members from Rio's Rocinha favela as part of a continuing effort to clean up the 2016 Olympic city.
>
> At around 4am last Saturday, armoured personnel carriers clattered into the gigantic hillside slum. Bulletproof and sniper-manned helicopters soared over the redbrick homes searching for gunmen.[114]

Brazilian sensitivities to 'slum' embarrassments are widely shared. When Bangkok hosted the annual Asia-Pacific Economic Cooperation (APEC) summit in 2003, a huge welcome banner for international delegates was erected that stretched for half a kilometre (1,600 ft), obscuring the Thai Tien 'slum' behind it.[115] It is alleged that Chinese authorities 'removed hundreds of thousands of families' from Beijing 'slums' before the 2008 Olympic Games.[116] In the lead-up to the Commonwealth Games in Delhi in 2010 it was announced that 'large bamboo partitions would be erected along the Capital's main roads near major drains and slum clusters to make the city more presentable during the Commonwealth Games.'[117] The preparations in Delhi were relatively mild compared with those undertaken before the 2010 FIFA World Cup in South Africa, where a 'slum-free agenda' was vigorously pursued from the mid-2000s to rid its cities of social eyesores before the tournament began. The most blatant example was the N2 Gateway 'housing project' in Cape Town beside the N2 highway from the airport to the city centre, which was essentially an old-style slum clearance project carried out in the face of protests by shanty town residents. As one critic remarked, 'City governments have become increasingly engaged in remodelling their places for the "visitors class", the needs of the residents have gone out of sight.'[118]

WHEREAS CAPE TOWN'S N2 Gateway Project was undertaken under the guise of slum upgrading and with a pledge to rehouse shanty town residents, the twenty-first century has witnessed a surge in unrepentant slum clearance in the style of that carried out during the slum wars of the twentieth century. Jockin Arputham, president of Shack/Slum Dwellers International, complained in 2004,

> we talk of stopping demolitions, but there are so many cities where whole slums are being demolished. In Accra, and many other places in Africa, slums are being bulldozed. Some countries which have signed up for the Millennium Development Goals are continuing to demolish slums. The phrase 'cities without slums' is being interpreted by some municipalities to mean that slums should be removed and slum dwellers sent far from the city, thrown out of where they were living.[119]

It has aptly been said that in the present day 'Forced evictions and involuntary resettlement of individuals, families and communities rank among the most widespread human rights violations in the world.'[120]

The new wave of slum clearances is in part the result of government infrastructure projects such as road and railway construction and electricity supply works. In 2004 some 2,000 people in Kibera were evicted to make way for a road bypass, without any offer of compensation or resettlement.[121] In Mumbai, several thousand families were evicted in one night as railway authorities resumed demolitions in 2000.[122] It was estimated in 2007 that up to 400,000 squatters would be removed as the city's busy airport expands. As one woman complained,

> This place was a marsh when we moved in. It was full of boot-leggers. We built it with rubble and cement, and made it a safe place to live. Now they want the land back. Why didn't they claim it all these years when it was no good?[123]

Other clearances are the direct result of explicit government slum elimination programmes. In 2005 Zimbabwe embarked upon a slum clearance campaign styled Operation Murambatsvina, as a result of which some 700,000 people lost their homes. During the early 2000s the government of Delhi, then dominated by the Bharatiya Janata Party (BJP), also undertook 'massive bulldozing interventions . . . packing off slums and polluting industries'. Ironically, Delhi's minister of urban development at the time was the same Jagmohan Malhotra who had launched large-scale slum clearances in Delhi on behalf of Indira and Sanjay Gandhi during the Emergency in 1975–7.[124] Mumbai also experienced waves of government-ordered 'slum' clearances during the first decade of the new century, and every few months in between the municipal police were ordered to break up squatter settlements and informal markets.[125] Early in 2005 over 30,000 homes were destroyed in one such government slum clearance sweep. In 2007 the state government 'placed advertisements . . . inviting Indian and foreign developers to raze the tin shanties and maze of open drains that make up the Dharavi slum'.[126] Often the legal system endorses these clearances. The Supreme Court of India in 2000 authorized the removal of 'slums' in Delhi, and high court decisions in Delhi and Mumbai endorsed 'slum' repossessions to clear away encroachments along railway lines. In Kampala, objections by residents to police-backed clearances by the Kampala Capital City Authority were dismissed by the courts in 2012.

Government clearance schemes are paralleled by private enterprise redevelopments. Often the two overlap. Government bulldozers arrived in Nairobi's Deep Sea shanty town without warning one night in 2005 in support of a private redevelopment proposal, demolishing the homes of about 850 families. Private developers seek to reap profits by transforming marginal city land into marketable property. The trend is also clear in Delhi. In 2007, bulldozers supported by riot police attempted to clear the Shankar Gardens shanty town. One resident, Puja, summed up the situation thus: "'The big people do not care for us,' she said. "We have been here for years and they just wanted to get rid of us to make Delhi look beautiful.'" According to activists, her experience typifies redevelopments in the national capital, as 'shacks and shantytowns have disappeared from the edge of the capital to make room for shopping complexes and cinema halls.'[127] In Mumbai, meanwhile, as it attempts to rival Shanghai as a global financial centre,

> the property-development boom has gathered pace, and the land that squatters occupy appears increasingly valuable. Dharavi, one of the most prominent slums in Mumbai, is estimated to be worth $2 billion. The pressure to clear it – for environmental and social reasons that mask the land grab – is mounting daily. Financial powers backed by the state push for forcible slum clearance, in some cases violently taking possession of terrain occupied for a whole generation. Capital accumulation through real-estate activity booms, since the land is acquired at almost no cost.[128]

Novelist Aravind Adiga recently highlighted these tensions in *Last Man in Tower*.[129] Perlman detected similar trends in the renewed drive to clear the favelas of Rio de Janeiro:

> I had thought that this issue was long dead and buried, but evidently, it is resurrected from time to time as policy-makers see the potential use of the favela territory for land speculation and capital accumulation (often under the pretext of environmental protection).[130]

Government and private enterprise redevelopment projects, together with court backing for them, are reinforced by ongoing middle-class disdain for slum dwellers, who in India are blamed for 'holding up ... much-needed modernisation by clinging to illegal land'.[131] The same situation is occurring in Brazil, where the middle class of Rio de Janeiro are demanding the clearance of areas occupied by the favelas for their own use.[132] As one Brazilian urban planner says, 'the poor are being pushed further out of the city to make way for the growing middle class who can pay top prices for new luxury developments built where the slums used to be.'[133] Drawing out the battle lines, a spokesperson for the favela federation of Rio de Janeiro declared, 'We won't let them come into the favelas that we have built with our blood and sweat and destroy everything we have managed to achieve.'[134] In India, the same battle lines have been drawn: 'Developers [in Mumbai] hope to raze slums and make vast profits from commercial projects, but slum residents have other ideas.'[135] Yet another slum war looms.

Going full circle

There is another twist to these twenty-first-century slum wars. Encouraged by the United Nations Millennium Development Goals, they are entirely set in the developing world, but it is the developed world that is most engrossed in sustaining them and observing their results. Yet the latter, notwithstanding its preoccupation with foreign slums, has experienced intensifying urban social inequalities since the late twentieth century even as the word 'slum' faded from self-analysis of this disturbing trend. Moreover, redevelopment facelifts have been undertaken in disadvantaged urban areas of the developed world that have much in common with the twenty-first-century slum wars of the developing world.

Joseph Stiglitz calls the United States the most unequal of the world's developed nations. He used World Bank measures to estimate that the number of Americans living in extreme poverty in 2011 was 1.5 million, twice as many as in 1996.[136] In Britain, the Archbishop of Canterbury's Commission on Urban Priority Areas drew attention in 1985 to the 'challenge of increasing inequality and social disintegration'.[137] Subsequent social commentary in post-Thatcher Britain has been similarly bleak:

> Homelessness, poverty, declining educational and moral standards, increasing crime and lawlessness, sporadic violent unrest, derelict land and crumbling buildings: any or all of these phenomena blight much of urban Britain in the mid-1990s.[138]

Occasionally 'slum' epithets do still give colour to descriptions of inequality and alienation in the developed world. The British public housing estates that were built to rehouse 'slum' dwellers during the 1950s and '60s are derided as 'architect-designed and system-built

modern slums'.[139] Conservative newspaper commentator Bruce
Anderson railed against these 'sink' estates as being 'slums full of lay-
abouts and sluts'.[140] In the late 1990s liberal journalist Nick Davies
echoed the language that had been used over a century earlier by
Mayhew, Sims and Mearns, likening his experiences in visiting disadvantaged neighbourhoods to those of 'some Victorian explorer
penetrating a distant jungle'.[141] Davies's description of the inner-city
Leeds district of Hyde Park was redolent of James Cuming Walters's
descriptions of Birmingham almost a century earlier:

> poverty has wounded this community . . . It has bruised the
> minds and bodies of those who live with it, spoiling their
> health, undermining their self-respect, spreading hopelessness
> and sadness, loneliness and anxiety, provoking frustration and
> anger and crime and alcoholism and drug abuse, corroding all
> the fibre of daily life to the point where a place like Hyde Park
> almost ceases to exist as a community and becomes instead
> a collection of strangers, living with or without each other's
> support, in surroundings for which many of them can feel
> nothing but estrangement.[142]

Davies remarked that 'it was as if I crossed an invisible frontier
and cut a path into a different country.'[143] However, such language is
rarely used in the developed world to describe domestic social affairs. It
is used instead to characterize urbanization in the developing world. A
complacent consensus holds that however bad contemporary domestic
inequalities might be in the developed world, they do not compare
with 'the state of complete material deprivation in which people once
lived on the streets of Victorian England and in which they continue
to live on the streets of Calcutta'.[144] In the Australian city of Adelaide,
which is consistently rated as one of the world's 'most liveable cities',
there was a brief stirring of concern in 2011–12 to make the city
'slum-proof': the concerns were triggered not by home-grown social
disadvantage but by revelations that international students from the
developing world were being crammed into tiny rental apartments by
unscrupulous landlords.[145]

Recurring bouts of rioting in British, American and French cities
since the 1980s, and terrorist attacks in London (2005), Paris (2015)
and Brussels (2016), have drawn attention to the simmering tensions

– grounded in social class, race and religious differences – that are being generated in the cities of the developed world by their 'growing pockets of abandonment and deprivation'.[146] This has led in turn to 'intense period[s] of contemplation and reflection regarding issues of race, ethnicity, identity, segregation and social harmony'.[147] However these outbursts are no longer blamed explicitly on slums but more loosely upon an accumulating urban 'underclass'.[148] Ted Cantle, chairman of the independent review team appointed by the British government to investigate the causes of the rioting in English cities in 2001, remarked that 'the team was particularly struck by the depth of polarisation of our towns and cities.'[149] Sometimes such outbursts are attributed to the 'rapid and near-terminal decline' of once-dominant heavy industries and the communities that sustained them, as a result of global economic restructuring.[150] Sometimes they are associated with the neoliberal withdrawal of state action in order to facilitate the free operations of the marketplace. Sometimes they are linked to the related trend of inner-city gentrification, the 'middle-class colonisation' of collapsing working-class city communities.[151] But all these discussions are overshadowed by sensational slumland news stories from the developing world about drug-related violence in the favelas of Latin America, and communal bloodletting in the slums of South Asia and sub-Saharan Africa.

Yet in the developed world, slum deceits do continue insidiously to influence domestic urban development options. The assumptions that were embedded in public knowledge by the word 'slum' have continued to shape choices even after the word itself has largely been reapplied elsewhere. Since the 1980s, programmes of 'renewal' and 'regeneration', usually undertaken through profit-driven partnerships between state and private developers, have resulted in the rebuilding of cities on a comparable scale to that undertaken during the explicit slum wars earlier in the twentieth century. In the United States,

> Decrepit downtown areas were transformed, from Atlanta to
> Baltimore to Cleveland – and indeed Lost Angeles. City after
> city sprouted posh hotels, skyscrapers and renovated business
> districts. Yet the traditional urban problems – crime, home-
> lessness, welfare dependency, loss of jobs and unemployment
> – persisted. And new problems – AIDS, crack and guns galore
> – emerged.[152]

Billions of dollars of public and private investment poured into the redevelopment of districts in cities such as New York, Baltimore and Boston before the global financial crisis of 2007–8, resulting in the displacement of hundreds of thousands of residents, most of them African American.[153] The federal government's HOPE VI revitalization programme, begun in 1993, has resulted in the dramatic reshaping of inner-city neighbourhoods as public housing authorities demolish 'distressed public housing' and build new mixed-use developments.[154] In Canada, redevelopment of Vancouver's 'gritty' southern downtown district caused massive displacement.[155] In Thatcherite Britain a surge in what was generally called 'property-led regeneration' channelled public and private sector investment through urban development corporations that redesigned London's Docklands district (where the last dock had closed in 1981) and undertook major revitalization projects in 'derelict' areas of Birmingham, Manchester and Liverpool.[156] This approach continued under John Major's Conservative government that succeeded Thatcher from 1990 to 1997. The assurance was repeatedly given – in response to criticisms that the redevelopments prioritized economic returns over social well-being, and were undertaken with insufficient attention to local needs and local participation – that benefits would 'trickle down' to disadvantaged communities (a deceit that had already been used a century earlier). In continental Europe, notwithstanding growing concern since the 1990s about the social ill effects of global economic restructuring, and a spate of European Union (EU) policy papers on social exclusion and cohesion and the need for a 'bottom-up approach' to urban regeneration, it was nevertheless being said in the new century that 'professional and political forms of knowledge still tend to dominate.' As a result, despite 'the rhetoric around greater citizen participation across the EU both national and sub-national government has still to genuinely embrace this approach'.[157]

IT IS IN ENGLAND, where slum deceits originated in the early nineteenth century, that they have most nearly come full circle by the early twenty-first century. Paradoxically, this is not the result of the Conservatives' property-led renewal drive but of the professedly progressive reformist policies begun by the government that replaced them in 1997: those of New Labour under Prime Minister Tony Blair. New Labour's urban programme was maintained by Gordon Brown when he succeeded Blair as prime minister in 2007.

New Labour entered office acknowledging the urban problems that had resulted from economic restructuring and social polarization, and decrying the insufficiency of previous attempts to encourage community participation in city regeneration. Blair established a Social Exclusion Unit in 1997 to develop a new policy agenda. Its *Bringing Britain Together: A National Strategy for Neighbourhood Renewal* (1998) laid down the parameters for bolder policy approaches, and in the same year the government set up an Urban Task Force led by Lord (Richard) Rogers to reassess the broader causes of 'urban decline' in England and solutions to them. Its final report, *Towards an Urban Renaissance* (1999), provided the foundations for the government's subsequent white paper *Our Towns and Cities: The Future – Delivering an Urban Renaissance* (2000). New Labour's policy reassessments were expressed in new programmes, announced in 2001 and 2002, that were intended to begin the revitalization process using '"trailblazer" or "pathfinder" areas that act as policy laboratories'.[158] Endorsing the initiatives, Blair declared:

> When we came into office, we inherited a country where hundreds of neighbourhoods were scarred by unemployment, educational failure and crime. They had become progressively more cut off from the prosperity and opportunities that most of us take for granted. Communities were breaking down. Public services were failing. People had started to lose hope.[159]

There is an undercurrent to Blair's words: behind the rhetoric of New Labour's progressive reform programme lingered the old slum deceits. 'Slums' were nowhere mentioned in government policy documents and reports; instead there were 'poor neighbourhoods', 'deprived areas' and 'low demand or unpopular neighbourhoods'.[160] These places were supposedly 'caught in an accelerating spiral of decline that leads to neighbourhood abandonment', a consequence of demographic and economic decline, but also of 'crime and anti-social behaviour, poor condition housing . . . and poverty'.[161] In England, it was contended that these alarming symptoms of urban decline were concentrated in the north and Midlands. It was therefore here that the experimental 'pathfinder' projects began, championed especially by John Prescott (deputy prime minister 1997–2007). Pathfinder initiatives sought to regenerate these places by 'tackling crime, anti-social behaviour and drugs, [and] empowering communities'.[162] Residents had to be made active and responsible citizens; locales had to be given sustainable functional relevance.

The first of New Labour's strategies to achieve its urban renaissance was the Neighbourhood Management Pathfinder Programme, which started during 2001 in a selection of 'deprived neighbourhoods'. The programme was intended to improve local services and livelihoods by appointing neighbourhood managers and support staff with responsibility for developing and implementing community management plans, and for

> reaching out to, and involving, local residents and community groups [by] publishing neighbourhood newsletters, holding community fun days, establishing 'open forums' and identifying 'street reps' to report on local issues.[163]

Undoubtedly well intentioned, the programme nonetheless exhibited similar top-down paternalism to that in community development projects in the developing world since the 1950s, and Britain's own slum-mending efforts since the nineteenth century.

The second New Labour strategy, announced in 2002, was the Housing Market Renewal Pathfinder programme, an aspirational fifteen-year undertaking that was initially rolled out with £500 million in funding in nine Pathfinder areas of acute housing 'low demand' and 'abandonment' in England's north and Midlands: Liverpool and the broader Merseyside region, Manchester–Salford, Newcastle–Gateshead, South Yorkshire, East Lancashire, Oldham–Rochdale, North Staffordshire, Birmingham–Sandwell and Humberside. Three additional Pathfinder areas were added in 2005, and funding was doubled. The aim was to revitalize those communities that had been most hit by the social costs of economic restructuring. 'Low demand' in the housing market – 'reflected in very low house prices, high vacancy rates, and in extreme cases abandonment of multi-tenure neighbourhoods'[164] – was assumed to identify the communities most at risk. Prescott declared in 2005 that 850,000 homes in the north and Midlands were at risk from low demand.[165] The Housing Market Renewal Pathfinder programme sought to bring about 'improvements in the quality and choice of housing, as well as the desirability of neighbourhoods' in these urban crisis areas.[166] The programme put into effect the latest findings of British social science research. The Centre for Urban and Regional Studies at the University of Birmingham had estimated that some 1.5 million homes nationally were at risk, and a research team led by Professor Ian Cole at Sheffield Hallam University reported that almost 500,000 public housing properties in England 'were blighted by low demand', with an equivalent number of private properties 'resting on a knife-edge'.[167]

New Labour's bottom line, which it paradoxically held in common with the Conservatives' regeneration programmes of the 1980s and '90s, was to provide 'a general encouragement for private sector interest in deprived areas'. The Housing Market Renewal Pathfinder initiative was

> designed to encourage private sector interest in deprived areas and to generate market growth in areas where a lack of market activity had trapped many households and stunted inward investment.[168]

Encouragement for market growth meant finding profitable new uses for city land, and creating new 'mixed' communities in which a selection of former residents could be acculturated alongside affluent newcomers.

Pathfinder thus had much in common with other large public–private regeneration projects in Britain, such as the Clyde River waterfront redevelopment in Scotland, which overlapped with regeneration of Glasgow's 'problem' neighbourhoods in the city's East End in the lead-up to the 2014 Commonwealth Games, and London's ongoing Docklands redevelopment. Yet as the archbishop of Canterbury's *Faithful Cities* report cautioned in 2006, as it reassessed the findings of an earlier inquiry in 1985,

> A trip down the Thames from the Tower of London to the Thames Barrier and beyond illustrates how little of regenerated Docklands riverside has been left for public space: where there is public space, it appears neither to have received adequate investment nor to have been designed to serve the needs of new local communities. It seems to bear witness to a model of regeneration in which the powerful forces of commerce sideline the needs of local people if they do not generate economic returns.[169]

Notwithstanding the rhetoric of achieving a new renaissance, New Labour merely continued in the early twenty-first century the historical reliance on the old trickle-down approach to 'slum' improvement that had been trialled a century earlier, and that had been reintroduced by the Conservatives during the 1990s. As the *Faithful Cities* report observed,

> The regeneration industry [still] works with a 'trickle-down' model, which assumes that the gentrification of poor areas, and the erection of shiny new buildings, public and private, will transform the fortunes of the deprived. This assumption is rarely tested.[170]

It has often been said that the Pathfinder programme and its equivalents 'can be viewed as "state-managed" gentrification'.[171]

Despite the talk of inclusiveness in the new urban renaissance, Pathfinder and other urban redevelopment projects in Britain conspicuously failed to harness the knowledge and aspirations of local communities. *Faithful Cities* reported that

> Many people have expressed real anger to us. They believe that the promise at the heart of civil renewal – of citizens having influence and some power in the governance of their neighbourhoods and cities – has been broken.[172]

In Liverpool, the declarations of support by city officials for community-led regeneration have been called 'misleading in the extreme'. One residents' representative recalled that 'I tried to bring forward what my neighbours were saying but they didn't want to know.'[173] In Newcastle's West End district, which became a focus area for the Housing Market Renewal Pathfinder programme, residents complained that 'they have been consulted to death . . . and nothing ever happens.'[174] Nothing ever happens, that is, for the better.

Pathfinder promised better homes and communities. However, it delivered few new homes and little in the way of improved local services, and yet destroyed many viable communities. The old slum stereotypes, seemingly now a spectacle of the developing world, were responsible for this fiasco. Although New Labour never referred to slums or to a new slum war, its opponents in Pathfinder areas often did. Pathfinder 'placed demolition back on the urban policy agenda'.[175] Between 2002, when Pathfinder began, and 2008 some 40,000 houses were refurbished but only 1,000 new homes built, whereas 10,000 houses that were 'demonstrably unfit' had been demolished.[176] Residents' groups attempted to save their neighbourhoods, court challenges were mounted and a national campaign, Fight for Our Homes, warned that 'Britain is on the brink of the biggest mass demolition since the slum clearances of the 1960s.'[177] Critics agreed that Pathfinder represented 'the biggest programme of demolition since the slum clearances of the 1950s and 1960s', and some observers drew analogies with the first determined slum war during the 1930s.[178] A local woman in Salford objected, 'We are not slums, and we are not scum, we deserve a better life.'[179] In Merseyside's Bootle clearance area, posters appeared in house windows declaring 'No More Bulldozers'.[180] In Newcastle, members of the Scotswood Neighbourhood Residents Association recall that 'we lined the streets as they came in with their bulldozers and booed.'[181] In Oldham, window posters announced 'Vote Labour? Never Again!'[182] One protester pointed to the boarded-up Victorian terrace homes awaiting demolition and upmarket redevelopment and declared 'it's disgusting. It's social cleansing.'[183]

The protesters had powerful allies. The *Sunday Times* remarked upon the illogicality that

> to regenerate . . . a community . . . you must first knock its houses down and disperse the people . . . Houses by the thousand . . . are being lined up for the bulldozers in an agonizing, slow-motion replay of the community-wrecking slum clearances of the 1960s.[184]

Jonathan Glancey wrote in *The Guardian* that

> the government's dim and nasty 'Housing Market Renewal Pathfinder' initiative of 2002 . . . has led to countless boarded-up houses in parts of northern cities . . . that should and could be perfectly decent homes in perfectly decent streets. Instead they have been sold off, decadently and wastefully, to maximise profits for developers at the expense of local people.[185]

The mainstream heritage organizations SAVE Britain's Heritage and English Heritage expressed outrage that great swathes of Victorian and Edwardian terrace housing were being destroyed. Researchers reported that although residents were aware of

> poor housing conditions, inadequate transport, retail and services provision, changing population profiles and crime and anti-social behaviour, a significant proportion of households were nevertheless happy with both their home and their neighbourhood.[186]

Architects, housing experts and urban planners deplored the use of compulsory purchase orders to board up or demolish solid and affordable homes that 'should be lived in'.[187] Ian Cole, who had once warned about the proliferation of housing blight in the north and Midlands, cautioned in 2012 that countervailing attachments to place might also be at play, and that social life within low-income working-class neighbourhoods was therefore 'not necessarily straight and unremittingly downhill, as deindustrialization and economic restructuring take their toll'. He mused that 'residents' perceptions may offer a different set of priorities and understandings to those of the policy-makers, but this 'collective memory' of place often remains unheeded or invisible.'[188]

Social justice campaigners pointed out that residents had saved, bought and renovated houses that officialdom now condemned, and that the compulsory purchase prices being offered were far less than the prices for new housing. Residents' complaints were circulated that when Pathfinder areas were announced, local officials undertook that they were 'going to improve living standards, but instead they are putting us out on the streets. They are not giving us any money so we can buy houses in good areas.'[189] It was widely alleged that clearance areas were being 'deliberately managed for decline' in order to maximize the profits to be generated between the original purchase prices and a site's subsequent market value when cleared for development.[190] Anna Minton's damning book *Ground Control: Fear and Happiness in the Twenty-first-century City* (2009) drew attention to the words of a Liverpool taxi driver as she went to view Pathfinder's effects:

> It's terrible what they're doing. They're knocking down all the houses so someone can make some money out of it. They've

broken up neighbourhoods who were perfectly happy in these homes.[191]

Labour was defeated in the 2010 British election and replaced by a Conservative government under Prime Minister David Cameron in coalition with the Liberal Democrats. The Housing Market Renewal Pathfinder programme was halted in the same year. A subsequent assessment report concluded that notwithstanding the expenditure of £5 billion, the Pathfinder projects

> were often resented by local communities and created as many problems as they solved. This topdown approach has not worked, often resulting in blighted areas where large-scale demolition and clearance projects have been stopped in their tracks, leaving some families isolated in abandoned streets.
> There was widespread public controversy over an obsession with demolition over refurbishment, the lack of transparency[,] large profits by developers, the demolition of our nation's Victorian heritage.[192]

It was a damning assessment, and the legacy of these mistakes continued after Pathfinder ended, because in the cities of England's north and Midlands tens of thousands of residents were left 'trapped in streets filled with demolished or boarded-up houses'.[193] Here was yet another sad outcome of the twenty-first century's obsession with shadow cities.

THE END DATE for the Millennium Development Goals was reached in 2015. Drawing attention to this global milestone, the United Nations declared that 'the world has the opportunity to build on their successes and momentum', and expressed satisfaction that

> The lives of those living in slums have improved significantly in the last 15 years. Between 2000 and 2014, more than 320 million people gained access to either improved water, improved sanitation, durable housing or less crowded housing conditions, which means that the MDG target was largely surpassed. The proportion of urban population living in slums in the

developing regions fell from approximately 39 per cent in 2000 to 30 per cent in 2014.[194]

Improvements in housing, sanitation and water supply are to be welcomed, of course, but how much more could have been achieved had problems and solutions not been framed in terms of slums? This question can be broadened further, to apply not only to the fifteen years of the Millennium Development Goals but to the previous two centuries during which the slum deceits have had currency. Looking beyond the Millennium Development Goals and calling for a 'bold new agenda . . . to transform the world' for the better, the United Nations mused that 'The global community stands at a historic cross-roads in 2015.'[195] Yes it does, but to choose the best road forward it needs to learn from history and put the slum deceits behind it.

CONCLUSION

South Delhi, 2006. We pay for a guide and take photographs of the towering red Qutb Minar that symbolizes the thirteenth-century power of the Delhi Sultanate. As we drive away from the World Heritage Site, my friend pulls off the busy road. He is aware of my deep interest in 'slums', and here is a small squatter settlement to investigate. He talks with the inhabitants who agree that, for a small fee, I can wander around and photograph. The surroundings are rubble-strewn, but the huts and living areas are swept clean. The occupants' bright dress contrasts with the drab ochre grey of the bare hard-packed earth. Children crowd around, demanding more money. Their tone is bantering, but my friend thinks he detects a sinister undercurrent. 'Get back to the car,' he yells. 'Quick!' We slam the doors and accelerate away. I feel fear, and then shame.

I have spent my career studying 'slums' but I have formed no lasting friendships with any of the inhabitants of low-income neighbourhoods. This is in part because I am an historian, and many of the people and places I know best therefore belong to the past. But it is also because of the subconscious effect on my feelings of the prevailing slum deceits. My suspicion and alarm in Delhi were shameful because they had no clear cause. But they are understandable. They were products of the negative associations that permeate the word 'slum'. I consciously reject those associations, but unconsciously I perpetuate them.

E. P. Richards, an engineer, city planner and the first chairman of the Calcutta Improvement Trust, likewise struggled to understand disadvantaged neighbourhoods because his attitudes were also skewed by slum stereotypes. He reported in 1914:

> From the humanitarian aspect, it is a maximum evil that human beings should pass their lives and propagate our species in slums. We all know that to live in a slum steadily lowers the whole moral and physical tone of men, women, and children, prevents and destroys their happiness, and breeds among them discontent, sedition, anarchy, vice, misery, sickness, pain, and death. Disease, crime, intemperance, and insanity are, of course, well known to be absolutely and directly bound up with slum results. A city which produces slums is damaging the whole community and race.[1]

The word 'slum' distorts reality. That is its essence. We perpetuate this distortion through our own guiding principles and actions whenever we use the word to describe poor neighbourhoods and attempt to 'improve' them. As Herbert Gans remarked, 'The term "slum" is an evaluative, not an analytic, concept.'[2] Slums are merely products of our imagination and our conceits; in reality there are no 'slum' neighbourhoods, no 'slum cities', no 'slum-minded' inhabitants. We invent them to explain to ourselves the ugly traits, the logical incongruities and the social inequalities of modern capitalist cities. Robert Neuwirth said of the 'shadow cities' of the developing world, 'A slum is the apotheosis of everything that people who do not live in a slum fear.'[3] Sociologist Loic Wacquant identified much the same reaction when he studied areas of 'advanced marginality' in the cities of the developed world, and he suggested that 'perception contributes powerfully to fabricating reality – hotbeds of violence, vice and social dissolution.' He observed:

> Whether or not these areas are in fact dilapidated and dangerous . . . matters little in the end: when it becomes widely shared and diffused, the prejudicial belief that they are suffices to set off socially noxious consequences.[4]

Slum deceits emerge out of the relationships of power in economics, politics and society. As urban planning academic Peter Marcuse contends, 'Every society uses mechanisms of social control to maintain its basic structures of power and its arrangements for the distribution of the resources of society.'[5] However, disturbingly, the deceits are perpetuated not only by elites but by the self-interest and complacency of us all as we contemplate other people and places, and position them in relation to ourselves:

> *We* follow the rules, *we* live in nice strong houses, *we* have roads and street lighting. *We* have children who are well behaved and go to school. *We* have regular jobs.
>
> The other half – *they* – live in squalid conditions. *Their* ragged children pester us for money and vandalize the place. *They* carry diseases and have lice. All the criminals live in *those* places. *Their* houses are dark and dangerous.
>
> It is hard to grasp how powerful and self-reinforcing the 'them' and 'us' perceptions can be.[6]

'Slum' can neither describe nor explain urban social inequality, and it impedes progressive reform. As grass-roots activists from the developing world caution, 'The term "slum" usually has derogatory connotations and can suggest that a settlement needs replacement or can legitimate the eviction of its residents.'[7]

We can grasp these things by learning from history, by heeding the effects of slum stereotypes over the past two centuries. Unless we do so we will continue to repeat past mistakes and we will go full circle. In England, where the slum deceits began, the recent Housing Market Renewal Pathfinder programme was clearly not informed by history. Neither was the United Nations' ambitious 'Cities Without Slums' programme in the developing world. UN-Habitat, its chief advocate, echoed the original English regulatory phrase 'unfit for habitation' which had formed the basis for the first unhelpful interventions against 'slums' in the nineteenth century.[8]

A FRIEND AND COLLEAGUE remarked after reading a draft of my concluding comments that

> it ends a bit downbeat: no reform agenda, just a general hope that showing what was wrong about the past will help us do better in the future. Yet everything in the preceding 100,000 words indicates that we won't learn from the past,

not because we don't know what happened but because we don't want to know.

The criticism is fair, but I dare not attempt to do more. Many slum polemicists have confidently proposed interventions and reforms, but they were undercut by blinkered self-confidence. All I can hope to do is to encourage debate, and thus to challenge my friend's axiom that we don't want to know because we don't want to act.

THERE ARE UGLY PLACES and behaviours in today's cities that blight the lives of vulnerable people. Interventions are needed to assist them. This is as true for residents of low-income communities in Baltimore or Bristol as it is for those living in the favelas of Rio de Janeiro, Jakarta's kampungs or the hutments of Mumbai and Lagos.

However, any interventions must complement the efforts that are already being made by residents in even the most disadvantaged city precincts to better their lives. Today progressives and neoliberals agree that good things are happening in 'slums':

> all things considered, slum growth is a force for good. It could be an even stronger driver of development if leaders stopped treating slums as a problem to be cleared and started treating them as a population to be serviced, providing access to reliable land titles, security, paved roads, water and sewer lines, schools, and clinics.[9]

There is an emerging consensus that we should 'cast . . . off long-held prejudices about slums' if interventions on behalf of the urban poor are to work.[10] Governments, commentators, think tanks and aid agencies now suggest that positive social effects can result from the unimpeded workings of the informal housing sector and the informal economy in today's shadow cities. Recognition even extends to the possibility that viable community life may flourish in such settlements. As AbdouMaliq Simone recently urged,

> If we pay attention only to the misery and not to the often complex forms of deliberation, calculation, and engagement through which residents try to do more than simply register

the factualness of a bare existence, do we not inevitably make these conditions worse? If we are not willing to find a way to live and discover within the worlds these residents have made, however insalubrious, violent, and banal they might often be, do we not undermine the very basis on which we would work to make cities more liveable for all?[11]

But none of this is sufficient if we are to avoid going full circle. Even astute and sympathetic observers, such as Kalpana Sharma in her depictions of social inequality in Mumbai, still refer to poor communities as 'slums'.[12] It is time to take the logical next step, and instead of attempting to reform a fundamentally ugly and judgemental word, to drop it entirely from our vocabulary. It is time to heed the viewpoints and achievements of the urban poor. Slum deceits have endured around the world for two centuries because the local knowledge and common-sense activities of poor communities have not been heeded, respected and effectively partnered. We must reject the slum stereotypes that stymie social reform programmes and seek to justify city redevelopment projects that profit a few at the expense of entire communities.

Ending the slum wars does not mean that we give up renewing and improving our cities. The myriad cities of our new 'urban century' are dynamic and ever-evolving entities, and although their cityscapes often reveal long histories they are less museums of the past than they are habitats for effective living in the present. Ongoing renewal of their fabric can sustain the vitality of cities and enhance the well-being of their inhabitants. Many neighbourhoods are constrained by topography, choked by traffic or polluting industries, and their quality of life is compromised by the size of allotments, tenuous legal title, and the age, design and quality of existing housing. Redevelopment in such places and new housing for their inhabitants can be a blessing, especially if they are complemented by broader social programmes. There is plenty of historical evidence in Britain from the 1930s onwards of inner-city residents rejoicing at being relocated to new housing estates, as there is from the recent past in Latin America and South Asia. But there is also evidence of other relocated residents regretting the change, and of houses and neighbourhoods destroyed that could have been successfully refurbished. Neighbourhood renewal must be anchored in the opinions of the communities that make up cities; it should not be imposed on them. There must be no repeats of the experiences endured by the inhabitants of places such as Hungate, Boston's West End, District Six, Yamuna Pushta or Recife.

The outcomes of urban renewal thus depend upon the governing assumptions that sustain the renewal process. Community improvement projects must be measurable in terms of public good rather than private profit. Projects must be designed and implemented by disinterested professionals. And, most of all, project design and implementation must be informed by recognition that, as Gans insisted, effective living environments are shaped by those who occupy them. The fashioning of such environments is best undertaken when planners and residents come together to work out agreed goals, strategies and accountabilities. To date, there has been more rhetoric than achievement in these regards. Slum stereotypes, and the scenarios for change that they imply, impede the necessary convergence.

This book does not explicitly propose a specific reform agenda for taking the next step, of enhancing poor neighbourhoods rather than damning them as slums. However, it does seek to influence those who do, and the broader community that will need to endorse them. I am an historian, not a futurologist. I use history to expose the deceits of the word 'slum', hopeful that knowledge of past mistakes can help us all to make better choices to shape a fairer and more inclusive world in the new urban century.

REFERENCES

INTRODUCTION

1 United Nations Millennium Declaration, *United Nations General Assembly* 55/2 (18 September 2000), clauses 11 and 19.
2 United Nations, *The Millennium Development Goals Report 2012* (New York, 2012), p. 3.
3 Goal 11.1 in United Nations, *Transforming Our World: The 2030 Agenda for Sustainable Development*, www.sustainabledevelopment.un.org, accessed 6 June 2016.
4 *Oxford English Dictionary Online*, www.oed.com, accessed 30 May 2016.
5 See for example David Harvey, *Rebel Cities* (New York, 2012), *The Enigma of Capital* (London, 2010), *A Brief History of Neoliberalism* (Oxford, 2005), *Social Justice and the City* (1973); and Joseph Stiglitz, *The Great Divide: Unequal Societies and What We Can Do About Them* (London, 2015), *The Price of Inequality* (New York, 2012), *Making Globalization Work* (London, 2006), *Globalization and Its Discontents* (London, 2002), Mike Davis, *Planet of Slums* (London, 2006).
6 See my initial statement of this argument in Alan Mayne, *The Imagined Slum: Newspaper Representation in Three Cities, 1870–1914* (Leicester, 1993).
7 Michael Harrington, *The Other America: Poverty in the United States*, revd edn (New York, 1971), pp. 148–9.
8 Peter Marris, 'The Meaning of Slums and Patterns of Change', *International Journal of Urban and Regional Research*, III/1–4 (1979), p. 420.
9 United Nations Human Settlements Programme, *The Challenge of Slums: Global Report on Human Settlements 2003* (London, 2003), p. 9.
10 United Nations Development Programme, UNDP *Support to the Implementation of Sustainable Development Goal 1*, p. 8, www.undp.org, accessed 6 June 2016.
11 Quoted in Seth Koven, *Slumming: Sexual and Social Politics in Victorian London* (Princeton, NJ, 2004), p. 194.
12 Vandana Desai, *Community Participation and Slum Housing: A Study of Bombay* (New Delhi, 1995), p. 252.
13 Michael Dewit, 'Slum Perceptions and Cognitions', in *Living in India's Slums: A Case Study of Bangalore*, ed. Hans Schenk (New Delhi, 2001), p. 107.

14 S. Devadas Pillai, 'Slums and Squatters', in *Slums and Urbanization*, ed. A. R. Desai and S. Devadas Pillai (Bombay, 1990), p. 165.

15 Liverpool Shelter Neighbourhood Action Project (SNAP), *Another Chance for Cities: SNAP69/72* (London, 1972), p. 101.

16 Lou Antolihao, *Culture of Improvisation: Informal Settlements and Slum Upgrading in a Metro Manila Locality* (Quezon City, 2004), p. 79; Janice Perlman, *Favela: Four Decades of Living on the Edge in Rio de Janeiro* (Oxford, 2010), p. 23.

17 Robert Roberts, *The Classic Slum: Salford Life in the First Quarter of the Century*, first published 1971 (London, 1990), p. 49.

18 See the list of White's publications at the 'London Historian Jerry White' website www.jerrywhite.co.uk.

19 James Symonds, 'The Poverty Trap? Abject and Object Perspectives on the Lives of Slum Dogs and Other Down-and-outs', in York Archaeological Trust, 'Poverty in Depth: New International Perspectives' Symposium pre-event 'Discussion Pieces' (York, 2009).

20 Pillai, 'Slums and Squatters', p. 164, emphasis original.

21 ABS-CBN News, 'Next Travel Stop: Indonesia's Slums', 7 June 2009.

1 'SLUM' AND 'SLUMMING'

1 Charles Abrams, *The Language of Cities: A Glossary of Terms* (New York, 1971), p. 286. See Marie Huchzermeyer, 'Troubling Continuities: Use and Utility of the Term "Slum"', in *The Routledge Handbook on Cities of the Global South*, ed. Susan Parnell and Sophie Oldfield (London, 2014), p. 86.

2 Herbert B. Ames, *The City below the Hill*, first published 1897 (Toronto, 1972), p. 6.

3 'Developed' and 'developing' world are themselves problematic terms, which I shall nevertheless use in preference to the still more problematic terms 'first', 'second', 'third' (and 'fourth') worlds.

4 Drew D. Gray, *London's Shadows: The Dark Side of the Victorian City* (London, 2010), p. 1.

5 S. Martin Gaskell, ed., *Slums* (Leicester, 1990), p. 2.

6 Jawaharlal Nehru, *An Autobiography*, first published 1936 (New Delhi, 2004), p. 609.

7 *The Freedom Charter*, 26 June 1955, www.anc.org.za. Marie Huchzermeyer, *Cities with 'Slums': From Informal Settlement Eradication to a Right to the City in Africa* (Claremont, South Africa, 2011), p. 170.

8 United Nations Human Settlements Programme, *2007 Annual Report* (Nairobi, 2008), p. 30.

9 David Harvey, 'The Right to the City', *New Left Review*, LIII (2008), p. 33.

10 Center for Habitat Studies and Development, *Mozambique, Cities without Slums. Analysis of the Situation and Proposal of Intervention Strategies* (Maputo, 2006), p. 6.

11 Alan Gilbert, 'Extreme Thinking about Slums and Slum Dwellers: A Critique', *SAIS Review*, XXIX/1 (2009), p. 37.

12 Xing Quan Zhang, 'Chinese Housing Policy 1949–1978: The Development of a Welfare System', *Planning Perspectives*, XII/4 (1997), p. 434.

13 B. Chatterjee and Zakia Khan, eds, *Report of the Seminar on Slum Clearance* (Bombay, 1958), pp. v–vi.
14 Ministry of Housing and Poverty Alleviation, *India: Urban Poverty Report 2009* (New Delhi, 2009), p. xv.
15 Ben C. Arimah, *Slums as Expressions of Social Exclusion: Explaining the Prevalence of Slums in African Countries* (Nairobi, 2011), p. 1.
16 Dennis Rodgers, Jo Beall and Ravi Kanbur, 'Re-thinking the Latin American City', in *Latin American Urban Development into the 21st Century: Towards a Renewed Perspective on the City*, ed. Dennis Rodgers, Jo Beall and Ravi Kanbur (Basingstoke, 2012), pp. 10, 16.
17 United Nations Human Settlements Programme, *Harmonious Cities: State of the World's Cities 2008/2009* (London, 2008), p. iii.
18 Gaskell, *Slums*, p. 1.
19 Barry M. Doyle, 'Mapping Slums in a Historic City: Representing Working Class Communities in Edwardian Norwich', *Planning Perspectives*, XVI/1 (2001), p. 51.
20 See, however, Seth Koven, *Slumming: Sexual and Social Politics in Victorian London* (Princeton, NJ, 2004).
21 David Sibley, *Geographies of Exclusion: Society and Difference in the West* (London, 1995), p. 57.
22 Tyler Anbinder, *Five Points: The 19th-century New York City Neighborhood That Invented Tap Dance, Stole Elections, and Became the World's Most Notorious Slum* (New York, 2001).
23 Gareth Stedman Jones, *Outcast London: A Study in the Relationship between Classes in Victorian Society* (Oxford, 1971); Richard Dennis, *English Industrial Cities of the Nineteenth Century: A Social Geography* (Cambridge, 1984).
24 Anthony S. Wohl, *The Eternal Slum: Housing and Social Policy in Victorian London* (London, 1977).
25 David Englander, *Landlord and Tenant in Urban Britain, 1838–1918* (Oxford, 1983), p. x.
26 J. A. Yelling, *Slums and Slum Clearance in Victorian London* (London, 1986), p. 1.
27 J. A. Yelling, *Slums and Redevelopment: Policy and Practice in England, 1918–45, with Particular Reference to London* (London, 1992), p. 2; Yelling, *Slums and Slum Clearance*, pp. 1–2.
28 Yelling, *Slums and Redevelopment*, p. 2.
29 Sam Bass Warner, Jr, 'The Management of Multiple Urban Images', in *The Pursuit of Urban History*, ed. Derek Fraser and Anthony Sutcliffe (London, 1983), pp. 383–94.
30 C. J. Dennis, *The Moods of Ginger Mick* (Sydney, 1916), p. 69; C. J. Dennis, *The Songs of A Sentimental Bloke* (Sydney, 1916), p. 40.
31 See for example Ellen Ross, *Slum Travelers: Ladies and London Poverty, 1860–1920* (Berkeley, CA, 2007); Koven, *Slumming*, pp. 228–81.
32 Herbert J. Gans, *The Urban Villagers: Group and Class in the Life of Italian-Americans*, updated and expanded edition (New York, 1982), p. xiii.
33 Robert M. Dowling, *Slumming in New York: From the Waterfront to Mythic Harlem* (Urbana, IL, 2007), p. 4.

34 Peter Stallybrass and Allon White, *The Politics and Poetics of Transgression* (Ithaca, NY, 1986), p. 139.
35 See Fabian Frenzel, *Slumming It: The Tourist Valorization of Urban Poverty* (London, 2016).
36 Gregory David Roberts, *Shantaram: A Novel* (Sydney, 2003). A sequel, *The Mountain Shadow* (London, 2015), has recently been published.
37 'Walking Thru Kibera', Kibera Slum Foundation, www.kslum.org, accessed 19 November 2006.
38 'Journey through the Slums of Singapore', www.princessemilyng. blogspot.com.au, 19 May 2007.
39 John Stanley James, 'Sydney Common Lodging Houses' (1878), in *The Vagabond Papers*, ed. Michael Cannon (Melbourne, 1983), p. 47.
40 Victor Mallet, 'A Tour of Mumbai's Slums', *Financial Times*, www. ft.com, 6 February 2009.
41 Eric Weiner, 'Slum Visits: Tourism or Voyeurism?', *New York Times*, www.nytimes.com, 9 March 2008.
42 ABS-CBN News, 'Next Travel Stop: Indonesia's Slums', www.abs-cbnnews.com, 7 June 2009.
43 *Sydney Morning Herald*, 'Singapore's Slum Deal', www.smh.com.au, 8 April 2007.
44 Julia Meschkank, 'Investigations into Slum Tourism in Mumbai: Poverty Tourism and the Tensions between Different Constructions of Reality', *GeoJournal*, LXXVI/1 (February 2011), p. 48.
45 Amnesty International, 'Indonesia – Tourists in the Slums', in *Slum Stories: Human Rights Live Here*, www.slumstories.org, August 2008.
46 Stuart Grudgings, 'Best View in Rio? Pushing Limits of Slum Tourism', *The Independent*, www.independent.co.uk, 23 October 2011.
47 See the 'CaringSharing' link on Roberts's website, www.shantaram.com.
48 Riddhi Shah, 'Sun, Sand and Slums: With Slum Tourism Becoming the Latest Exotica, India's Poverty-ridden Underbelly is getting Dollar-rich Visitors', *India Today*, 9 October 2006, p. 76.
49 Bethe Dufresne, 'The Ethics and Economics of Slum Tours', *Commonweal*, CXXXVII/22 (2010), pp. 9–11.
50 Graeme Davison, 'Introduction', in *The Outcasts of Melbourne: Essays in Social History*, ed. Graeme Davison, David Dunstan and Chris McConville (Sydney, 1985), p. 3.
51 *The Times*, 10 January 1928, p. 11, 'London Housing'.
52 Charles Abrams, *Man's Struggle for Shelter in an Urbanizing World* (Cambridge, MA, 1964), p. 4.
53 United Nations Human Settlements Programme, *The Challenge of Slums: Global Report on Human Settlements 2003* (London, 2003), p. 84.
54 Ibid., p. 10.
55 United Nations Human Settlements Programme and Cities Alliance, *Analytical Perspective of Pro-poor Slum Upgrading Frameworks* (Nairobi, 2006), p. 1.
56 Mike Davis, *Planet of Slums* (London, 2006), p. 22.
57 Richard Martin and Ashna Mathema, *Development Poverty and Politics: Putting Communities in the Driver's Seat* (New York, 2010), p. 15.

58 United Nations Human Settlements Programme, *Harmonious Cities*,
   p. 106.
59 United Nations Development Programme, *Sustainable Development
   Goals: UNDP Support to the Implementation of Sustainable Development
   Goal 1, Poverty Reduction*, p. 3, www.undp.org, accessed 9 June 2016.
60 Charles J. Stokes, 'A Theory of Slums', *Land Economics*, XXXVIII/3 (1962),
   p. 189.
61 S. Devadas Pillai, 'Slums and Squatters', in *Slums and Urbanization*,
   ed. A. R. Desai and S. Devadas Pillai (Bombay, 1990), p. 164.
62 United Nations Human Settlements Programme, *Challenge of Slums*, p. vi.
63 See Susan Parnell and Sophie Oldfield, eds, *The Routledge Handbook
   on Cities of the Global South* (London, 2014).
64 Ibid., p. 9.
65 Ashish Bose, 'Urbanization and Slums', in *Urbanization and Slums*,
   ed. Prodipto Roy and Shangon Das Gupta (New Delhi, 1995), pp. 19, 23.
66 S. Ramanathan, 'Foreword', in Raj Nandy, *Squatters: Human Resource
   Dimension. The Case of Faridabad – A 'Ringtown' of National Capital
   Region* (New Delhi, 1987), p. v.
67 A. R. Desai and S. D. Pillai, *A Profile of an Indian Slum* (Bombay, 1972),
   pp. 2, 6.
68 Mridula Bhatnagar, *Urban Slums and Poverty* (Jaipur, 2010), p. vii;
   Bela Bhattacharya, *Slums and Pavement Dwellers of Calcutta Metropolis*
   (Calcutta, 1997), p. 1; R. N. Thakur and M. S. Dhadave, *Slum and
   Social System* (New Delhi, 1987), p. 7.
69 P. R. Nayak in *Report of the Seminar on Slum Clearance*, ed. B. Chatterjee
   and Zakia Khan (Bombay, 1958), pp. 17 (emphasis added), 35, 18, 38.
70 P. R. Nayak, 'Director's Report', ibid., pp. 165, 167.
71 A. R. Desai and S. Devadas Pillai, eds, *Slums and Urbanization*, 2nd edn
   (Bombay, 1990), p. 125. Nayak's definition appears on pp. 136–7.
72 Ibid., pp. 5–6.
73 Shveta Mathur and Sakshi Chadha, 'Creating Inclusive Cities for
   Poverty Reduction', in *Poverty and Deprivation in Urban India*, ed. Sabir
   Ali (New Delhi, 2007), p. 187.
74 Amitabh Kundu, 'Keynote Address', ibid., p. 23.
75 Vyjayanthi Rao, 'Slum as Theory: The South/Asian City and
   Globalization', *International Journal of Urban and Regional Research*,
   XXX/1 (2006), pp. 225–32; Ananya Roy, 'Slumdog Cities: Rethinking
   Subaltern Urbanism', *International Journal of Urban and Regional
   Research*, XXXV/2 (2011), pp. 223–38; Pushpa Arabindoo, 'Rhetoric of the
   "Slum"', *City: Analysis of Urban Trends, Culture, Theory, Policy, Action*,
   XV/6 (2011), pp. 636–46.
76 S. L. Goel and S. S. Dhaliwal, *Slum Improvement through Participatory
   Urban-based Community Structures* (New Delhi, 2004), pp. 29, 62.
77 M.K.A. Siddiqui and Y. Hossain, *Life in the Slums of Calcutta: A Study
   of Parsi Bagan Bustee* (New Delhi, 2002), p. 49.
78 Anupurna Rathor, *Slum Dwellers: Curse on Development* (New Delhi,
   2003), p. 36.
79 D. Ravindra Prasad and A. Malla Reddy, *Environmental Improvement
   of Urban Slums: The Indian Experience* (Hyderabad, 1994), pp. 2–3.

80 Arti Mishra, *Women in Slums: Impact of Environmental Pollution* (New Delhi, 2004), p. 159.

81 Noor Mohammad, *Slum Culture and Deviant Behaviour* (Delhi, 1983), pp. 1, 51.

82 Mridula Bhatnagar, *Urban Slums and Poverty*, p. 37. See also the similar findings in Sudesh Nangia and Sukhadeo Thorat, *Slum in a Metropolis: The Living Environment* (New Delhi, 2000), p. 18.

83 Amitabh Kundu, 'Foreword', in WaterAid India, *Profiling 'Informal City' of Delhi: Policies, Norms, Institutions and Scope for Intervention* (New Delhi, 2005), p. v.

84 IRIN: Humanitarian News and Analysis, 'Indonesia: Jakarta's Slums Struggle with Sanitation', www.irinnews.org, 16 April 2010.

85 Christine Bodewes, *Parish Transformation in Urban Slums: Voices of Kibera, Kenya* (Nairobi, 2005), p. 9.

86 United Nations Human Settlements Programme, *Challenge of Slums*, p. 9.

87 AbdouMaliq Simone, *City Life from Jakarta to Dakar: Movements at the Crossroads* (New York, 2010), p. 17.

88 David Patrick and William Geddie, eds, *The Illustrated Chambers's Encyclopaedia: A Dictionary of Universal Knowledge* (London, 1924), vol. IX, p. 450 and vol. V, pp. 816–21.

89 C. Govindan Nair, 'Causation and Definition of Slums', in Chatterjee and Khan, *Report of the Seminar on Slum Clearance*, pp. 74–5.

90 Janice Perlman, *Favela: Four Decades of Living on the Edge in Rio de Janeiro* (Oxford, 2010), pp. 36–7.

91 'Slum', n.2, *Oxford English Dictionary Online*, www.oed.com, accessed 4 September 2013.

92 Desai and Pillai, *Profile of an Indian Slum*, p. 2.

93 Government of India, *Report of the Committee on Slum Statistics/Census*, Ministry of Housing and Urban Poverty Alleviation (New Delhi, 2010), p. 2.

94 C. Chandramouli, *Housing Stock, Amenities & Assets in Slums – Census 2011*, Registrar General and Census Commissioner, Census of India, 2011, PowerPoint presentation available at www.censusindia.gov.in.

95 Cities Alliance, *Cities without Slums Action Plan*, www.citiesalliance.org, 1999, p. 6.

96 United Nations Human Settlements Programme, *Challenge of Slums*, p. 12.

97 United Nations Human Settlements Programme, *Harmonious Cities*, pp. 92, 90.

98 Ibid., p. 106.

99 Ibid., p. 92.

100 United Nations Human Settlements Programme, *Challenge of Slums*, p. 12.

101 *The Hindu*, 21 May 2009, p. 1, '"Slumdog" Fame Rubina's Home Demolished'.

102 Simone, *City Life from Jakarta to Dakar*, p. 26.

103 Kundu, 'Keynote Address', p. 20.

104 Joseph Stiglitz, *Making Globalization Work* (New York, 2006), p. 9.

105 Alan Mayne, 'Tall Tales but True? New York's "Five Points" Slum', *Journal of Urban History*, XXXIII/2 (2007), p. 322.

106 Peter Stallybrass and Allon White, *The Politics and Poetics of Transgression* (Ithaca, NY, 1986), pp. 3, 5.
107 Pillai, 'Slums and Squatters', p. 165.

2 THE ATTRACTION OF REPULSION

1 Adna F. Weber, *The Growth of Cities in the Nineteenth Century: A Study in Statistics* (Ithaca, NY, 1967), p. 1.
2 Lewis Mumford, *The Culture of Cities* (London, 1938), p. 161.
3 *The Times*, 24 February 1934, p. 17, 'Disgrace of the Slums'.
4 Marie Huchzermeyer, 'Troubling Continuities: Use and Utility of the Term "Slum"', in *The Routledge Handbook on Cities of the Global South*, ed. Susan Parnell and Sophie Oldfield (London, 2014), p. 86.
5 Winifred Foley, *A Child in the Forest*, first published 1974 (London, 1977), pp. 14, 16.
6 Le Corbusier, *When the Cathedrals were White* (1944), quoted in *New York: An Illustrated Anthology*, comp. Michael Marqusee (London, 1988), p. 16.
7 David M. Scobey, *Empire City: The Making and Meaning of the New York City Landscape* (Philadelphia, 2002), p. 10.
8 P. D. Smith, *City: A Guidebook for the Urban Age* (London, 2012), p. xi.
9 Eric E. Lampard, 'The Urbanizing World', in *The Victorian City: Images and Realities*, ed. H. J. Dyos and Michael Wolff (London, 1973), vol. I, p. 9.
10 Guther Barth, *Instant Cities: Urbanization and the Rise of San Francisco and Denver* (New York, 1975).
11 Maury Klein and Harvey A. Kantor, *Prisoners of Progress: American Industrial Cities 1850–1920* (New York, 1976), p. xii.
12 F. B. Smith, *The People's Health, 1830–1910* (Canberra, 1979), p. 223.
13 H. J. Dyos, 'The Slums of Victorian London', *Victorian Studies*, XI/1 (September 1967), p. 27.
14 Stephen V. Ward, *Planning and Urban Change*, 2nd edn (London, 2004), p. 12.
15 Vance Palmer, 'Thirty Years, and a New England', *Herald*, 13 July 1935.
16 Michael Harrington, *The Other America: Poverty in the United States*, revd edn (New York, 1971), p. 21.
17 Herbert B. Ames, *The City below the Hill*, first published 1897 (Toronto, 1972), p. 114.
18 Dyos, 'The Slums of Victorian London', p. 27.
19 J. Cuming Walters, *Further Scenes in Slum-land* (Birmingham, 1901), p. 4.
20 *Report of the National Advisory Commission on Civil Disorders* (New York, 1968), pp. 245–6.
21 Anne Stevenson, Elaine Martin and Judith O'Neill, *High Living: A Study of Family Life in Flats* (Melbourne, 1967), p. 10.
22 *San Francisco Chronicle*, 3 July 1900, p. 6, editorial: 'Rebuilding Chinatown'.
23 E. P. Hennock, *Fit and Proper Persons: Ideal and Reality in Nineteenth-century Urban Government* (London, 1973).
24 Francis H. McLean, Robert E. Todd and Frank B. Sanborn, *The Report of the Lawrence Survey* (Lawrence, MA, 1912), p. III.

25 Liverpool Shelter Neighbourhood Action Project (SNAP), *Another Chance for Cities: SNAP69/72* (London, 1972), p. 9.

26 Hugh Wilson and Lewis Womersley, Roger Tym and Associates, Jamieson Mackay and Partners, *Change or Decay: Final Report of the Liverpool Inner Area Study* (London, 1977), p. 1.

27 Harrington, *The Other America*, pp. 1–2.

28 John Stubbs, *The Hidden People: Poverty in Australia* (Melbourne, 1966), p. 1.

29 B. Seebohm Rowntree, *Poverty: A Study of Town Life* (London, 1902), p. vii.

30 Ibid., p. 5.

31 Robert A. Beauregard, *Voices of Decline: The Postwar Fate of U.S. Cities* (New York, 2003), p. 57.

32 Anthony S. Wohl, ed., *The Bitter Cry of Outcast London, with Leading Articles from the Pall Mall Gazette of October 1883 and Articles by Lord Salisbury Joseph Chamberlain and Foster Crozier* (Leicester, 1970), p. 55.

33 Robert A. Woods, 'The Social Awakening in London', in *The Poor in Great Cities: Their Problems and What is Being Done to Solve Them* (London, 1896), p. 4.

34 *Sydney Morning Herald*, 22 March 1884, 14 January 1884, quoted in A.J.C. Mayne, *Fever, Squalor and Vice: Sanitation and Social Policy in Victorian Sydney* (Brisbane, 1982), p. 130.

35 *The Congregationalist*, XII (November 1883), quoted in Wohl, *The Bitter Cry*, p. 35.

36 Dyos, 'The Slums of Victorian London', p. 27.

37 'Flash' and 'Cant', in *The Oxford Companion to the English Language*, ed. Tom McArthur (Oxford, 1992), pp. 406, 188. See also 'Slang', pp. 940–43; 'Vulgar', p. 1098.

38 Ibid., p. 942.

39 See Francis Grose, *Dictionary of the Vulgar Tongue: A Dictionary of Buckish Slang, University Wit, and Pickpocket Eloquence* (London, 1811); James Hardy Vaux, 'A Vocabulary of the Flash Language', in *Memoirs of James Hardy Vaux* (London, 1819), vol. II; Jon Bee, *Slang: A Dictionary of the Turf, the Ring, the Chase, the Pit, of Bon-Ton, and the Varieties of Life* (London, 1823); John Camden Hotten, *A Dictionary of Modern Slang, Cant, and Vulgar Words* (London, 1859); *Oxford English Dictionary Online*, 'slum, n.', 'slum, v.', www.oed.com, accessed 16 September 2013.

40 Vaux, 'A Vocabulary of the Flash Language', pp. 187, 200, 206. Although the 'Vocabulary' was first circulated in 1812, it was not published until 1819.

41 See 'slum' and 'slumber' in Eric Partridge, *Origins: A Short Etymological Dictionary of Modern English*, 4th edn (London, 1966), p. 3092.

42 J. Cuming Walters, *Scenes in Slum-land* (Birmingham, 1901), p. 5; Mearns, in Wohl, *The Bitter Cry*, p. 62.

43 H. J. Dyos and D. A. Reeder, 'Slums and Suburbs', in *The Victorian City: Images and Realities*, ed. H. J. Dyos and Michael Wolff (London, 1973), vol. I, p. 362.

44 W. G. Hoskins, *The Making of the English Landscape* (London, 1955), pp. 172–3.

45 Quoted in Dyos, 'The Slums of Victorian London', p. 8.
46 Bernard Blackmantle (Charles Molloy Westmacott), *The English Spy: An Original Work, Characteristic, Satirical and Humorous, Comprising Scenes and Sketches in Every Rank of Society* (London, 1825), vol. II, p. 29. Project Gutenberg eBook, www.gutenberg.org, accessed 18 September 2013.
47 *Argus*, 11 February 1857, quoted by Graeme Davison and David Dunstan, '"This Moral Pandemonium": Images of Low Life', in *The Outcasts of Melbourne: Essays in Social History*, ed. Graeme Davison, David Dunstan and Chris McConville (Sydney, 1985), p. 30.
48 Wiseman, quoted in Anthony S. Wohl, *The Eternal Slum: Housing and Social Policy in Victorian London* (London, 1977), p. 5.
49 Webster's Dictionary, quoted in F. Oswald Barnett, *The Unsuspected Slums* (Melbourne, 1933), p. 8.
50 Barnett, *The Unsuspected Slums*, p. 8.
51 Howard Marshall, *Slum* (London, 1933), p. 12.
52 W. T. Stead, 'Is it Not Time?', *Pall Mall Gazette*, 16 October 1883, quoted in Wohl, *The Bitter Cry*, p. 81. See Gertrude Himmelfarb, *The Idea of Poverty: England in the Early Industrial Age* (New York, 1984), p. 307.
53 *Voice* (New York), 7 March 1889, quoted in *Oxford English Dictionary Online*, 'slummer, n. 2', www.oed.com, accessed 17 September 2013.
54 *The Times*, 13 December 1933, p. 7, 'Bishop of London and the Speculative Builder'.
55 *Boston Journal*, 1 October 1884, quoted in *Oxford English Dictionary Online*, 'slum v. 4a', www.oed.com, accessed 13 October 2013. Joseph Hatton, *Reminiscences of J. L. Toole* (London, 1889), quoted ibid., 'slummer, n. 1', accessed 17 September 2013.
56 Mrs Cecil Chesterton, *I Lived in a Slum* (London, 1936), p. 11.
57 John Forster, *The Life of Charles Dickens* (Boston, MA, 1875), vol. I, p. 39 (first published 1872–4).
58 See Dickens, 'The City of the Absent', first published in *All the Year Round* in 1863, and incorporated as chapter 23 in *The Uncommercial Traveller* (London, 1866, 1875).
59 Rosemary O'Day and David Englander, *Mr Charles Booth's Inquiry: Life and Labour of the People in London Reconsidered* (London, 1993), p. 194.
60 Victor Turner, *On the Edge of the Bush: Anthropology as Experience*, ed. Edith L. B. Turner (Tuscon, AZ, 1985), p. 184.
61 Robert H. Wiebe, *The Search for Order, 1877–1920* (New York, 1967), p. xiv.
62 The *Sun* newspaper, 1849, quoted in Himmelfarb, *The Idea of Poverty*, p. 351.
63 This phrase was repeatedly used during the 1930s by British minister of health Sir Edward Hilton Young. See, for example, *The Times*, 11 December 1933, p. 7, 'Sir Hilton Young on the Slums'.
64 Ames, *City below the Hill*, p. 7.
65 Walters, *Scenes in Slum-land*, p. 15.
66 Keith Gandal, *The Virtues of the Vicious: Jacob Riis, Stephen Crane, and the Spectacle of the Slum* (New York, 1997), p. 8.

67 Cited in Wohl, *The Bitter Cry*, p. 58.
68 *Time*, 29 August 1977, 'The American Underclass', p. 18, www.content. time.com, accessed 20 November 2013.
69 John Freeman, *Lights and Shadows of Melbourne Life* (London, 1888), p. 15.
70 *The Times*, 7 September 1928, p. 14, 'Sanitary Inspectors' Conference'.
71 Marshall, *Slum*, p. 8.
72 George R. Sims, *How the Poor Live* (London, 1883), p. 1.
73 Walters, *Scenes in Slum-land*, p. 3.
74 Barnett, *The Unsuspected Slums*, p. 18.
75 *Time*, 'The American Underclass', p. 18.
76 Walters, *Further Scenes in Slum-land*, p. 20.
77 Walters, *Scenes in Slum-land*, p. 18.
78 Marshall, *Slum*, p. 36.
79 Jeremy Harrison, ed., *Reprieve for Slums: A Shelter Report* (London, 1972), p. 3.
80 Sims, *How the Poor Live*, p. 55.
81 Ibid., p. 57.
82 Wohl, *The Bitter Cry*, p. 61.
83 B. S. Townroe, *Britain Rebuilding: The Slum and Overcrowding Campaigns* (London, 1936), p. 138.
84 Housing Management Sub-Committee of the Central Housing Advisory Committee, *Moving from the Slums: Seventh Report of the Housing Management Sub-Committee of the Central Housing Advisory Committee* (London, 1956), p. 13.
85 *New Society*, 18 November 1976, quoted in *Oxford English Dictionary Online*, 'sink, n.2g', www.oed.com, accessed 17 November 2013.
86 Walter Besant, 'A Riverside Parish', in *The Poor in Great Cities*, p. 273.
87 Walters, *Further Scenes in Slum-land*, p. 25. Walters, *Scenes in Slum-land*, p. 1.
88 Barnett, *The Unsuspected Slums*, p. 25.
89 *Time*, 'The American Underclass', p. 18.
90 Ramsay Mailler, *The Slums Are Still with Us* (Melbourne, 1944), p. 10.
91 Walters, *Scenes in Slum-land*, p. 18.
92 *Time*, 'The American Underclass', p. 18.
93 Barnett, *The Unsuspected Slums*, p. 25; F. Oswald Barnett and W. O. Burt, *Housing the Australian Nation* (Melbourne, 1942), p. 42; *The Times*, 5 December 1931, p. 7, 'Persistence of Slum Habits'.
94 *Argus*, 14 May 1910, p. 18, 'Melbourne's Slum Tangle'.
95 F. B. Boyce, *Fourscore Years and Seven: The Memoirs of Archdeacon Boyce, for over Sixty Years a Clergyman of the Church of England in New South Wales* (Sydney, 1934), p. 97.
96 Walters, *Scenes in Slum-land*, p. 3.
97 *Evening News* (Sydney), 16 March 1887, in Alan Mayne, *Representing the Slum: Popular Journalism in a Late Nineteenth Century City* (Melbourne, 1990), p. 176.
98 T. Brennan, *Reshaping a City* (Glasgow, 1959), p. 139.
99 Harrison, *Reprieve for Slums*, p. 15.

100 Walters, *Scenes in Slum-land*, p. 6. Jacob A. Riis, *How the Other Half Lives: Studies among the Tenements of New York* (New York, 1890), p. 138.
101 *Argus*, 11 May 1910, p. 13, 'Melbourne's Slum-Tangle'.
102 *Time*, 'The American Underclass', p. 18.
103 Barnett, *The Unsuspected Slums*, p. 9.
104 Sims, *How the Poor Live*, pp. 25, 27.
105 Wohl, *The Bitter Cry*, p. 73.
106 *The Times*, 14 June 1932, p. 11, 'Overcrowding in London'.
107 Statement by Sons of the American Revolution, in *Reports of the United States Immigration Commission* (Washington, DC, 1911), vol. XLI, p. 7.
108 Robert Hunter, *Poverty* (New York, 1904), p. 262.
109 William T. Elsing, 'Life in New York Tenement-Houses as Seen by a City Missionary', originally published in *Scribner's Magazine*, June 1892, and reprinted in Woods, *The Poor in Great Cities*, p. 56.
110 Howard B. Grose, *Aliens or Americans?* (New York, 1906), p. 198.
111 Ibid., p. 196.
112 Hunter, *Poverty*, p. 265.
113 Robert E. Park and Herbert A. Miller, *Old World Traits Transplanted*, first published 1921 (New York, 1969), pp. 234, 61.
114 Charles B. Davenport, *Heredity in Relation to Eugenics* (New York, 1911), pp. 214, 219.
115 William C. Oates, House of Representatives, 19 February 1891, in *Congressional Record: Containing the Proceedings and Debates of the Fifty-First Congress, Second Session* (Washington, DC, 1891), vol. XXII, p. 2948.
116 *Annual Report of the Surgeon-General of the Public Health Service of the United States for the Fiscal Year 1921* (Washington, DC, 1921), p. 162.
117 Henry Cabot Lodge, House of Representatives, 19 February 1891, in *Congressional Record*, pp. 2956, 2958.
118 *Sun* (Melbourne), 12 October 1955, 16 October 1955, quoted in Alan Mayne, 'A Just War: The Language of Slum Representation in Twentieth-Century Australia', *Journal of Urban History*, XX/1 (1995), p. 86.
119 Woods, 'Social Awakening in London', p. 3.
120 Bill Luckin, 'Revisiting the Idea of Degeneration in Urban Britain, 1830–1900', *Urban History*, XXX/2 (2006), p. 243.
121 Hunter, *Poverty*, pp. 312, 313, 314.
122 Ibid., p. 315.
123 John Sandes, 'The Ambassador's "Double": What he thought of Australia', in *Australia To-Day*, 1 November 1912, p. 71.
124 E. J. Holloway, 'Foreword', in Barnett and Burt, *Housing the Australian Nation*, p. 3.
125 Jacob A. Riis, *The Battle with the Slum* (New York, 1902), p. 1.
126 *Annual Report of the Surgeon-General of the Public Health and Marine-Hospital Service of the United States for the Fiscal Year 1904* (Washington, DC, 1904), p. 199.
127 'A Day with the Slum Sisters', *War Cry*, 3 August 1907, p. 3.
128 Christopher Addison, *The Betrayal of the Slums* (London, 1922), pp. 10, 80.
129 R.M., *The Congested Areas of our City: Their Dangers, and a Suggested Outline for their Relief* (Melbourne, 1936), p. 7.

130 Donald J. Wilding, 'Report on Slum Conditions' (Melbourne, 1947), p. 2.
131 Ibid., p. 3.
132 Esther Romeyn, *Street Scenes: Staging the Self in Immigrant New York, 1880–1924* (Minneapolis, 2008), p. xix.
133 *Herald*, 6 July 1908, p. 2, 'Abolish the Slums'; *Argus*, 12 May 1910, p. 7, 'Melbourne's Slum Tangle'; *Punch*, 16 March 1922, p. 42, 'The Unseen Side of Melbourne'.
134 U.S. Commissioner of Immigration to Commissioner-General, 2 May 1899, enclosure in Commissioner-General of Immigration, Report on Japanese Immigration, 14 May 1900, in *House Documents*, 56-1, No. 686, p. 20.
135 *Argus* (Melbourne), 12 May 1910, p. 7.
136 *Call*, 1 June 1900, p. 6, 'Chinatown and the Chances'. Ibid., 1 July 1900, p. 11, 'Widen Streets of Chinatown and Purge Place of its Evils'.
137 Enclosure in Surgeon A. H. Glennan to Surgeon General Walter Wyman, 15 May 1903, in *House Documents*, 58-2, No. 338, p. 259.
138 *Call*, 1 June 1900, p. 6, 'Chinatown and the Chances'.
139 *Examiner*, 4 July 1900, p. 9, 'Health Board has Report on Plague'. *Chronicle*, 20 January 1903, p. 9, 'Chinese will Reward Murder'.
140 Ibid., 7 August 1904, p. 5, 'How White Women Doctors are Called in by the Wealthy to Cure Ills of Chinatown'.
141 *Examiner*, 18 January 1900, p. 2, 'Oriental Vengeance like a Tiger Asleep in Chinatown'.
142 *Sunday Examiner Magazine*, 18 March 1900, 'Why Chinese Murderers Escape; Showing Chinatown's Loopholes for Highbinders'.
143 Ibid.
144 *Argus*, 26 November 1912, p. 5, 'Alleged Chinese Opium Den'; ibid., 10 August 1911, p. 7, 'Trip to Chinatown'.
145 *Chronicle*, 16 December 1903, p. 9, 'Raid Highbinder Den; Capture Hatchet Men'.
146 Wilson et al., *Change or Decay*, p. 92.
147 Riis, *How the Other Half Lives*, p. 115.
148 Louis Wirth, 'The Ghetto' (first published 1927), in Louis Wirth, *On Cities and Social Life: Selected Papers* (Chicago, IL, 1964), p. 95.
149 David Ward, 'The Ethnic Ghetto in the United States: Past and Present', *Transactions of the Institute of British Geographers*, n.s., VII (1982), p. 271.
150 The quotation used as this section's title comes from Central Housing Advisory Committee, *Moving from the Slums*, p. 2.
151 Stubbs, *The Hidden People*, p. 2.
152 Wohl, *The Bitter Cry*, p. 61.
153 Chesterton, *I Lived in a Slum*, p. 86.
154 Barry M. Doyle, 'Mapping Slums in a Historic City: Representing Working Class Communities in Edwardian Norwich', *Planning Perspectives*, XVI/1 (2001), p. 50.
155 David Ward, *Poverty, Ethnicity, and the American City, 1840–1925: Changing Conceptions of the Slum and the Ghetto* (Cambridge, 1989), p. 40.
156 John S. Williams in the Senate, 5 August 1882, *Congressional Record:*

Containing the Proceedings and Debates of the Forty-seventh Congress, First Session (Washington, DC, 1882), p. 6951.

157 *Call*, 6 September 1896, p. 24, 'San Francisco's Barriers Against Oriental Plagues. The Best Equipped Quarantine Station in the World'.

158 U.S. Senate, 28 June 1832, in *Gales & Seaton's Register of Debates in Congress*, 22-1 (1832), pp. 1128–9.

159 Sims, *How the Poor Live*, p. 54.

160 B. S. Townroe, *The Slum Problem* (London, 1930), pp. 28–9.

161 B. Seebohm Rowntree, *Poverty and Progress: A Second Social Survey of York* (London, 1941), p. 446.

162 SNAP, *Another Chance for Cities*, 1972, p. 19.

163 Citizens' Association of New York, Report upon the Sanitary Conditions of the City (1865), quoted in Scobey, *Empire City*, p. 149.

164 The phrase was used in Honoré Frégier's *Des Classes dangereuses de la population dans les grandes villes* (Paris, 1840); 'dangerous class' was used in the authorized 1888 English translation of Karl Marx and Friedrich Engels, *The Communist Manifesto* (London, 1848).

165 Freeman, *Lights and Shadows of Melbourne Life*, p. 14.

166 Robert M. Dowling, *Slumming in New York: From the Waterfront to Mythic Harlem* (Urbana, IL, 2007), p. 32.

167 Gareth Stedman Jones, *Outcast London: A Study in the Relationship between Classes in Victorian Society* (Oxford, 1971).

168 *The Times*, 14 March 1928, p. 13, 'Mr Lloyd George on Slums of Kensington'.

169 Ibid., 29 October 1928, p. 16, 'Churches and Slum Clearance'.

170 Richard M. Brown, 'Historical Patterns of Violence in America', in *Violence in America: Historical and Comparative Perspectives*, ed. Hugh D. Graham and Ted R. Gurr (New York, 1969), p. 53.

171 Stanley Buder, *Pullman: An Experiment in Industrial Order and Community Planning 1880–1930* (New York, 1967), p. 192.

172 *Report of the National Advisory Commission on Civil Disorders* (New York, 1968), p. 203.

173 Michael Carriere, 'Chicago, the South Side Planning Board, and the Search for (Further) Order: Toward an Intellectual Lineage of Urban Renewal in Postwar America', *Journal of Urban History*, XXXIX/3 (2012), p. 413.

174 F. Oswald Barnett and A. G. Pearson, *The Poverty of the People of Australia* (Melbourne, 1944), pp. 7–8.

175 Ibid., p. 2.

176 Rowntree, *Poverty and Progress*, p. 276.

177 B. Seebohm Rowntree and G. R. Lavers, *Poverty and the Welfare State. A Third Social Survey of York dealing only with Economic Questions* (London, 1951), p. 32.

178 Charles J. Stokes, 'A Theory of Slums', *Land Economics*, XXXVIII/3 (1962), pp. 187–97.

179 Gerald D. Suttles, *The Social Order of the Slum: Ethnicity and Territory in the Inner City* (Chicago, IL, 1968), p. 25.

180 O'Day and Englander, *Mr Charles Booth's Inquiry*, p. 37.

181 R. Unwin, *Town Planning in Practice: An Introduction to the Art of*

Designing Cities and Suburbs (London, 1909), p. 271. Veiller quoted in Robert M. Fogelson, *Downtown: Its Rise and Fall, 1880–1950* (New Haven, CT, 2001), p. 328.

182 E. W. Russell, *The Slum Abolition Movement in Victoria, 1933–37* (Melbourne, 1972), p. 35.

183 Ibid., p. 24.

184 Joseph Kirkland, 'Among the Poor of Chicago', in *The Poor in Great Cities*, pp. 215–16.

185 Seth Koven, *Slumming: Sexual and Social Politics in Victorian London* (Princeton, NJ, 2004), p. 236.

186 Tucker, 16 March 1932, quoted in John Handfield, *Friends and Brothers: A Life of Gerard Kennedy Tucker, Founder of the Brotherhood of St. Laurence and Community Aid Abroad* (Melbourne, 1980), p. 95.

187 Tucker, *How It Began and How It Goes On* (1943), quoted ibid., p. 93.

188 Alexander Einar Pratt, *Letting in the Light: Faith, Fact and Fun in Melbourne's Poorer Parts* (Melbourne, 1933), p. 9.

189 Woods, 'The Social Awakening in London', p. 8. 'A Day with the Slum Sisters', *War Cry*, 3 August 1907, p. 3.

190 Marshall, *Slum*, p. 19.

191 *The Times*, 10 October 1933, p. 15, 'Slum Clearance'.

192 Ward, *Poverty, Ethnicity, and the American City*, p. 67.

193 Wohl, *The Eternal Slum*, p. 255. See Mark Swenarton, *Homes Fit for Heroes: The Politics and Architecture of Early State Housing in Britain* (London, 1981).

194 Catherine Bauer, *Modern Housing* (Boston, MA, 1934), p. 266.

195 P. Booth and M. Huxley, '1909 and All That: Reflections on the Housing, Town Planning, Etc. Act 1909', *Planning Perspectives*, XXVII/2 (2012), p. 273.

196 *The Poor in Great Cities*, p. viii. Housing Investigation and Slum Abolition Board, *First (Progress) Report: Slum Reclamation. Housing for the Lower-Paid Worker* (Melbourne, 1937), p. 45.

197 Addison, *Betrayal of the Slums*.

198 Barnett and Pearson, *Poverty of the People*, pp. 5–6.

199 F. Oswald Barnett, 'The Economics of the Slums', M. Comm. thesis, University of Melbourne, 1931, p. 85.

200 Russell, *Slum Abolition Movement in Victoria*, p. 28.

201 Townroe, *Britain Rebuilding*, p. 139.

202 Walters, *Scenes in Slum-land*, pp. 18, 15.

203 Stokes, 'A Theory of Slums', p. 194.

204 David A. Kirby, *Slum Housing and Residential Renewal: The Case in Urban Britain* (London, 1979), pp. 6, 40.

205 Gandal, *The Virtues of the Vicious*, p. 74.

206 Romeyn, *Street Scenes*, p. 55.

207 *Manchester City News*, 'Mr. J. Cuming Walters', no date [December 1931], newspaper cuttings, Birmingham Central Library.

208 *Chronicle*, 16 August 1903, Sunday Supplement p. 5, 'Chinese Boy is Running an Undertaking Establishment to keep Himself in School'. Ibid., 21 April 1901, p. 12, 'Government Lays Strong Hand on Chinese Slave Trade'.

209 Paula Rabinowitz, 'Margaret Bourke-White's Red Coat; or, Slumming in the 1930s', in *Radical Revisions: Rereading 1930s Culture*, ed. Bill Mullen and Sherry Lee Linkon (Urbana, IL, 1996), p. 198.
210 Romeyn, *Street Scenes*, p. 129.
211 Timothy J. Gilfoyle, *City of Eros: New York City, Prostitution, and the Commercialization of Sex, 1790–1920* (New York, 1992), p. 144.
212 Ibid., p. 183.
213 Pratt, *Letting in the Light*, p. 15.
214 R.M., *Congested Areas of our City*, p. 1.
215 *Examiner*, 22 March 1900, p. 7, 'To Stop Vulgar Shows in Chinatown'.
216 Walters, *Scenes in Slum-land*, p. 24.
217 Montague Grover, 'Big Lon. and Little Lon: Sinister Streets of Other Days', *The Bulletin*, 7 June 1933, p. 36.
218 *Chronicle*, 4 April 1903, p. 16, 'Ask Removal Of Chinatown'.
219 Ibid., 23 January 1903, p. 9, 'Chinese Observe Ancient Custom'.
220 Maren Stange, 'Jacob Riis and Urban Visual Culture: The Lantern Slide Exhibition as Entertainment and Ideology', *Journal of Urban History*, xv/3 (1989), p. 275.
221 Suttles, *The Social Order of the Slum*, p. 24.
222 Simon Pepper, *Housing Improvement: Goals and Strategy* (London, 1971), p. 90.
223 Ronald F. Henderson, Alison Harcourt and R.J.A. Harper, *People in Poverty: A Melbourne Survey* (Melbourne, 1970).
224 Ward, *Planning and Urban Change*, p. 184.
225 Henderson, Harcourt and Harper, *People in Poverty*, p. 139.
226 *Report of the National Advisory Commission on Civil Disorders*, p. 606.
227 Stubbs, *The Hidden People*, p. 128.
228 P. J. Hollingworth, *The Powerless Poor: A Comprehensive Guide to Poverty in Australia* (Melbourne, 1972), p. 145.
229 *Report of the National Advisory Commission on Civil Disorders*, pp. 410, 398.
230 Harrington, *The Other America*, p. xv.
231 Ida Susser and Jane Schneider, 'Wounded Cities: Destruction and Reconstruction in a Globalized World', in *Wounded Cities: Destruction and Reconstruction in a Globalized World*, ed. Jane Schneider and Ida Susser (Oxford, 2003), p. 6.

3 THE WAR ON SLUMS

1 *The Times*, 13 December 1933, p. 7, 'Parliament'.
2 See Jacob A. Riis, *A Ten Years' War: An Account of the Battle with the Slum in New York* (Boston, MA, 1900); *The Battle with the Slum* (New York, 1902).
3 Michael S. Gibson and Michael J. Langstaff, *An Introduction to Urban Renewal* (London, 1982), p. 11. See also John English, Ruth Madigan and Peter Norman, *Slum Clearance: The Social and Administrative Context in England and Wales* (London, 1976), p. 44; John Burnett, *A Social History of Housing, 1815–1970* (London, 1980), p. 279.
4 William J. Collins and Katherine L. Shester, *Slum Clearance and Urban*

Renewal in the United States (Cambridge, MA, 2011), p. 4.

5 Herbert J. Gans, *The Urban Villagers: Group and Class in the Life of Italian-Americans*, updated and expanded edition (New York, 1982), p. 386.

6 *The Times*, 20 January 1925, p. 9, 'A Gigantic Evil'.

7 United States Housing Authority, *The United States Housing Act of 1937, as Amended* (Washington DC, 1939), section 2 (3), p. 2.

8 Anthony S. Wohl, *Endangered Lives: Public Health in Victorian Britain* (London, 1983), p. 145.

9 Donald J. Wilding, 'Report on Slum Conditions' (Melbourne, 1947), p. 1.

10 *Birmingham Daily Post*, 13 March 1913, quoted in Alan Mayne, *The Imagined Slum: Newspaper Representation in Three Cities, 1870–1914* (Leicester, 1993), p. 92.

11 Catherine Bauer, *Modern Housing* (Boston, MA, 1934), p. xxxv.

12 Unhealthy Areas Committee, *Second and Final Report of the Committee appointed by the Minister of Health to Consider and Advise on the Principles to be Followed in Dealing with Unhealthy Areas* (London, 1921), p. 7.

13 Marian Bowley, *Housing and the State, 1919–1944* (London, 1945), p. 135.

14 Burnett, *A Social History of Housing*, p. 237.

15 Bowley, *Housing and the State*, p. 140. See Dougall Meston, *The Housing Act, 1935, with an Introduction, Notes and Index* (London, 1935).

16 J. A. Yelling, 'The Origins of British Redevelopment Areas', *Planning Perspectives*, III/3 (1988), p. 282.

17 See for example Carl Brown, 'MPS Debate Homes Fit for Habitation Bill', in INSIDE HOUSING, 19 October 2015, www.insidehousing.co.uk, accessed 30 June 2016.

18 Memorandum, 'Houses Unfit for Human Habitation', 25 October 1912, Town Clerk's Office, 12/6587.

19 F. Oswald Barnett and W. O. Burt, *Housing the Australian Nation* (Melbourne, 1942), p. 27.

20 Housing Commission of Victoria (HCV), *The Enemy within Our Gates* (Melbourne, 1966), n.p.

21 Mabel L. Walker, *Urban Blight and Slums* (Cambridge, MA, 1938), p. 3.

22 Jane Jacobs, *The Death and Life of Great American Cities: The Failure of Town Planning*, first published 1961 (Harmondsworth, 1965), p. 289.

23 Bauer, *Modern Housing*, p. 243.

24 Walker, *Urban Blight and Slums*, p. vii.

25 Ralph da Costa Nunez and Ethan G. Sribnick, *Family Poverty and Homelessness in New York City: The Poor Among Us* (New York, 2015), p. 154.

26 Lewis Mumford, *The Culture of Cities* (London, 1938), pp. 8, 245–8.

27 Robert A. Beauregard, *Voices of Decline: The Postwar Fate of U.S. Cities* (New York, 2003), p. 59.

28 Ibid., p. 73.

29 Housing Investigation and Slum Abolition Board, *First (Progress) Report: Slum Reclamation. Housing for the Lower-paid Worker* (Melbourne, 1937), pp. 3, 9. M. W. Peacock, 'Melbourne's Workers Need Homes!', *Australian Quarterly*, XII/4 (1940), p. 105.

30 Ramsay Mailler, *The Slums Are Still with Us* (Melbourne, 1944), p. 7.
31 Walter Bunning, *Homes in the Sun: The Past, Present and Future of Australian Housing* (Sydney, 1945), p. 8.
32 John R. Gold, 'A SPUR to Action?: The Society for the Promotion of Urban Renewal, "anti-scatter" and the Crisis of City Reconstruction, 1957–1963', *Planning Perspectives*, XXVII/2 (2012), pp. 199–223.
33 Robert M. Fogelson, *Downtown: Its Rise and Fall, 1880–1950* (New Haven, CT, 2001), p. 377.
34 Robert A. Caro, *The Power Broker: Robert Moses and the Fall of New York* (New York, 1974), p. 777.
35 David Harvey, 'The Right to the City', *New Left Review*, LIII (2008), p. 27.
36 Jon C. Teaford, *The Rough Road to Renaissance: Urban Revitalization in America, 1940–1985* (Baltimore, 1990), p. 112.
37 Jim Yelling, 'The Development of Residential Urban Renewal Policies in England: Planning for Modernization in the 1960s', *Planning Perspectives*, XIV/1 (1999), p. 3.
38 Douglas S. Robertson, 'Pulling in Opposite Directions: The Failure of Post War Planning to Regenerate Glasgow', *Planning Perspectives*, XIII/1 (1998), p. 54.
39 *The Times*, 25 November 1932, p. 7, 'House of Lords'.
40 Ministry of Housing and Local Government Welsh Office, *Old Houses into New Homes* (London, 1968), p. 1.
41 English, Madigan and Norman, *Slum Clearance*, p. 9.
42 David A. Kirby, *Slum Housing and Residential Renewal: The Case in Urban Britain* (London, 1979), p. 15.
43 Housing Investigation and Slum Abolition Board, *First (Progress) Report*, p. 17.
44 Carlton Association, *Housing Survival in Carlton* (Carlton, 1969), n.p.
45 *The Times*, 24 January 1934, p. 7, 'Local Authorities' Programmes'.
46 Herbert Gans, *People and Plans: Essays on Urban Problems and Solutions* (New York, 1968), p. 210.
47 Central Housing Advisory Committee Sub-committee on Standards of Housing Fitness, *Our Older Homes: A Call for Action* (London, 1966), p. 8.
48 Ministry of Housing and Local Government Welsh Office, *Old Houses into New Homes*, p. 9.
49 Carlton Association, *Housing Survival in Carlton*.
50 Liverpool Shelter Neighbourhood Action Project (SNAP), *Another Chance for Cities: SNAP69/72* (London, 1972), p. 35.
51 *The Times*, 6 October 1933, p. 13, 'Attacking the Slums'; p. 7, 'Slum Clearance'.
52 Bowley, *Housing and the State*, p. 152.
53 Neville Chamberlain, chairman's interim report (March 1920) in Unhealthy Areas Committee, *Second and Final Report*, p. 6.
54 *The Times*, 16 December 1932, p. 6, 'The Housing Bill'.
55 Manchester and District Regional Survey Society, *Social Studies of a Manchester City Ward. No. 3: Housing Needs of Ancoats in Relation to the Greenwood Act* (Manchester, 1930), p. 4.

56 R.P.P. Rowe, 'A Work of Slum Reclamation', in *The Times*, 8 April 1931, p. 11.

57 *The Times*, 25 November 1932, p. 7, 'House of Lords'.

58 Rowe, 'A Work of Slum Reclamation', p. 11.

59 *The Times* leader, 8 April 1931, p. 11, 'Good Landlords for Bad'.

60 Unhealthy Areas Committee, *Second and Final Report*, pp. 8, 9.

61 *The Times*, 10 October 1933, p. 15.

62 See Simon Pepper, *Housing Improvement: Goals and Strategy* (London, 1971), p. 16; Gibson and Langstaff, *An Introduction to Urban Renewal*, pp. 11, 51.

63 Wilding, 'Report on Slum Conditions', p. 15.

64 Gans, *People and Plans*, p. 222.

65 *The Times* leader, 27 November 1933, p. 15, 'Housing the Poorest'.

66 HCV, *State Housing* (Melbourne, 1965), p. 7.

67 Patricia L. Garside, '"Unhealthy Areas": Town Planning, Eugenics and the Slums', *Planning Perspectives*, III (1988), p. 30.

68 *The Times* 13 January 1932, p. 9.

69 Ibid., 31 October 1933, p. 11, 'Slum Dweller's Questions'.

70 *The Great Crusade* was the title of a 1936 promotional film; see Stephen V. Ward, *Planning and Urban Change*, 2nd edn (London, 2004), p. 60. 'A Good War' is the title of chapter 3 in B. S. Townroe, *Britain Rebuilding: The Slum and Overcrowding Campaigns* (London, 1936).

71 See for example *Age* (Melbourne), 8 October 1912, 'Anti-slum Crusade'.

72 *British Parliamentary Debates*, vol. CCLXXII, 5th series, 7 July 1933, p. 650.

73 *The Times*, 16 December 1932, p. 6, 'The Housing Bill'.

74 Harrington, *The Other America: Poverty in the United States*, revd edn (New York, 1971), pp. 163, 166.

75 Samuel Zipp, *Manhattan Projects: The Rise and Fall of Urban Renewal in Cold War New York* (Oxford, 2010), p. 5.

76 Norman Dennis, *Public Participation and Planners' Blight* (London, 1972), pp. 240, 241.

77 David Adams, 'Everyday Experiences of the Modern City: Remembering the Post-war Reconstruction of Birmingham', *Planning Perspectives*, XXVI/2 (2011), p. 244.

78 Beauregard, *Voices of Decline*, pp. 111–12.

79 Howard Marshall, *Slum* (London, 1933), p. 166. *The Times* editorial leader, 19 September 1928, p. 15, 'Housing Facts and Fallacies'; editorial, 18 May 1933, p. 15, 'The Campaign against Slums'.

80 Ibid., 5 October 1933, p. 7, 'Labour and Housing'; 31 October 1933, p. 11, 'Slum Dweller's Questions'.

81 Townroe, *Britain Rebuilding*, p. 36. Townroe had used the same passage in his earlier book *The Slum Problem* (London, 1930), p. 208(b).

82 Lindsay Thompson, December 1966, in HCV, *The Enemy within Our Gates*.

83 Townroe, *The Slum Problem*, pp. 1, 3.

84 *The Times*, 21 June 1928, p. 8, 'Slum Clearance'; Pepper, *Housing Improvement*, p. 102.

85 *The Times* leader, 8 April 1931, p. 11, 'Good Landlords for Bad'.

86 Kirby, *Slum Housing and Residential Renewal*, p. 65.

87 Nunez and Sribnick, *Family Poverty and Homelessness*, p. 126.

88 *The Times*, 20 November 1931, p. 7, 'New Homes for Old'; 8 December 1931, p. 11, 'New Homes for Old'.

89 *Herald*, 13 August 1936, quoted in E. W. Russell, *The Slum Abolition Movement in Victoria, 1933–37* (Melbourne, 1972), p. 8.

90 *The Medical Officer*, 15 April 1933, 'Slum Clearance', in Town Clerk's correspondence files, 33/3960.

91 Harrington, *The Other America*, p. 5.

92 Caro, *The Power Broker*, pp. 19, 20. See John T. Metzger, 'Rebuilding Harlem: Public Housing and Urban Renewal, 1920–1960', *Planning Perspectives*, IX/3 (1994), p. 276.

93 David Harvey, *The Urban Experience* (Oxford, 1989), pp. 192–3

94 *The Times*, 8 February 1933, p. 7, 'Slum Clearance'; 6 October 1933, p. 7, 'Slum Clearance'.

95 Bowley, *Housing and the State*, p. 152.

96 Gibson and Langstaff, *An Introduction to Urban Renewal*, p. 24.

97 John Handfield, *Friends and Brothers: A Life of Gerard Kennedy Tucker, Founder of the Brotherhood of St. Laurence and Community Aid Abroad* (Melbourne, 1980), p. 101.

98 HCV, *The Enemy within Our Gates*.

99 See Rachel Weber, 'Extracting Value from the City: Neoliberalism and Urban Redevelopment', in *Spaces of Neoliberalism: Urban Restructuring in North America and Western Europe* (Oxford, 2002), ed. Neil Brenner and Nik Theodore, pp. 172–93.

100 *New York Times*, 26 May 1957, quoted in Caro, *The Power Broker*, p. 1009.

101 See Ella Howard, *Homeless: Poverty and Place in Urban America* (Philadelphia, PA, 2013).

102 Christopher Klemek, *The Transatlantic Collapse of Urban Renewal: Postwar Urbanism from New York to Berlin* (Chicago, IL, 2011), pp. 40, 47.

103 Final Report of the Commonwealth Housing Commission, 1944, quoted in Anne Stevenson, Elaine Martin and Judith O'Neill, *High Living: A Study of Family Life in Flats* (Melbourne, 1967), p. 14.

104 Brotherhood of St Laurence, *What's Wrong with Victoria's Housing Programme?* (Melbourne, 1954), p. 7.

105 See Kaye Hargreaves, ed., *'This House Not For Sale': Conflicts between the Housing Commission and Residents of Slum Reclamation Areas* (Melbourne, 1976).

106 Housing Management Sub-Committee of the Central Housing Advisory Committee, *Moving from the Slums: Seventh Report of the Housing Management Sub-Committee of the Central Housing Advisory Committee* (London, 1956), p. 1.

107 Macmillan in the House of Commons, November 1953, quoted in Kirby, *Slum Housing and Residential Renewal*, p. 72.

108 Andrew Tallon, *Urban Regeneration in the UK*, 2nd edn (Abingdon, 2013), p. 35.

109 *Birmingham Evening Mail*, quoted in Adams, 'Everyday Experiences of the Modern City', p. 244.

110 Graham Towers, *Building Democracy: Community Architecture in the Inner Cities* (London, 1995), p. 227

111 Quoted in Pepper, *Housing Improvement*, p. 103.

112 Rob Atkinson, 'Narratives of Policy: The Construction of Urban Problems and Urban Policy in the Official Discourse of British Government 1969–1998', *Critical Social Policy*, xx/2 (2000), p. 217.

113 Lord Melchett, in *The Times*, 21 June 1928, p. 8, 'Slum Clearance'.

114 John H. Reeves, *Housing the Forgotten Tenth: An Investigation of the 'Problem Tenant'* (Melbourne, 1944), p. 9.

115 Carlton Association, *Housing Survival in Carlton*.

116 Hilda Jennings, *Societies in the Making: A Study of Development and Redevelopment within a County Borough* (London, 1962), pp. 81–2.

117 Ibid., p. 96.

118 Gans, *People and Plans*, p. 219.

119 Ministry of Housing and Local Government Welsh Office, *Old Houses into New Homes*, p. 10.

120 Carlton Association, *Housing Survival in Carlton*.

121 Gans, *People and Plans*, p. 212.

122 English, Madigan and Norman, *Slum Clearance*, p. 177.

123 Jennings, *Societies in the Making*, pp. 84–5.

124 English, Madigan and Norman, *Slum Clearance*, p. 172.

125 Norman Dennis, *People and Planning: The Sociology of Housing in Sunderland* (London, 1970), pp. 177, 196–7.

126 English, Madigan and Norman, *Slum Clearance*, p. 178.

127 Val Wilson, *Rich in All but Money: Life in Hungate 1900–1938*, revd edn (York, 2007), p. 150.

128 Fogelson, *Downtown: Its Rise and Fall*, p. 331.

129 Townroe, *The Slum Problem*, pp. 3–4.

130 J. Cuming Walters, *Further Scenes in Slum-land* (Birmingham, 1901), p. 12.

131 *The Times*, 5 December 1931, p. 7, 'Persistence of Slum Habits'.

132 Unhealthy Areas Committee, *Second and Final Report*, p. 9.

133 Ward, *Planning and Urban Change*, p. 140.

134 Gans, *People and Plans*, p. 204.

135 English, Madigan and Norman, *Slum Clearance*, p. 186.

136 Unhealthy Areas Committee, *Second and Final Report*, p. 9.

137 H. A. Hill, *The Complete Law of Housing, including the Housing Act, 1925, the Housing Act, 1930* (London, 1931), p. lii.

138 English, Madigan and Norman, *Slum Clearance*, p. 76.

139 Gans, *People and Plans*, pp. 220, 214.

140 Harrington, *The Other America*, p. 148.

141 HCV, *State Housing*, p. 7.

142 *Architects' Journal*, quoted in Simon Pepper and Peter Richmond, 'Stepney and the Politics of High-rise Housing: Limehouse Fields to John Scurr House, 1925–1937', *The London Journal*, xxxiv/1 (2009), p. 41.

143 Housing Management Sub-Committee, *Moving from the Slums*, p. 7.

144 *The Times*, 12 February 1934, p. 14, 'Slum Clearance in London'.

145 Ibid., 26 July 1928, p. 10, 'Block Dwellings'; 21 June 1928, p. 8, 'Slum Clearance'.

146 Ibid., 16 November 1931, p. 9, 'L.C.C. and Peckham Tenants'.
147 Jennings, *Societies in the Making*, pp. 99, 154–5.
148 Housing Management Sub-Committee, *Moving from the Slums*, p. 3.
149 *The Times*, 16 December 1932, p. 6, 'The Housing Bill'.
150 Michael Young and Peter Willmott, *Family and Kinship in East London* (London, 1957), p. 86.
151 English, Madigan and Norman, *Slum Clearance*, p. 119.
152 Manchester University Settlement, *Ancoats: A Study of a Clearance Area. Report of a Survey made in 1937–1938* (Manchester, 1945), p. 4.
153 Young and Willmott, *Family and Kinship in East London*, p. 85.
154 Gans, *People and Plans*, p. 215. See Gans, *The Urban Villagers*.
155 Dennis, *People and Planning*, p. 213.
156 Sidney Jacobs, *The Right to a Decent House* (London, 1976), p. 25.
157 George R. Sims, *How the Poor Live* (London, 1883), p. 128.
158 Caro, *The Power Broker*, pp. 893, 970.
159 Gans, *People and Plans*, p. 212.
160 Jennings, *Societies in the Making*, p. 89.
161 Hilda Jennings, *University Settlement Bristol: Sixty Years of Change 1911–1971* (Bristol, 1971), p. 48.
162 Towers, *Building Democracy*, p. 227
163 Dennis, *Public Participation and Planners' Blight*, p. 53.
164 Ibid., p. 79.
165 Gibson and Langstaff, *An Introduction to Urban Renewal*, p. 222.
166 Pepper, *Housing Improvement*, p. 87.
167 A. Stones, 'Stop Slum Clearance – Now', in *Built Environment*, 1972, quoted in Gibson and Langstaff, *An Introduction to Urban Renewal*, p. 47.
168 Hugh Wilson and Lewis Womersley, Roger Tym and Associates, Jamieson Mackay and Partners, *Change or Decay: Final Report of the Liverpool Inner Area Study* (London, 1977), p. 47.
169 Caro, *The Power Broker*, pp. 865, 859.
170 Ibid., p. 520.
171 *Daily Telegraph*, 15 January 1884, 'Inspection and Condemnation of Rookeries', quoted in Alan Mayne, *Representing the Slum: Popular Journalism in a Late Nineteenth Century City* (Melbourne, 1990), p. 165.
172 Dennis, *Public Participation and Planners' Blight*, pp. 147–8.
173 *The Times* editorial leader, 18 April 1933, p. 11, 'The Slums'.
174 Caro, *The Power Broker*, pp. 850–84.
175 Zipp, *Manhattan Project*, p. 204. Metzger, 'Rebuilding Harlem', pp. 276–7.
176 Gerald D. Suttles, *The Social Order of the Slum: Ethnicity and Territory in the Inner City* (Chicago, IL, 1968), p. 22.
177 Klemek, *The Transatlantic Collapse of Urban Renewal*, pp. 170–73.
178 Laura Madokoro, 'Chinatown and Monster Homes: The Splintered Chinese Diaspora in Vancouver', *Urban History Review*, XXXIX/2 (2011), p. 18.
179 See Renate Howe, ed., *New Houses for Old: Fifty Years of Public Housing in Victoria 1938–1988* (Melbourne, 1988), pp. 155–6.
180 Zipp, *Manhattan Project*, p. 358. See Caro, *The Power Broker*, p. 1044.

181 Gans, *People and Plans*, p. 204.

182 See Wilson et al., *Change or Decay*, pp. 136–7.

183 See Peter Shapley, 'Planning, Housing and Participation in Britain, 1968–1976', *Planning Perspectives*, xxvi/1 (2011), pp. 75–90.

184 Gibson and Langstaff, *An Introduction to Urban Renewal*, pp. 204–45.

185 Zula Nittim, 'The Coalition of Resident Action Groups', in *Twentieth Century Sydney: Studies in Urban and Social History*, ed. Jill Roe (Sydney, 1980), pp. 231–47.

186 Gans, *People and Plans*, pp. 36–7.

187 Chris Wallace-Crabbe, 'A Mental Carlton', undated typescript in author's possession.

188 *Oxford English Dictionary Online*, 'gentrification, n.', www.oed.com, accessed 26 May 2014. Wallace-Crabbe, 'A Mental Carlton'.

189 See Klemek, *The Transatlantic Collapse of Urban Renewal*, pp. 145–60.

190 Ibid., pp. 219–24.

191 See Madokoro, 'Chinatown and Monster Homes'.

192 *Age* (Melbourne), 4 July 1969, 'Old Houses – New Powers'.

193 Hargreaves, *'This House Not For Sale'*, p. 7.

194 Carlton Association, *Housing Survival in Carlton*.

195 Hargreaves, *'This House Not For Sale'*, pp. 37, 57.

196 *Age* (Melbourne), 17 August 1973, 'Hamer Didn't Let It Happen'.

197 Hargreaves, *'This House Not For Sale'*, p. 12.

198 Gibson and Langstaff, *An Introduction to Urban Renewal*, p. 101.

199 Jacobs, *The Death and Life of Great American Cities*, p. 285.

200 *Age* (Melbourne) editorial, 12 June 1969, 'When is a Slum?'

201 See David Lowenthal, *The Heritage Crusade and the Spoils of History* (Cambridge, 1998).

202 Pepper, *Housing Improvement*, p. 101.

203 J. B. Cullingworth, *Housing in Transition: A Case Study in the City of Lancaster 1958–1962* (London, 1963), pp. 119–20.

204 Kirby, *Slum Housing and Residential Renewal*, p. 74.

205 Ward, *Planning and Urban Change*, p. 147. Kirby, *Slum Housing and Residential Renewal*, p. 75.

206 R. Crosland, 'Government Change Gear in their Housing Policy', *Building Societies Gazette*, February 1976, quoted in Kirby, *Slum Housing and Residential Renewal*, p. 77.

207 Klemek, *The Transatlantic Collapse of Urban Renewal*, p. 203.

4 ORIENTALIZING THE SLUM

1 'Third World', n. (and adj.); 'Developing World', n., *Oxford English Dictionary Online*, www.oed.com, accessed 17 July 2014.

2 'Orient', n. and adj.; 'Orientalism', n., ibid. See Edward W. Said, *Orientalism* (London, 1978).

3 'Report on the Question of the Housing of the Population of Hongkong', 14 May 1902, in *Hong Kong Government Gazette Extraordinary*, 10 June 1902, p. 997.

4 H. V. Lanchester, *Town Planning in Madras: A Review of the Conditions*

and Requirements of City Improvement and Development in the Madras Presidency (London, 1918), p. 6.

5 Alan Smart, *The Shek Kip Mei Myth: Squatters, Fires and Colonial Rule in Hong Kong, 1950–1963* (Hong Kong, 2006), p. 46.

6 *Hong Kong Legislative Council*, 13 October 1938, p. 119.

7 Teo Siew Eng and Lily Kong, 'Public Housing in Singapore: Interpreting "Quality" in the 1990s', *Urban Studies*, xxxiv/3 (1997), p. 441.

8 Indian Plague Commission, *Report of the Indian Plague Commission with Appendices and Summary* (London, 1901), vol. v, p. 362.

9 Indian Plague Commission, *Minutes of Evidence taken by the Indian Plague Commission with Appendices* (London, 1900), vol. ii, pp. 449–50.

10 E. P. Richards, *Report on the Condition, Improvement and Town Planning of the City of Calcutta and Contiguous Areas* (Ware, Hertfordshire, 1914), pp. 229, 231.

11 A. R. Burnett-Hurst, *Labour and Housing in Bombay: A Study in the Economic Conditions of the Wage-earning Classes in Bombay* (Westminster, 1925), p. 31. Indian Plague Commission, *Report of the Indian Plague Commission*, vol. v, appendix iii, p. 449. Corporation of Madras, *Annual Report of the Health Officer of the City of Madras for the Year 1925* (Madras, 1926), p. 31.

12 Annual Report of the Medical Officer of Health for 1937, in *Report on the Administration of the Delhi Municipality for the Year 1937–38*, vol. ii, p. 64.

13 Sir Bhalchandra Krishna, *Overcrowding in Bombay and the Problem of Housing the Poor and Working Classes* (Bombay, 1904), p. 7.

14 J. M. Linton Bogle, *Town Planning in India* (Bombay, 1929), p. 7.

15 Richards, *Report on the Condition, Improvement and Town Planning of the City of Calcutta*, pp. 229, 238.

16 Prashant Kidambi, *The Making of an Indian Metropolis: Colonial Governance and Public Culture in Bombay, 1890–1920* (Aldershot, 2007), pp. 203–33.

17 Corporation of Madras, *Annual Report of the Health Officer of the City of Madras for the Year 1917* (Madras, 1918), p. 2.

18 Corporation of Madras, *Annual Report of the Health Officer of the City of Madras for the Year 1922* (Madras, 1923), p. 3. Corporation of Madras, *Annual Report of the Health Officer of the City of Madras for the Year 1925* (Madras, 1926), p. 32.

19 Corporation of Madras, *Annual Report of the Health Officer of the City of Madras for the Year 1926* (Madras, 1927), pp. 2, 3. Corporation of Madras, *Annual Report of the Health Officer of the City of Madras for the Year 1928* (Madras, 1929), p. ii.

20 Krishna, *Overcrowding in Bombay*, pp. 20, 10, 11.

21 Ibid., p. 23.

22 Chunilal Bose, *Health of Calcutta* (Calcutta, 1928), p. 4.

23 Jawaharlal Nehru, *An Autobiography*, first published 1936 (New Delhi, 2004), p. 29.

24 Ibid., p. 151.

25 Jawaharlal Nehru, *The Discovery of India*, first published 1946 (New Delhi, 2004), p. 391.

26 Tommy Koh, 'The Singapore of my Dreams', *Southeast Asian Affairs* (2009), p. 305.

27 Kidambi, *The Making of an Indian Metropolis*, p. 211.

28 Nehru, *An Autobiography*, p. 151

29 Dr Arthur Geddes, quoted in Bharat Sevak Samaj, *Slums of Old Delhi: Report of the Socio-economic Survey of the Slum Dwellers of Old Delhi City* (Delhi, 1958), appendix 1, pp. 217–18.

30 Stephen Legg, *Spaces of Colonialism: Delhi's Urban Governmentalities* (Oxford, 2007), p. 43.

31 Vincent I. Ogu, 'Evolutionary Dynamics of Urban Land Use Planning and Environmental Sustainability in Nigeria', *Planning Perspectives*, xiv/4, p. 351.

32 Andrew Byerley, 'Displacements in the Name of (Re)development: The Contested Rise and Contested Demise of Colonial "African" Housing Estates in Kampala and Jinja', *Planning Perspectives*, xxiv/4 (2013), p. 550.

33 Nehru, *An Autobiography*, p. 452.

34 Kidambi, *The Making of an Indian Metropolis*, pp. 236–7.

35 Robert Home, *Of Planting and Planning: The Making of British Colonial Cities*, 2nd edn (London, 2013), p. 57. See also Robert Home, 'Shaping Cities of the Global South: Legal Histories of Planning and Colonialism', in *The Routledge Handbook on Cities of the Global South*, ed. Susan Parnell and Sophie Oldfield (London, 2014), pp. 75–85.

36 Marie Huchzermeyer, *Tenement Cities: From 19th Century Berlin to 21st Century Nairobi* (Trenton, NJ, 2011), p. 130.

37 Bogle, *Town Planning in India*, p. 6.

38 Corporation of Madras, *Annual Report of the Health Officer of the City of Madras for the Year 1918* (Madras, 1919), p. 1.

39 Bombay Plague Committee, *Report of the Bombay Plague Committee* (Bombay, 1898), p. 130.

40 Burnett-Hurst, *Labour and Housing in Bombay*, p. 5. See David Arnold, *Colonizing the Body: State Medicine and Epidemic Disease in Nineteenth-century India* (Berkeley, CA, 1993), pp. 200–239.

41 Patrick Geddes, *Town Planning towards City Development: A Report to the Durbar of Indore. Part I* (Indore, 1918), p. 14.

42 Bombay Plague Committee, *Report*, p. 67. W. L. Harvey, *Report of the Municipal Commissioner on the Plague in Bombay for the Year Ending 31st May 1899* (Bombay, 1899), p. 25. W. L. Harvey, *Report of the Municipal Commissioner on the Plague in Bombay for the Year Ending 31st May 1900* (Bombay, 1901), p. 16.

43 'Memorandum by Mr. W. H. Owen', in *Report of the Housing Commission 1935* (Hong Kong, 1938), p. 272.

44 Patrick Geddes, 'Report on the Towns in the Madras Presidency' (1915), in *Patrick Geddes in India*, ed. Jacqueline Tyrwhitt (London, 1947), p. 72. Geddes, *Town Planning towards City Development. Part I*, p. 14.

45 Burnett-Hurst, *Labour and Housing in Bombay*, p. 31.

46 Lanchester, *Town Planning in Madras*, p. vii.

47 J. P. Orr, *Social Reform and Slum Reform: Part I – General. A Lecture delivered by J. P. Orr, Esq., c.s.i., i.c.s., to the Social Services League,*

Bombay, in the Servants of India Society's Hall, Bombay, on 3rd September 1917 (Bombay, 1917), p. 1.

48 Margaret Jones, 'Tuberculosis, Housing and the Colonial State: Hong Kong, 1900–1950', *Modern Asian Studies*, XXXVII/3 (2003), p. 681.

49 Indian Plague Commission, *Minutes of Evidence taken by the Indian Plague Commission*, question 1090, p. 47.

50 C. A. Bentley, *Diploma in Public Health Manual* (Calcutta, 1921), pp. 158–9, 164–5.

51 Indian Plague Commission, *Minutes of Evidence taken by the Indian Plague Commission*, question 975, p. 44.

52 Ibid., question 908, p. 41; question 26,667, p. 364.

53 T. Frederick Pearse, *Report on Plague in Calcutta for the Year Ending 30th June 1904* (Calcutta, 1905), pp. 1, 8.

54 Indian Plague Commission, *Report of the Indian Plague Commission*, vol. V, p. 491.

55 Patrick Geddes, *Reports on Re-planning of Six Towns in Bombay Presidency 1915* (Bombay, 1965), p. 20.

56 Bombay Plague Committee, *Report*, p. 70.

57 Krishna, *Overcrowding in Bombay*, pp. 24, 35.

58 Lanchester, *Town Planning in Madras*, p. 57.

59 H. M. Crake, *Report on Plague in Calcutta for the Year Ending 30th June 1910* (Calcutta, 1910), n.p.

60 Richards, *Report on the Condition, Improvement and Town Planning of the City of Calcutta*, pp. xv, 2–4. Calcutta Improvement Trust, *The Calcutta Improvement Act, 1911 and Allied Matters* (Calcutta, 1974), p. 18.

61 Corporation of Madras, *Annual Report of the Health Officer for the Year 1922* (Madras, 1923), p. 3. *Annual Report of the Director of Town-planning for the Year 1937–38* (Madras, 1939), p. 14.

62 Delhi Improvement Trust, *Administration Report of the Delhi Improvement Trust for Years 1937–1939* (New Delhi, 1940), p. 4.

63 Ibid., p. 2.

64 'Annual Report of the Medical Officer of Health for 1937', in Delhi Municipality, *Report on the Administration of the Delhi Municipality for the Year 1937–38* (Delhi, 1938), vol. I, p. 65. See the body of work since the mid-2000s by Stephen Legg (University of Nottingham) on colonial Delhi.

65 Geddes, *Town Planning towards City Development, Part I*, p. 15.

66 Patrick Geddes, *Town Planning towards City Development: A Report to the Durbar of Indore. Part II* (Indore, 1918), pp. 103–4.

67 City of Bombay Improvement Trust, *Administration Report for the Year Ending 31st March 1906* (Bombay, 1906), p. ii.

68 Report of the Health Officer, 1903–4, quoted in Kidambi, *The Making of an Indian Metropolis*, p. 89.

69 J. P. Orr, *Social Reform and Slum Reform. Part II: Bombay Past and Present* (Bombay, 1917), p. 23.

70 Calcutta Improvement Trust, *The Calcutta Improvement Act*, p. 29.

71 Calcutta Improvement Trust, *Annual Report of the Calcutta Improvement Trust for the Year 1913–14* (Calcutta, 1914), p. 7.

72 Calcutta Improvement Trust, *Annual Report of the Calcutta Improvement Trust for the Year 1912–13* (Calcutta, 1913), p. II.

73 Calcutta Improvement Trust, *Annual Report of the Calcutta Improvement Trust for the Year 1917–18* (Calcutta, 1918), p. 22.
74 City of Bombay Improvement Trust, *Administration Report for the Year Ending 31st March 1899* (Bombay, 1899), p. 5. City of Bombay Improvement Trust, *Administration Report for the Year Ending 31st March 1900* (Bombay, 1900), p. 5.
75 City of Bombay Improvement Trust, *Administration Report for the Year Ending 31st March 1902* (Bombay, 1902), pp. 3, 5. City of Bombay Improvement Trust, *Administration Report for the Year Ending 31st March 1903* (Bombay, 1903), p. xiv.
76 City of Bombay Improvement Trust, *Administration Report for the Year Ending 31st March 1900* (Bombay, 1900), p. 3.
77 City of Bombay Improvement Trust, *Administration Report for the Year Ending 31st March 1918* (Bombay, 1918), p. 114.
78 City of Bombay Improvement Trust, *Administration Report for the Year Ending 31st March 1917* (Bombay, 1917), p. 1.
79 City of Bombay Improvement Trust, *Administration Report for the Year Ending 31st March 1912* (Bombay, 1912), p. 33.
80 Orr, *Social Reform and Slum Reform. Part II*, p. 23.
81 Burnett-Hurst, *Labour and Housing in Bombay*, p. 31.
82 Richards, *Report on the Condition, Improvement and Town Planning of the City of Calcutta*, pp. 257, 301.
83 Ibid., p. 262.
84 Ibid., p. 263.
85 Ibid., p. 282.
86 Bogle, *Town Planning in India*, pp. 75–6.
87 Delhi Improvement Trust, *Administration Report*, 1937–1939, p. 23. See Legg, *Spaces of Colonialism*, ch. 4.
88 Calcutta Improvement Trust, *Annual Report on the Operations of the Calcutta Improvement Trust for the Year 1947–48* (Calcutta, 1948), p. 7.
89 Delhi Municipality, *Report on the Administration of the Delhi Municipality for the Year 1938–39* (Delhi, 1939), vol. I, pp. 24, 25.
90 Government of Bombay, *Report of the Town Planning and Valuation Department for the Period from 1st April 1936 to 31st March 1938* (Bombay, 1938), p. 2.
91 Brenda S. A. Yeoh, *Contesting Space in Colonial Singapore: Power Relations and the Urban Built Environment* (Singapore, 2003), p. 152.
92 Ibid., p. 162.
93 Singapore Improvement Trust, 1932, quoted ibid., p. 164.
94 Singapore Improvement Trust, 1948, quoted in Loh Kah Seng, 'Dangerous Migrants and the Informal Mobile City of Postwar Singapore', *Mobilities*, v/2 (2010), p. 201.
95 Smart, *The Shek Kip Mei Myth*, p. 61.
96 Hong Kong Legislative Council, *Official Report of Proceedings*, 30 September 1964, p. 356. See Alan Smart, *Making Room: Squatter Clearance in Hong Kong* (Hong Kong, 1992).
97 Hong Kong Legislative Council, *Official Report of Proceedings*, 30 September 1964, p. 356.

98 C. Y. Jim, 'Urban Renewal and Environmental Planning in Hong Kong', *The Environmentalist*, XIV/3 (1994), p. 179.

99 Ibid., p. 171.

100 Byerley, 'Displacements in the Name of (Re)development', pp. 3–8

101 Godwin Arku, 'The Economics of Housing Programmes in Ghana, 1929–66', *Planning Perspectives*, XXIV/3 (2009), p. 286.

102 United Nations Economic and Social Council, 'The Ghana Roof Loan Scheme', typescript, 10 January 1969, p. 3, in UN Economic Commission for Africa, www.repository.uneca.org.

5 NEW SLUMS IN A POSTCOLONIAL WORLD

1 Jawaharlal Nehru, 'Foreword', in Bharat Sevak Samaj, *Slums of Old Delhi: Report of the Socio-economic Survey of the Slum Dwellers of Old Delhi City* (Delhi, 1958), p. 7.

2 Ben C. Arimah (UN-Habitat), 'Slums as Expressions of Social Exclusion: Explaining the Prevalence of Slums in African Countries', p. 4, www. oecd.org, accessed 27 June 2014. United Nations Human Settlements Programme, *The Challenge of Slums: Global Report on Human Settlements 2003* (London, 2003), p. 129.

3 G. Arku, 'The Economics of Housing Programmes in Ghana, 1929–66', *Planning Perspectives*, XXIV/3 (2009), pp. 281–300.

4 Andrew Byerley, 'Displacements in the Name of (Re)development: The Contested Rise and Contested Demise of Colonial "African" Housing Estates in Kampala and Jinja', *Planning Perspectives*, XXIV/4 (2013), p. 10.

5 Amnesty International, Kenya, *The Unseen Majority: Nairobi's Two Million Slum-dwellers* (London, 2009), p. 7.

6 Lim Yew Hock in 1958, quoted in Loh Kah Seng, 'Dangerous Migrants and the Informal Mobile City of Postwar Singapore', *Mobilities*, V/2 (2010), p. 197.

7 Lee Kuan Yew in the 1968 *Singapore Year Book*, quoted in Yue-man Yeung, *National Development Policy and Urban Transformation in Singapore: A Study of Public Housing and the Marketing System* (Chicago, IL, 1973), p. 173.

8 Johnny Liang Heng Wong, 'Creating a Sustainable Living Environment for Public Housing in Singapore', in *Climate Change and Sustainable Urban Development in Africa and Asia*, ed. B. Yuen and A. Kumssa (London, 2011), p. 119.

9 Sim Lou Lee, Lim Lan Yuan and Tay Kah Poh, 'Shelter for All: Singapore's Strategy for Full Home Ownership by the Year 2000', *Habitat International*, XVII/1 (1993), p. 96.

10 Loh Kah Seng, 'Conflict and Change at the Margins: Emergency Kampong Clearance and the Making of Modern Singapore', *Asian Studies Review*, XXXIII/2 (2009), p. 140.

11 Lee, Yuan and Poh, 'Shelter for All', p. 86.

12 See Peter Lloyd, 'Poverty: Attitudes and Policies of Dominant Groups', in *Slums of Hope? Shanty Towns of the Third World* (Manchester, 1979), pp. 41–68.

13 Indian Planning Commission, *Sixth Five Year Plan, 1980–85* (New Delhi, 1981), p. 389.

14 Loh Kah Seng, '*Kampong*, Fire, Nation: Towards a Social History of Postwar Singapore', *Journal of Southeast Asian Studies*, XL/3 (2009), p. 624.

15 Housing and Development Board, *Annual Report*, 1963, quoted in Seng, 'Conflict and Change at the Margins', p. 152.

16 David Arnold, *Police Power and Colonial Rule: Madras, 1859–1947* (Delhi, 1986), p. 33.

17 Ministry of Works, Housing and Supply, *Slum Clearance Scheme: Grant of Loans and Subsidies to State Governments for Slum Clearance/ Improvement Projects* (1957), p. 9, GOI Ministry of Home Affairs, Delhi Section. National Archives of India, 14/11/58 – Delhi.

18 Seng, 'Conflict and Change at the Margins', p. 140.

19 Arimah, 'Slums as Expressions of Social Exclusion', p. 14.

20 Byerley, 'Displacements in the Name of (Re)development', p. 12.

21 P. R. Nayak in *Report of the Seminar on Slum Clearance*, ed. B. Chatterjee and Zakia Khan (Bombay, 1958), p. 17.

22 V.S.C. Bonarjee, 'Some Problems and Solutions on Town Planning in India', reprinted in *The Calcutta Improvement Act, 1911 and Allied Matters*, ed. Calcutta Improvement Trust (Calcutta, 1974), p. 7.

23 Charles Abrams, *Man's Struggle for Shelter in an Urbanizing World* (Cambridge, MA, 1964), p. 119.

24 Ministry of Health memorandum, 16 March 1959, in Ministry of Home Affairs, Seminar on 'Urbanisation in India – Urban Trends and Problems in a Developing Country', National Archives of India, 25/42/59 – Delhi.

25 Deputy Secretary A. V. Venkatasubban, Ministry of Home Affairs, 'Master Plan, Urbanisation and Housing Problems of Delhi', 16 May 1959, National Archives of India, 32/24/59 – Delhi.

26 A. R. Desai and S. D. Pillai, *A Profile of an Indian Slum* (Bombay, 1972), pp. 29–30.

27 S. B. Bhasme, *Report of the Commission of Inquiry on the Worli and Naigaum B.D.D. Chawls Disturbances, Bombay* (Bombay, 1976), p. 324.

28 Tamil Nadu Slum Clearance Board, *Socio-economic Survey of Madras Slums* (Madras, 1975), pp. 37, 41.

29 Indian Planning Commission, *First Five Year Plan* (Delhi, 1953), p. 233.

30 Working Group on Housing and Urban Development for the Third Five Year Plan, Paper No. III, 'Regional Planning' (1959), p. 3, in Ministry of Home Affairs, 'Master Plan, Urbanisation and Housing Problems of Delhi', National Archives of India, 32/24/59 – Delhi.

31 M.K.A. Siddiqui, 'Life in the Slums of Calcutta: Some Aspects', *Economic and Political Weekly*, IV/50 (1969), p. 1917.

32 William J. Cousins and Catherine Goyder, *Changing Slum Communities: Urban Community Development in Hyderabad* (New Delhi, 1979), p. 6.

33 Vandana Desai, *Community Participation and Slum Housing: A Study of Bombay* (New Delhi, 1995), p. 139.

34 Tamil Nadu Slum Clearance Board, *Socio-economic Survey of Madras Slums* (Madras, 1975), p. 13.

35 Indian Planning Commission, *First Five Year Plan*, p. 247.
36 Memorandum, 24 October 1958, Ministry of Home Affairs, National Archives of India, 15/46/58 – Delhi.
37 Calcutta Improvement Trust, *Annual Report on the Operations of the Calcutta Improvement Trust for the Year 1951–52* (Calcutta, 1952), p. 25.
38 Meeting of Standing Committee of the Congress Party on Rehabilitation, 8 September 1959, Ministry of Home Affairs, National Archives of India, 32/40/59 – Delhi.
39 S. Mullick (Joint Secretary, Ministry of Health) to Hari Sharma (Joint Secretary, Ministry of Home Affairs), 16 May 1957, Ministry of Home Affairs, National Archives of India, 27/17/57 – Delhi
40 Memorandum by A. P. Nathan, 24 October 1958, Ministry of Home Affairs, National Archives of India, 15/46/58–Delhi.
41 Bharat Sevak Samaj, *Slums of Old Delhi*, p. 8.
42 DDA to Ministry of Home Affairs, 11 February 1959, p. 21, Ministry of Home Affairs, National Archives of India, 33/1/59 – Delhi.
43 Ministry of Home Affairs, *Report of Fact Finding Committee: Slum Clearance Demolitions, etc, and Firing in Turkman Gate During the Emergency, June 25, 1975–March 21, 1977* (New Delhi, 1977), p. 27.
44 Chief Commissioner Delhi to Secretary Ministry of Health, 9 February 1957, Ministry of Home Affairs, National Archives of India, 27/17/57 – Delhi.
45 Prime Minister's Principal Private Secretary to Chief Commissioner Delhi, 7 February 1957, p. 5, Ministry of Home Affairs, National Archives of India, 27/17/57 – Delhi.
46 Notes, 21 March 1957, pp. 1–2, Ministry of Home Affairs, National Archives of India, 27/17/57 – Delhi.
47 Meeting of the Delhi Advisory Committee, 20 July 1959, Ministry of Home Affairs, National Archives of India, 33/1/59 – Delhi.
48 Prime Minister's Principal Private Secretary to Chief Commissioner Delhi, 7 February 1957, Ministry of Home Affairs, National Archives of India, 27/17/57 – Delhi.
49 Nehru, 'Foreword', p. 7.
50 'A Pilot Project for Social and Economic Welfare Work in the Slums of Delhi by Bharat Sewak Samaj, Delhi Pradesh' (1956), p. 1, Ministry of Home Affairs, National Archives of India, 8/69/57 – Delhi.
51 Ibid., p. 2.
52 Bharat Sevak Samaj, *Slums of Old Delhi*, p. 1.
53 Secret Cabinet Meeting, 6 August 1957, in 'Decision taken by the Ad Hoc Committee of the Cabinet at its meeting held on 24.5.1957 regarding (i) Unauthorized occupation of land and (ii) Slum Clearance', Appendix III, Ministry of Home Affairs, National Archives of India, 27/17/57 – Delhi.
54 See Brij Krishna Chandiwala (President, Bharat Sevak Samaj) to G. B. Plant (Minister of Home Affairs), 14 April 1957, Ministry of Home Affairs, National Archives of India, 8/69/57 – Delhi; Bharat Sevak Samaj, *Slums of Old Delhi*, appendix 1, 'An Approach to the Problem of Slums in Delhi', pp. 215–22.

55 Secret minutes of a Cabinet meeting, 9 April 1957, Ministry of Home Affairs, National Archives of India, 27/4/57 – Delhi.

56 Nehru, 'Foreword', p. 8.

57 G. Mukharji (chairman, Delhi Improvement Trust), 'Note on the Slum Problem in Delhi', appendix II, Ministry of Home Affairs, National Archives of India, 27/17/57 – Delhi.

58 H. C. Arora, ed., *The Slum Areas (Improvement and Clearance) Act, 1956 as Amended up to Date* (Delhi, 1974), p. 1.

59 Ibid., pp. 4, 8–9.

60 P. R. Nayak in Chatterjee and Khan, *Report of the Seminar on Slum Clearance*, p. 35.

61 M. K. Moitra, 'Environmental Improvement of Slums: The Calcutta Experience', *Building and Environment*, XXVI/3 (1991), p. 253.

62 Arjun Appadurai, 'Deep Democracy: Urban Governmentality and the Horizon of Politics', *Environment and Urbanization*, XIII/2 (2001), p. 27.

63 Indian Planning Commission, *Second Five Year Plan* (New Delhi, 1956), p. 561.

64 Quoted in Ministry of Home Affairs, *Report of Fact Finding Committee*, p. 31.

65 Ibid.

66 Marshall B. Clinard, *Slums and Community Development: Experiments in Self-help* (New York, 1966), p. viii.

67 Ibid., pp. 3, 11.

68 Chatterjee and Khan, *Report of the Seminar on Slum Clearance*, p. 30.

69 A. R. Desai and S. D. Pillai, *A Profile of an Indian Slum* (Bombay, 1972), pp. 2, 19, 18.

70 K. N. Venkatarayappa, *Slums: A Study in Urban Problem* (New Delhi, 1972), pp. 4, 15.

71 Ibid., p. 50.

72 Noor Mohammad, *Slum Culture and Deviant Behaviour* (Delhi, 1983), pp. 1, 3.

73 Ibid., p. 134.

74 P. P. Shrivastav, '"City for the Citizen" or "Citizen for the City": The Search for an Appropriate Strategy for Slums and Housing for the Urban Poor in Developing Countries – The Case of Delhi', *Habitat International*, VI/1 (1982), p. 201.

75 Arjun Appadurai, 'Spectral Housing and Urban Cleansing: Notes on Millennial Mumbai', *Public Culture*, XII/3 (2000), pp. 631, 629.

76 Indian Planning Commission, *First Five Year Plan*, p. 235.

77 Indian Planning Commission, *Second Five Year Plan*, p. 561.

78 Liza Weinstein, 'Demolition and Dispossession: Toward an Understanding of State Violence in Millennial Mumbai', *Studies in Comparative International Development*, XLVIII (2013), p. 296.

79 Tamil Nadu Slum Clearance Board, *Socio-economic Survey of Madras Slums* (Madras, 1975), p. 6.

80 S. Mullick (joint secretary, Ministry of Health), 'Note on Unauthorised Occupation of Open Lands in the Urban Areas of Delhi', appendix I, Ministry of Home Affairs, National Archives of India, 27/17/57 – Delhi.

81 Mukharji, 'Note on the Slum Problem in Delhi'.

82 Partha Chatterjee, *The Politics of the Governed: Reflections on Popular Politics in Most of the World* (New York, 2004), p. 54.

83 Indian Planning Commission, *Third Five Year Plan* (New Delhi, 1961), pp. 46, 73.

84 Shrivastav, '"City for the Citizen" or "Citizen for the City"', p. 201.

85 B. K. Shivalingappa, 'Slum Clearance in Bangalore: Problems and Programmes', in Indian Institute of Public Administration, *Slum Clearance and Improvement* (New Delhi, 1979), p. 114.

86 'Note on Slum Clearance Schemes of the Delhi Development Authority', pp. 22–3, attachment in G. Mukharji (now vice chairman, Delhi Development Authority) to the Ministry of Home Affairs, 11 February 1959, Ministry of Home Affairs, National Archives of India, 33/1/59 – Delhi.

87 Ibid., p. 26.

88 Nehru, 'Foreword', p. 8.

89 Indian Planning Commission, *Second Five Year Plan*, p. 561.

90 Indian Planning Commission, *Third Five Year Plan*, p. 688.

91 Indian Planning Commission, *Fourth Five Year Plan, 1969–74* (New Delhi, 1970), p. 402.

92 Indian Planning Commission, *Sixth Five Year Plan*, p. 392.

93 Nehru, 'Foreword', p. 8.

94 'An Approach to the Problem of Slums in Delhi', in Bharat Sevak Samaj, *Slums of Old Delhi*, appendix 1, p. 219.

95 'Pilot Project for Social and Economic Welfare Work', p. 1.

96 Memorandum by P. R. Nayak, 22 March 1958, in 'Urban Community Development Schemes in Delhi', Ministry of Home Affairs, National Archives of India, 23/17/58 – Delhi.

97 Clinard, *Slums and Community Development*, p. 146.

98 Ibid., p. 172.

99 Cousins and Goyder, *Changing Slum Communities*, p. 14.

100 Clinard, *Slums and Community Development*, pp. 146, 155, 156.

101 Cousins and Goyder, *Changing Slum Communities*, pp. 14, 15, 20.

102 A. Malla Reddy, *Slum Improvement: The Hyderabad Experience* (Delhi, 1996), p. 21.

103 Venkatarayappa, *Slums*, pp. 89–90.

104 Clinard, *Slums and Community Development*, p. 269.

105 Desai, *Community Participation and Slum Housing*, pp. 67, 68.

106 Paul D. Wiebe, *Social Life in an Indian Slum* (Delhi, 1975), pp. 7, 4.

107 A. N. Krishnamurthy and Solomon J. Benjamin, 'The Indian Experience of Community Participation: Public Projects and the Grassroots', in *Slum Upgradation: Emerging Issue and Policy Implications*, ed. R. L. Sehgal (New Delhi, 1998), p. 404.

108 Deva Raj, 'Slums and the Urban Community', in Indian Institute of Public Administration, *Slum Clearance and Improvement*, p. 9.

109 M. B. Achwal, 'Environmental Improvement in Slums', ibid., p. 51.

110 Mohit Bhattacharya, 'Policy on Slums', ibid., pp. 32, 33.

111 Hans Schenk, 'Slums and Government Authorities: The Karnataka State Slum Clearance Board', in *Living in India's Slums: A Case Study of Bangalore*, ed. Hans Schenk (New Delhi, 2001), p. 271.

112 Ministry of Home Affairs, *Report of Fact Finding Committee*, pp. 48, 55.
113 Quoted in Margaret Antony and G. Maheswaran, *Social Segregation and Slums: The Plight of Dalits in the Slums of Delhi* (New Delhi, 2001), p. 34.
114 Weinstein, 'Demolition and Dispossession', p. 298.
115 Interview by Rasna Warah with Jockin Arputham, 2002, originally published by UN-Habitat as 'If You Want to Mobilize People, Go to the Public Toilets', and reproduced in 'Squatter Cities and Slums: Where the Sidewalks End', Worldwatch Institute, www.worldwatch.org, accessed 27 November 2015.
116 S. Devada Pillai, 'Slums and Squatters', in *Slums and Urbanization*, ed. A. R. Desai and S. Devadas Pillai, 2nd edn (Bombay, 1990), p. 159.
117 Vandana Desai, 'Dharavi, the Largest Slum in Asia: Development of Low-income Housing in India', *Habitat International*, xii/2 (1988), p. 73.
118 Janice Perlman, *Favela: Four Decades of Living on the Edge in Rio de Janeiro* (Oxford, 2010), pp. 27, 53.
119 Janice E. Perlman, *The Myth of Marginality: Urban Poverty and Politics in Rio de Janeiro* (Berkeley, 1976), p. 246.
120 Jose Arthur Rios, 'Social Transformation and Urbanization: The Case of Rio de Janeiro', *Urban Anthropology*, iii/1 (1974), p. 97.
121 Perlman, *Favela*, p. 12.
122 Celine d'Cruz and Patience Mudimu, 'Community Savings that Mobilize Federations, Build Women's Leadership and Support Slum Upgrading', *Environment and Urbanization*, xxv/1 (2013), p. 33.
123 *Vancouver Declaration on Human Settlements*, Part iii, clause 6, www.unhabitat.org, accessed 12 October 2005.
124 Ibid., Part iii, clause 8.

6 LITTLE PALACES

1 Ruzbeh N. Bharucha, *Yamuna Gently Weeps: A Journey into the Yamuna Pushta Slum Demolitions* (New Delhi, 2006), p. 43.
2 Janice Perlman, *Favela: Four Decades of Living on the Edge in Rio de Janeiro* (Oxford, 2010), p. 79.
3 Manchester and District Regional Survey Society, *Social Studies of a Manchester City Ward. No. 3: Housing Needs of Ancoats in Relation to the Greenwood Act* (Manchester, 1930), p. 10.
4 Hilda Jennings, *University Settlement Bristol: Sixty Years of Change 1911–1971* (Bristol, 1971), p. 44.
5 Sidney Jacobs, *The Right to a Decent House* (London, 1976), p. 25.
6 See the documentary film by Lindy Wilson, *Last Supper in Horstley Street* (1983).
7 Patrick McAuslan, *Urban Land and Shelter for the Poor* (London, 1985), p. 117.
8 Raj Nandy, *Squatters: Human Resource Dimension. The Case of Faridabad – A 'Ringtown' of National Capital Region* (New Delhi, 1987), p. 50.
9 United Nations Human Settlements Programme, *An Urbanizing World: Global Report on Human Settlements, 1996* (Oxford, 1996), p. 245.
10 Ibid., p. xxviii.

11 Charles Abrams, *Man's Struggle for Shelter in an Urbanizing World* (Cambridge, MA, 1964), p. 5.

12 Jeremy Seabrook, *Life and Labour in a Bombay Slum* (London, 1987), p. 152.

13 Quoted in Van Wilson, *Rich in All but Money: Life in Hungate, 1900– 1938*, revd edn (York, 2007), p. 26.

14 *Herald*, 3 June 1957, quoted in Alan Mayne, 'A Just War: The Language of Slum Representation in Twentieth-century Australia', *Journal of Urban History*, XX/1 (1995), p. 101.

15 AbdouMaliq Simone, *City Life from Jakarta to Dakar: Movements at the Crossroads* (New York, 2010), p. 34.

16 Richard Martin and Ashna Mathema, *Development Poverty and Politics: Putting Communities in the Driver's Seat* (New York, 2010), p. 28.

17 James Holston, *Insurgent Citizenship: Disjunctions of Democracy and Modernity in Brazil* (Princeton, NJ, 2008).

18 See Shaohua Chen and Martin Ravallion, *The Developing World is Poorer than We Thought, but No Less Successful in the Fight against Poverty* (World Bank, 2008), available at www.openknowledge.worldbank.org.

19 Nagamma Shilpiri, quoted in Jonas Bendiksen, *The Places We Live* (New York, 2008), n.p.

20 Michael Young and Peter Willmott, *Family and Kinship in East London* (London, 1957), p. 8.

21 Liverpool Shelter Neighbourhood Action Project (SNAP), *Another Chance for Cities: SNAP69/72* (London, 1972), p. 73.

22 Rosita Mertens, *Forced Relocation of Slum Dwellers in Bangalore, India: Slum Dwellers, Landlords and the Government* (Amsterdam, 1996), p. 57.

23 Sudesh Nangia and Sukhadeo Thorat, *Slum in a Metropolis: The Living Environment* (New Delhi, 2000), p. 107.

24 D. Ravindra Prasad and A. Malla Reddy, *Environmental Improvement of Urban Slums: The Indian Experience* (Hyderabad, 1994), pp. 43, 51.

25 Tulshi Kumar Das, *Culture of Slum Dwellers: A Study of a Slum in Dhaka* (Dhaka, 2003), p. 96.

26 Jerry White, *Campbell Bunk: The Worst Street in North London between the Wars* (London, 2003), p. 49.

27 Joseph E. Stiglitz, *The Price of Inequality* (New York, 2012), p. 103. See also Alok Jha, 'Poverty Saps Capacity for Tough Tasks', *Guardian Weekly*, 6 September 2013, p. 12.

28 White, *Campbell Bunk*, p. 69.

29 Simone, *City Life from Jakarta to Dakar*, p. 83.

30 Asok Sen, *Life and Labour in a Squatters' Colony* (Calcutta, 1992), pp. 125–6.

31 Manchester and District Regional Survey Society, *Social Studies of a Manchester City Ward*, p. 10.

32 Ajay K. Mehra, *The Politics of Urban Development: A Study of Old Delhi* (New Delhi, 1991), p. 99.

33 H. U. Bijlani and Prodipto Roy, eds, *Slum Habitat: Hyderabad Slum Improvement Project* (New Delhi, 1991), p. 62.

34 Mark Jacobson and Jonas Bendiksen, 'Dharavi: Mumbai's Shadow City', *National Geographic Magazine*, CCXI/5 (2007), p. 87.

35 Interview by Rasna Warah with Jockin Arputham, 2002, originally
   published by UN-Habitat as 'If You Want to Mobilize People, Go to the
   Public Toilets', and reproduced in 'Squatter Cities and Slums: Where
   the Sidewalks End', Worldwatch Institute, www.worldwatch.org,
   accessed 27 November 2015.
36 Arjun Appadurai, 'Spectral Housing and Urban Cleansing: Notes on
   Millennial Mumbai', *Public Culture*, XII/3 (2000), p. 636.
37 R. L. Sehgal, ed., *Slum Upgradation: Emerging Issue and Policy
   Implications* (New Delhi, 1998), p. 1.
38 Owen M. Lynch, 'Political Mobilisation and Ethnicity among Adi-
   Dravidas in a Bombay Slum', *Economic and Political Weekly*, IX/39
   (1974), p. 186.
39 White, *Campbell Bunk*, p. xvi.
40 Henri Lefebvre, *The Production of Space* (Oxford, 1991), pp. 362, 370.
41 R. K. Gerrand, 'City Has Grown Up Around Cottage', *Herald*,
   25 July 1951.
42 Lefebvre, *The Production of Space*, pp. 373–4.
43 John F. C. Turner, 'An Introductory Perspective', in *Building
   Community: A Third World Case Book*, ed. Bertha Turner (London,
   1988), p. 13.
44 Ibid., p. 13. Turner, 'Housing as a Verb', in *Freedom to Build: Dweller
   Control of the Housing Process*, ed. John F. C. Turner and Robert Fichter
   (New York, 1972), pp. 152, 162.
45 White, *Campbell Bunk*, p. xvi.
46 Mridula Bhatnagar, *Urban Slums and Poverty* (Jaipur, 2010), p. 37.
47 Hans Schenk, 'Living in Bangalore's Slums', in *Living in India's Slums:
   A Case Study of Bangalore*, ed. Hans Schenk (New Delhi, 2001), p. 27.
48 Barry M. Doyle, 'Mapping Slums in a Historic City: Representing
   Working Class Communities in Edwardian Norwich', *Planning
   Perspectives*, XVI/1 (2001), p. 47.
49 *Birmingham Daily Post*, 31 October 1905, p. 11, 'Municipal Elections'.
50 Oscar Arias, 'Foreword', in Ivo Imparato and Jeff Ruster, *Slum
   Upgrading and Participation: Lessons from Latin America* (Washington
   DC, 2003), p. vii.
51 D. P. Pattanayak, 'Foreword', in K. S. Rajyashree, *An Ethnolinguistic
   Survey of Dharavi: A Slum in Bombay* (Mysore, 1986), n.p.
52 Marie Huchzermeyer, *Cities with 'Slums': From Informal Settlement
   Eradication to a Right to the City in Africa* (Claremont, South Africa,
   2011), p. 75.
53 Jaya Shrivastava, quoted in Bharucha, *Yamuna Gently Weeps*, p. 207.
54 Quoted in Michael Carriere, 'Chicago, the South Side Planning Board,
   and the Search for (Further) Order: Toward an Intellectual Lineage of
   Urban Renewal in Postwar America', *Journal of Urban History*, XXXIX/3
   (2012), p. 412.
55 Hugh Wilson and Lewis Womersley, Roger Tym and Associates,
   Jamieson Mackay and Partners, *Change or Decay: Final Report of the
   Liverpool Inner Area Study* (London, 1977), p. 43.
56 Christine Bodewes, *Parish Transformation in Urban Slums: Voices
   of Kibera, Kenya* (Nairobi, 2005), p. 56.

57 Marwa A. Khalifa, 'Redefining Slums in Egypt: Unplanned versus Unsafe Areas', *Habitat International*, XXXV (2011), p. 40.

58 Loh Kah Seng, 'Dangerous Migrants and the Informal Mobile City of Postwar Singapore', *Mobilities*, V/2 (2010), p. 209.

59 D. J. Dwyer, *People and Housing in Third World Cities: Perspectives on the Problem of Spontaneous Settlements* (London, 1979), p. 94.

60 Ibid., pp. 201, 204.

61 Charles J. Stokes, 'A Theory of Slums', *Land Economics*, XXXVIII/3 (1962), p. 188.

62 Imparato and Ruster, *Slum Upgrading and Participation*, p. 37.

63 United Nations Human Settlements Programme, *Housing and Urban Development in Ghana, with Special Reference to Low-income Housing* (Nairobi, 2004), p. 22.

64 Director's Report in *Report of the Seminar on Slum Clearance*, ed. B. Chatterjee and Zakia Khan (Bombay, 1958), p. 165.

65 Biswaroop Das, 'Slum Dwellers in Indian Cities: The Case of Surat in Western India', *QEH Working Papers* (Oxford, 1998), p. 3.

66 Pratibha Joshi, 'Slum Improvements in Greater Bombay', in Indian Institute of Public Administration, *Slum Clearance and Improvement* (New Delhi, 1979), p. 69.

67 Marshall B. Clinard, *Slums and Community Development: Experiments in Self-help* (New York, 1966), p. 141.

68 K. N. Venkatarayappa, *Slums: A Study in Urban Problem* (New Delhi, 1972), p. 12.

69 L. R. Singh, *Slums of Allahabad: A Socio-economic Profile* (Allahabad, 1984), Preface, n.p.

70 Noor Mohammad, *Slum Culture and Deviant Behaviour* (Delhi, 1983), pp. 41, 43.

71 Ashok K. Gupta, *Slums in New Industrial Towns: A Study of Durg-Bhilai in Madhya Pradesh* (Delhi, 1993), p. 106.

72 Sudha Kaldate, *Slums and Housing Problems* (Jaipur, 1989), p. 63.

73 M.K.A. Siddiqui and Y. Hossain, *Life in the Slums of Calcutta: A Study of Parsi Bagan Bustee* (New Delhi, 2002), p. 49.

74 Vandana Desai, 'Dharavi, the Largest Slum in Asia: Development of Low-income Housing in India', *Habitat International*, XII/2 (1988), p. 69.

75 A. Malla Reddy, *Slum Improvement: The Hyderabad Experience* (Delhi, 1996), pp. 157, 152.

76 Bodewes, *Parish Transformation in Urban Slums*, p. 9.

77 Father Joe Maier, *Welcome to the Bangkok Slaughterhouse: The Battle for Human Dignity in Bangkok's Bleakest Slums* (Singapore, 2005), pp. 25, 122.

78 Andrew H. Malcolm, 'Crack, Bane of Inner City, is now Gripping Suburbs', *New York Times*, 1 October 1989, p. 1. See also 'The Crack Legacy', *Washington Post*, 10 September 1989, pp. A1, 22–3.

79 'Dinkins Speech: Retaking the City', ibid., 23 August 1989, p. B4.

80 'The Case for Ed Koch – and His Duty', editorial leader, ibid., 3 September 1989, p. E12.

81 Bharat Sevak Samaj, 5 May 1956, 'An Approach to the Problem of Slums in Delhi', in Bharat Sevak Samaj, *Slums of Old Delhi: Report of*

the Socio-economic Survey of the Slum Dwellers of Old Delhi City (Delhi, 1958), appendix 1, p. 217.

82 B. H. Mehta, 'Social Aspects of the Slum Problem', in *Report of the Seminar on Slum Clearance*, ed. Chatterjee and Khan, p. 81.

83 Director's Report, ibid., p. 167.

84 Satish Sinha, *Slum Eradication and Urban Renewal: Patna* (New Delhi, 1985), p. 3. Venkatarayappa, *Slums*, p. 50.

85 Ibid., p. 73.

86 Girish K. Mistra, 'Municipal Services in Slums of Nyderabad: An Evaluation', in *Slum Upgradation*, ed. Sehgal, p. 317.

87 Bhatnagar, *Urban Slums*, p. 115.

88 Michael Dewit, 'Slum Perceptions and Cognitions', in *Living in India's Slums*, ed. Schenk, pp. 100–101.

89 Bhatnagar, *Urban Slums*, p. 159.

90 Mitu Sengupta, 'Hollow Message', *Frontline*, XXVI/6 (14–27 March 2009), available at www.frontline.in.

91 Ibid.

92 *The Hindu*, 23 February 2009, p. 1, 'Slumdog Surefire Favourite'.

93 George Abraham, 'A Billion Stories Now', *The Hindu Magazine*, 25 January 2009, available at www.thehindu.com/thehindu/mag.

94 Gethin Chamberlain, 'Mumbai's Beating Heart', *Guardian Weekly*, 9 January 2009, pp. 25–6.

95 Bendiksen, *The Places We Live*.

96 'Charles Abrams: A Biography', Charles Abrams: Papers and Files, Department of Manuscripts and University Archives, Cornell University, 1975, available at www.rmc.library.cornell.edu.

97 David A. Kirby, *Slum Housing and Residential Renewal: The Case in Urban Britain* (London, 1979), p. 9.

98 Norman Dennis, *People and Planning: The Sociology of Housing in Sunderland* (London, 1970), p. 296.

99 Bodewes, *Parish Transformation in Urban Slums*, p. 53.

100 B. K. Shivalingappa, 'Slum Clearance in Bangalore: Problems and Programmes', in Indian Institute of Public Administration, *Slum Clearance and Improvement*, pp. 118–19.

101 Calcutta Improvement Trust, *Annual Report on the Operations of the Calcutta Improvement Trust for the Year 1925–26* (Calcutta, 1926), pp. 18–19.

102 Maier, *Welcome to the Bangkok Slaughterhouse*, p. 106.

103 Huchzermeyer, *Cities with 'Slums'*, pp. 82–3.

104 Asok Sen, *Life and Labour in a Squatters' Colony*, p. 123, emphasis added.

105 Gerald D. Suttles, *The Social Order of the Slum: Ethnicity and Territory in the Inner City* (Chicago, IL, 1968), pp. 3, 8.

106 Clinard, *Slums and Community Development*, p. 309.

107 Janice E. Perlman, *The Myth of Marginality: Urban Poverty and Politics in Rio de Janeiro* (Berkeley, CA, 1976), pp. 1, 13.

108 Huchzermeyer, *Cities with 'Slums'*, p. 26.

109 See M. J. Daunton, *House and Home in the Victorian City: Working-class Housing, 1850–1914* (London, 1983), pp. 263–85.

110 Jerry White, *Rothschild Buildings: Life in an East End Tenement Block, 1887–1920* (London, 1980), pp. 36, 38–9, 44.

111 See Alan Mayne and Tim Murray, eds, *The Archaeology of Urban Landscapes: Explorations in Slumland* (Cambridge, 2001).

112 Manchester University Settlement, *Ancoats: A Study of a Clearance Area. Report of a Survey Made in 1937–1938* (Manchester, 1945), p. 14.

113 Manchester and District Regional Survey Society, *Social Studies of a Manchester City Ward*, p. 10.

114 Manchester University Settlement, *Ancoats*, p. 14.

115 Hilda Jennings, *Societies in the Making: A Study of Development and Redevelopment within a County Borough* (London, 1962), p. 171.

116 Liverpool Shelter Neighbourhood Action Project, *Another Chance for Cities*, p. 53.

117 Wilson et al., *Change or Decay*, p. 46.

118 Jacobs, *The Right to a Decent House*, p. 22.

119 Bendiksen, *The Places We Live*.

120 Robert Neuwirth, *Shadow Cities: A Billion Squatters, a New Urban World* (New York, 2005), p. 83.

121 Simone, *City Life from Jakarta to Dakar*, p. 225.

122 K. Ranga Rao and M.S.A. Rao, *Cities and Slums: A Study of a Squatters' Settlement in the City of Vijayawada* (New Delhi, 1984), p. 100.

123 Vandana Desai, *Community Participation and Slum Housing: A Study of Bombay* (New Delhi, 1995), p. 179.

124 Neuwirth, *Shadow Cities*, p. 111.

125 Venkatarayappa, *Slums*, p. 7.

126 B. Mema and Shagufta Jamal, *Environmental Perception of Slum Dwellers* (New Delhi, 2004), pp. 60, 63.

127 Charles Kenny, 'In Praise of Slums: Why Millions of People Choose to Live in Urban Squalor', *Foreign Policy*, 13 August 2012, p. 29.

128 Bendiksen, *The Places We Live*.

129 Jacobs, *The Right to a Decent House*, p. 24.

130 Suttles, *The Social Order of the Slum*, p. 75.

131 Wilson et al., *Change or Decay*, p. 46.

132 Rajyashree, *An Ethnolinguistic Survey of Dharavi*, p. 28.

133 Bendiksen, *The Places We Live*.

134 Manchester University Settlement, *Ancoats*, p. 14.

135 Alan Gilbert, 'Love in the Time of Enhanced Capital Flows: Reflections on the Links between Liberalization and Informality', in *Urban Informality: Transnational Perspectives from the Middle East, Latin America, and South Asia*, ed. Ananya Roy and Nezar AlSayyad (Lanham, MD, 2004), p. 36.

136 See Florian Urban, 'La Perla – 100 Years of Informal Architecture in San Juan, Puerto Rico', *Planning Perspectives*, XXX/4 (2015), pp. 495–536.

137 Rudolf C. Heredia, *Settlements and Shelter: Alternative Housing for the Urban Poor in Bombay* (New Delhi, 1986), p. 31. See Eugenie L. Birch, Shahana Chattaraj and Susan M. Wachter, eds, *Slums: How Informal Real Estate Markets Work* (Philadelphia, PA, 2016).

138 Turner, quoted in Alan Gilbert, 'On the Absence of Ghettos in Latin American Cities', in *The Ghetto: Contemporary Global Issues and Controversies*, ed. Ray Hutchinson and Bruce D. Haynes (Boulder, CO, 2012), p. 204. John F. C. Turner, *Housing by People: Towards Autonomy*

in Building Environments (London, 1976), p. 52. John F. C. Turner, 'The Reeducation of a Professional', in *Freedom to Build*, ed. Turner and Fichter, p. 145.

139 Bendiksen, *The Places We Live.*

140 Jose Arthur Rios, 'Social Transformation and Urbanization: The Case of Rio de Janeiro', *Urban Anthropology*, III/1 (1974), p. 96.

141 Perlman, *The Myth of Marginality*, p. 13.

142 Neuwirth, *Shadow Cities*, pp. 36, 42, 55.

143 Martijn Koster and Monique Nuijten, 'From Preamble to Post-project Frustrations: The Shaping of a Slum Upgrading Project in Recife, Brazil', *Antipode*, XLIV/1 (2011), p. 178.

144 Quoted in Seabrook, *Life and Labour in a Bombay Slum*, p. 152.

145 Sen, *Life and Labour in a Squatters' Colony*, p. 31.

146 Seabrook, *Life and Labour in a Bombay Slum*, p. 15.

147 Amnesty International, Kenya, *The Unseen Majority: Nairobi's Two Million Slum-Dwellers* (London, 2009), p. 8.

148 Geddes, 'Report on the Towns in the Madras Presidency' (1915), in *Patrick Geddes in India*, ed. Jaqueline Tyrwhitt (London, 1947), p. 64.

149 Anna Tibaijuka, 'Introduction', in United Nations Human Settlements Programme, *The Challenge of Slums: Global Report on Human Settlements 2003* (London, 2003), p. vi.

150 Alan R. Johnson, *Leadership in a Slum: A Bangkok Case Study* (Oxford, 2009), p. 46.

151 Paul D. Wiebe, *Social Life in an Indian Slum* (Delhi, 1975), p. 100.

152 Anna Davin, *Growing Up Poor: Home, School and Street in London, 1870–1914* (London, 1996), pp. 34–5.

153 Manchester University Settlement, *Ancoats*, p. 13.

154 Seabrook, *Life and Labour in a Bombay Slum*, p. 68.

155 Jacobson and Bendiksen, 'Dharavi: Mumbai's Shadow City', pp. 68–93.

156 Dan McDougall, 'Success in a Slum', reprinted in the *Guardian Weekly*, 16 March 2007, p. 29. See Shahana Chattaraj, 'Property Markets without Property Rights: Dharavi's Informal Real Estate Market', in *Slums*, ed. Birch, Chattaraj and Wachter, pp. 94–106.

157 Sengupta, 'Hollow Message'.

158 Das, 'Slum Dwellers in Indian Cities', p. 36.

159 Bodewes, *Parish Transformation in Urban Slums*, p. 66.

160 See Gilbert, 'On the Absence of Ghettos in Latin American Cities', pp. 191–224.

161 Heredia, *Settlements and Shelter*, p. 22.

162 Bharucha, *Yamuna Gently Weeps*, p. 14.

163 Manchester University Settlement, *Ancoats*, p. 13.

164 Young and Willmott, *Family and Kinship in East London*, p. 81. See Jennings, *Societies in the Making*, p. 50.

165 White, *Rothschild Buildings*, pp. 70, 101.

166 Arthur William Jephson, *My Work in London* (London, 1910), quoted in Davin, *Growing Up Poor*, p. 35.

167 Suttles, *The Social Order of the Slum*, p. 3.

168 Herbert J. Gans, *People and Plans: Essays on Urban Social Problems and Solutions* (New York, 1968), p. 213.

169 Young and Willmott, *Family and Kinship in East London*, p. 85.
170 Jennings, *Societies in the Making*, pp. 48, 57, 63.
171 Karen Evans, "'It's all right 'round here if you're a local': Community in the Inner City', in *Contested Communities: Experiences, Struggles, Policies*, ed. Paul Hoggett (Bristol, 1997), p. 45.
172 M.K.A. Siddiqui, 'Life in the Slums of Calcutta: Some Aspects', *Economic and Political Weekly*, IV/50 (1969), p. 1917.
173 Sanjay K. Roy, 'Life in Calcutta Slums', in *Urbanization and Slums*, ed. Prodipto Roy and Shangon Das Gupta (New Delhi, 1995), p. 99.
174 Wiebe, *Social Life in an Indian Slum*, p. 154
175 Ibid., pp. 166, 156.
176 Margaret Antony and G. Maheswaran, *Social Segregation and Slums: The Plight of Dalits in the Slums of Delhi* (New Delhi, 2001), p. 40.
177 Rajyashree, *An Ethnolinguistic Survey of Dharavi*, p. 70.
178 Rob Crilly, 'Life is Good in My Nairobi Slum, Says Barack Obama's Younger Brother', *The Times*, 22 August 2008.
179 Maier, *Welcome to the Bangkok Slaughterhouse*, p. 23.
180 Bendiksen, *The Places We Live*.
181 Dennis Rodgers, 'Slum Wars of the 21st Century: The New Geography of Conflict in Central America', *Crisis States Working Papers*, series 2, paper 7 (February 2007), p. 10.
182 S. Devadas Pillai, 'Slums and Squatters', in *Slums and Urbanization*, ed. A. R. Desai and S. Devadas Pillai, 2nd edn (Bombay, 1990), p. 165.
183 United Nations Human Settlements Programme, *An Urbanizing World*, p. 419.
184 Bharucha, *Yamuna Gently Weeps*, p. 17.
185 Gans, *People and Plans*, pp. 4–11.
186 John F. C. Turner, 'An Introductory Perspective', in Turner, *Building Community*, p. 13.
187 Ashok Ranjan Basu, *Urban Squatter Housing in Third World* (Delhi, 1988), p. 251.
188 Ibid., p. 232.
189 McAuslan, *Urban Land and Shelter for the Poor*, p. 11.
190 Interview by Rasna Warah with Jockin Arputham.
191 Geddes, 'Report on the Towns in the Madras Presidency, 1915: Madura', in Tyrwhitt, *Patrick Geddes in India*, p. 53.
192 Geddes, 'Town Planning in Balrampur: A Report to the Honourable the Maharaja Bahadur, 1917', ibid., p. 84. Geddes, 'Report on the Towns in the Madras Presidency, 1915', ibid., p. 61.
193 See Jane Jacobs, *The Death and Life of Great American Cities: The Failure of Town Planning*, first published 1961 (Harmondsworth, 1965); Sam Bass Warner, Jr, *The Urban Wilderness: A History of the American City* (New York, 1972).
194 Dwyer, *People and Housing in Third World Cities*, pp. 93, 95.
195 Amos Rapoport, 'Spontaneous Settlements as Vernacular Design', in *Spontaneous Shelter: International Perspectives and Prospects*, ed. Carl V. Patton (Philadelphia, PA, 1988), p. 52.
196 Ibid., pp. 51–2, 72.
197 Ibid., p. 61.

198 Ibid., pp. 69–70.
199 Perlman, *The Myth of Marginality*, p. 196. See also Janice E. Perlman, 'The Formalization of Informal Real Estate Transactions in Rio's Favelas', in *Slums*, ed. Birch, Chattaraj and Wachter, pp. 58–82.
200 Neuwirth, *Shadow Cities*, p. 57.
201 Witold Rybczynski and Vikram Bhatt, 'Understanding Slums: The Use of Public Space', in *Slum Upgradation*, ed. Sehgal, p. 132.
202 Ibid., p. 136, emphasis added.
203 T. K. Majumdar, 'The Problem of Squatter Settlements: A Sociological Perspective', in Indian Institute of Public Administration, *Slum Clearance and Improvement*, p. 20.
204 Alan Gilbert, 'Land, Housing, and Infrastructure in Latin America's Cities', in *The Mega-city in Latin America*, ed. Alan Gilbert (Tokyo, 1996), p. 78.
205 Dwyer, *People and Housing in Third World Cities*, p. 250.
206 '20-year-old Rubbish Dump Turned into a Lush Garden', www.1millionwomen.com.au, accessed 24 July 2016.

7 BUILDING COMMUNITIES?

1 United Nations, *The Millennium Development Goals Report 2009* (New York, 2009), p. 47. United Nations, *The Millennium Development Goals Report 2015* (New York, 2015), p. 60.
2 Indian Planning Commission, *Sixth Five Year Plan 1980–85* (New Delhi, 1981), p. 392.
3 Raina Naidu and Kusnal Deb, 'Slum Improvement: A Study of Hyderabad', in *Slum Upgradation: Emerging Issue and Policy Implications*, ed. R. L. Sehgal (New Delhi, 1998), p. 260.
4 Ibid., p. 263.
5 Joop W. de Wit, *Poverty, Policy and Politics in Madras Slums: Dynamics of Survival, Gender and Leadership* (New Delhi, 1996), p. 120.
6 PM Global Infrastructure Inc, *Assessment of the UN-Habitat Slum Upgrading Facility. Final Report* (2006), p. 16, available at unhabitat.org.
7 United Nations Human Settlements Programme and United Nations Environment Programme, *Sustainable Cities Programme, 1990–2000: A Decade of United Nations Support for Broad-based Participatory Management of Urban Development* (Nairobi, 2001), p. 3.
8 United Nations Human Settlements Programme, *An Urbanizing World: Global Report on Human Settlements, 1996* (Oxford, 1996), p. 428.
9 Arjun Appadurai, 'Deep Democracy: Urban Governmentality and the Horizon of Politics', *Environment and Urbanization*, XIII/2 (2001), p. 36.
10 Celine d'Cruz and Patience Mudimu, 'Community Savings that Mobilize Federations, Build Women's Leadership and Support Slum Upgrading', *Environment and Urbanization*, XXV/1 (2013), p. 32.
11 Ibid., p. 33.
12 Kamukam Ettyang, 'Empowering the Urban Poor to Realize the Right to Housing: Community-Led Slum Upgrading in Huruma-Nairobi', in *Slum Upgrading Programmes in Nairobi: Challenges in Implementation*, ed. Rosa Flores Fernandez (Nairobi, 2011), p. 153.

13 Vincentian Missionaries Social Development Foundation Incorporated (VMSDFI), Manila, 'Meet the Philippines Homeless People's Federation', *Environment and Urbanization*, XIII/2 (2001), p. 76.
14 Hans Schenk, 'Living in Bangalor's Slums', in *Living in India's Slums: A Case Study of Bangalore*, ed. Hans Schenk (New Delhi, 2001), p. 26.
15 Tasneem A. Siddiqui, 'Foreword', in *Shelter for the Shelterless: The Story of Khuda ki Basti*, ed. Aquila Ismail (Karachi, 2002), p. 10.
16 Cities Alliance, *Cities Without Slums Action Plan*, 1999, p. 2, available at www.citiesalliance.org.
17 Patrick McAuslan, *Urban Land and Shelter for the Poor* (London, 1985), p. 119.
18 'Address by the Executive Director of the United Nations Centre for Human Settlements (Habitat) on the State of Human Settlements', in Report of the Commission on Human Settlements on the Work of its Sixth Session (New York, 1983), p. 43, available at www.unhabitat.org.
19 Ivo Imparato and Jeff Ruster, *Slum Upgrading and Participation: Lessons from Latin America* (Washington, DC, 2003), pp. 340–41.
20 United Nations Human Settlements Programme, *Harmonious Cities: State of the World's Cities 2008/2009* (London, 2008), p. 58.
21 United Nations Economic and Social Council, *In-depth Evaluation of the United Nations Human Settlements (UN-Habitat) Programme* (2005), p. 30, available at www.unhabitat.org.
22 Cities Alliance, *Cities Without Slums Action Plan*, p. 6.
23 Ibid., p. 1.
24 United Nations Human Settlements Programme, *Harmonious Cities*, p. 209.
25 United Nations Human Settlements Programme, *The Challenge of Slums: Global Report on Human Settlements 2003* (London, 2003), p. 136.
26 R. N. Sharma and A. Narender, 'Policies and Strategies for Slum Improvement and Renewal: The Bombay Experience', in *Urban Explosion of Mumbai: Restructuring of Growth*, ed. M. D. David (Mumbai, 1996), p. 204. Vinit Mukhija, *Squatters as Developers? Slum Redevelopment in Mumbai* (Aldershot, 2003), p. 27.
27 See Rosita Mertens, *Forced Relocation of Slum Dwellers in Bangalore, India: Slum Dwellers, Landlords and the Government* (Amsterdam, 1996).
28 Paul D. Wiebe, *Social Life in an Indian Slum* (Delhi, 1975), p. 165.
29 T. M. Vinod Kumar, 'Slums: Present Status and Strategies for Improvement', in *Urbanization and Slums*, ed. Prodipto Roy and Shangon Das Gupta (New Delhi, 1995), p. 340.
30 William J. Cousins and Catherine Goyder, *Changing Slum Communities: Urban Community Development in Hyderabad* (New Delhi, 1979), p. 87.
31 A. Malla Reddy, *Slum Improvement: The Hyderabad Experience* (Delhi, 1996), pp. 152, 147, 155.
32 Vidyadhar K. Phatak, 'Shelter Strategy for Bombay', in David, *Urban Explosion of Mumbai*, p. 194. Mukhija, *Squatters as Developers*, p. 141.
33 Silke Kapp and Ana Paula Baltazar, 'The Paradox of Participation: A Case Study on Urban Planning in Favelas and a Plea for Autonomy', *Bulletin of Latin American Research*, XXXI/2 (2012), pp. 169, 160.
34 Rasna Warah with Jockin Arputham, 2002, originally published by

UN-Habitat as 'If You Want to Mobilize People, Go to the Public Toilets', and reproduced in 'Squatter Cities and Slums: Where the Sidewalks End', Worldwatch Institute, www.worldwatch.org, accessed 27 November 2015.

35 Vandana Desai, *Community Participation and Slum Housing: A Study of Bombay* (New Delhi, 1995), p. 225.

36 Jeremy Seabrook, *Life and Labour in a Bombay Slum* (London, 1987), p. 82.

37 See D. Ravindra Prasad and A. Malla Reddy, *Environmental Improvement of Urban Slums: The Indian Experience* (Hyderabad, 1994); Sehgal, *Slum Upgradation*, pp. 1–32

38 Prodipto Roy, 'Urbanization and Slum Improvement: A Middle Range Theory', in *Urbanization and Slums*, ed. Roy and Gupta, p. 347.

39 Janice Perlman, *Favela: Four Decades of Living on the Edge in Rio de Janeiro* (Oxford, 2010), pp. 280, 282.

40 John F. C. Turner, 'Issues and Conclusions', in *Building Community: A Third World Case Book*, ed. Bertha Turner (London, 1988), p. 180.

41 David Satterthwaite, 'From Professionally Driven to People-Driven Poverty Reduction: Reflections on the Role of Shack/Slum Dwellers International', *Environment and Urbanization*, XIII/2 (2001), p. 135.

42 United Nations Human Settlements Programme, *The Challenge of Slums*, p. vi.

43 United Nations Human Settlements Programme, *An Urbanizing World*, p. 205.

44 *Istanbul Declaration on Human Settlements*, clause 1, UN General Assembly resolutions 51/177 (16 December 1996) and 53/242 (28 July 1999). See also *The Habitat Agenda Goals and Principles, Commitments and the Global Plan of Action*, available at www.unhabitat.org.

45 UN Millennium Project, *Investing in Development: A Practical Plan to Achieve the Millennium Development Goals* (London, 2005), pp. 2–3.

46 *United Nations Millennium Declaration*, UN General Assembly, 55/2 (18 September 2000), clause 1.

47 Ibid., clause 19.1. See the full list of Millennium Goals and Targets in UN Millennium Project, *Investing in Development*, pp. xviii–xix.

48 *United Nations Millennium Declaration*, clause 19.6.

49 Cities Alliance, *2001 Annual Report*, p. 11; Cities Alliance, *2002 Annual Report*, p. 2, available at www.citiesalliance.org. See Marie Huchzermeyer, 'Troubling Continuities: Use and Utility of the Term "Slum"', in *The Routledge Handbook on Cities of the Global South*, ed. Susan Parnell and Sophie Oldfield (London, 2014), p. 93.

50 United Nations Human Settlements Programme, *The Challenge of Slums*, p. vii.

51 Ibid., p. 189.

52 United Nations Human Settlements Programme, *Harmonious Cities*, p. 90.

53 United Nations Human Settlements Programme, *The Challenge of Slums*, pp. xxv, 12.

54 UN-Habitat and Cities Alliance, *Analytical Perspective of Pro-poor Slum Upgrading Frameworks* (Nairobi, 2006), p. 1.

55 Ibid., p. 2.
56 United Nations Human Settlements Programme, *The Challenge of Slums*, p. 167.

8 SHADOW CITIES

1 Ban Ki-moon, 'Foreword', in United Nations Human Settlements Programme, *Harmonious Cities: State of the World's Cities 2008/2009* (London, 2008), p. v. United Nations Human Settlements Programme, *2007 Annual Report* (Nairobi, 2008), p. 8.
2 'A Message from the Executive Director', ibid., p. 5.
3 Mike Davis, *Planet of Slums* (London, 2006).
4 David Harvey, *The Enigma of Capital and the Crises of Capitalism* (London, 2010), p. vi.
5 United Nations Human Settlements Programme, *The Challenge of Slums: Global Report on Human Settlements* (London, 2003), p. 2.
6 Harvey, *Enigma of Capital*, p. 6.
7 Ibid., p. 10.
8 See Loic Wacquant, *Urban Outcasts: A Comparative Sociology of Advanced Marginality* (Cambridge, 2008).
9 Fay and Anna Wellenstein, 'Keeping a Roof over One's Head: Improving Access to Safe and Decent Shelter', in *The Urban Poor in Latin America*, ed. Marianne Fay (Washington, DC, 2005), p. 92.
10 Lynne Hancock and Gerry Mooney, '"Welfare Ghettos" and the "Broken Society": Territorial Stigmatization in the Contemporary UK', *Housing, Theory and Society*, XXX/1 (2013), p. 47.
11 Robert Neuwirth, *Shadow Cities: A Billion Squatters, a New Urban World* (New York, 2005), pp. 242, 249.
12 Shaohua Chen and Martin Ravallion, 'The Developing World Is Poorer than We Thought, but No Less Successful in the Fight against Poverty', World Bank Policy Research Working Paper 4703 (August 2008).
13 Martin Ravallion, Shaohua Chen and Prem Sangraula, *New Evidence on the Urbanization of Global Poverty* (World Bank, 2007), available at www.openknowledge.worldbank.org.
14 The term was first popularized by Gerard Piel, 'The Urbanization of Poverty Worldwide', *Challenge*, XL/1 (1997), pp. 58–68.
15 UN-Habitat Slum Upgrading Facility, *Guarantees for Slum Upgrading: Lessons on How to Use Guarantees to Address Risk and Access Commercial Loans for Slum Upgrading* (Nairobi, 2009), p. 1.
16 Harris Beider, 'Conclusion', in *Neighbourhood Renewal and Housing Markets: Community Engagement in the U.S. and UK*, ed. Harris Beider (Oxford, 2008), p. 331.
17 Philip Inman, 'Oxfam says Gains of Wealthiest are Hindering Fight to End Inequality', *Guardian Weekly*, 25 January 2013, p. 11.
18 Toby Helm, 'Part-time and Temporary Jobs Condemn Millions to Low Pay', ibid., 6 September 2013, p. 15.
19 Peter Kerr, 'Suburbs and a Blighted City Foresee a Future in Common', *New York Times*, 7 September 1989, pp. A1, B2.
20 Ewen MacAskill, 'Washington Divided by Cuts', ibid., 5 August 2011, p. 1.

21 United Nations Human Settlements Programme, *Harmonious Cities*, p. 65.

22 Amitabh Kundu, Keynote Address in *Poverty and Deprivation in Urban India*, ed. Sabir Ali (New Delhi, 2007), p. 20.

23 Jason Burke, 'India's Super-rich see their Wealth Soar', *Guardian Weekly*, 1 August 2014, p. 10.

24 Kofi Annan, 'Foreword', in United Nations Centre for Human Settlements, *Cities in a Globalizing World: Global Report on Human Settlements 2001* (London, 2001), p. v.

25 Neuwirth, *Shadow Cities*, p. 22.

26 United Nations Centre for Human Settlements, *Cities in a Globalizing World*, p. 79.

27 Stephanie McCummen, 'Slumming it in Kenya's Back Streets, *Guardian Weekly*, 4 April 2008, p. 28.

28 'Tour of Mathare Slum', www.youtube.com, 10 March 2012.

29 *Life in Favela of Rocinha, Rio de Janeiro, Brazil*, www.lifeinrocinha. blogspot.com, accessed 30 November 2015. See also the BBC's portrait of Rocinha through the eyes of six of its residents: BBC News, 'Favela Life: Rio's City within a City', 9 June 2014, www.bbc.com.

30 'Forced Evictions', Office of the High Commissioner for Human Rights, www.ohchr.org, accessed 30 November 2015. See UN-Habitat and UN Commission on Human Rights, *Forced Evictions* (New York and Geneva, 2014).

31 Nelson Mandela, 'While Poverty Persists, there is no Freedom', *Guardian Weekly*, 10 November 2006, p. 17.

32 Randeep Ramesh, 'Banker to Poor wins Nobel Peace Prize', *Guardian Weekly*, 20 October 2006, p. 5.

33 Roy Brockman and GHK International, *Slum Upgrading Facility: Mid-term Review* (2009), www.unhabitat.org, accessed 3 June 2011.

34 UN-Habitat, *Conference Report: Making Slums History – A Global Challenge for 2020* (2012), p. 7, www.unhabitat.org, accessed 8 August 2013.

35 Andrew Harding, 'Nairobi Slum Life: Escaping Kibera', BBC News, 15 October 2002, www.news.bbc.co.uk.

36 BBC News, 'Favela Life: Rio's City within a City'.

37 Xavier de Souza Briggs, *Democracy as Problem Solving: Civic Capacity in Communities across the Globe* (Cambridge, MA, 2008), p. 53.

38 United Nations Human Settlements Programme, *Harmonious Cities*, p. 19.

39 See Dennis Rodgers, Jo Beall and Ravi Kanbur, 'Re-thinking the Latin American City', in *Latin American Urban Development into the 21st Century: Towards a Renewed Perspective on the City*, ed. Dennis Rodgers, Jo Beall and Ravi Kanbur (Basingstoke, 2012), pp. 3–33.

40 Tom Phillips, 'Blood, Sweat and Fears in the Favelas of Rio', *Guardian*, 29 October 2005, www.gu.com. BBC News, 'Inside Rio's Violent Favelas', 4 July 2007, www.news.bbc.co.uk.

41 Cities Alliance, *2009 Annual Report*, p. 59, available at www.citiesalliance.org.

42 Briggs, *Democracy as Problem Solving*, p. 90.

43 R. N. Sharma and A. Narender, 'Policies and Strategies for Slum
   Improvement and Renewal: The Bombay Experience', in *Urban
   Explosion of Mumbai: Restructuring of Growth*, ed. M. D. David
   (Mumbai, 1996), p. 199.
44 Jawaharlal Nehru National Urban Renewal Mission, *Recommendations
   and Summary of the Workshop Proceedings on 'Jawaharlal Nehru National
   Urban Renewal Mission: Issues and Opportunities'*, held on Friday 22nd
   September 2006 at Chidambaram Conference Hall, SICCI, Esplanade,
   Chennai, p. 2, www.unhabitat.org, accessed 17 April 2008.
45 United Nations Human Settlements Programme, *The Challenge
   of Slums*, p. 189.
46 Kofi Annan, 'Foreword', ibid., p. v.
47 United Nations Human Settlements Programme, *UN-HABITAT Global
   Activities Report 2013: Our Presence and Partnerships* (Nairobi, 2013),
   p. xii. United Nations Human Settlements Programme, *Harmonious
   Cities*, p. 90.
48 Ibid., pp. 106, 113.
49 United Nations, *The Millennium Development Goals Report 2013* (New
   York, 2013), p. 50. United Nations, *The Millennium Development Goals
   Report 2011* (New York, 2011), p. 57.
50 United Nations Human Settlements Programme, *The Challenge of
   Slums*, p. xxxii.
51 United Nations Human Settlements Programme, *Harmonious Cities*, p. 57.
52 Dennis Rodgers, 'Slum Wars of the 21st Century: The New Geography
   of Conflict in Central America', *Crisis States Working Papers*, series 2,
   paper 7 (February 2007), p. 10. Rodgers, Beall and Kanbur, 'Re-thinking
   the Latin American City', p. 15.
53 Rodgers, 'Slum Wars of the 21st Century', p. 12.
54 Janice Perlman, 'Megacity's Violence and its Consequences in Rio de
   Janeiro', in *Megacities: The Politics of Urban Exclusion and Violence in
   the Global South*, ed. Kees Koonings and Dirk Kruijt (London, 2009),
   p. 53. Janice Perlman, *Favela: Four Decades of Living on the Edge in Rio
   de Janeiro* (Oxford, 2010), pp. xxi–xxii.
55 Ibid., p. 316.
56 Rodgers, Beall and Kanbur, 'Re-thinking the Latin American City',
   p. 16.
57 Prakash Louis, 'Preface', in Margaret Antony and G. Maheswaran,
   Social Segregation and Slums: The Plight of Dalits in the Slums of Delhi
   (New Delhi, 2001), p. 4.
58 *Jakarta Globe*, 19 March 2010, 'Clearing Indonesia's Slums through
   Education', available at www.jakartaglobe.beritasatu.com.
59 Cities Alliance, *2006 Annual Report*, p. 28, available at
   www.citiesalliance.org.
60 Austin Zeiderman, 'The Fetish and the Favela: Notes on Tourism and
   the Commodification of Place in Rio de Janeiro, Brazil', 27 March
   2006, Breslauer Symposium, University of California at Berkeley, http://
   eprints.cdlib.org, accessed 30 November 2015.
61 Andrew Harding, 'Nairobi Slum Life: Into Kibera', BBC News,
   4 October 2002, www.news.bbc.co.uk.

62 Andrew Harding, 'Nairobi Slum Life: Kibera's Children', BBC News, 10 October 2002, www.news.bbc.co.uk.

63 Charles Kenny, 'In Praise of Slums: Why Millions of People Choose to Live in Urban Squalor', *Foreign Policy*, 13 August 2012, p. 29.

64 See Fabian Frenzel, *Slumming It: The Tourist Valorization of Urban Poverty* (London, 2016).

65 Kibera Slum Foundation, *Walking Thru Kibera* (2006), www.youtube. com, accessed 1 November 2011.

66 Manfred Rolfes, 'Poverty Tourism: Theoretical Reflections and Empirical Findings Regarding an Extraordinary Form of Tourism', *GeoJournal*, LXXV (2010), p. 422.

67 Julia Meschkank, 'Investigations into Slum Tourism in Mumbai: Poverty Tourism and the Tensions between Different Constructions of Reality', *GeoJournal*, LXXVI (2011), p. 56.

68 Rory Carroll, 'Welcome to Chávez-land', *Guardian Weekly*, 26 January 2007, p. 18.

69 Rolfes, 'Poverty Tourism', p. 439.

70 Cities Alliance, *2012 Annual Report*, p. 3; Cities Alliance, *2006 Annual Report*, p. 3, both available at www.citiesalliance.org.

71 UN Millennium Project, *Investing in Development*, p. 1.

72 See UN-Habitat, *Conference Report: Making Slums History*.

73 UN-Habitat and Cities Alliance, *Analytical Perspective of Pro-poor Slum Upgrading Frameworks* (Nairobi, 2006), p. 2.

74 United Nations Human Settlements Programme, *Harmonious Cities*, p. 209.

75 Cities Alliance, *2001 Annual Report*, p. 4, available at www.citiesalliance. org.

76 Ibid., p. 20.

77 UN-Habitat, *Kenya Slum Upgrading Project (KENSUP)*, (2010), www.unhabitat.org, accessed 1 September 2011.

78 Cities Alliance, *2004 Annual Report*, p. 21, available at www.citiesalliance.org.

79 UN-Habitat, *UN-HABITAT and the Kenya Slum Upgrading Programme* (Nairobi, 2007), pp. 13, 3.

80 Ibid., p. 19.

81 See the accumulating body of work on Recife by University of Wageningen researcher Monique Nuijten.

82 Anna Tibaijuka, 'Introduction', in United Nations Human Settlements Programme, *The Challenge of Slums*, p. vi.

83 Asian Development Bank, In Brief: 'ADB's Poverty Reduction Strategy' (2008), www.adb.org, accessed 17 December 2009. See ADB, *Poverty and Environment Fund* (2003), accessed 7 October 2005.

84 Ban Ki-moon, 'Foreword', in United Nations, *The Millennium Development Goals Report 2012* (New York, 2012), p. 3.

85 United Nations Economic and Social Council, *In-depth Evaluation of the United Nations Human Settlements (UN-Habitat) Programme* (2005), p. 28, available at www.unhabitat.org.

86 United Nations, *The Millennium Development Goals Report 2015* (New York, 2015), p. 60.

87 Amnesty International, Kenya, *The Unseen Majority: Nairobi's Two Million Slum-Dwellers* (London, 2009), p. 13.

88 Monique Nuijten, 'The Perversity of the "Citizenship Game": Slum-upgrading in the Urban Periphery of Recife, Brazil', *Critique of Anthropology*, XXXIII/1 (2013), p. 16.

89 Martijn Koster and Monique Nuijten, 'From Preamble to Post-project Frustrations: The Shaping of a Slum Upgrading Project in Recife, Brazil', *Antipode*, XLIV/1 (2012), p. 177.

90 Koster and Nuijten, 'From Preamble to Post-project Frustrations', pp. 182, 184.

91 Ibid., p. 192.

92 Nuijten, 'The Perversity of the "Citizenship Game"', p. 16.

93 Ivo Imparato and Jeff Ruster, *Slum Upgrading and Participation: Lessons from Latin America* (Washington, DC, 2003), p. 308.

94 Ibid., p. 391.

95 Sapana Doshi, 'The Politics of Persuasion: Gendered Slum Citizenship in Neoliberal Mumbai', in *Urbanizing Citizenship: Contested Spaces in Indian Cities*, ed. Renu Desai and Romola Sanyal (New Delhi, 2012), p. 82.

96 UN-Habitat and Cities Alliance, *Analytical Perspective of Pro-poor Slum Upgrading Framework*, p. ii.

97 A. K. Jain, 'Slum Housing as a Tool of Poverty Reduction', in Ali, *Poverty and Deprivation in Urban India*, p. 447.

98 Gita Dewan Verma, *Slumming India: A Chronicle of Slums and Their Saviours* (New Delhi, 2002), p. 15.

99 *The Hindu*, 23 February 2009, p. 3, 'Rehabilitation Project Launched'.

100 See Vinit Mukhija, 'Rehousing Mumbai: Formalizing Slum Land Markets through Redevelopment', in *Slums: How Informal Real Estate Markets Work*, ed. Eugenie Birch, Shahana Chattaraj and Susan M. Wachter, pp. 125–39.

101 Jason Burke, 'Street Artists Fight to Save Delhi Slum', *Guardian Weekly*, 11 April 2014, p. 29.

102 Amnesty International, Kenya, *The Unseen Majority*, pp. 22–9.

103 Koster and Nuijten, 'From Preamble to Post-project Frustrations', p. 188.

104 Tom Phillips, 'Urbanism for the Masses', *Guardian Weekly*, 31 December 2010, p. 28.

105 Simon Jenkins, 'Slum or Utopia?', ibid., 30 May 2014, pp. 26–9. See Damian McIver, 'Rio 2016: Popular Favela Reduced to 20 Concrete Houses for Olympics, Residents Say', Australian Broadcasting Commission, 8 August 2016, www.abc.net.au; USA TODAY, 'Residents Lose Homes to Make Way for Rio Olympics', 29 June 2016, www.usatoday.com.

106 BBC News, 'Rio Plans to Clear Slums Ahead of 2016 Olympic Games', 28 July 2010 and 5 March 2012, www.bbc.com.

107 Ibid., 'Google to Amend Rio Maps over Brazil Favela Complaints', 26 April 2011.

108 Cities Alliance, *2012 Annual Report*, p. 15.

109 BBC News, 'Rio Olympics: Favela Poor Evicted as City Spruced Up', 1 July 2011, www.bbc.com.

110 Robert Gay, 'From Popular Movements to Drug Gangs to Militias: An Anatomy of Violence in Rio de Janeiro', in *Megacities*, ed. Koonings and Kruijt, p. 29.

111 BBC News, 'Brazilian Forces Seize Rio Drug Trafficker Stronghold', 28 November 2010, www.bbc.com. See Tom Phillips, 'Police "Conquer" Gang-controlled Rio Slum', *Guardian Weekly*, 3 December 2010, p. 6.

112 BBC News, 'Brazil Army to Take Up "Peacekeeping" in Rio Slums', 5 December 2010, www.bbc.com.

113 Ibid., 'Brazil Police Occupy Rio Favela in World Cup Operation', 20 June 2011.

114 Tom Phillips, 'Rio Favela Stormed in Olympic Clean-up', *Guardian Weekly*, 18 November 2011, p. 14.

115 Alan R. Johnson, *Leadership in a Slum: A Bangkok Case Study* (Oxford, 2009), p. 37.

116 Simon Romero, 'Slum Dwellers are Defying Brazil's Grand Design for Olympics', *New York Times*, 5 March 2012, A1.

117 *The Hindu*, 6 September 2009, p. 4: 'Delhi Govt. Accused of Betraying Slum Dwellers'.

118 Caroline Newton, 'The Reverse Side of the Medal: About the 2010 FIFA World Cup and the Beautification of the N2 in Cape Town', *Urban Forum*, XX (2009), p. 98. See Marie Huchzermeyer, *Cities with 'Slums': From Informal Settlement Eradication to a Right to the City in Africa* (Claremont, South Africa, 2011), pp. 121ff.

119 'Statement from Mr Jockin Arputham, President of Shack/Slum Dwellers International, at the opening plenary of the Second World Urban Forum, Barcelona September 2004', p. 1, www.unhabitat.org, accessed 2 September 2005.

120 Michael Hooper and Leonard Ortolano, 'Confronting Urban Displacement: Social Movement Participation and Post-eviction Resettlement Success in Dar es Salaam, Tanzania', *Journal of Planning Education and Research*, XXXII/3 (2012), p. 278.

121 Amnesty International, Kenya, *The Unseen Majority*, pp. 18–19.

122 Kalpana Sharma, *Rediscovering Dharavi: Stories from Asia's Largest Slum* (New Delhi, 2000), pp. 194–7.

123 Anupama Katakam, 'Ground Realities', *Frontline*, XXIV/12 (16–29 June 2007), available at www.frontline.in.

124 Verma, *Slumming India*, p. 46.

125 See Liza Weinstein, 'Demolition and Dispossession: Toward an Understanding of State Violence in Millennial Mumbai', *Studies in Comparative International Development*, XLVIII (2013), pp. 285–307.

126 'India Tycoon Builds Tower Block Home', *Guardian Weekly*, 8 June 2007, p. 8.

127 Randeep Ramesh, 'Delhi Poor Swept Aside by Tide of "Progress"', ibid., 2 February 2007, p. 5.

128 David Harvey, 'The Right to the City', *New Left Review*, LIII (2008), p. 35.

129 Aravind Adiga, *Last Man in Tower* (London, 2011).

130 Perlman, *Favela*, p. xxiii.

131 BBC News, 'In Pictures: Life in Dharavi' (2008), www. news.bbc.co.uk, accessed 13 October 2015.

132 Phillips, 'Blood, Sweat and Fears'.

133 BBC News, 'Rio Olympics: Favela Poor Evicted as City Spruced Up'.

134 Phillips, 'Blood, Sweat and Fears'.

135 Nishika Patel, 'Battle over Mumbai's Slums', *The Guardian*, 11 March 2011, www.the.guardian.com.

136 Joseph E. Stiglitz, *The Price of Inequality* (New York, 2012), pp. 16, 21–2.

137 Report of the Archbishop of Canterbury's Commission on Urban Priority Areas, *Faith in the City: A Call for Action by Church and Nation* (London, 1985), p. 5.

138 Graham Towers, *Building Democracy: Community Architecture in the Inner Cities* (London, 1995), p. xiii.

139 Commission on Urban Priority Areas, *Faith in the City*, p. 20.

140 Bruce Anderson in *The Spectator*, August 1996, quoted in Nick Davies, *Dark Heart: The Shocking Truth about Hidden Britain* (London, 1998), pp. 303–4.

141 Ibid., p. viii.

142 Ibid., pp. 114–15.

143 Ibid., p. vii.

144 Ibid., p. 113.

145 *The Advertiser*, 'Slum Busters', 13 March 2012, p. 1; *Sunday Mail*, 'City Slum Lords', 18 December 2011, p. 1.

146 David Harvey, *The Urban Experience* (Oxford, 1989), p. 40.

147 David Robinson, 'Living Parallel Lives? Housing, Residential Segregation and Community Cohesion in England', in *Neighbourhood Renewal & Housing Markets*, ed. Beider, p. 164.

148 See Anna Haworth and Tony Manzi, 'Managing the "Underclass": Interpreting the Moral Discourse of Housing Management', *Urban Studies*, XXXVI/1 (1999), pp. 153–65.

149 Home Office, *Community Cohesion: A Report of the Independent Review Team* (London, 2001), p. 9.

150 Katy Bennett, Huw Beynon and Ray Hudson, *Coalfields Regeneration: Dealing with the Consequences of Industrial Decline* (Bristol, 2000), p. 1.

151 Chris Hamnett, 'Gentrification and the Middle-class Remaking of Inner London, 1961–2001', *Urban Studies*, XL/12 (2003), p. 2416.

152 'America's Cities: Doomed to Burn?', *The Economist*, 9 May 1992, p. 21.

153 Derek S. Hyra, 'Conceptualizing the New Urban Renewal: Comparing the Past to the Present', *Urban Affairs Review*, XLVIII/4 (2012), pp. 498–527.

154 Susan J. Popkin, 'Race and Public Housing Transformation in the United States', in *Neighbourhood Renewal & Housing Markets*, ed. Beider, p. 138.

155 Mark Davidson and Loretta Lees, 'New-build Gentrification: Its Histories, Trajectories, and Critical Geographies', *Population, Space and Place*, XVI (2010), p. 397.

156 Keith Shaw and Fred Robinson, 'UK Regeneration Policies in the Early Twenty-First Century: Continuity or Change?' *Town Planning Review*, LXXXI/2 (2010), p. 125.

157 Rob Atkinson, 'The Emerging "Urban Agenda"' and the European Spatial Development Perspective: Towards an EU Urban Policy?',

European Planning Studies, IX/3 (2001), p. 395. Atkinson, 'The White Paper on European Governance: Implications for Urban Policy', *European Planning Studies*, X/6 (2002), p. 787.

158 Paul Chatterton and David Bradley, 'Bringing Britain Together? The Limitations of Area-based Regeneration Policies in Addressing Deprivation', *Local Economy*, XV/2 (2000), p. 100.

159 Tony Blair, 'Foreword', in Social Exclusion Unit, *A New Commitment to Neighbourhood Renewal: National Strategy Action Plan* (London, 2001), p. 4.

160 See ibid., p. 7; also Department of the Environment, Transport and the Regions, *Our Towns and Cities: The Future – Delivering an Urban Renaissance* (London, 2000).

161 Hilary Armstrong, minister for local government and the regions, 'Foreword', in Department for Communities and Local Government, *Unpopular Housing: Report of Policy Action Team* VII (1999), www.communities.gov.uk, accessed 30 June 2011.

162 Neighbourhood Renewal Unit, *National Evaluation of the Neighbourhood Management Pathfinder Programme* (London, 2006), p. 6.

163 Neighbourhood Renewal Unit, *Neighbourhood Management Pathfinder Programme: Interim Evaluation First Annual Report 2002/03* (Wetherby, West Yorkshire, 2003), n.p.

164 Department for Communities and Local Government, *Key Messages and Evidence on the Housing Market Renewal Pathfinder Programme 2003–2009* (London, 2009), p. 8.

165 John Prescott, 'Foreword', in Office of the Deputy Prime Minister, *Sustainable Communities: Homes for All* (London, 2005), p. 2.

166 Department for Communities and Local Government, *Key Messages and Evidence*, p. 4.

167 *The Guardian*, 6 January 2000, 'North's Sink Estates are "Beyond Saving"', www.theguardian.com.

168 Rowland Atkinson, *Does Gentrification Help or Harm Urban Neighbourhoods? An Assessment of the Evidence-base in the Context of the New Urban Agenda*, Centre for Neighbourhood Research Paper 5 (Bristol, 2002), p. 19.

169 Commission on Urban Life and Faith, *Faithful Cities: A Call for Celebration, Vision and Justice* (London, 2006), p. 64.

170 Ibid., p. 47.

171 Shaw and Robinson, 'UK Regeneration Policies in the Early Twenty-first Century', p. 139.

172 Commission on Urban Life and Faith, *Faithful Cities*, p. 52.

173 David Webb, '"Problem Neighbourhoods" in a Part-linear, Part-network Regime: Problems with, and Possible Responses to, the Housing Market Renewal Leviathan', PhD thesis, Newcastle University, 2010, pp. 194, 197.

174 Andrea Armstrong, 'Creating Sustainable Communities in "NewcastleGateshead"', PhD thesis, Durham University, 2010, p. 154.

175 Ibid., p. 71

176 Town and Country Planning Association, *Housing Market Renewal* (London, 2006), n.p. House of Commons Committee of Public

Accounts, *Housing Market Renewal: Pathfinders* (London, 2008), pp. 5, 7. Department for Communities and Local Government, *Key Messages and Evidence*, p. 4.

177 'Fight For Our Homes', www.fightforourhomes.com, accessed 9 February 2010. This protest forum began *c*. 2005 and no longer exists.

178 Anna Minton, *Ground Control: Fear and Happiness in the Twenty-first-century City* (London, 2009), p. 83. Adam Wilkinson, *Pathfinder* (London, 2006), pp. 9, 73.

179 Department for Communities and Local Government, *Unpopular Housing*.

180 Wilkinson, *Pathfinder*, p. 28.

181 Armstrong, 'Creating Sustainable Communities', p. 250

182 Anna Minton, 'Razing the Roots', *The Guardian*, 17 June 2009, p. 2.

183 Quoted in Minton, *Ground Control*, p. 86.

184 Richard Girling, 'Save our Streets', *Sunday Times*, 19 September 2004.

185 Jonathan Glancey, 'The Lights Are On, but No One Is Home', *Guardian Weekly*, 21 August 2009, p. 41.

186 I. Cole and J. Flint, *Demolition, Relocation and Affordable Rehousing* (York, 2007), p. 13.

187 Minton, *Ground Control*, p. 83.

188 Ian Cole, 'Whose Place? Whose History? Contrasting Narratives and Experiences of Neighbourhood Change and Housing Renewal', *Housing, Theory and Society*, xxx/1 (2013), pp. 78, 80.

189 Webb, 'Problem Neighbourhoods', p. 234.

190 Wilkinson, *Pathfinder*, p. 10. See Minton, *Ground Control*, p. 90.

191 Minton, *Ground Control*, p. 89.

192 Wendy Wilson, *Housing Market Renewal Pathfinders*, House of Commons Library, 4 June 2013, p. 5, available online at www.parliament.uk.

193 *Guardian Weekly*, 26 November 2010, p. 12, 'End of Housing Renewal Traps the Poorest in Dead Streets'.

194 United Nations, *The Millennium Development Goals Report 2015*, pp. 9, 60.

195 Ibid., p. 9.

CONCLUSION

1 E. P. Richards, *Report on the Condition, Improvement and Town Planning of the City of Calcutta and Contiguous Areas* (Ware, Hertfordshire, 1914), p. 239.

2 Herbert J. Gans, *The Urban Villagers: Group and Class in the Life of Italian-Americans*, updated and expanded edition (New York, 1982), p. 350.

3 Robert Neuwirth, *Shadow Cities: A Billion Squatters, a New Urban World* (New York, 2005), p. 16.

4 Loic Wacquant, *Urban Outcasts: A Comparative Sociology of Advanced Marginality* (Cambridge, 2008), pp. 1, 239.

5 Peter Marcuse, 'De-spacialization and Dilution of the Ghetto: Current Trends in the United States', in *The Ghetto: Contemporary Global Issues*

and Controversies, ed. Ray Hutchinson and Bruce D. Haynes (Boulder, CO, 2012), p. 36.

6 Richard Martin and Ashna Mathema, *Development Poverty and Politics: Putting Communities in the Driver's Seat* (New York, 2010), p. 19.

7 Celine d'Cruz and Patience Mudimu, 'Community Savings that Mobilize Federations, Build Women's Leadership and Support Slum Upgrading', *Environment and Urbanization*, XXV/1 (2013), p. 31.

8 United Nations Human Settlements Programme, *Harmonious Cities: State of the World's Cities 2008/2009* (London, 2008), p. xiii.

9 Charles Kenny, 'In Praise of Slums: Why Millions of People Choose to Live in Urban Squalor', *Foreign Policy*, 13 August 2012, p. 29.

10 S. Devadas Pillai, 'Slums and Squatters', in *Slums and Urbanization*, ed. A. R. Desai and S. Devadas Pillai, 2nd edn (Bombay, 1990), p. 164.

11 AbdouMaliq Simone, *City Life from Jakarta to Dakar: Movements at the Crossroads* (New York, 2010), p. 333.

12 Kalpana Sharma, *Rediscovering Dharavi: Stories from Asia's Largest Slum* (New Delhi, 2000), p. xvi.

SELECT BIBLIOGRAPHY

Abrams, Charles, *Man's Struggle for Shelter in an Urbanizing World*
    (Cambridge, MA, 1964)
Ali, Sabir, ed., *Poverty and Deprivation in Urban India* (New Delhi, 2007)
——, *Slums within Slums: A Study of Resettlement Colonies in Delhi* (New
    Delhi, 1990)
Arabindoo, Pushpa, 'Rhetoric of the "Slum": Rethinking Urban Poverty',
    City: Analysis of Urban Trends, Culture, Theory, Policy, Action, xv/6
    (2011), pp. 636–46
Atkinson, Rob, 'Discourses of Partnership and Empowerment in
    Contemporary British Urban Regeneration', *Urban Studies*, xxxvi/1
    (1999), pp. 59–72
Atkinson, Rowland, and Keith Kintrea, 'Disentangling Area Effects:
    Evidence from Deprived and Non-deprived Neighbourhoods', *Urban
    Studies*, xxxviii/12 (2001), pp. 2277–98
Basu, Ashok Ranjan, *Urban Squatter Housing in Third World* (Delhi, 1988)
Beauregard, Robert A., *Voices of Decline: The Postwar Fate of U.S. Cities* (New
    York, 2003)
Beider, Harris, ed., *Neighbourhood Renewal and Housing Markets: Community
    Engagement in the U.S. and UK* (Oxford, 2008)
Bendiksen, Jonas, *The Places We Live* (New York, 2008)
Bennett, Katy, Huw Beynon and Ray Hudson, *Coalfields Regeneration:
    Dealing with the Consequences of Industrial Decline* (Bristol, 2000)
Bharucha, Ruzbeh N., *Yamuna Gently Weeps: A Journey into the Yamuna
    Pushta Slum Demolitions* (New Delhi, 2006)
Bijlani, H. U. and Prodipto Roy, eds, *Slum Habitat: Hyderabad Slum
    Improvement Project* (New Delhi, 1991)
Birch, Eugenie L., Shahana Chattaraj and Susan M. Wachter, eds,
    Slums: How Informal Real Estate Markets Work (Philadelphia,
    PA, 2016)
Caro, Robert A., *The Power Broker: Robert Moses and the Fall of New York*
    (New York, 1974)
Clinard, Marshall B., *Slums and Community Development: Experiments
    in Self-help* (New York, 1966)
Cole, Ian, 'Whose Place? Whose History? Contrasting Narratives and

Experiences of Neighbourhood Change and Housing Renewal',
Housing, Theory and Society, XXX/1 (2013), pp. 65–83

Cousins, William J. and Catherine Goyder, *Changing Slum Communities:
Urban Community Development in Hyderabad* (New Delhi, 1979)

Davin, Anna, *Growing Up Poor: Home, School and Street in London 1870–
1914* (London, 1996)

Davis, Mike, *Planet of Slums* (London, 2006)

de Wit, Joop W., *Poverty, Policy and Politics in Madras Slums: Dynamics
of Survival, Gender and Leadership* (New Delhi, 1996)

Dennis, Norman, *Public Participation and Planners' Blight* (London, 1972)

——, *People and Planning: The Sociology of Housing in Sunderland* (London,
1970)

Desai, A. R., and S. Devadas Pillai, *Slums and Urbanization*, 2nd edn
(Bombay, 1990)

——, eds, *A Profile of an Indian Slum* (Bombay, 1972)

Desai, Renu, and Romola Sanyal, eds, *Urbanizing Citizenship: Contested
Spaces in Indian Cities* (New Delhi, 2012)

Desai, Vandana, *Community Participation and Slum Housing: A Study of
Bombay* (New Delhi, 1995)

Doshi, Sapana, 'The Politics of the Evicted: Redevelopment, Subjectivity,
and Difference in Mumbai's Slum Frontier', *Antipode*, XLV/4 (2012),
pp. 844–65

Dowling, Robert M., *Slumming in New York: From the Waterfront to Mythic
Harlem* (Urbana, IL, 2007)

Drakakis-Smith, D. W., 'Urban Renewal in an Asian Context: A Case Study
in Hong Kong', *Urban Studies*, XIII (1976), pp. 295–305

Dwyer, D. J., *People and Housing in Third World Cities: Perspectives on the
Problem of Spontaneous Settlements* (London, 1979)

Dyos, H. J., 'The Slums of Victorian London', *Victorian Studies*, XI/1 (1967),
pp. 5–40

—— and D. A. Reeder, 'Slums and Suburbs', in *The Victorian City: Images
and Realities*, ed. H. J. Dyos and Michael Wolff (London, 1973), vol. I,
pp. 359–86

English, John, Ruth Madigan and Peter Norman, *Slum Clearance: The Social
and Administrative Context in England and Wales* (London, 1976)

Fay, Marianne, ed., *The Urban Poor in Latin America* (Washington, DC, 2005)

Fernandez, Rosa Flores, ed., *Slum Upgrading Programmes in Nairobi:
Challenges in Implementation* (Nairobi, 2011)

Frenzel, Fabian, *Slumming It: The Tourist Valorization of Urban Poverty*
(London, 2016)

Gandal, Keith, *The Virtues of the Vicious: Jacob Riis, Stephen Crane, and the
Spectacle of the Slum* (New York, 1997)

Gans, Herbert J., *People and Plans: Essays on Urban Problems and Solutions*
(New York, 1968)

——, *The Urban Villagers: Group and Class in the Life of Italian-Americans*,
updated and expanded edition (New York, 1982)

Garside, Patricia, '"Unhealthy Areas": Town Planning, Eugenics and the
Slums', *Planning Perspectives*, III (1988), pp. 24–46

Gaskell, S. Martin, ed., *Slums* (Leicester, 1990)

Gibson, Michael S., and Michael J. Langstaff, *An Introduction to Urban Renewal* (London, 1982)

Gilbert, Alan, 'Extreme Thinking about Slums and Slum Dwellers: A Critique', *SAIS Review*, XXIX/1 (2009), pp. 35–48

——, 'The Return of the Slum: Does Language Matter?', *International Journal of Urban and Regional Research*, XXXI/4 (2007), pp. 697–713

——, ed., *The Mega-city in Latin America* (Tokyo, 1996)

—— and Peter M. Ward, eds, *Housing, the State and the Poor: Policy and Practice in Three Latin American Cities* (Cambridge, 1985)

Goetz, Edward G., 'The Politics of Poverty Deconcentration and Housing Demolition', *Journal of Urban Affairs*, XXII/2 (2000), pp. 157–73

Hancock, Lynn, and Gerry Mooney, '"Welfare Ghettos" and the "Broken Society": Territorial Stigmatization in the Contemporary UK', *Housing, Theory and Society*, XXX/1 (2013), pp. 46–64

Hansen, Karen Tranberg, and Mariken Vaa, eds, *Reconsidering Informality: Perspectives from Urban Africa* (Uppsala, 2004)

Harvey, David, *Rebel Cities: From the Right to the City to the Urban Revolution* (London, 2013)

——, *The Enigma of Capital and the Crises of Capitalism* (London, 2010)

Heredia, Rudolf C., *Settlements and Shelter: Alternative Housing for the Urban Poor in Bombay* (New Delhi, 1986)

Hoban, Martin, and Peter Beresford, 'Regenerating Regeneration', *Community Development Journal*, XXXVI/4 (2001), pp. 312–20

Hoggett, Paul, ed., *Contested Communities: Experiences, Struggles, Policies* (Bristol, 1997)

Hollington, Michael, *Dickens and the Grotesque* (London, 1984)

Home, Robert, *Of Planting and Planning: The Making of British Colonial Cities*, 2nd edn (London, 2013)

Howard, Ella, *Homeless: Poverty and Place in Urban America* (Philadelphia, PA, 2013)

Huchzermeyer, Marie, *Cities with 'Slums': From Informal Settlement Eradication to a Right to the City in Africa* (Claremont, South Africa, 2011)

——, *Tenement Cities: From 19th Century Berlin to 21st Century Nairobi* (Trenton, NJ, 2011)

Hutchinson, Ray, and Bruce D. Haynes, eds, *The Ghetto: Contemporary Global Issues and Controversies* (Boulder, CO, 2012)

Hyra, Derek S., 'Conceptualizing the New Urban Renewal: Comparing the Past to the Present', *Urban Affairs Review*, XLVIII/4 (2012), pp. 498–527

Imparato, Ivo, and Jeff Ruster, *Slum Upgrading and Participation: Lessons from Latin America* (Washington, DC, 2003)

Indian Institute of Public Administration, *Slum Clearance and Improvement* (New Delhi, 1979)

Jacobs, Sidney, *The Right to a Decent House* (London, 1976)

Jim, C. Y., 'Urban Renewal and Environmental Planning in Hong Kong', *The Environmentalist*, XIV/3 (1994), pp. 163–81

Johnson, Alan R., *Leadership in a Slum: A Bangkok Case Study* (Oxford, 2009)

Jones, Gavin W., and Pravin Visaria, eds, *Urbanization in Large Developing Countries: China, Indonesia, Brazil and India* (Oxford, 1997)

Kidambi, Prashant, *The Making of an Indian Metropolis: Colonial Governance and Public Culture in Bombay, 1890–1920* (Aldershot, 2007)

Kirby, David A., *Slum Housing and Residential Renewal: The Case in Urban Britain* (London, 1979)

Klemek, Christopher, *The Transatlantic Collapse of Urban Renewal: Postwar Urbanism from New York to Berlin* (Chicago, IL, 2011)

Koonings, Kees, and Dirk Kruijt, eds, *Megacities: The Politics of Urban Exclusion and Violence in the Global South* (London, 2009)

Koven, Seth, *Slumming: Sexual and Social Politics in Victorian London* (Princeton, NJ, 2004)

Langford, Malcolm, Andy Sumner and Alicia Ely Yamin, eds, *The Millennium Development Goals and Human Rights: Past, Present and Future* (Cambridge, 2013)

Lloyd, Peter, *Slums of Hope? Shanty Towns of the Third World* (Harmondsworth, 1979)

McAuslan, Patrick, *Urban Land and Shelter for the Poor* (London, 1985)

MacLeod, Gordon, and Craig Johnstone, 'Stretching Urban Renaissance: Privatizing Space, Civilizing Place, Summoning "Community"', *International Journal of Urban and Regional Research*, XXXVI/1 (2012), pp. 1–28

Maeckelbergh, Marianne, 'Mobilizing to Stay Put: Housing Struggles in New York City', *International Journal of Urban and Regional Research*, XXXVI/4 (2012), pp. 655–73

Marris, Peter, 'The Meaning of Slums and Patterns of Change', *International Journal of Urban and Regional Research*, III/1–4 (1979), pp. 419–41

Martin, Richard, and Ashna Mathema, *Development Poverty and Politics: Putting Communities in the Driver's Seat* (New York, 2010)

Mayne, Alan, *The Imagined Slum: Newspaper Representation in Three Cities, 1870–1914* (Leicester, 1993)

—— and Tim Murray, eds, *The Archaeology of Urban Landscapes: Explorations in Slumland* (Cambridge, 2001)

Mehra, Ajay K., *The Politics of Urban Development: A Study of Old Delhi* (New Delhi, 1991)

Mertens, Rosita, *Forced Relocation of Slum Dwellers in Bangalore, India: Slum Dwellers, Landlords and the Government* (Amsterdam, 1996)

Minton, Anna, *Ground Control: Fear and Happiness in the Twenty-first-century City* (London, 2009)

Mukhija, Vinit, *Squatters as Developers? Slum Redevelopment in Mumbai* (Aldershot, 2003)

Narayan, Deepa, *Voices of the Poor: Can Anyone Hear Us?* (New York, 2000)

Neuwirth, Robert, *Shadow Cities: A Billion Squatters, a New Urban World* (New York, 2005)

Nevin, Brendan, 'Housing Market Renewal in Liverpool: Locating the Gentrification Debate in History, Context and Evidence', *Housing Studies*, XXV/5 (2010), pp. 715–33

Newman, Kathe, and Elvin K. Wyly, 'The Right to Stay Put, Revisited: Gentrification and Resistance to Displacement in New York City', *Urban Studies*, XLIII/1 (2006), pp. 23–57

Nijman, Jan, 'A Study of Space in Mumbai's Slums', *Tijdschrift voor Economische en Sociale Geografie*, CI/1 (2009), pp. 4–17

——, 'Against the Odds: Slum Rehabilitation in Neoliberal Mumbai', *Cities*, xxv (2008), pp. 73–85

Nuijten, Monique, 'The Perversity of the "Citizenship Game": Slum-upgrading in the Urban Periphery of Recife, Brazil', *Critique of Anthropology*, XXXIII/1 (2013), pp. 8–25

Parnell, Susan, and Sophie Oldfield, eds, *The Routledge Handbook on Cities of the Global South* (London, 2014)

Payne, Helen and Brian Littlechild, eds, *Ethical Practice and the Abuse of Power in Social Responsibility: Leave No Stone Unturned* (London, 2000)

Pepper, Simon, *Housing Improvement: Goals and Strategy* (London, 1971)

——, and Peter Richmond, 'Homes Unfit for Heroes: The Slum Problem in London and Neville Chamberlain's Unhealthy Areas Committee, 1919–21', *Town Planning Review*, LXXX/2 (2009), pp. 143–71

Perlman, Janice E., *Favela: Four Decades of Living on the Edge in Rio de Janeiro* (Oxford, 2010)

——, *The Myth of Marginality: Urban Poverty and Politics in Rio de Janeiro* (Berkeley, CA, 1976)

Pooley, C. G., 'Housing for the Poorest Poor: Slum-clearance and Rehousing in Liverpool, 1890–1918', *Journal of Historical Geography*, XI/1 (1985), pp. 70–88

Prasad, D. Ravindra, and A. Malla Reddy, *Environmental Improvement of Urban Slums: The Indian Experience* (Hyderabad, 1994)

Rao, Vyjayanthi, 'Slum as Theory: The South/Asian City and Globalization', *International Journal of Urban and Regional Research*, XXX/1 (2006), pp. 225–32

Reddy, A. Malla, *Slum Improvement: The Hyderabad Experience* (Delhi, 1996)

Rodgers, Dennis, 'Slum Wars of the 21st Century: The New Geography of Conflict in Central America', *Crisis States Working Papers*, series 2, paper 7 (February 2007)

——, Jo Beall and Ravi Kanbur, eds, *Latin American Urban Development into the 21st Century: Towards a Renewed Perspective on the City* (Basingstoke, 2012)

Romeyn, Esther, *Street Scenes: Staging the Self in Immigrant New York, 1880–1924* (Minneapolis, MN, 2008)

Ross, Ellen, *Slum Travelers: Ladies and London Poverty, 1860–1920* (Berkeley, CA, 2007)

Roy, Ananya, 'Slumdog Cities: Rethinking Subaltern Urbanism', *International Journal of Urban and Regional Research*, XXXV/2 (2011), pp. 223–38

—— and Nezar AlSayyad, eds, *Urban Informality: Transnational Perspectives from the Middle East, Latin America, and South Asia* (Lanham, MD, 2004)

Roy, Maitreyi Bardhan, *Calcutta Slums: Public Policy in Retrospect* (Calcutta, 1994)

Roy, Prodipto, and Shangon Das Gupta, eds, *Urbanization and Slums* (New Delhi, 1995)

Schenk, Hans, ed., *Living in India's Slums: A Case Study of Bangalore* (New Delhi, 2001)

Schneider, Jane, and Ida Susser, eds, *Wounded Cities: Destruction and Reconstruction in a Globalized World* (Oxford, 2003)

Seabrook, Jeremy, *Life and Labour in a Bombay Slum* (London, 1987)

Sehgal, R. L., ed., *Slum Upgradation: Emerging Issue and Policy Implications* (New Delhi, 1998)

Seng, Loh Kah, 'Conflict and Change at the Margins: Emergency Kampong Clearance and the Making of Modern Singapore', *Asian Studies Review*, xxxiii/2 (2009), pp. 139–59

Sharma, Kalpana, *Rediscovering Dharavi: Stories from Asia's Largest Slum* (New Delhi, 2000)

Sibley, David, *Geographies of Exclusion: Society and Difference in the West* (London, 1995)

Siddiqui, M.K.A., 'Life in the Slums of Calcutta; Some Aspects', *Economic and Political Weekly*, iv/50 (1969), pp. 1919–21

Simone, AbdouMaliq, *City Life from Jakarta to Dakar: Movements at the Crossroads* (New York, 2010)

Smart, Alan, *The Shek Kip Mei Myth: Squatters, Fires and Colonial Rule in Hong Kong, 1950–1963* (Hong Kong, 2006)

—, *Making Room: Squatter Clearance in Hong Kong* (Hong Kong, 1992)

Smith, P. J., 'Slum Clearance as an Instrument of Sanitary Reform: The Flawed Vision of Edinburgh's First Slum Clearance Scheme', *Planning Perspectives*, ix (1994), pp. 1–27

Stallybrass, Peter, and Allon White, *The Politics and Poetics of Transgression* (Ithaca, NY, 1986)

Stokes, Charles J., 'A Theory of Slums', *Land Economics*, xxxviii/3 (1962), pp. 187–97

Suttles, Gerald D., *The Social Order of the Slum: Ethnicity and Territory in the Inner City* (Chicago, IL, 1968)

Tagg, John, *Disciplinary Frame: Photographic Truths and the Capture of Meaning* (Minneapolis, MN, 2009)

Tallon, Andrew, *Urban Regeneration in the UK*, 2nd edn (Abingdon, 2013)

Teaford, Jon C., *The Rough Road to Renaissance: Urban Revitalization in America, 1940–1985* (Baltimore, MD, 1990)

Towers, Graham, *Building Democracy: Community Architecture in the Inner Cities* (London, 1995)

United Nations Human Settlements Programme, *Harmonious Cities: State of the World's Cities 2008/2009* (London, 2008)

—, *The Challenge of Slums: Global Report on Human Settlements 2003* (London, 2003)

—, *Cities in a Globalizing World: Global Report on Human Settlements 2001* (London, 2001)

—, *An Urbanizing World: Global Report on Human Settlements, 1996* (Oxford, 1996)

Verma, Gita Dewan, *Slumming India: A Chronicle of Slums and Their Saviours* (New Delhi, 2002)

Wacquant, Loic, *Urban Outcasts: A Comparative Sociology of Advanced Marginality* (Cambridge, 2008)

Walkowitz, Judith R., *City of Dreadful Delight: Narratives of Sexual Danger in Late-Victorian London* (Chicago, IL, 1992)

Ward, David, *Poverty, Ethnicity, and the American City, 1840–1925: Changing Conceptions of the Slum and the Ghetto* (Cambridge, 1989)

Ward, Stephen V., *Planning and Urban Change* (London, 2004)

Weinstein, Liza, 'Demolition and Dispossession: Toward an Understanding of State Violence in Millennial Mumbai', *Studies in Comparative International Development*, XLVIII (2013), pp. 285–307

Werlin, Herbert, 'The Slum Upgrading Myth', *Urban Studies*, XXXVI/9 (1999), pp. 1523–34

White, Jerry, *Campbell Bunk: The Worst Street in North London Between the Wars* (London, 2003)

——, *Rothschild Buildings: Life in an East End Tenement Block, 1887–1920* (London, 1980)

Wiebe, Paul D., *Social Life in an Indian Slum* (Delhi, 1975)

Wilkinson, Adam, *Pathfinder* (London, 2006)

Winkler, Tanja, 'Prolonging the Global Age of Gentrification: Johannesburg's Regeneration Policies', *Planning Theory*, VIII/4 (2009), pp. 362–81

Wise, Sarah, *The Blackest Streets: The Life and Death of a Victorian Slum* (London, 2009)

Wohl, Anthony S., ed., *The Eternal Slum: Housing and Social Policy in Victorian London* (London, 1977)

——, *The Bitter Cry of Outcast London, with Leading Articles from the Pall Mall Gazette of October 1883 and Articles by Lord Salisbury, Joseph Chamberlain and Foster Crozier* (Leicester, 1970)

Yadav, C. S., *Land Use in Big Cities: A Study of Delhi* (Delhi, 1979)

Yelling, J. A., *Slums and Redevelopment: Policy and Practice in England, 1918–45, with Particular Reference to London* (London, 1992)

——, 'The Origins of British Redevelopment Areas', *Planning Perspectives*, III (1988), pp. 282–96

——, *Slums and Slum Clearance in Victorian London* (London, 1986)

Yeoh, Brenda S. A., *Contesting Space in Colonial Singapore: Power Relations and the Urban Built Environment* (Singapore, 2003)

Young, Michael, and Peter Willmott, *Family and Kinship in East London* (London, 1957)

Zipp, Samuel, *Manhattan Projects: The Rise and Fall of Urban Renewal in Cold War New York* (Oxford, 2010)

ACKNOWLEDGEMENTS

This book draws upon findings accumulated during an academic career that stretches back over forty years and it is therefore impossible to acknowledge here all those who contributed to it.

I thank the Australian Research Council for funding support that, although not directly associated with this book, nonetheless contributed to its development. I especially acknowledge the research funding given to me both by Caroline McMillen while she was Deputy Vice Chancellor for Research at the University of South Australia and by India's Jawaharlal Nehru University.

I appreciate the support I received from librarians at the British Library, the Bancroft Library at the University of California, Berkeley, the Nehru Library, the Library of Congress, the Birmingham Central Library, the University of South Australia and Flinders University, and from archivists in diverse places, from District Six in Cape Town to Museum Melbourne.

I am grateful to Jim Dyos for influencing the direction of my research career, and to Tony Wohl, Richard Rodger, Graeme Davison and Asa Briggs for encouraging me to pursue that path. Alan Gilbert and Gareth Jones introduced me to research in Latin America, as did Vivian Bickford-Smith in sub-Saharan Africa, and Amita Singh, Darvesh Gopal, Rabindranath Bhattacharyya and Kapil Kumar in India. Amitabh Kundu has especially informed my understanding of contemporary social disadvantage in India. Mary Beaudry and Becky Yamin have been stimulating companions in the United States, as has Richard Harris in Canada. Simon Gunn and his colleagues in the University of Leicester's Centre for Urban History have enriched my work in Britain.

Richard Dennis read my original manuscript, pointing out several potential disasters and suggesting improvements. Ben Hayes, the commissioning editor at Reaktion, initially suggested that I should write this book, and maintained his enthusiasm when mine faltered and the years passed by. Martha Jay, Reaktion's managing editor, and her colleagues transformed my text into the book you have before you.

I have been helped by many research assistants over the years, among whom I especially thank Kasia Zygmuntowicz and Annmarie Reid.

I remember as well the squatters whom I met in New Delhi and Cape Town. This book has been written with them in mind.

INDEX